Honda Civic Owners Workshop Manual

John S Mead

Models covered
Honda Civic Hatchback; 'Base', DX, S & Si
Honda Civic Sedan
Honda Civic Wagon
Honda Civic CRX; 'Standard', HF & Si
1342 cc & 1488 cc

Does not cover 16-valve CRX or Wagon 4WD

ABCDE
FGHIJ
KLMNO
PQ

Haynes Publishing Group
Sparkford Nr Yeovil
Somerset BA22 7JJ England

Haynes Publications, Inc
861 Lawrence Drive
Newbury Park
California 91320 USA

Acknowledgements

Thanks are due to the Champion Sparking Plug Company Limited who supplied the illustrations showing the spark plug conditions, to Sykes-Pickavant Limited who provided some of the workshop tools, and to all those people at Sparkford who helped in the production of this manual.

A book in the **Haynes Owners Workshop Manual Series**

Printed by J. H. Haynes & Co. Ltd, Sparkford, Nr Yeovil, Somerset BA22 7JJ, England

ISBN 1 85010 227 9

Library of Congress Catalog Card Number 86–83213

Contents

Honda Civic S

About this manual

Its aim

The aim of this manual is to help you get the best value from your vehicle. It can do so in several ways. It can help you decide what work must be done (even should you choose to get it done by a garage), provide information on routine maintenance and servicing, and give a logical course of action and diagnosis when random faults occur. However, it is hoped that you will use the manual by tackling the work yourself. On simpler jobs it may even be quicker than booking the car into a garage and going there twice, to leave and collect it. Perhaps most important, a lot of money can be saved by avoiding the costs a garage must charge to cover its labour and overheads.

The manual has drawings and descriptions to show the function of the various components so that their layout can be understood. Then the tasks are described and photographed in a step-by-step sequence so that even a novice can do the work.

Its arrangement

The manual is divided into twelve Chapters, each covering a logical sub-division of the vehicle. The Chapters are each divided into Sections, numbered with single figures, eg 5; and the Sections into paragraphs (or sub-sections), with decimal numbers following on from the Section they are in, eg 5.1, 5.2, 5.3 etc.

It is freely illustrated, especially in those parts where there is a detailed sequence of operations to be carried out. There are two forms of illustration: figures and photographs. The figures are numbered in sequence with decimal numbers, according to their position in the Chapter – eg Fig. 6.4 is the fourth drawing/illustration in Chapter 6. Photographs carry the same number (either individually or in related groups) as the Section or sub-section to which they relate.

There is an alphabetical index at the back of the manual as well as a contents list at the front. Each Chapter is also preceded by its own individual contents list.

References to the 'left' or 'right' of the vehicle are in the sense of a person in the driver's seat facing forwards.

Unless otherwise stated, nuts and bolts are removed by turning anti-clockwise, and tightened by turning clockwise.

Vehicle manufacturers continually make changes to specifications and recommendations, and these, when notified, are incorporated into our manuals at the earliest opportunity.

Whilst every care is taken to ensure that the information in this manual is correct, no liability can be accepted by the authors or publishers for loss, damage or injury caused by any errors in, or omissions from, the information given.

Introduction to the Honda Civic

Introduced in 1984, the Civic range covered by this Manual comprises 3-door Hatchback, 5-door Shuttle (estate), and sporty CRX coupe models for the UK market, and a similar line up for North America (where the Shuttle is known as a Wagon) with the addition of a four-door Sedan model.

All models are powered by four-cylinder single overhead camshaft engines available in carburettor or fuel-injected form depending on model. The engine is transversely mounted at the front, and drives the front wheels through a 4 or 5-speed manual transmission or Hondamatic automatic transmission.

An extensive range of standard equipment is fitted, and a wide range of options is available to suit most requirements.

Four-wheel-drive Shuttle/Wagon models and a twin overhead camshaft CRX model are available, but these are not covered by this Manual.

Honda Civic Shuttle

Honda Civic CRX

General dimensions, weights and capacities

Dimensions

UK models

Overall length:	
Hatchback	3810 mm (150.0 in)
Shuttle	3990 mm (157.1 in)
CRX	3675 mm (144.7 in)
Overall width:	
Hatchback	1635 mm (64.4 in)
Shuttle	1650 mm (65.0 in)
CRX	1625 mm (63.9 in)
Overall height:	
Hatchback	1340 mm (52.8 in)
Shuttle	1490 mm (58.7 in)
CRX	1290 mm (50.8 in)
Ground clearance	165 mm (6.5 in)
Wheelbase:	
Hatchback	2380 mm (93.7 in)
Shuttle	2450 mm (96.5 in)
CRX	2200 mm (86.6 in)
Track:	
Front	1400 mm (55.1 in)
Rear	1415 mm (55.7 in)

North American models

Overall length:	
Hatchback	3845 mm (151.4 in)
Sedan	4145 mm (163.2 in)
Wagon	4030 mm (158.7 in)
CRX:	
Standard and HF	3675 mm (144.7 in)
Si	3755 mm (147.8 in)
Overall width	1625 mm (63.9 in)
Overall height:	
Hatchback	1335 mm (52.6 in)
Sedan	1385 mm (54.5 in)
Wagon	1480 mm (58.3 in)
CRX	1290 mm (50.8 in)
Ground clearance:	
Hatchback	160 mm (6.3 in)
Sedan	160 mm (6.3 in)
Wagon	165 mm (6.4 in)
CRX	165 mm (6.4 in)
Wheelbase:	
Hatchback	2380 mm (93.7 in)
Sedan	2450 mm (96.5 in)
Wagon	2450 mm (96.5 in)
CRX	2200 mm (86.6 in)
Track:	
Front	1400 mm (55.1 in)
Rear	1415 mm (55.7 in)

Weights (kerb with oil, coolant and full fuel tank)

UK models
Hatchback:
    Manual transmission .... 805 kg (1775.0 lb)
    Automatic transmission .... 820 kg (1808.1 lb)
Shuttle:
    Manual transmission .... 890 kg (1962.4 lb)
    Automatic transmission .... 905 kg (1995.5 lb)
CRX .... 820 kg (1808.1 lb)

North American models
Hatchback:
    Standard .... 854 kg (1887.0 lb)
    DX:
        Manual transmission .... 888 kg (1958.0 lb)
        Automatic transmission .... 909 kg (2004.0 lb)
    Si .... 922 kg (2033.0 lb)
Sedan:
    Manual transmission .... 936 kg (2064.0 lb)
    Automatic transmission .... 973 kg (2145.0 lb)
Wagon:
    Manual transmission .... 945 kg (2083.0 lb)
    Automatic transmission .... 966 kg (2130.0 lb)
CRX:
    Manual transmission:
        Standard .... 825 kg (1819.0 lb)
        HF .... 777 kg (1713.0 lb)
        Si .... 854 kg (1883.0 lb)
    Automatic transmission .... 839 kg (1849.0 lb)

Capacities

Engine oil with filter change .... 3.5 litres (6.2 Imp pt/3.7 US qt)
Manual transmission .... 2.3 litres (4.1 Imp pt/2.4 US qt)
Automatic transmission (fluid change) .... 2.4 litres (4.2 Imp pt/2.5 US qt)
Cooling system:
    UK models:
        1300 manual transmission .... 3.4 litres (5.9 Imp pt/3.6 US qt)
        1500 manual transmission .... 4.2 litres (7.4 Imp pt/4.4 US qt)
        1300 automatic transmission .... 3.9 litres (6.8 Imp pt/4.1 US qt)
        1500 automatic transmission .... 4.2 litres (7.4 Imp pt/4.4 US qt)
    North American models:
        1300 .... 4.4 litres (7.7 Imp pt/4.6 US qt)
        1500 .... 5.5 litres (9.7 Imp pt/5.8 US qt)
Fuel tank:
    UK models .... 45 litres (9.9 Imp gal/11.9 US gal)
    North American models:
        Hatchback .... 45 litres (9.9 Imp gal/11.9 US gal)
        Sedan and Wagon .... 46 litres (10.1 Imp gal/12.1 US gal)
    CRX:
        Standard .... 41 litres (9.0 Imp gal/10.8 US gal)
        HF .... 38 litres (8.4 Imp gal/10.0 US gal)
        Si .... 45 litres (9.9 Imp gal/11.9 US gal)

Jacking, towing and wheel changing

To avoid repetition, the procedure for raising the vehicle, in order to carry out work under it, is not included before each relevant operation described in this Manual.

It is to be preferred, and it is certainly recommended, that the vehicle is positioned over an inspection pit or raised on a lift. Where these facilities are not available, use ramps or jack up the vehicle strictly in accordance with the following guide. Once the vehicle is raised, supplement the jack with axle stands.

Jacking

To lift the front of the car (both wheels) locate the jack under the jacking bracket. Support the car with axle stands placed under the forward jacking points under the sills.

Raise the rear of the car by placing the jack under the rear jacking bracket.

Support the car with axle stands placed under the rearmost jacking points under the sills.

Towing

If the car is being towed, use the hooks provided, but have the ignition key in position (1) so that the steering does not lock. Remember that the brake pedal will require greater effort as the vacuum servo assistance will not be available.

Ensure that the transmission is in neutral.

If the car is fitted with automatic transmission it is recommended that the front wheels are raised off the ground when being towed. If

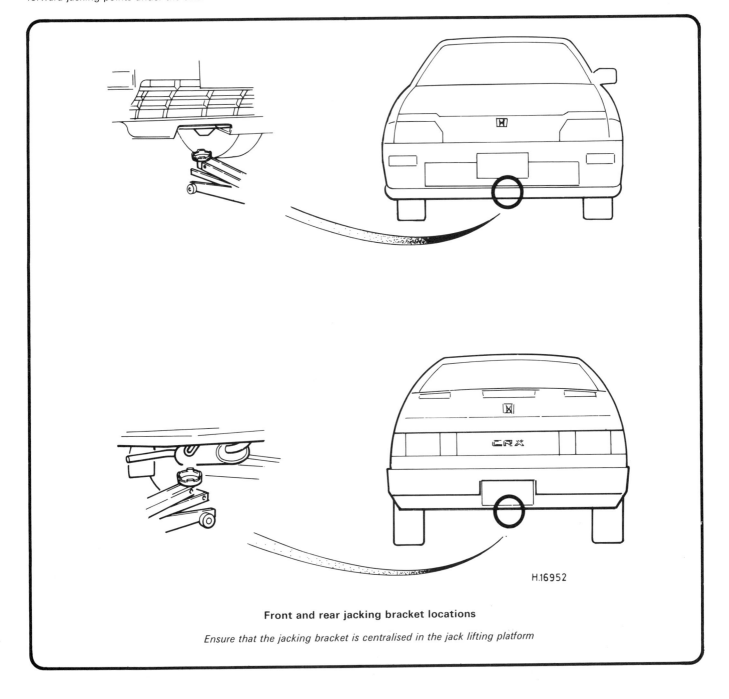

H.16952

Front and rear jacking bracket locations

Ensure that the jacking bracket is centralised in the jack lifting platform

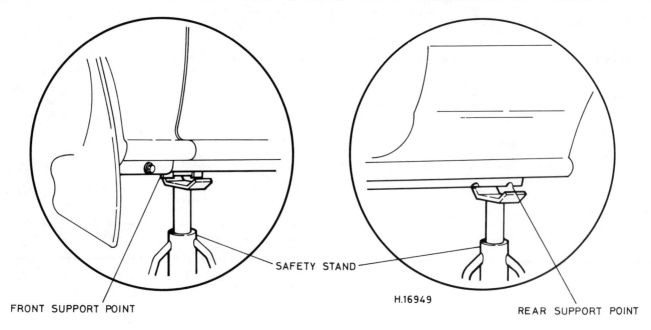

FRONT SUPPORT POINT   SAFETY STAND   H.16949   REAR SUPPORT POINT

Axle stand support points

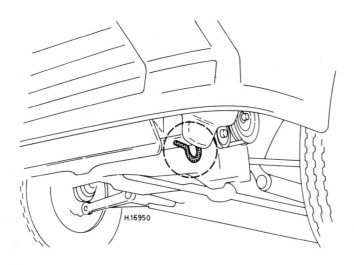

Towing hook location

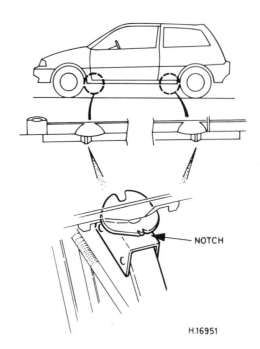

NOTCH

H.16951

this is not possible, restrict the towing speed to 48 km/h (30 mph) and the distance towed to 48 km (30 miles).

Wheel changing

To change a roadwheel, remove the spare wheel from the well in the luggage compartment.

Remove the jack, wheelbrace and trim removal lever fom the container ahead of the spare wheel.

Prise off the hub cap or roadwheel trim according to model.

Make sure that the handbrake is fully applied and chock the wheel opposite to the one being removed.

Release but do not remove the wheel nuts.

Locate the jack from the tool kit under the reinforced jacking point below the sill nearest to the roadwheel being changed. Do not jack up under the tubular bars adjacent to the jacking points. The correct points of lift are marked with a triangle.

Raise the car, remove the wheel nuts and roadwheel.

Fit the spare wheel, tighten the nuts until the roadwheel cannot be held against rotation.

Lower the jack and tighten the roadwheel nuts fully. Fit the wheel trim or hub cap.

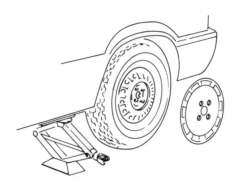

Wheel changing details

Buying spare parts and vehicle identification numbers

Buying spare parts

Spare parts are available from many sources, for example: Honda garages, other garages and accessory shops, and motor factors. Our advice regarding spare parts sources is as follows:

Officially appointed Honda garages – This is the best source for parts which are peculiar to your car and are not generally available (eg complete cylinder heads, internal gearbox components, badges, interior trim etc). It is also the only place at which you should buy parts if your vehicle is still under warranty – non-Honda components may invalidate the warranty. To be sure of obtaining the correct parts it will always be necessary to give the storeman your car's vehicle identification number, and if possible, to take the 'old' part along for positive identification. Many parts are available on a factory exchange scheme – any parts returned should always be clean! It obviously makes good sense to go straight to the specialists on your car for this type of part for they are best equipped to supply you.

Other garages and accessory shops – These are often very good places to buy materials and components needed for the maintenance of your car (eg oil filters, spark plugs, bulbs, drivebelts, oils and greases, touch-up paint, filler paste, etc). They also sell general accessories, usually have convenient opening hours, charge lower prices and can often be found not far from home.

Motor factors – Good factors will stock all of the more important components which wear out relatively quickly (eg clutch components, pistons, valves, exhaust systems, brake cylinders/pipes/hoses/seals and pads etc). Motor factors will often provide new or reconditioned components on a part exchange basis – this can save a considerable amount of money.

Vehicle identification numbers

Modifications are a continuing and unpublicised process in vehicle manufacture, quite apart from major model changes. Spare parts manuals and lists are compiled upon a numerical basis, the individual vehicle numbers being essential to correct identification of the component required.

When ordering spare parts, always give as much information as possible. Quote the car model, year of manufacture, body and engine numbers as appropriate.

On UK models the chassis and engine numbers are stamped on a plate located on the right-hand side of the front body panel (photo). The chassis number is also stamped on the engine compartment bulkhead.

On North American models the vehicle identification number is stamped on a plate attached to the top left-hand side of the facia and also on the engine compartment bulkhead.

Additionally on all models the engine number is stamped on the top edge of the cylinder block adjacent to the transmission mating face. The transmission number is located on the upper face of the transmission casing.

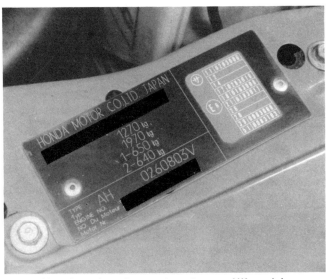

Chassis and engine number plate on UK models

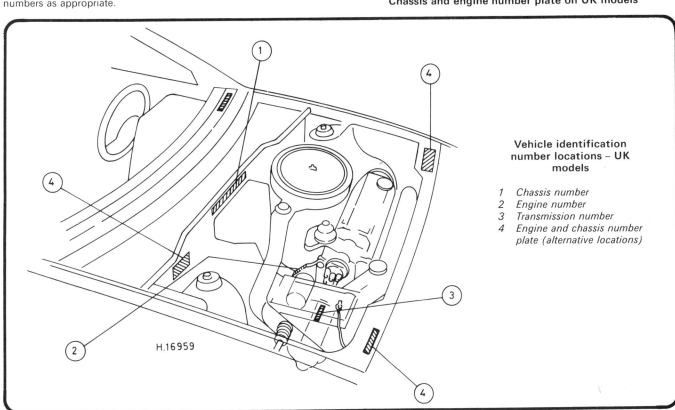

Vehicle identification number locations – UK models

1 *Chassis number*
2 *Engine number*
3 *Transmission number*
4 *Engine and chassis number plate (alternative locations)*

H.16959

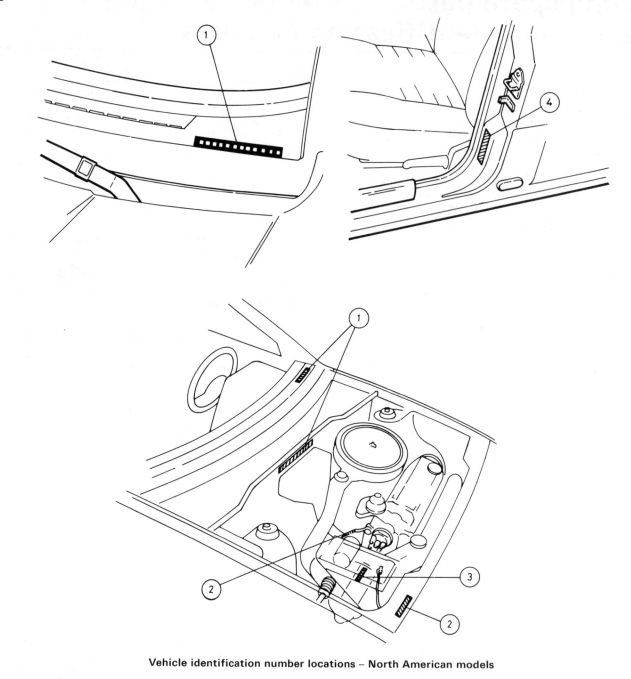

Vehicle identification number locations – North American models

1 *Vehicle identification number*   2 *Engine number*   3 *Transmission*   4 *FMVSS label*

Use of English

As this book has been written in England, it uses the appropriate English component names, phrases, and spelling. Some of these differ from those used in America. Normally, these cause no difficulty, but to make sure, a glossary is printed below. In ordering spare parts remember the parts list may use some of these words:

English	American	English	American
Accelerator	Gas pedal	Leading shoe (of brake)	Primary shoe
Aerial	Antenna	Locks	Latches
Anti-roll bar	Stabiliser or sway bar	Methylated spirit	Denatured alcohol
Big-end bearing	Rod bearing	Motorway	Freeway, turnpike etc
Bonnet (engine cover)	Hood	Number plate	License plate
Boot (luggage compartment)	Trunk	Paraffin	Kerosene
Bulkhead	Firewall	Petrol	Gasoline (gas)
Bush	Bushing	Petrol tank	Gas tank
Cam follower or tappet	Valve lifter or tappet	'Pinking'	'Pinging'
Carburettor	Carburetor	Prise (force apart)	Pry
Catch	Latch	Propeller shaft	Driveshaft
Choke/venturi	Barrel	Quarterlight	Quarter window
Circlip	Snap-ring	Retread	Recap
Clearance	Lash	Reverse	Back-up
Crownwheel	Ring gear (of differential)	Rocker cover	Valve cover
Damper	Shock absorber, shock	Saloon	Sedan
Disc (brake)	Rotor/disk	Seized	Frozen
Distance piece	Spacer	Sidelight	Parking light
Drop arm	Pitman arm	Silencer	Muffler
Drop head coupe	Convertible	Sill panel (beneath doors)	Rocker panel
Dynamo	Generator (DC)	Small end, little end	Piston pin or wrist pin
Earth (electrical)	Ground	Spanner	Wrench
Engineer's blue	Prussian blue	Split cotter (for valve spring cap)	Lock (for valve spring retainer)
Estate car	Station wagon	Split pin	Cotter pin
Exhaust manifold	Header	Steering arm	Spindle arm
Fault finding/diagnosis	Troubleshooting	Sump	Oil pan
Float chamber	Float bowl	Swarf	Metal chips or debris
Free-play	Lash	Tab washer	Tang or lock
Freewheel	Coast	Tappet	Valve lifter
Gearbox	Transmission	Thrust bearing	Throw-out bearing
Gearchange	Shift	Top gear	High
Grub screw	Setscrew, Allen screw	Trackrod (of steering)	Tie-rod (or connecting rod)
Gudgeon pin	Piston pin or wrist pin	Trailing shoe (of brake)	Secondary shoe
Halfshaft	Axleshaft	Transmission	Whole drive line
Handbrake	Parking brake	Tyre	Tire
Hood	Soft top	Van	Panel wagon/van
Hot spot	Heat riser	Vice	Vise
Indicator	Turn signal	Wheel nut	Lug nut
Interior light	Dome lamp	Windscreen	Windshield
Layshaft (of gearbox)	Countershaft	Wing/mudguard	Fender

General repair procedures

Whenever servicing, repair or overhaul work is carried out on the car or its components, it is necessary to observe the following procedures and instructions. This will assist in carrying out the operation efficiently and to a professional standard of workmanship.

Joint mating faces and gaskets

Where a gasket is used between the mating faces of two components, ensure that it is renewed on reassembly, and fit it dry unless otherwise stated in the repair procedure. Make sure that the mating faces are clean and dry with all traces of old gasket removed. When cleaning a joint face, use a tool which is not likely to score or damage the face, and remove any burrs or nicks with an oilstone or fine file.

Make sure that tapped holes are cleaned with a pipe cleaner, and keep them free of jointing compound if this is being used unless specifically instructed otherwise.

Ensure that all orifices, channels or pipes are clear and blow through them, preferably using compressed air.

Oil seals

Whenever an oil seal is removed from its working location, either individually or as part of an assembly, it should be renewed.

The very fine sealing lip of the seal is easily damaged and will not seal if the surface it contacts is not completely clean and free from scratches, nicks or grooves. If the original sealing surface of the component cannot be restored, the component should be renewed.

Protect the lips of the seal from any surface which may damage them in the course of fitting. Use tape or a conical sleeve where possible. Lubricate the seal lips with oil before fitting and, on dual lipped seals, fill the space between the lips with grease.

Unless otherwise stated, oil seals must be fitted with their sealing lips toward the lubricant to be sealed.

Use a tubular drift or block of wood of the appropriate size to install the seal and, if the seal housing is shouldered, drive the seal down to the shoulder. If the seal housing is unshouldered, the seal should be fitted with its face flush with the housing top face.

Screw threads and fastenings

Always ensure that a blind tapped hole is completely free from oil, grease, water or other fluid before installing the bolt or stud. Failure to do this could cause the housing to crack due to the hydraulic action of the bolt or stud as it is screwed in.

When tightening a castellated nut to accept a split pin, tighten the nut to the specified torque, where applicable, and then tighten further to the next split pin hole. Never slacken the nut to align a split pin hole unless stated in the repair procedure.

When checking or retightening a nut or bolt to a specified torque setting, slacken the nut or bolt by a quarter of a turn, and then retighten to the specified setting.

Locknuts, locktabs and washers

Any fastening which will rotate against a component or housing in the course of tightening should always have a washer between it and the relevant component or housing.

Spring or split washers should always be renewed when they are used to lock a critical component such as a big-end bearing retaining nut or bolt.

Locktabs which are folded over to retain a nut or bolt should always be renewed.

Self-locking nuts can be reused in non-critical areas, providing resistance can be felt when the locking portion passes over the bolt or stud thread.

Split pins must always be replaced with new ones of the correct size for the hole.

Special tools

Some repair procedures in this manual entail the use of special tools such as a press, two or three-legged pullers, spring compressors etc. Wherever possible, suitable readily available alternatives to the manufacturer's special tools are described, and are shown in use. In some instances, where no alternative is possible, it has been necessary to resort to the use of a manufacturer's tool and this has been done for reasons of safety as well as the efficient completion of the repair operation. Unless you are highly skilled and have a thorough understanding of the procedure described, never attempt to bypass the use of any special tool when the procedure described specifies its use. Not only is there a very great risk of personal injury, but expensive damage could be caused to the components involved.

Tools and working facilities

Introduction

A selection of good tools is a fundamental requirement for anyone contemplating the maintenance and repair of a motor vehicle. For the owner who does not possess any, their purchase will prove a considerable expense, offsetting some of the savings made by doing-it-yourself. However, provided that the tools purchased are of good quality, they will last for many years and prove an extremely worthwhile investment.

To help the average owner to decide which tools are needed to carry out the various tasks detailed in this manual, we have compiled three lists of tools under the following headings: *Maintenance and minor repair, Repair and overhaul,* and *Special.* The newcomer to practical mechanics should start off with the *Maintenance and minor repair* tool kit and confine himself to the simpler jobs around the vehicle. Then, as his confidence and experience grow, he can undertake more difficult tasks, buying extra tools as, and when, they are needed. In this way, a *Maintenance and minor repair* tool kit can be built-up into a *Repair and overhaul* tool kit over a considerable period of time without any major cash outlays. The experienced do-it-yourselfer will have a tool kit good enough for most repair and overhaul procedures and will add tools from the *Special* category when he feels the expense is justified by the amount of use to which these tools will be put.

It is obviously not possible to cover the subject of tools fully here. For those who wish to learn more about tools and their use there is a book entitled *How to Choose and Use Car Tools* available from the publishers of this manual.

Maintenance and minor repair tool kit

The tools given in this list should be considered as a minimum requirement if routine maintenance, servicing and minor repair operations are to be undertaken. We recommend the purchase of combination spanners (ring one end, open-ended the other); although more expensive than open-ended ones, they do give the advantages of both types of spanner.

    Combination spanners - 10, 11, 12, 13, 14 & 17 mm
    Adjustable spanner - 9 inch
    Spark plug spanner (with rubber insert)
    Spark plug gap adjustment tool
    Set of feeler gauges
    Screwdriver - 4 in long x $^1/_4$ in dia (flat blade)
    Screwdriver - 4 in long x $^1/_4$ in dia (cross blade)
    Combination pliers - 6 inch
    Hacksaw (junior)
    Tyre pump
    Tyre pressure gauge
    Oil can
    Fine emery cloth (1 sheet)
    Wire brush (small)
    Funnel (medium size)

Repair and overhaul tool kit

These tools are virtually essential for anyone undertaking any major repairs to a motor vehicle, and are additional to those given in the *Maintenance and minor repair* list. Included in this list is a comprehensive set of sockets. Although these are expensive they will be found invaluable as they are so versatile - particularly if various drives are included in the set. We recommend the ½ in square-drive type, as this can be used with most proprietary torque wrenches. If you cannot afford a socket set, even bought piecemeal, then inexpensive tubular box spanners are a useful alternative.

The tools in this list will occasionally need to be supplemented by tools from the *Special* list.

    Sockets (or box spanners) to cover range in previous list
    Reversible ratchet drive (for use with sockets)
    Extension piece, 10 inch (for use with sockets)
    Universal joint (for use with sockets)
    Torque wrench (for use with sockets)
    'Mole' wrench - 8 inch
    Ball pein hammer
    Soft-faced hammer, plastic or rubber
    Screwdriver - 6 in long x $^5/_{16}$ in dia (flat blade)
    Screwdriver - 2 in long x $^5/_{16}$ in square (flat blade)
    Screwdriver - 1$^1/_2$ in long x $^1/_4$ in dia (cross blade)
    Screwdriver - 3 in long x $^1/_8$ in dia (electricians)
    Pliers - electricians side cutters
    Pliers - needle nosed
    Pliers - circlip (internal and external)
    Cold chisel - $^1/_2$ inch
    Scriber
    Scraper
    Centre punch
    Pin punch
    Hacksaw
    Valve grinding tool
    Steel rule/straight-edge
    Allen keys
    Selection of files
    Wire brush (large)
    Axle-stands
    Jack (strong trolley or hydraulic type)

Special tools

The tools in this list are those which are not used regularly, are expensive to buy, or which need to be used in accordance with their manufacturers' instructions. Unless relatively difficult mechanical jobs are undertaken frequently, it will not be economic to buy many of these tools. Where this is the case, you could consider clubbing together with friends (or joining a motorists' club) to make a joint purchase, or borrowing the tools against a deposit from a local garage or tool hire specialist.

The following list contains only those tools and instruments freely available to the public, and not those special tools produced by the vehicle manufacturer specifically for its dealer network. You will find occasional references to these manufacturers' special tools in the text of this manual. Generally, an alternative method of doing the job without the vehicle manufacturers' special tool is given. However, sometimes, there is no alternative to using them. Where this is the case and the relevant tool cannot be bought or borrowed, you will have to entrust the work to a franchised garage.

Valve spring compressor
Piston ring compressor
Balljoint separator
Universal hub/bearing puller
Impact screwdriver
Micrometer and/or vernier gauge
Dial gauge
Stroboscopic timing light
Dwell angle meter/tachometer
Universal electrical multi-meter
Cylinder compression gauge
Lifting tackle
Trolley jack
Light with extension lead

Buying tools

For practically all tools, a tool factor is the best source since he will have a very comprehensive range compared with the average garage or accessory shop. Having said that, accessory shops often offer excellent quality tools at discount prices, so it pays to shop around.

Remember, you don't have to buy the most expensive items on the shelf, but it is always advisable to steer clear of the very cheap tools. There are plenty of good tools around at reasonable prices, so ask the proprietor or manager of the shop for advice before making a purchase.

Care and maintenance of tools

Having purchased a reasonable tool kit, it is necessary to keep the tools in a clean serviceable condition. After use, always wipe off any dirt, grease and metal particles using a clean, dry cloth, before putting the tools away. Never leave them lying around after they have been used. A simple tool rack on the garage or workshop wall, for items such as screwdrivers and pliers is a good idea. Store all normal wrenches and sockets in a metal box. Any measuring instruments, gauges, meters, etc, must be carefully stored where they cannot be damaged or become rusty.

Take a little care when tools are used. Hammer heads inevitably become marked and screwdrivers lose the keen edge on their blades from time to time. A little timely attention with emery cloth or a file will soon restore items like this to a good serviceable finish.

Working facilities

Not to be forgotten when discussing tools, is the workshop itself. If anything more than routine maintenance is to be carried out, some form of suitable working area becomes essential.

It is appreciated that many an owner mechanic is forced by circumstances to remove an engine or similar item, without the benefit of a garage or workshop. Having done this, any repairs should always be done under the cover of a roof.

Wherever possible, any dismantling should be done on a clean, flat workbench or table at a suitable working height.

Any workbench needs a vice: one with a jaw opening of 4 in (100 mm) is suitable for most jobs. As mentioned previously, some clean dry storage space is also required for tools, as well as for lubricants, cleaning fluids, touch-up paints and so on, which become necessary.

Another item which may be required, and which has a much more general usage, is an electric drill with a chuck capacity of at least 5/16 in (8 mm). This, together with a good range of twist drills, is virtually essential for fitting accessories such as mirrors and reversing lights.

Last, but not least, always keep a supply of old newspapers and clean, lint-free rags available, and try to keep any working area as clean as possible.

Spanner jaw gap comparison table

Jaw gap (in)	Spanner size
0.250	1/4 in AF
0.276	7 mm
0.313	5/16 in AF
0.315	8 mm
0.344	11/32 in AF; 1/8 in Whitworth
0.354	9 mm
0.375	3/8 in AF
0.394	10 mm
0.433	11 mm
0.438	7/16 in AF
0.445	3/16 in Whitworth; 1/4 in BSF
0.472	12 mm
0.500	1/2 in AF
0.512	13 mm
0.525	1/4 in Whitworth; 5/16 in BSF
0.551	14 mm
0.563	9/16 in AF
0.591	15 mm
0.600	5/16 in Whitworth; 3/8 in BSF
0.625	5/8 in AF
0.630	16 mm
0.669	17 mm
0.686	11/16 in AF
0.709	18 mm
0.710	3/8 in Whitworth; 7/16 in BSF
0.748	19 mm
0.750	3/4 in AF
0.813	13/16 in AF
0.820	7/16 in Whitworth; 1/2 in BSF
0.866	22 mm
0.875	7/8 in AF
0.920	1/2 in Whitworth; 9/16 in BSF
0.938	15/16 in AF
0.945	24 mm
1.000	1 in AF
1.010	9/16 in Whitworth; 5/8 in BSF
1.024	26 mm
1.063	11/16 in AF; 27 mm
1.100	5/8 in Whitworth; 11/16 in BSF
1.125	11/8 in AF
1.181	30 mm
1.200	11/16 in Whitworth; 3/4 in BSF
1.250	11/4 in AF
1.260	32 mm
1.300	3/4 in Whitworth; 7/8 in BSF
1.313	15/16 in AF
1.390	13/16 in Whitworth; 15/16 in BSF
1.417	36 mm
1.438	17/16 in AF
1.480	7/8 in Whitworth; 1 in BSF
1.500	11/2 in AF
1.575	40 mm; 15/16 in Whitworth
1.614	41 mm
1.625	15/8 in AF
1.670	1 in Whitworth; 11/8 in BSF
1.688	111/16 in AF
1.811	46 mm
1.813	113/16 in AF
1.860	11/8 in Whitworth; 11/4 in BSF
1.875	17/8 in AF
1.969	50 mm
2.000	2 in AF
2.050	11/4 in Whitworth; 13/8 in BSF
2.165	55 mm
2.362	60 mm

Conversion factors

Length (distance)
Inches (in)	X	25.4	= Millimetres (mm)	X 0.0394	= Inches (in)
Feet (ft)	X	0.305	= Metres (m)	X 3.281	= Feet (ft)
Miles	X	1.609	= Kilometres (km)	X 0.621	= Miles

Volume (capacity)
Cubic inches (cu in; in^3)	X	16.387	= Cubic centimetres (cc; cm^3)	X 0.061	= Cubic inches (cu in; in^3)
Imperial pints (Imp pt)	X	0.568	= Litres (l)	X 1.76	= Imperial pints (Imp pt)
Imperial quarts (Imp qt)	X	1.137	= Litres (l)	X 0.88	= Imperial quarts (Imp qt)
Imperial quarts (Imp qt)	X	1.201	= US quarts (US qt)	X 0.833	= Imperial quarts (Imp qt)
US quarts (US qt)	X	0.946	= Litres (l)	X 1.057	= US quarts (US qt)
Imperial gallons (Imp gal)	X	4.546	= Litres (l)	X 0.22	= Imperial gallons (Imp gal)
Imperial gallons (Imp gal)	X	1.201	= US gallons (US gal)	X 0.833	= Imperial gallons (Imp gal)
US gallons (US gal)	X	3.785	= Litres (l)	X 0.264	= US gallons (US gal)

Mass (weight)
Ounces (oz)	X	28.35	= Grams (g)	X 0.035	= Ounces (oz)
Pounds (lb)	X	0.454	= Kilograms (kg)	X 2.205	= Pounds (lb)

Force
Ounces-force (ozf; oz)	X	0.278	= Newtons (N)	X 3.6	= Ounces-force (ozf; oz)
Pounds-force (lbf; lb)	X	4.448	= Newtons (N)	X 0.225	= Pounds-force (lbf; lb)
Newtons (N)	X	0.1	= Kilograms-force (kgf; kg)	X 9.81	= Newtons (N)

Pressure
Pounds-force per square inch (psi; lbf/in^2; lb/in^2)	X	0.070	= Kilograms-force per square centimetre (kgf/cm^2; kg/cm^2)	X 14.223	= Pounds-force per square inch (psi; lbf/in^2; lb/in^2)
Pounds-force per square inch (psi; lbf/in^2; lb/in^2)	X	0.068	= Atmospheres (atm)	X 14.696	= Pounds-force per square inch (psi; lbf/in^2; lb/in^2)
Pounds-force per square inch (psi; lbf/in^2; lb/in^2)	X	0.069	= Bars	X 14.5	= Pounds-force per square inch (psi; lbf/in^2; lb/in^2)
Pounds-force per square inch (psi; lbf/in^2; lb/in^2)	X	6.895	= Kilopascals (kPa)	X 0.145	= Pounds-force per square inch (psi; lbf/in^2; lb/in^2)
Kilopascals (kPa)	X	0.01	= Kilograms-force per square centimetre (kgf/cm^2; kg/cm^2)	X 98.1	= Kilopascals (kPa)

Torque (moment of force)
Pounds-force inches (lbf in; lb in)	X	1.152	= Kilograms-force centimetre (kgf cm; kg cm)	X 0.868	= Pounds-force inches (lbf in; lb in)
Pounds-force inches (lbf in; lb in)	X	0.113	= Newton metres (Nm)	X 8.85	= Pounds-force inches (lbf in; lb in)
Pounds-force inches (lbf in; lb in)	X	0.083	= Pounds-force feet (lbf ft; lb ft)	X 12	= Pounds-force inches (lbf in; lb in)
Pounds-force feet (lbf ft; lb ft)	X	0.138	= Kilograms-force metres (kgf m; kg m)	X 7.233	= Pounds-force feet (lbf ft; lb ft)
Pounds-force feet (lbf ft; lb ft)	X	1.356	= Newton metres (Nm)	X 0.738	= Pounds-force feet (lbf ft; lb ft)
Newton metres (Nm)	X	0.102	= Kilograms-force metres (kgf m; kg m)	X 9.804	= Newton metres (Nm)

Power
Horsepower (hp)	X	745.7	= Watts (W)	X 0.0013	= Horsepower (hp)

Velocity (speed)
Miles per hour (miles/hr; mph)	X	1.609	= Kilometres per hour (km/hr; kph)	X 0.621	= Miles per hour (miles/hr; mph)

Fuel consumption*
Miles per gallon, Imperial (mpg)	X	0.354	= Kilometres per litre (km/l)	X 2.825	= Miles per gallon, Imperial (mpg)
Miles per gallon, US (mpg)	X	0.425	= Kilometres per litre (km/l)	X 2.352	= Miles per gallon, US (mpg)

Temperature
Degrees Fahrenheit = (°C x 1.8) + 32   Degrees Celsius (Degrees Centigrade; °C) = (°F - 32) x 0.56

*It is common practice to convert from miles per gallon (mpg) to litres/100 kilometres (l/100km),
where mpg (Imperial) x l/100 km = 282 and mpg (US) x l/100 km = 235

Safety first!

Professional motor mechanics are trained in safe working procedures. However enthusiastic you may be about getting on with the job in hand, do take the time to ensure that your safety is not put at risk. A moment's lack of attention can result in an accident, as can failure to observe certain elementary precautions.

There will always be new ways of having accidents, and the following points do not pretend to be a comprehensive list of all dangers; they are intended rather to make you aware of the risks and to encourage a safety-conscious approach to all work you carry out on your vehicle.

Essential DOs and DON'Ts

DON'T rely on a single jack when working underneath the vehicle. Always use reliable additional means of support, such as axle stands, securely placed under a part of the vehicle that you know will not give way.

DON'T attempt to loosen or tighten high-torque nuts (e.g. wheel hub nuts) while the vehicle is on a jack; it may be pulled off.

DON'T start the engine without first ascertaining that the transmission is in neutral (or 'Park' where applicable) and the parking brake applied.

DON'T suddenly remove the filler cap from a hot cooling system – cover it with a cloth and release the pressure gradually first, or you may get scalded by escaping coolant.

DON'T attempt to drain oil until you are sure it has cooled sufficiently to avoid scalding you.

DON'T grasp any part of the engine, exhaust or catalytic converter without first ascertaining that it is sufficiently cool to avoid burning you.

DON'T allow brake fluid or antifreeze to contact vehicle paintwork.

DON'T syphon toxic liquids such as fuel, brake fluid or antifreeze by mouth, or allow them to remain on your skin.

DON'T inhale dust – it may be injurious to health (see *Asbestos* below).

DON'T allow any spilt oil or grease to remain on the floor – wipe it up straight away, before someone slips on it.

DON'T use ill-fitting spanners or other tools which may slip and cause injury.

DON'T attempt to lift a heavy component which may be beyond your capability – get assistance.

DON'T rush to finish a job, or take unverified short cuts.

DON'T allow children or animals in or around an unattended vehicle.

DO wear eye protection when using power tools such as drill, sander, bench grinder etc, and when working under the vehicle.

DO use a barrier cream on your hands prior to undertaking dirty jobs – it will protect your skin from infection as well as making the dirt easier to remove afterwards; but make sure your hands aren't left slippery.

DO keep loose clothing (cuffs, tie etc) and long hair well out of the way of moving mechanical parts.

DO remove rings, wristwatch etc, before working on the vehicle – especially the electrical system.

DO ensure that any lifting tackle used has a safe working load rating adequate for the job.

DO keep your work area tidy – it is only too easy to fall over articles left lying around.

DO get someone to check periodically that all is well, when working alone on the vehicle.

DO carry out work in a logical sequence and check that everything is correctly assembled and tightened afterwards.

DO remember that your vehicle's safety affects that of yourself and others. If in doubt on any point, get specialist advice.

IF, in spite of following these precautions, you are unfortunate enough to injure yourself, seek medical attention as soon as possible.

Asbestos

Certain friction, insulating, sealing, and other products – such as brake linings, brake bands, clutch linings, torque converters, gaskets, etc – contain asbestos. *Extreme care must be taken to avoid inhalation of dust from such products since it is hazardous to health*. If in doubt, assume that they *do* contain asbestos.

Fire

Remember at all times that petrol (gasoline) is highly flammable. Never smoke, or have any kind of naked flame around, when working on the vehicle. But the risk does not end there – a spark caused by an electrical short-circuit, by two metal surfaces contacting each other, by careless use of tools, or even by static electricity built up in your body under certain conditions, can ignite petrol vapour, which in a confined space is highly explosive.

Always disconnect the battery earth (ground) terminal before working on any part of the fuel or electrical system, and never risk spilling fuel on to a hot engine or exhaust.

It is recommended that a fire extinguisher of a type suitable for fuel and electrical fires is kept handy in the garage or workplace at all times. Never try to extinguish a fuel or electrical fire with water.

Fumes

Certain fumes are highly toxic and can quickly cause unconsciousness and even death if inhaled to any extent. Petrol (gasoline) vapour comes into this category, as do the vapours from certain solvents such as trichloroethylene. Any draining or pouring of such volatile fluids should be done in a well ventilated area.

When using cleaning fluids and solvents, read the instructions carefully. Never use materials from unmarked containers – they may give off poisonous vapours.

Never run the engine of a motor vehicle in an enclosed space such as a garage. Exhaust fumes contain carbon monoxide which is extremely poisonous; if you need to run the engine, always do so in the open air or at least have the rear of the vehicle outside the workplace.

If you are fortunate enough to have the use of an inspection pit, never drain or pour petrol, and never run the engine, while the vehicle is standing over it; the fumes, being heavier than air, will concentrate in the pit with possibly lethal results.

The battery

Never cause a spark, or allow a naked light, near the vehicle's battery. It will normally be giving off a certain amount of hydrogen gas, which is highly explosive.

Always disconnect the battery earth (ground) terminal before working on the fuel or electrical systems.

If possible, loosen the filler plugs or cover when charging the battery from an external source. Do not charge at an excessive rate or the battery may burst.

Take care when topping up and when carrying the battery. The acid electrolyte, even when diluted, is very corrosive and should not be allowed to contact the eyes or skin.

If you ever need to prepare electrolyte yourself, always add the acid slowly to the water, and never the other way round. Protect against splashes by wearing rubber gloves and goggles.

When jump starting a car using a booster battery, for negative earth (ground) vehicles, connect the jump leads in the following sequence: First connect one jump lead between the positive (+) terminals of the two batteries. Then connect the other jump lead first to the negative (−) terminal of the booster battery, and then to a good earthing (ground) point on the vehicle to be started, at least 18 in (45 cm) from the battery if possible. Ensure that hands and jump leads are clear of any moving parts, and that the two vehicles do not touch. Disconnect the leads in the reverse order.

Mains electricity

When using an electric power tool, inspection light etc, which works from the mains, always ensure that the appliance is correctly connected to its plug and that, where necessary, it is properly earthed (grounded). Do not use such appliances in damp conditions and, again, beware of creating a spark or applying excessive heat in the vicinity of fuel or fuel vapour.

Ignition HT voltage

A severe electric shock can result from touching certain parts of the ignition system, such as the HT leads, when the engine is running or being cranked, particularly if components are damp or the insulation is defective. Where an electronic ignition system is fitted, the HT voltage is much higher and could prove fatal.

Routine maintenance

Maintenance is essential for ensuring safety, and desirable for the purpose of getting the best in terms of performance and economy from your car. Over the years the need for periodic lubrication has been greatly reduced if not totally eliminated. This has unfortunately tended to lead some owners to think that, because no such action is required, the items either no longer exist, or will last forever. This is certainly not the case; it is essential to carry out regular visual examination as comprehensively as possible in order to spot any possible defects at an early stage before they develop into major expensive repairs.

The following service schedules are a list of the maintenance requirements and the intervals at which they should be carried out, as recommended by the manufacturers. Where applicable these procedures are covered in greater detail throughout this manual, near the beginning of each Chapter.

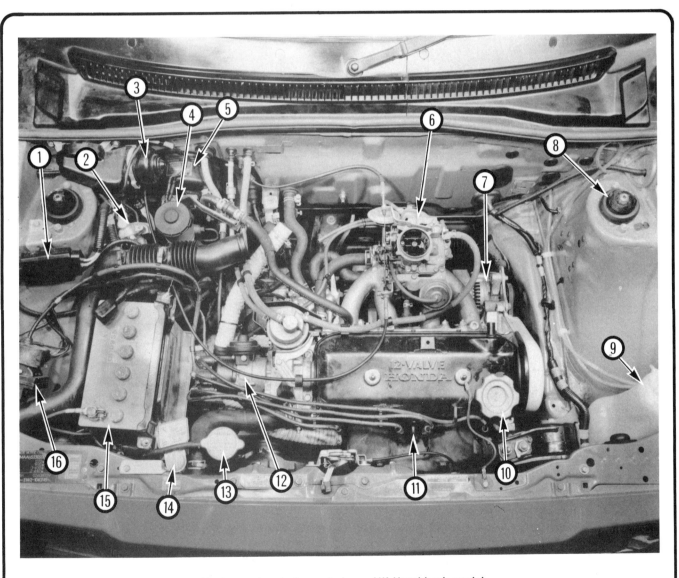

Engine and underbonnet view – UK Hatchback model

1 Fusible links
2 Brake pressure regulating valve
3 Windscreen wiper motor
4 Brake master cylinder reservoir
5 Brake servo
6 Carburettor
7 Alternator
8 Suspension strut upper mounting
9 Windscreen washer reservoir
10 Oil filler cap
11 Oil level dipstick
12 Distributor
13 Radiator filler cap
14 Coolant reservoir
15 Battery
16 Ignition coil

Front underbody view – UK
Hatchback model

1 Brake caliper
2 Suspension lower arm
3 Transmission
4 Oil drain plug
5 Tie-rod outer balljoint
6 Radius arm
7 Torque tube
8 Exhaust flexible joint
9 Exhaust intermediate section
10 Gearchange remote control
   rod
11 Torque rod
12 Driveshaft inner constant
   velocity joint

Rear underbody view – UK Hatchback model

1 Exhaust pipe
2 Fuel pump cover
3 Trailing arm front mounting
4 Fuel tank drain plug
5 Shock absorber lower mounting
6 Rear axle beam
7 Panhard rod
8 Stabilizer control arm
9 Coil spring
10 Rear brake hose
11 Trailing arm

At weekly intervals or before a long journey

Engine, cooling system and brakes:
 Check the engine oil level (Chapter 1)
 Check the coolant level (Chapter 2)
 Check the brake fluid level in the master cylinder (Chapter 9)
Battery, lights and wipers:
 Check the operation of all interior and exterior lights, wipers and washers (Chapter 12)
 Check and if necessary top up the washer reservoir (Chapter 12)
 Check and if necessary top up the battery – where applicable (Chapter 12)
Tyres:
 Check the tyre pressures (Chapter 10)
 Visually examine the tyres for wear and tread damage (Chapter 10)
General:
 Clean the windscreen and if necessary the windows
 Clean the headlamp and rear lamp lenses

Every 6000 miles (10 000 km) for UK models/7500 miles (12 000 km) for North American models, or 6 months – whichever comes first

Engine (Chapter 1)
 Renew the engine oil and filter
Braking system (Chapter 9)
 Inspect and if necessary renew the front disc pads

Every 12 000 miles (20 000 km) for UK models/15 000 miles (24 000 km) for North American models, or annually – whichever comes first

Engine (Chapter 1)
 Renew the engine oil and filter
 Check and adjust the valve clearances
Fuel, exhaust and emission control systems (Chapter 3)
 Renew the air cleaner element (UK models only)
 Check and if necessary adjust the idle speed and mixture (UK models only)
 Check the condition and security of the exhaust system
Ignition system (Chapter 4)
 Check and if necessary adjust the ignition timing (UK models only)
 Renew the spark plugs (UK models only)
Clutch (Chapter 5)
 Check the clutch adjustment
Manual transmission (Chapter 6)
 Check and if necessary top up the transmission oil
Automatic transmission (Chapter 7)
 Renew the transmission fluid (UK models only)
 Check and if necessary top up the transmission fluid (North American models only)
Driveshafts (Chapter 8)
 Check the condition of the driveshaft constant velocity joints
Braking system (Chapter 9)
 Inspect and if necessary renew the front disc pads
 Check the operation of the handbrake
Suspension and steering (Chapter 10)
 Check the condition of and security of all suspension and steering mountings, joints and linkages
 Check the power-assisted steering fluid level (where applicable)
 Check the front wheel alignment

Every 24 000 miles (40 000 km) for UK models/30 000 miles (48 000 km) for North American models, or 2 years – whichever comes first

In addition to all the items in the previous service, carry out the following:
Engine (Chapter 1)
 Renew the crankcase ventilation system PCV valve and blow-by filter
Cooling system (Chapter 2)
 Check the condition and security of all cooling system hoses, pipes and connections
Fuel, exhaust and emission control systems (Chapter 3)
 Renew the air cleaner element (North American models only)
 Renew the fuel filter (UK models only)
 Check the condition of the fuel tank, pipes and connections
 Check the operation of the accelerator and choke controls
Ignition system (Chapter 4)
 Clean and inspect the distributor cap and ignition leads and wiring
 Renew the spark plugs (North American models only)
Manual transmission (Chapter 6)
 Renew the transmission oil
Automatic transmission (Chapter 7)
 Renew the transmission fluid (North American models only)
Braking system (Chapter 9)
 Inspect the condition of the brake pipes, hoses and unions
 Check the condition of the rear brake shoes, drums and wheel cylinders
 Renew the brake fluid
Suspension and steering (Chapter 10)
 Check the condition of the steering pump drivebelt
Bodywork and fittings (Chapter 11)
 Check the condition of the air conditioning compressor drivebelt (where applicable)

Every 36 000 miles (60 000 km) for UK models/45 000 miles (72 000 km) for North American models, or 3 years – whichever comes first

In addition to all the items previously listed, carry out the following:
Cooling system (Chapter 2)
 Renew the coolant in the cooling system (North American models only)

Every 48 000 miles (80 000 km) for UK models/60 000 miles (96 000 km) for North American models, or 4 years – whichever comes first

In addition to all the items previously listed, carry out the following:
Cooling system (Chapter 2)
 Renew the coolant in the cooling system (UK models only)
Fuel, exhaust and emission control systems (Chapter 3)
 Renew the fuel filter (North American models only)
 Check and if necessary adjust the idle speeds and mixture (North American models only)
 Have the emission control equipment checked and serviced by a dealer (North American models only)
 Check the operation of the air cleaner intake air control system
Ignition system (Chapter 4)
 Check and if necessary adjust the ignition timing (North American models only)

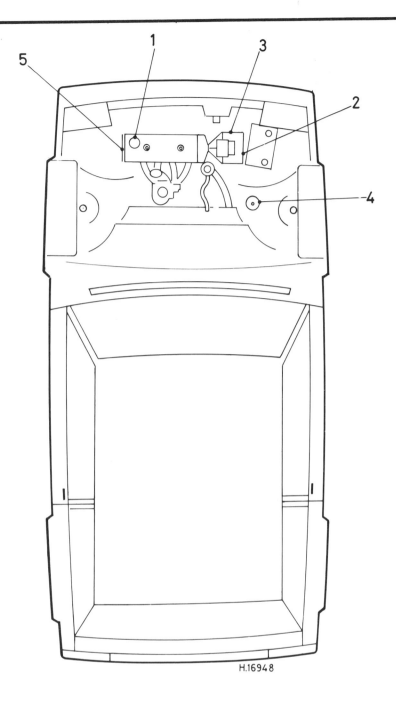

H.16948

Recommended lubricants and fluids

Component or system	Lubricant type or specification
Engine (1)	SAE 10W/40 multigrade engine oil (or multigrade engine oil with a viscosity rating suitable for the environmental temperature in which the vehicle is operated – see owner's handbook)
Manual transmission (2)	SAE 10W/40 multigrade engine oil (as above)
Automatic transmission (3)	Dexron automatic transmission fluid
Brake fluid (4)	Brake fluid to FMVSS 116, DOT 3 or 4 specification
Power-assisted steering (5)	Honda power steering fluid
General greasing	Multi-purpose grease

Fault diagnosis

Introduction

The vehicle owner who does his or her own maintenance according to the recommended schedules should not have to use this section of the manual very often. Modern component reliability is such that, provided those items subject to wear or deterioration are inspected or renewed at the specified intervals, sudden failure is comparatively rare. Faults do not usually just happen as a result of sudden failure, but develop over a period of time. Major mechanical failures in particular are usually preceded by characteristic symptoms over hundreds or even thousands of miles. Those components which do occasionally fail without warning are often small and easily carried in the vehicle.

With any fault finding, the first step is to decide where to begin investigations. Sometimes this is obvious, but on other occasions a little detective work will be necessary. The owner who makes half a dozen haphazard adjustments or replacements may be successful in curing a fault (or its symptoms), but he will be none the wiser if the fault recurs and he may well have spent more time and money than was necessary. A calm and logical approach will be found to be more satisfactory in the long run. Always take into account any warning signs or abnormalities that may have been noticed in the period preceding the fault – power loss, high or low gauge readings, unusual noises or smells, etc – and remember that failure of components such as fuses or spark plugs may only be pointers to some underlying fault.

The pages which follow here are intended to help in cases of failure to start or breakdown on the road. There is also a Fault Diagnosis Section at the end of each Chapter which should be consulted if the preliminary checks prove unfruitful. Whatever the fault, certain basic principles apply. These are as follows:

Verify the fault. This is simply a matter of being sure that you know what the symptoms are before starting work. This is particularly important if you are investigating a fault for someone else who may not have described it very accurately.

Don't overlook the obvious. For example, if the vehicle won't start, is there petrol in the tank? (Don't take anyone else's word on this particular point, and don't trust the fuel gauge either!) If an electrical fault is indicated, look for loose or broken wires before digging out the test gear.

Cure the disease, not the symptom. Substituting a flat battery with a fully charged one will get you off the hard shoulder, but if the underlying cause is not attended to, the new battery will go the same way. Similarly, changing oil-fouled spark plugs for a new set will get you moving again, but remember that the reason for the fouling (if it wasn't simply an incorrect grade of plug) will have to be established and corrected.

Don't take anything for granted. Particularly, don't forget that a 'new' component may itself be defective (especially if it's been rattling round in the boot for months), and don't leave components out of a fault diagnosis sequence just because they are new or recently fitted. When you do finally diagnose a difficult fault, you'll probably realise that all the evidence was there from the start.

Electrical faults

Electrical faults can be more puzzling than straightforward mechanical failures, but they are no less susceptible to logical analysis if the basic principles of operation are understood. Vehicle electrical wiring exists in extremely unfavourable conditions – heat, vibration and chemical attack – and the first things to look for are loose or corroded connections and broken or chafed wires, especially where the wires pass through holes in the bodywork or are subject to vibration.

All metal-bodied vehicles in current production have one pole of the battery 'earthed', ie connected to the vehicle bodywork, and in nearly all modern vehicles it is the negative (–) terminal. The various electrical components – motors, bulb holders etc – are also connected to earth, either by means of a lead or directly by their mountings. Electric current flows through the component and then back to the battery via the bodywork. If the component mounting is loose or corroded, or if a good path back to the battery is not available, the circuit will be incomplete and malfunction will result. The engine and/or gearbox are also earthed by means of flexible metal straps to the body or subframe; if these straps are loose or missing, starter motor, generator and ignition trouble may result.

Assuming the earth return to be satisfactory, electrical faults will be due either to component malfunction or to defects in the current supply. Individual components are dealt with in Chapter 12. If supply wires are broken or cracked internally this results in an open-circuit, and the easiest way to check for this is to bypass the suspect wire temporarily with a length of wire having a crocodile clip or suitable connector at each end. Alternatively, a 12V test lamp can be used to verify the presence of supply voltage at various points along the wire and the break can be thus isolated.

If a bare portion of a live wire touches the bodywork or other earthed metal part, the electricity will take the low-resistance path thus formed back to the battery: this is known as a short-circuit. Hopefully a short-circuit will blow a fuse, but otherwise it may cause burning of the insulation (and possibly further short-circuits) or even a fire. This is why it is inadvisable to bypass persistently blowing fuses with silver foil or wire.

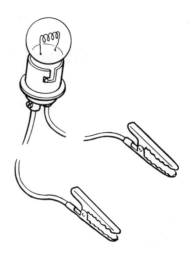

A simple test lamp is useful for tracing electrical faults

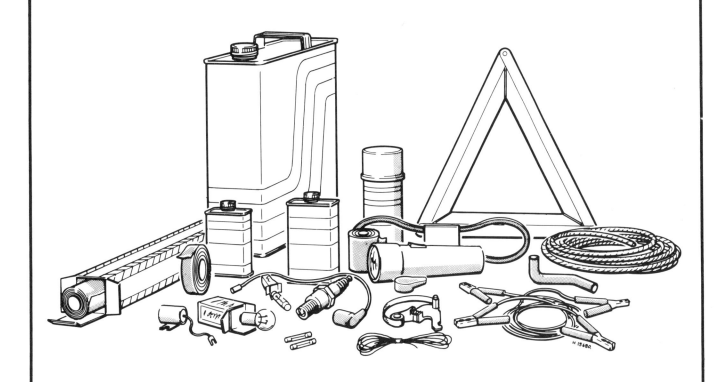

Carrying a few spares may save you a long walk!

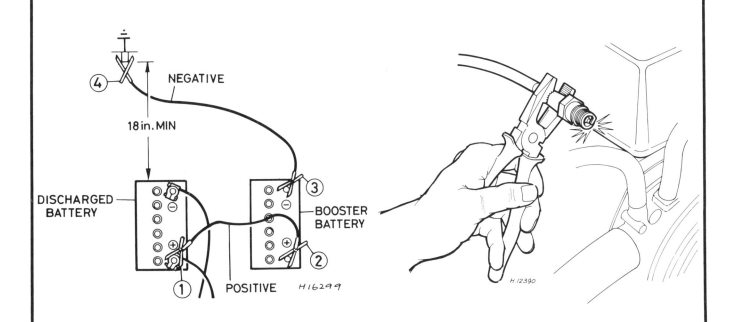

Jump start lead connections for negative earth vehicles –
connect leads in order shown

Crank engine and check for spark. Note use of insulated
tool to hold plug lead

Spares and tool kit

Most vehicles are supplied only with sufficient tools for wheel changing; the *Maintenance and minor repair* tool kit detailed in *Tools and working facilities,* with the addition of a hammer, is probably sufficient for those repairs that most motorists would consider attempting at the roadside. In addition a few items which can be fitted without too much trouble in the event of a breakdown should be carried. Experience and available space will modify the list below, but the following may save having to call on professional assistance:

Spark plugs, clean and correctly gapped
HT lead and plug cap – long enough to reach the plug furthest from the distributor
Distributor rotor
Drivebelt(s) – emergency type may suffice
Spare fuses
Set of principal light bulbs
Tin of radiator sealer and hose bandage
Exhaust bandage
Roll of insulating tape
Length of soft iron wire
Length of electrical flex
Torch or inspection lamp (can double as test lamp)
Battery jump leads
Tow-rope
Ignition waterproofing aerosol
Litre of engine oil
Sealed can of hydraulic fluid
Emergency windscreen
Worm drive clips
Tube of filler paste

If spare fuel is carried, a can designed for the purpose should be used to minimise risks of leakage and collision damage. A first aid kit and a warning triangle, whilst not at present compulsory in the UK, are obviously sensible items to carry in addition to the above.

When touring abroad it may be advisable to carry additional spares which, even if you cannot fit them yourself, could save having to wait while parts are obtained. The items below may be worth considering:

Clutch and throttle cables
Cylinder head gasket
Alternator brushes
Tyre valve core

One of the motoring organisations will be able to advise on availability of fuel etc in foreign countries.

Engine will not start

Engine fails to turn when starter operated
Flat battery (recharge, use jump leads, or push start)
Battery terminals loose or corroded
Battery earth to body defective
Engine earth strap loose or broken
Starter motor (or solenoid) wiring loose or broken
Automatic transmission selector in wrong position, or inhibitor switch faulty
Ignition/starter switch faulty
Major mechanical failure (seizure)
Starter or solenoid internal fault (see Chapter 12)

Starter motor turns engine slowly
Partially discharged battery (recharge, use jump leads, or push start)
Battery terminals loose or corroded
Battery earth to body defective
Engine earth strap loose
Starter motor (or solenoid) wiring loose
Starter motor internal fault (see Chapter 12)

Starter motor spins without turning engine
Flat battery
Starter motor pinion sticking on sleeve
Flywheel gear teeth damaged or worn
Starter motor mounting bolts loose

Engine turns normally but fails to start
Damp or dirty HT leads and distributor cap (crank engine and check for spark)
No fuel in tank (check for delivery at carburettor)
Excessive choke (hot engine) or insufficient choke (cold engine)
Fouled or incorrectly gapped spark plugs (remove, clean and regap)
Other ignition system fault (see Chapter 4)
Other fuel system fault (see Chapter 3)
Poor compression (see Chapter 1)
Major mechanical failure (eg camshaft drive)

Engine fires but will not run
Insufficient choke (cold engine)
Air leaks at carburettor or inlet manifold
Fuel starvation (see Chapter 3)
Ballast resistor defective, or other ignition fault (see Chapter 4)

Engine cuts out and will not restart

Engine cuts out suddenly – ignition fault
Loose or disconnected LT wires
Wet HT leads or distributor cap (after traversing water splash)
Coil or condenser failure (check for spark)
Other ignition fault (see Chapter 4)

Engine misfires before cutting out – fuel fault
Fuel tank empty
Fuel pump defective or filter blocked (check for delivery)
Fuel tank filler vent blocked (suction will be evident on releasing cap)
Carburettor needle valve sticking
Carburettor jets blocked (fuel contaminated)
Other fuel system fault (see Chapter 3)

Engine cuts out – other causes
Serious overheating
Major mechanical failure (eg camshaft drive)

Engine overheats

Ignition (no-charge) warning light illuminated
Slack or broken drivebelt – retension or renew (Chapter 12)

Ignition warning light not illuminated
Coolant loss due to internal or external leakage (see Chapter 12)
Thermostat defective
Low oil level
Brakes binding
Radiator clogged externally or internally
Electric cooling fan not operating correctly
Engine waterways clogged
Ignition timing incorrect or automatic advance malfunctioning
Mixture too weak

Note: *Do not add cold water to an overheated engine or damage may result*

Low engine oil pressure

Gauge reads low or warning light illuminated with engine running
Oil level low or incorrect grade
Defective gauge or sender unit
Wire to sender unit earthed
Engine overheating
Oil filter clogged or bypass valve defective
Oil pressure relief valve defective
Oil pick-up strainer clogged
Oil pump worn or mountings loose
Worn main or big-end bearings

Note: *Low oil pressure in a high-mileage engine at tickover is not necessarily a cause for concern. Sudden pressure loss at speed is far more significant. In any event, check the gauge or warning light sender before condemning the engine.*

Engine noises

Pre-ignition (pinking) on acceleration
    Incorrect grade of fuel
    Ignition timing incorrect
    Distributor faulty or worn
    Worn or maladjusted carburettor
    Excessive carbon build-up in engine

Whistling or wheezing noises
    Leaking vacuum hose
    Leaking carburettor or manifold gasket
    Blowing head gasket

Tapping or rattling
    Incorrect valve clearances
    Worn valve gear
    Worn timing chain or belt
    Broken piston ring (ticking noise)

Knocking or thumping
    Unintentional mechanical contact (eg fan blades)
    Worn drivebelt
    Peripheral component fault (generator, water pump etc)
    Worn big-end bearings (regular heavy knocking, perhaps less under load)
    Worn main bearings (rumbling and knocking, perhaps worsening under load)
    Piston slap (most noticeable when cold)

Chapter 1 Engine

Contents

Specifications

General

Engine type	Four-cylinder overhead camshaft transversely mounted
Capacity:	
1300	1342 cc (81.8 cu in)
1500	1488 cc (90.7 cu in)
Bore	74.0 mm (2.91 in)
Stroke:	
1300	78.0 mm (3.07 in)
1500	86.5 mm (3.41 in)
Compression ratio:	
UK models	8.7:1
North American models:	
Hatchback except Si:	
1300	10.0:1
1500	9.2:1
Hatchback Si	8.7:1
Sedan	9.2:1
Wagon	9.2:1
1984 CRX:	
1300	10.0:1
1500	9.2:1
1985 CRX:	
Standard	9.6:1
HF	10.0:1
Si	8.7:1
1986 CRX:	
Standard	9.6:1
HF	8.7:1
Si	9.2:1
Firing order	1-3-4-2 (No.1 cylinder nearest timing belt)
Crankshaft rotation	Anti-clockwise (viewed from crankshaft pulley)
Compression pressures:	
Minimum:	
1300	9.3 bar (135.0 lbf/in²)
1500 with carburettor	10.2 bar (149.0 lbf/in²)
1500 with fuel-injection	10.7 bar (156.0 lbf/in²)
Maximum difference between cylinders	1.9 bar (28.0 lbf/in²)

Cylinder block
Material .... Light alloy with cast iron liners
Bore .... 74.00 to 74.02 mm (2.9133 to 2.9142 in)
Maximum bore taper .... 0.05 mm (0.002 in)
Reboring limit .... 0.5 mm (0.020 in)

Crankshaft
Number of main bearings 5
Main journal diameter:
    1300 .... 44.976 to 45.000 mm (1.770 to 1.771 in)
    1500 .... 49.976 to 50.000 mm (1.967 to 1.968 in)
Main journal running clearance .... 0.024 to 0.07 mm (0.0009 to 0.003 in)
Crankpin journal diameter:
    1300 .... 37.976 to 38.000 mm (1.495 to 1.496 in)
    1500 .... 41.976 to 42.000 mm (1.652 to 1.653 in)
Maximum crankshaft journal ovality .... 0.005 mm (0.0002 in)
Crankshaft endfloat .... 0.10 to 0.45 mm (0.004 to 0.018 in)

Connecting rods
Crankpin bore diameter:
    1300 .... 41.00 mm (1.61 in)
    1500 .... 45.00 mm (1.77 in)
Side play (on crankshaft) .... 0.15 to 0.40 mm (0.006 to 0.016 in)

Pistons
Skirt diameter .... 73.96 to 73.99 mm (2.912 to 2.913 in)
Clearance in cylinder .... 0.01 to 0.07 mm (0.0004 to 0.003 in)

Piston rings
Number:
  UK models .... Two compression, one oil control
  North American models:
    1300 .... One compression, one oil control
    1500 .... Two compression, one oil control
Clearance in groove (compression rings) ..... 0.03 to 0.13 mm (0.001 to 0.005 in)
End gap:
  Compression rings .... 0.15 to 0.6 mm (0.006 to 0.02 in)
  Oil control ring rails .... 0.20 to 0.8 mm (0.008 to 0.03 in)

Camshaft
Bearing running clearance .... 0.05 to 0.15 mm (0.002 to 0.006 in)
Endfloat .... 0.05 to 0.5 mm (0.002 to 0.02 in)
Cam lobe height:
  UK models:
    1300:
      Inlet .... 40.056 mm (1.5770 in)
      Exhaust .... 40.078 mm (1.5779 in)
    1500 carburettor engine:
      Inlet .... 40.370 mm (1.5894 in)
      Exhaust .... 40.391 mm (1.5902 in)
    1500 fuel-injected engine:
      Inlet .... 40.865 mm (1.6089 in)
      Exhaust .... 40.884 mm (1.6096 in)
  North American models
    1300:
      Inlet .... 39.739 mm (1.5645 in)
      Exhaust .... 39.762 mm (1.5654 in)
      Auxiliary .... 44.315 mm (1.7447 in)
    1500 carburettor engine:
      Inlet .... 40.370 mm (1.5894 in)
      Exhaust .... 40.391 mm (1.5902 in)
      Auxiliary .... 44.315 mm (1.7447 in)
    1500 fuel-injected engine – manual transmission:
      Inlet .... 40.865 mm (1.6089 in)
      Exhaust .... 40.391 mm (1.5902 in)
    1500 fuel-injected engine – automatic transmission:
      Inlet .... 40.884 mm (1.6096 in)
      Exhaust .... 40.391 mm (1.5902 in)

Rocker gear
Rocker arm-to-shaft clearance .... 0.018 to 0.08 mm (0.0007 to 0.003 in)

Cylinder head
Material .... Light alloy
Thickness (new) .... 90.0 mm (3.54 in)
Thickness (minimum after resurfacing) ..... 89.8 mm (3.53 in)

Maximum surface distortion	0.05 mm (0.002 in)
Valve seat angle	45°
Valve seat width	1.25 to 2.0 mm (0.049 to 0.008 in)

Valves

Stem diameter:	
Inlet	6.55 to 6.59 mm (0.258 to 0.2594 in)
Exhaust	6.52 to 6.56 mm (0.257 to 0.2583 in)
Auxiliary (North American models)	6.54 to 6.58 mm (0.257 to 0.2593 in)
Stem-to-guide clearance:	
Inlet	0.02 to 0.08 mm (0.001 to 0.003 in)
Exhaust	0.05 to 0.11 mm (0.002 to 0.004 in)
Auxiliary (North American models)	0.023 to 0.08 mm (0.001 to 0.003 in)
Valve seat angle	45°
Valve seat width:	
Inlet and exhaust	1.25 to 2.0 mm (0.049 to 0.08 in)
Auxiliary (North American models)	0.35 to 1.0 mm (0.014 to 0.04 in)
Valve clearance (cold):	
Inlet	0.17 to 0.22 mm (0.007 to 0.009 in)
Exhaust	0.22 to 0.27 mm (0.009 to 0.011 in)
Auxiliary (North American models)	0.17 to 0.22 mm (0.007 to 0.009 in)

Valve springs

Free length:	
UK models	46.6 to 47.6 mm (1.83 to 1.87 in)
North American models:	
1300:	
Inlet and exhaust	48.1 to 49.13 mm (1.89 to 1.93 in)
Auxiliary	31.0 to 31.7 mm (1.22 to 1.25 in)
1500 carburettor engine:	
Inlet and exhaust	46.6 to 47.6 mm (1.83 to 1.87 in)
Auxiliary	31.0 to 31.7 mm (1.22 to 1.25 in)
1500 fuel-injected engine:	
Inlet and exhaust inner	44.02 mm (1.733 in)
Inlet and exhaust outer	47.45 mm (1.868 in)

Lubrication system

Oil pump clearances:	
Outer rotor to body	0.1 to 0.2 mm (0.004 to 0.008 in)
Inner-to-outer rotor lobe gap	0.14 to 0.2 mm (0.006 to 0.008 in)
Rotor endfloat	0.03 to 0.15 mm (0.001 to 0.006 in)
Oil pressure (hot) at 3000 rpm	3.3 to 4.1 bar (48 to 60 lbf/in²)

Torque wrench settings

	Nm	lbf ft
Camshaft sprocket bolt	38	27
Rocker shafts/camshaft bearing caps to cylinder head	22	16
Cylinder head bolts and nuts:		
Stage 1	30	22
Stage 2	60	43
Rocker cover nuts	10	7
Timing belt upper cover	10	7
Timing belt lower cover	12	9
Timing belt tensioner adjuster bolt	45	35
Crankshaft pulley bolt	115	83
Sump nuts and bolts	12	9
Crankshaft main bearing monobloc bolts	50	36
Connecting rod big-end nuts	28	20
Crankshaft rear oil seal retainer	12	9
Flywheel to crankshaft	105	76
Drive plate to crankshaft	75	54
Oil pump housing to crankcase	12	9
Oil pump filter screen to pump housing	24	18
Oil pump filter screen to main bearing monobloc	12	9
Oil pump rear plate screws	5	4
Sump drain plug	45	33
Transmission-to-engine bolts	68	50
Transmission rear mounting-to-transmission bolts	65	47
Transmission rear bracket-to-mounting nuts	22	16
Transmission right-hand mounting-to-transmission bolts	45	33
Transmission right-hand mounting-to-body bolts	45	33
Engine left-hand mounting nuts and through bolt	65	47
Auxiliary valve holder nut	80	58

1 General description

The engine is of four-cylinder overhead camshaft type with a displacement of 1342 cc or 1488 cc, mounted transversely with the transmission at the front of the car.

The cylinder block, crankcase and cylinder head are of light alloy construction with cast-iron cylinder liners.

The crankshaft is supported in five main bearings, the caps for which are in the form of a monobloc casting.

Crankshaft endfloat is controlled by semi-circular thrust washers at number four journal.

The pistons are fitted with two compression rings and one oil control ring. The gudgeon pin is of press fit type in the connecting rod small end.

On UK models the cylinder head incorporates two inlet valves and one exhaust valve per cylinder. On North American models with carburettor induction the cylinder head may incoporrate either two inlet valves and one exhaust valve, or the more conventional single inlet and exhaust valve layout, according to model and year of manufacture. In addition, a small auxiliary valve is used to improve combustion and reduce exhaust emissions. All North American models with fuel-injection utilize the twin inlet valve and single exhaust valve arrangement. The valves on all engines are operated by individual rockers from the single belt driven camshaft.

The oil pump is driven directly from the crankshaft while the distributor is driven from a dog on the end of the camshaft.

The fuel pump is driven from an eccentric cam on the camshaft, on carburettor engine models.

Crankshaft rotation is anti-clockwise when viewed from the pulley end.

The procedures in this Chapter are applicable to all engine types and any differences will be described in the text where necessary.

2 Maintenance and inspection

1 At the intervals given in 'Routine Maintenance' at the beginning of this Manual, carry out the following operations on the engine.

2 Visually inspect the engine joint faces, gaskets and seals for any sign of oil or water leaks. Pay particular attention to the areas around the rocker cover, cylinder head, crankshaft front oil seal and sump joint faces. Rectify any leaks by referring to the appropriate Sections of this Chapter.

3 Place a suitable container beneath the oil drain plug located at the rear of the sump. Unscrew the plug using a spanner or socket and allow the oil to drain. Inspect the condition of the drain plug sealing washer, and renew it if necessary. Refit and tighten the plug after draining.

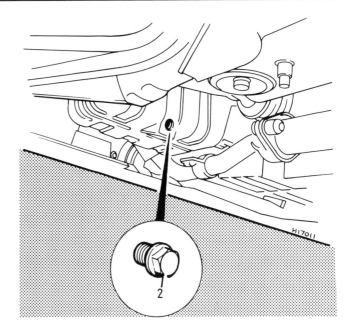

Fig. 1.1 Oil drain plug location (2) on engine sump (Sec 2)

4 Move the container to the rear of the engine under the oil filter.

5 Using a filter removing tool, slacken the filter, unscrew it from the engine and discard (photo). The filter is accessible from above working under the inlet manifold or, if preferred, raise and support the car and renew the filter from below.

6 Wipe the filter mating face with a rag, then lubricate the seal of a new filter with clean engine oil.

7 Screw the filter into position and tighten it by hand only, do not use any tools (photo).

8 Refill the engine using the correct grade of oil through the filler on the rocker cover (photo). Fill until the level reaches the upper mark on the dipstick.

9 Start the engine and check for leaks around the filter seal.

10 Switch off the engine, wait a few minutes and recheck the level on the dipstick. Top up if necessary and always maintain the level between the two marks on the dipstick.

11 At the intervals specified, check and if necessary adjust the valve

2.5 Removing the oil filter using a chain wrench

2.7 Fitting the new filter

2.8 Fill the engine with oil through the filler on the rocker cover

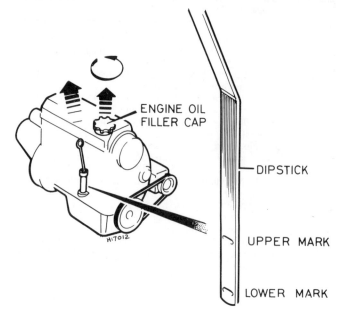

Fig. 1.2 Oil filler cap location and dipstick markings (Sec 2)

clearances as described in Section 5, and check the condition of the crankcase ventilation system as described in Section 3.

3 Lubrication and crankcase ventilation system – general

1   The lubrication system is of the forced feed type, the oil pump being of trochoid design and supplying oil under pressure to a full flow cartridge type filter which incorporates a bypass valve.
2   Oil then flows through the galleries and drillings to all the engine bearings and moving parts. Oil flow from the cylinder block to the cylinder head is regulated by a control orifice.
3   Crankcase ventilation is of the positive crankcase ventilation (PCV) valve type. The purpose of the system is to extract blow-by gases which have passed the piston rings and collected in the crankcase together with oil fumes and draw them into the inlet manifold where they are burned during the normal combustion processes.
4   The following service should be carried out at the intervals specified in 'Routine Maintenance'.

5   Remove the air cleaner as described in Chapter 3 (carburettor models only).
6   Release the clip which secures the PCV valve hose to the carburettor insulator or inlet manifold, and disconnect the hose (photo).
7   Remove the valve and hose assembly from the breather chamber, release the clip and disconnect the hose from the valve (photo).
8   Renew the valve and connect the hose to its small end. Fit the securing clip and fit the large end of the valve in the breather chamber. Fit the other end of the hose to the carburettor insulator or inlet manifold (as applicable). Refit the clip and the air cleaner (where applicable).
9   Unscrew the wing nut, disconnect the clips and remove the air cleaner cover. Lift out the element.
10   Remove the blow-by filter after extracting the screws which hold it to the side of the air cleaner (photos).
11   Renew the filter and fit it by reversing the removal operations.

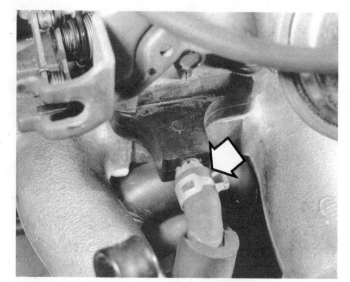

3.6 PCV valve hose clip (arrowed) at carburettor insulator

3.7 PCV valve hose attachment at crankcase breather chamber (arrowed) – manifold removed for clarity only

3.10A Extract the blow-by filter retaining screws ...

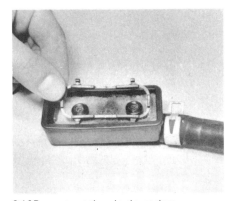
3.10B ... extract the plastic retainer ...

3.10C ... and remove the filter

4 Major operations possible without removing the engine

1 All major operations can be carried out with the engine in the car except for removal and refitting of the crankshaft and main bearings.
2 Attention to the flywheel and to the crankshaft rear oil seal is possible once the transmission has been removed as described in Chapter 6.

5 Valve clearances – adjustment

1 Disconnect the spark plug leads, the earth lead and the rocker cover breather hose. Remove the rocker cover (photo).
2 Apply a spanner to the crankshaft pulley bolt and turn the crankshaft in an anti-clockwise direction. Alternatively, engage top gear, raise one front roadwheel and turn it in the forward direction of travel. Keep turning until the 'UP' mark on the camshaft sprocket is uppermost and the marks on the sprocket are parallel with the upper surface of the cylinder head (Fig. 1.3). No. 1 piston is then at TDC on its compression stroke.
3 Check the valve clearances on number one cylinder. Viewed from the camshaft sprocket, inlet valves and auxiliary valves (where applicable) are on the right and exhaust valves on the left. Remember that the inlet and exhaust valve clearances are different.
4 Insert the feeler blade of appropriate thickness between the end of the valve stem and the rocker arm. It should be a stiff sliding fit, if not, release the adjuster screw locknut and turn the screw as necessary. Tighten the locknut (photo).
5 Rotate the crankshaft through 180° anti-clockwise and align the mark on the camshaft sprocket with the notch in the top of the timing belt cover (photo).
6 Check the valve clearances for number three cylinder, adjust if necessary.
7 Rotate the crankshaft through 180° anti-clockwise and align the camshaft sprocket marks with the upper surface of the cylinder head (photo).
8 Check the valve clearances for number four cylinder, adjust if necessary.
9 Rotate the crankshaft through 180° anti-clockwise and align the mark on the camshaft sprocket with the notch in the top of the timing belt cover (photo).
10 Check the valve clearances for number two cylinder, adjust if necessary.
11 Refit the rocker cover using a new gasket if necessary, connect the leads and breather hose (photo).

5.1 Rocker cover retaining nuts and earth lead (A) and breather hose (B)

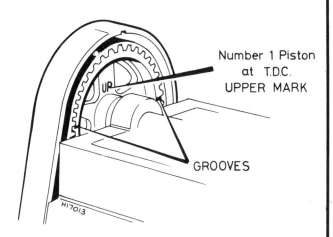
Number 1 Piston at T.D.C. UPPER MARK

GROOVES

H17013

Fig. 1.3 Camshaft sprocket position for No. 1 cylinder valve clearance adjustment (Sec 5)

5.4 Valve clearance adjustment

5.5 Camshaft sprocket mark and belt cover notch aligned (arrows) – position for adjusting No. 3 cylinder valve clearances

5.7 Camshaft sprocket marks aligned with head upper surface (arrows) – position for adjusting No. 4 cylinder valve clearances

5.9 Camshaft sprocket mark and belt cover notch aligned (A) with 'UP' mark as shown (B) – position for adjusting No. 2 cylinder valve clearances

6 Timing belt – adjustment

1   This is not a routine maintenance operation and it should only be required if the belt becomes noisy. Adjustment should be carried out with the engine cold.
2   Remove the alternator drivebelt as described in Chapter 12.
3   Remove the rocker cover.
4   Turn the crankshaft by means of its pulley bolt in an anti-clockwise direction to bring No. 1 piston to TDC on its compression stroke. In this position the white painted mark on the pulley will be aligned with the raised projection on the timing belt lower cover and the 'UP' mark on the camshaft sprocket will be uppermost with the two sprocket notches parallel with the top face of the cylinder head (see Fig. 1.4). The distributor rotor arm will be pointing toward the No. 1 cylinder segment in the cap.
5   Remove the timing belt adjuster access plug (photo).
6   Slacken the timing belt tensioner adjuster bolt. This is easily done by removing the plug in the splash shield under the wheel arch and inserting a socket and extension bar through the access hole and onto the bolt (photos).
7   Turn the crankshaft pulley bolt in an anti-clockwise direction to

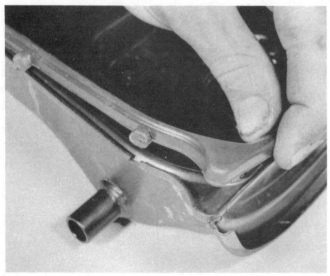

5.11 Fitting a new rocker cover gasket

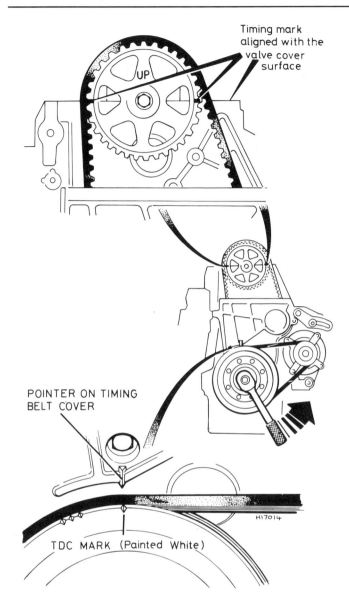

Timing mark aligned with the valve cover surface

UP

POINTER ON TIMING BELT COVER

TDC MARK (Painted White)

H17014

Fig. 1.4 Engine crankshaft and camshaft sprocket position for timing belt adjustment and renewal (Secs 6 and 7)

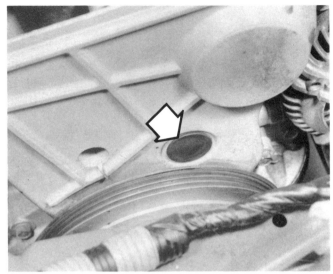

6.5 Timing belt adjuster access plug (arrowed)

6.6A Remove the plug in the wheel arch splash shield ...

6.6B ... for access through to the belt adjuster bolt

move the timing belt the distance of three teeth of the sprocket. This action will tension the belt automatically by means of the spring-loaded tensioner.
8 Tighten the tensioner bolt to the specified torque. (35 LB-FT)
9 Refit the tensioner bolt and access plugs.
10 Fit the alternator drivebelt and tension if (Chapter 12).

7 Timing belt – removal and refitting

1 Disconnect the battery negative lead.
2 Remove the rocker cover.
3 Remove the alternator drivebelt as described in Chapter 12.
4 Remove the timing belt upper cover.
5 Jack up the front of the car and support it on stands. Remove the left-hand front roadwheel and the splash shield under the wheel arch.
6 Set the engine with No. 1 piston at TDC on compression as described in Section 6 paragraph 4.
7 Engage a low gear and with an assistant fully applying the footbrake, unscrew the crankshaft pulley bolt.

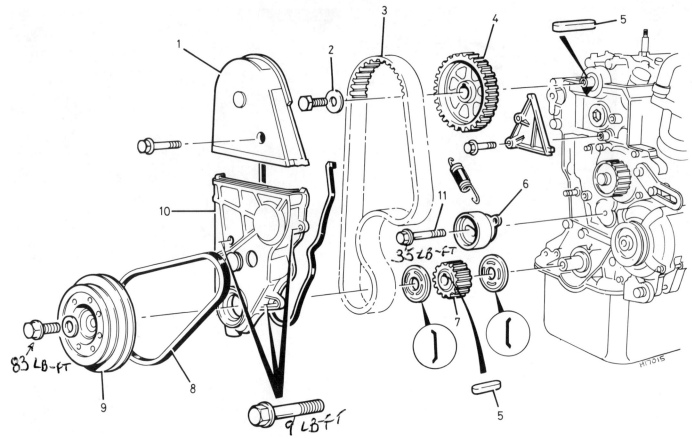

Fig. 1.5 Exploded view of the timing belt components (Sec 7)

1	Upper cover	4	Camshaft timing belt	7	Crankshaft timing belt	9	Crankshaft pulley
2	Washer		sprocket		sprocket	10	Lower cover
3	Timing belt	5	Key	8	Alternator belt	11	Adjustment bolt
		6	Belt tensioner				

8 Withdraw the crankshaft pulley and Woodruff key.
9 Remove the timing belt lower cover (photo).
10 Slacken the belt tensioner adjuster bolt, retract the tensioner and re-tighten the bolt (photo).

11 Remove the timing belt and the guide plate from the front of the crankshaft. *Do not turn the sprockets while the belt is off or the valve heads will contact the pistons* (photos).
12 If the belt is to be used again, mark it with the direction of rotation.

7.9 Timing belt lower cover bolt locations (arrowed)

7.10 Timing belt tensioner adjuster bolt (arrowed)

7.11A Removing the timing belt ...

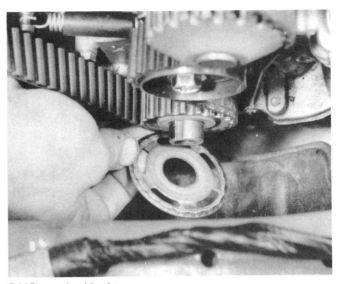

7.11B ... and guide plate

13 Check that the sprockets are still set at No. 1 TDC, then fit the belt to the sprockets.
14 Fit the guide plate to the crankshaft, convex side to the belt.
15 Fit the Woodruff key to the crankshaft followed by the lower cover and crankshaft pulley (photo).
16 Screw in and tighten the pulley bolt to the specified torque again holding the crankshaft against rotation as previously described.
17 Tension the belt as described in Section 6.
18 Fit the splash shield and roadwheel, then lower the car to the ground.
19 Refit the belt upper cover, rocker cover and alternator drivebelt, then reconnect the battery.

8 Camshaft front oil seal – renewal

1 Remove the rocker cover.
2 Remove the timing belt upper cover.
3 Remove the alternator drivebelt as described in Chapter 12.
4 Set the engine with No. 1 piston at TDC on compression as described in Section 6, paragraph 4.
5 Hold the camshaft sprocket still with a tool or rod passed through its spokes and release its retaining bolt.
6 Slacken the belt tensioner bolt and retract the tensioner (see Section 6).
7 Slip the timing belt from the camshaft sprocket, then withdraw the sprocket and key. **Do not** move the position of the camshaft.
8 Using a suitable tool, extract the camshaft oil seal.
9 Apply a smear of jointing compound to the oil seal recess in the housing, apply oil to the seal lips and drive it squarely home so that its lips face inwards (photo).
10 Refit the key and sprocket. Tighten the sprocket bolt to the specified torque.
11 Refit the timing belt and tension it as described in Section 6.
12 Refit the rocker cover and belt upper cover.
13 Refit the alternator drivebelt.

9 Crankshaft front oil seal – renewal

1 Remove the timing belt as described in Section 7. **Do not** rotate the crankshaft while the belt is off.
2 Using two screwdrivers, remove the crankshaft sprocket and inner guide plate. Prise out the oil seal.
3 Smear the inside of the oil seal housing recess with gasket cement and the seal lips with oil and drive the seal squarely into position. Fit the belt guide plate and sprocket.
4 Fit the timing belt and tension it as described in Sections 6 and 7.

7.15 Crankshaft pulley Woodruff key (arrowed)

8.9 Fitting the camshaft front oil seal

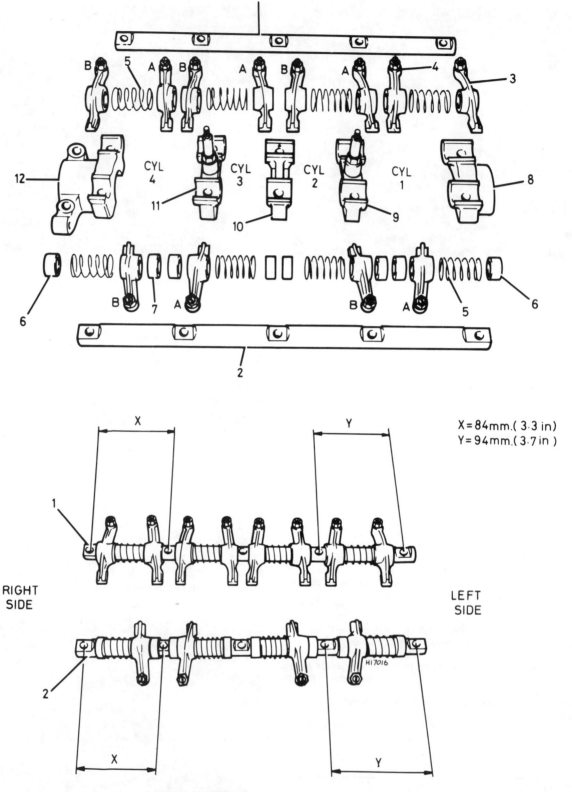

X = 84mm. (3·3 in)
Y = 94mm. (3·7 in)

RIGHT SIDE

LEFT SIDE

Fig. 1.6 Rocker shaft components – 12 valve engines (Sec 10)

1 Rocker shaft (Inlet) with 8 oil holes
2 Rocker shaft (Exhaust) with 4 oil holes
3 Rocker arm (Type A – 6 off)
4 Rocker arm (Type B – 6 off)
5 Rocker arm spring
6 Collar (Type A – 2 off)
7 Collar (Type B – 6 off)
8 Left end bearing cap
9 Left bearing cap
10 Centre bearing cap
11 Right bearing cap
12 Right end bearing cap

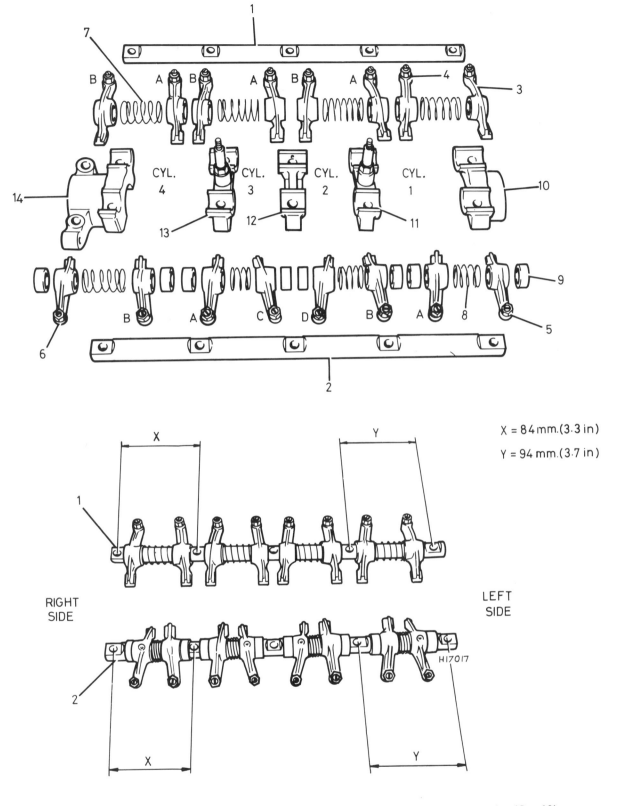

X = 84 mm. (3.3 in)

Y = 94 mm. (3.7 in)

RIGHT SIDE

LEFT SIDE

H17017

Fig. 1.7 Rocker shaft components – North American 12 valve engines with auxiliary valve (Sec 10)

1   Rocker shaft (Inlet) with 8 oil holes
2   Rocker shaft (Exhaust) with 4 oil holes
3   Rocker arm (Type A – 6 off)
4   Rocker arm (Type B – 6 off)
5   Rocker arm (Type C – 2 off)
6   Rocker arm (Type D – 2 off)
7   Rocker arm spring (Type A – 4 off)
8   Rocker arm spring (Type B – 4 off)
9   Collar (8 off)
10 Left end bearing cap
11 Left bearing cap
12 Centre bearing cap
13 Right bearing cap
14 Right end bearing cap

10 Rocker shafts – removal and refitting

1   Remove the rocker cover.
2   Unscrew the bolts securing the rocker shafts to the camshaft bearing caps. Slacken the bolts progressively a few turns at a time until valve spring tension is relieved (photo).
3   Hold the rocker shafts at each end to retain the components and lift them off the bearing brackets.
4   If the shafts are to be dismantled, note the location and orientation of the parts and slide them off the shafts.
5   Refitting is the reverse sequence to removal, but ensure that the rockers are not trapped by the bearing caps as the shafts are fitted. Tighten the retaining bolts progressively to the specified torque in the sequence shown in Fig. 1.8.
6   Adjust the valve clearances as described in Section 5.

11 Camshaft – removal and refitting

1   Remove the rocker cover.
2   Remove the alternator drivebelt as described in Chapter 12.
3   Set the engine with No. 1 piston at TDC on compression as described in Section 6, paragraph 4.
4   Hold the camshaft sprocket still with a tool or rod passed through its spokes and release its retaining bolt.
5   Slacken the belt tensioner bolt and retract the tensioner (see Section 6).
6   Slip the timing belt from the camshaft sprocket, then withdraw the sprocket and Woodruff key (photos).
7   Remove the rocker shafts as described in Section 10.
8   Remove the fuel pump as described in Chapter 3 (carburettor engine models only).
9   Remove the distributor as described in Chapter 4 and the distributor drive housing (carburettor engine models only). Recover the O-ring seal (photo).
10 Undo the bolts securing the camshaft rear bearing cap, then remove all five bearing caps. Keep the caps in strict order noting their fitted directions (photo).

10.2 Removing rocker shaft and camshaft bearing cap bolts

11 Remove the camshaft from the cylinder head and withdraw the front oil seal (photo).
12 To refit the camshaft, liberally lubricate the bearing journals and lay the camshaft in position in the cylinder head.
13 Turn the camshaft so that the keyway for the sprocket is uppermost.
14 Lubricate the lips of a new camshaft oil seal and place it in position with its open side inwards.
15 Lay the camshaft bearing caps over the camshaft journals. Note that the caps are numbered 1 to 5 from the timing belt end of the engine. Numbers 2 and 4 should have their arrows pointing toward the timing belt end. Read all numbers from the inlet manifold side. Apply

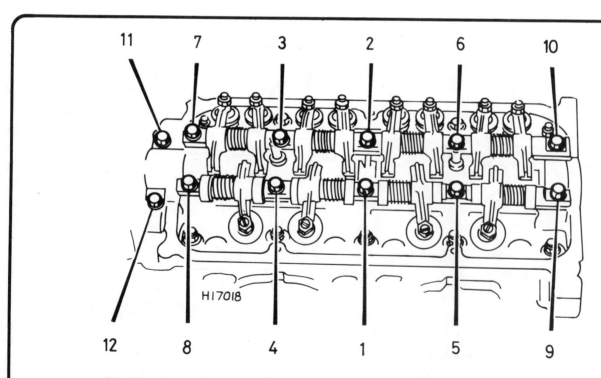

Fig. 1.8 Rocker shaft and camshaft bearing cap bolt tightening sequence (Secs 10 and 11)

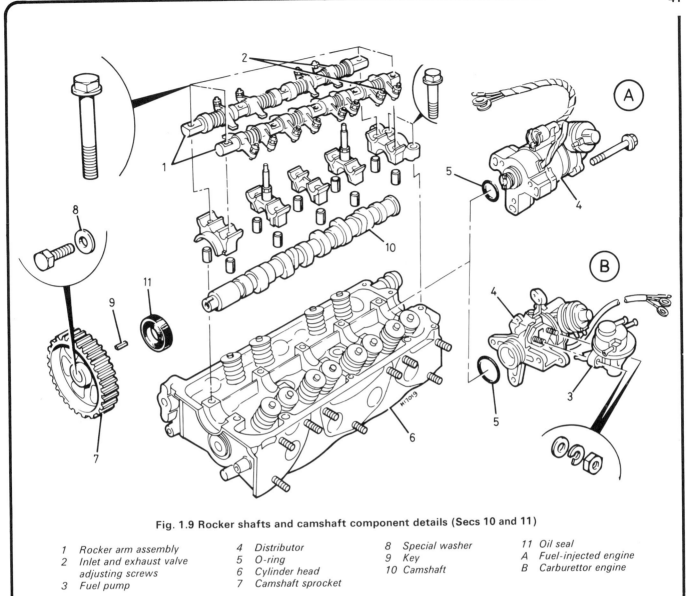

Fig. 1.9 Rocker shafts and camshaft component details (Secs 10 and 11)

1 Rocker arm assembly	4 Distributor	8 Special washer	11 Oil seal
2 Inlet and exhaust valve adjusting screws	5 O-ring	9 Key	A Fuel-injected engine
3 Fuel pump	6 Cylinder head	10 Camshaft	B Carburettor engine
	7 Camshaft sprocket		

11.6A Removing the bolt and camshaft sprocket ...

11.6B ... followed by the Woodruff key (arrowed)

11.9 Removing the distributor drive housing

11.10 Camshaft rear bearing cap removal

RTV sealant at the cylinder head joint faces of No. 1 and No. 5 bearing caps.

16 Place the rocker shafts in position with reference to Section 10, then tighten all the bolts two turns at a time in the order given in Fig. 1.8, to the specified torque.

17 Refit the camshaft sprocket and tighten the retaining bolt to the specified torque.

18 Refit the timing belt as described in Section 7.

19 Refit the distributor (Chapter 4) and, where applicable, the fuel pump (Chapter 3).

20 Adjust the valve clearances as described in Section 5.

12 Cylinder head (UK models) – removal and refitting

Carburettor engines

1 The cylinder head should only be removed from a cool engine, below 38°C (100°F).

2 Disconnect the battery negative lead.

3 Drain the cooling system, retaining the coolant for further use (Chapter 2).

4 Remove the air cleaner (Chapter 3).

5 Disconnect the brake servo vacuum hose from the inlet manifold. Also remove the coolant bypass hose.

6 Disconnect the radiator top hose from the cylinder head

7 Disconnect the hoses from the fuel pump and plug them.

8 Disconnect the throttle and choke controls from the carburettor (Chapter 3).

9 Unscrew the bolts which secure the support bracket to the inlet manifold and the crankcase (photos).

10 Disconnect the leads from the carburettor, ignition coil and coolant sender unit.

11 Detach the air cleaner hot air duct.

12 Remove the radiator heat baffle plate.

13 Remove the centre splash guard panel (photo).

14 Remove the hot air collector cover from the exhaust manifold.

15 Disconnect the exhaust downpipe and unbolt the exhaust manifold steady brackets.

16 Remove the rocker cover.

17 Remove the timing belt upper cover.

18 With a socket on the crankshaft pulley bolt, turn the crankshaft in an anti-clockwise direction until the 'UP' mark on the camshaft sprocket is uppermost and the timing marks on the sprocket are parallel with the top face of the cylinder head. No. 1 piston is now at TDC on its compression stroke.

19 Remove the alternator drivebelt (Chapter 12).

20 Slacken the belt tensioner adjusting bolt, retract the tensioner and slip the timing belt from the camshaft sprocket (see Section 6).

11.11 Withdrawing the camshaft from the cylinder head

12.9A Removing the inlet manifold bracket upper ...

12.9B ... and lower retaining bolts

12.13 Removing engine centre splash guard panel

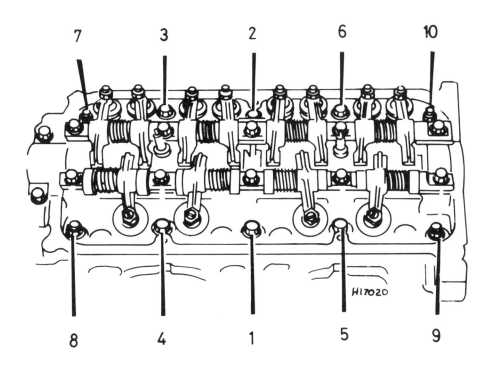

Fig. 1.10 Cylinder head bolt tightening sequence (Secs 12 and 13)

21 **Do not** rotate the crankshaft while the belt is off the sprocket.

22 Progressively slacken the cylinder head bolts and nuts, half a turn at a time in the reverse order of tightening (Fig. 1.10).

23 Remove the bolts and nuts and lift the cylinder head from the block. It is permissible to lever the head up if it is stuck, but use a suitable tool only between the lugs provided – **not** in the gasket joint. Positioning dowels are fitted, so lift the head straight up when removing it (photo).

24 Dismantling and decarbonising of the cylinder head is covered in Section 23.

25 Before refitting the cylinder head, make sure that all carbon and old gasket material has been removed from the cylinder head and block mating surfaces.

26 Check that the positioning dowels are fully located in the top of the block.

27 Place a new gasket on the cylinder block. Check that the timing marks are set as described in paragraph 18 with all valves closed (photo).

28 Carefully lower the head onto the block, insert the bolts (threads clean and lightly oiled) and screw the nuts onto the studs.

29 Tighten the bolts and nuts to the specified torque working in the sequence shown in Fig. 1.10. First tighten to half the tightening torque and then to full tightening torque.

30 Connect the timing belt to the camshaft sprocket with the timing marks correctly positioned as described in paragraph 18.

31 Tension the belt as described in Section 6.

12.23 Cylinder head removal

12.27 Locating a new cylinder head gasket on the cylinder block

32 If the valve gear has not been disturbed, then the valve clearances will not require checking or adjusting.

33 Fit the rocker cover and the timing belt upper cover.

34 Reconnect all hoses, control cables and electrical leads.

35 Reconnect the exhaust pipe, refit the hot air collector cover, radiator heat baffle plate and splash guard plate.

36 Fill and bleed the cooling system as described in Chapter 2.

Fuel-injected engines

37 The cylinder head should only be removed from a cool engine, below 38°C (100°F).

38 Disconnect the battery negative terminal.

39 Drain the cooling system, retaining the coolant for further use (Chapter 2).

40 Disconnect the air intake duct and vacuum hose.

41 Disconnect the brake servo vacuum hose from the inlet manifold.

42 Disconnect the radiator top hose from the cylinder head and the relevant heater hoses and bypass hoses from their outlets.

43 Disconnect the leads from the ignition coil, fuel cut-off solenoid valve and coolant sender unit.

44 Refer to Chapter 3 and depressurise the fuel system.

45 Disconnect the accelerator cable from the throttle body.

46 Disconnect the engine wiring sub-harness connectors on the inner wing valance.

47 Disconnect the fuel feed and return hoses.

48 Note their locations and disconnect the wiring connectors at the fuel system sensors.

49 Refer to Chapter 3 and remove the injector holder from the inlet manifold.

50 Remove the distributor as described in Chapter 4.

51 Disconnect the coolant hose between the inlet manifold and the thermostat housing.

52 The remainder of the procedure is the same as for carburettor engine models as described in paragraphs 13 to 36 inclusive.

13 Cylinder head (North American models) – removal and refitting

Carburettor engines

1 The cylinder head should only be removed from a cool engine, below 38°C (100°F).

2 Disconnect the battery negative terminal.

3 Drain the cooling system as described in Chapter 2, retaining the coolant for further use.

4 Refer to Chapter 3 and remove the air cleaner.

5 Disconnect the brake servo vacuum hose from the inlet manifold.

6 Disconnect the radiator top hose from the cylinder head.

7 Disconnect the coolant bypass hose and the relevant heater hoses from their outlets.

8 Disconnect the hoses at the fuel pump and plug them.

9 Disconnect the accelerator cable at the carburettor.

10 Refer to Chapter 4 and remove the distributor.

11 Disconnect the leads at the automatic choke and coolant sender unit.

12 Unscrew the bolts which secure the support bracket to the cylinder head and crankcase.

13 Detach the air cleaner hot air duct.

14 Disconnect the hoses from the charcoal canister.

15 Disconnect the No. 1 control box emission hoses from the tubing manifold.

16 On California and high altitude vehicles disconnect the air jet controller hoses.

17 On models equipped with air conditioning, disconnect the idle control solenoid hoses.

18 Remove the central splash guard panel under the engine.

19 Remove the hot air collector cover from the exhaust manifold.

20 Disconnect the exhaust downpipe and unbolt the exhaust manifold steady brackets.

21 Remove the rocker cover.

22 Remove the timing belt upper cover.

23 With a socket on the crankshaft pulley bolt, turn the crankshaft in an anti-clockwise direction until the 'UP' mark on the camshaft sprocket is uppermost and the timing marks on the sprocket are parallel with the top face of the cylinder head. No. 1 piston is now at TDC on its compression stroke.

24 Remove the alternator drivebelt (Chapter 12).

25 Slacken the belt tensioner adjusting bolt, retract the tensioner and slip the timing belt from the camshaft sprocket (see Section 6).

26 **Do not** rotate the crankshaft while the belt is off the sprocket.

27 Progressively slacken the cylinder head bolts and nuts, half a turn at a time in the reverse order of tightening (Fig. 1.10).

28 Remove the bolts and nuts and lift the cylinder head from the block. It is permissible to lever the head up if it is stuck, but use a suitable tool only between the lugs provided – **not** in the gasket joint. Positioning dowels are fitted, so lift the head straight up when removing it.

29 Dismantling and decarbonising of the cylinder head is covered in Section 23.

30 Before refitting the cylinder head, make sure that all carbon and old gasket material has been removed from the cylinder head and block mating surfaces.

31 Check that the positioning dowels are fully located in the top of the block.

32 Place a new gasket on the cylinder block. Check that the timing marks are set as described in paragraph 23 with all valves closed.

33 Carefully lower the head onto the block, insert the bolts (threads clean and lightly oiled) and screw the nuts onto the studs.

34 Tighten the bolts and nuts to the specified torque working in the sequence shown in Fig. 1.10. First tighten to half the tightening torque and then to full tightening torque.

35 Connect the timing belt to the camshaft sprocket with the timing marks correctly positioned as described in paragraph 23.

36 Tension the belt as described in Section 6.

37 If the valve gear has not been disturbed, then the valve clearances will not require checking or adjusting.

38 Fit the rocker cover and the timing belt upper cover.

39 Reconnect all hoses, control cables and electrical leads.

40 Reconnect the exhaust pipe, refit the hot air collector cover, and splash guard plate.

41 Fill and bleed the cooling system as described in Chapter 2.

Fuel-injected engines

42 The cylinder head should only be removed from a cool engine, below 38°C (100°F).

43 Disconnect the battery negative terminal.

44 Drain the cooling system as described in Chapter 2, retaining the coolant for further use.

45 Disconnect the air intake duct and vacuum hose.

46 Disconnect the brake servo vacuum hose from the inlet manifold.

47 Disconnect the radiator top hose from the cylinder head and the relevant heater hoses and bypass hoses from their outlets.

48 Disconnect the leads from the ignition coil, fuel cut-off solenoid valve and coolant sender unit.

49 Refer to Chapter 3 and depressurise the fuel system.

50 Disconnect the engine wiring sub-harness connectors and the fuel and emission system sensor connectors.

52 Disconnect the fuel feed and return hoses.

53 Remove the distributor as described in Chapter 4.

54 The remainder of the procedure is the same as for carburettor engine models as described in paragraphs 14 to 41 inclusive.

14 Sump – removal and refitting

1 Drain the engine oil.

2 Disconnect the exhaust downpipe from the manifold

3 Refer to Chapter 8 and disconnect the left-hand driveshaft from the transmission.

4 Unbolt and remove the stiffener bracket from between the engine and transmission (photo).

5 Progressively unscrew the six nuts and twleve bolts which hold the sump to the crankcase (photo).

6 Remove the cover plate from the lower part of the flywheel housing (photo).

7 Remove the sump and peel off the one-piece gasket (photo).

14.4 Engine/transmission stiffener bracket

14.5 Sump retaining bolt removal

14.6 Flywheel housing cover plate

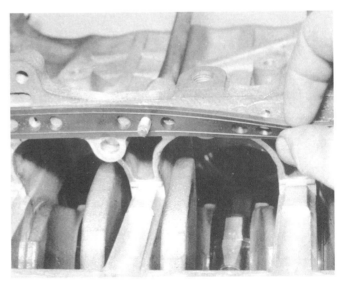
14.7 Removing the sump gasket

8 Before refitting, wipe the crankcase and sump mating surfaces clean and apply a bead of gasket cement between the studs and the main bearing cap, also to both sides of the gasket where it seats at the main bearing cap.
9 Position the new gasket and then offer the sump onto the studs and tighten all nuts and bolts to the specified torque. Refit the flywheel housing cover.
10 Refit the stiffener bracket.
11 Refit the driveshaft and exhaust downpipe, then fill the engine with oil.

15 Oil pump – removal and refitting

1 Remove the timing belt as described in Section 7 and the sump as described in Section 14.
2 Withdraw the crankshaft sprocket and the timing belt inner guide plate.
3 Undo the two nuts and two support bracket bolts and remove the filter screen assembly.
4 Undo the retaining bolts and remove the pump and housing from the front of the engine (photo).
5 Clean away all traces of sealant from the pump mating face and remove the filter screen gasket.
6 To refit the pump apply RTV sealant to the pump mating face and lubricate the oil seal lips with engine oil.
7 Place the pump in position, fit the retaining bolts and tighten to the specified torque.
8 Refit the filter screen using a new gasket.
9 Refit the timing belt inner guide plate and the crankshaft sprocket.
10 Refit the sump as described in Section 14 and the timing belt as decribed in Section 7.

16 Connecting rod big-end bearings and piston rings – renewal

1 These operations will normally be carried out at the time of complete engine overhaul, but the work may be done without removing the engine from the car where it is necessary to reduce oil consumption and to improve the oil pressure.
2 Refer to Section 14 and remove the sump.
3 Inspect the big-end caps for identification. They should be marked 1 to 4 from the crankshaft pulley end of the side nearest to the exhaust manifold. If not, mark them, with a centre punch on the cap and the adjacent surface of the connecting rod. Do not confuse the bearing shell code numbers (See Section 24).
4 Unscrew the big-end cap nuts, remove the cap with its shell

bearing. This is difficult owing to the monobloc construction of the main bearing caps. It can be done however if the crankshaft is rotated gently in both directions and the big-end cap removed through the monobloc apertures.
5 Push each connecting rod slightly upwards and remove the upper shell half. Only move the connecting rod upwards when the big-end is at the lowest point on its throw, otherwise if the piston is at TDC it might be possible for the top piston ring to pop out of the top of the cylinder.
6 If only new shells are to be fitted, fit them in matched pairs making

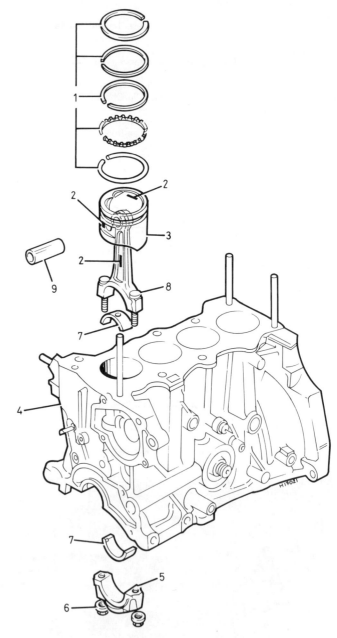

Fig. 1.11 Connecting rod, piston and piston ring components (Sec 16)

1 Piston rings
2 Identification marks
3 Piston
4 Engine block
5 Connecting rod big-end bearing cap
6 Connecting rod big-end bearing cap nut
7 Connecting rod big-end bearing shells
8 Connecting rod
9 Gudgeon pin

15.4 Removing the oil pump and housing from the crankcase

sure that their recesses in both the rod and cap are perfectly clean (see Section 24 regarding shell coding).

7 If the piston rings are to be renewed owing to heavy oil consumption, it is recommended that proprietary oil control sets are fitted.

8 Remove the cylinder head as described in Section 12 or 13.

9 Push the piston connecting rod assembly up and out of the top of the cylinder bore. If a heavy wear ridge is evident at the top of the bore, it will have to be carefully removed with a ridge reamer or by scraping in order to allow the ring to pass.

10 Remove the piston rings from the top of the piston. To avoid breaking a ring either during removal or refitting, slide two or three old feeler blades at equidistant points behind the top ring and slide it up them. Remove the other rings is a similar way (photo).

11 Clean carbon from the ring grooves, a segment of old piston ring is useful for this purpose.

12 Clean out the oil return holes in the piston ring grooves and fit the new piston rings. The top ring will be supplied stepped so that it does not impinge on the wear ridge.

13 Insert each piston ring in turn squarely into its bore and check the ring end gap. If it is not within the specified tolerance, carefully grind the end-face of the ring.

14 Now check each compression ring in its groove and measure the clearances with a feeler gauge. If it is tight the ring may be rubbed flat on a sheet of wet and dry paper laid flat on a piece of plate glass (photo).

15 Fit the rings to the piston using the feeler blade method as described for removal. Work from the top of the piston, fitting the oil control ring first.

16 Locate the compression ring gaps at 90° to each other on the thrust side (towards the dipstick guide tube). The expander of the oil control ring should have its gap on the opposite side to the gap in the second compression ring. The gaps in the rails of the oil control ring should be on either side of the expander gap. Repeat all the operations on the remaining pistons.

17 The cylinder bore should now be de-glazed using a glaze buster or fine glasspaper to enable the new rings to bed in.

18 Take care to remove all debris and then oil the bores and piston rings liberally.

19 Fit a piston ring compressor to the first piston and insert the rod complete with shell bearing into the bore so that the compressor stands flat on the block (photo).

20 Check that with the oil hole in the connecting rod towards the inlet manifold side of the block, the valve head cut-outs in the piston crowns are on the exhaust valve side of the engine.

21 Place the wooden handle of a hammer on the piston crown and tap the hammer head with the hand to drive the piston into the cylinder bore. The compressor will remain on the face of the block.

22 Lubricate the shell in the cap, fit the cap to its correctly numbered rod, and screw on the cap nuts to the specified torque (photo).

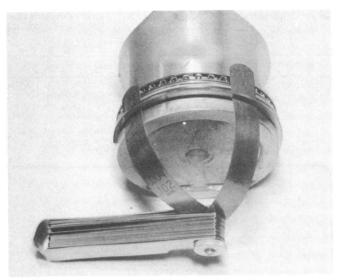

16.10 Using feeler blades to aid piston ring removal

16.14 Checking piston ring clearance in groove

16.19 Using a piston ring compressor to fit a piston into its cylinder

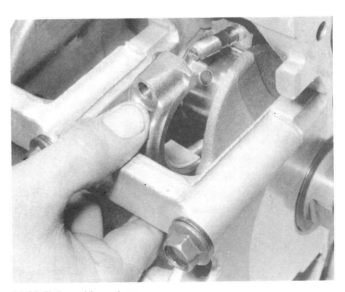

16.22 Fitting a big-end cap

23 Fit the remaining piston/connecting rods in a similar way.
24 Refit the cylinder head (section 12 or 13) and refit the sump (Section 14).

17 Engine/transmission mountings – renewal

1 The mountings may be renewed with the engine/transmission in the car provided the weight of the engine or transmission is taken on a hoist or by using a jack with a block of wood as an insulator.
2 The renewal procedure is straightforward and the layout of the mountings and their attachments is shown in Fig. 1.12.

3 If the rear mounting is to be renewed it will be necessary to disconnect the gear change selector rod and torque rod (manual transmission models) to provide access. Details of these procedures are given in Chapter 6.
4 When refitting, tighten all nuts and bolts to the specified torque.

18 Engine/transmission (UK models) – removal and separation

1 Refer to Chapter 11 and remove the bonnet.
2 Remove the battery and battery tray as described in Chapter 12.

Fig. 1.12 Engine mounting details (Sec 17)

3 Drain the engine oil as described in Section 2.
4 Drain the transmission oil/fluid as described in Chapter 6 (manual transmission) or 7 (automatic transmission).
5 Drain the cooling system as described in Chapter 2.
6 On carburettor engines remove the air cleaner as described in Chapter 3. On fuel-injected engines remove the air intake duct and vacuum hose.
7 Disconnect the brake servo vacuum hose from the inlet manifold.
8 Note the location of the engine wiring plugs and connectors and disconnect those affecting engine removal which include:

Ignition coil wiring
Engine wiring harness multi-plug connectos
Engine and transmission earth cables
Oil pressure switch
Temperature sender unit
Starter motor
Reversing lamp switch

9 On carburettor engines remove the fuel pump as described in Chapter 3 and disconnect the accelerator and choke cables.
10 Remove the distributor as described in Chapter 4.
11 Disconnect the radiator top and bottom hoses and the heater hoses.
12 Extract the wire clip and remove the speedometer cable from the pinion holder.
13 On carburettor engines proceed to paragraph 18. On fuel-injected engines proceed as follows.
14 Refer to Chapter 3 and depressurise the fuel system.
15 Disconnect the fuel feed and return hoses.
16 Disconnect the accelerator cable at the throttle body.
17 Disconnect the engine wiring sub-harness connectors on the inner wing valance.
18 Jack up the front of the car and support it on stands. Remove the front roadwheels.
19 Remove the splash shields under the engine and wheel arches.
20 On manual transmission models disconnect the clutch cable at the transmission (Chapter 5), then disconnect the gear change selector rod and torque rod (Chapter 6).
21 On automatic transmission models remove the centre console (Chapter 11) and place the selector lever in reverse. Extract the selector cable lock pin, remove the cable holder and cable guide bolts and withdraw the disconnected cable from the car.
22 Refer to Chapter 3 and remove the exhaust down pipe between the manifold and flexible joint.
23 On automaitc transmission models disconnect the transmission fluid cooler hoses at the transmission.
24 Place a jack beneath the left-hand front suspension lower arm. Remove the lower arm balljoint retaining nut and release the joint using a balljoint separator tool. The jack will take the full torque reaction of the torsion bar when the balljoint is released, so ensure that it is squarely and securely positioned. Slowly lower the jack and repeat the procedure on the right-hand side.
25 Disconnect the driveshafts from the transmission by inserting a lever between the inner driveshaft joint and the transmission casing. Prise against the spring pressure of the joint retaining clip to release the joint, then withdraw the driveshafts from the transmission.
26 Refer to Chapter 12 and remove the alternator.
27 Using a hoist or other suitable lifting gear securely attached to the engine using chains or rope slings, take the weight of the engine/transmission assembly.
28 Disconnect the engine/transmission mountings, then raise the power unit slightly and check that everything has been disconnected.
29 Lift the unit out of the engine compartment and lower it to the floor.
30 Support the engine and remove the starter motor and the cover plate from the face of the flywheel housing.
31 On automatic transmission models unscrew the bolts which secure the driveplate to the torque converter. These are accessible through the starter motor aperture, but the crankshaft will have to be rotated to bring each bolt into view.
32 Support the transmission and unscrew the bolts connecting the engine to the transmission.
33 Carefully withdraw the transmission making sure that on automatic transmission models the torque converter comes off with it and remains in place on the mainshaft (photo).

19 Engine/transmission (North American models) – removal and separation

1 Refer to Section 18 and carry out the operations described in paragraphs 1 to 12 inclusive.
2 On cars equipped with air conditioning, remove the idle control solenoid valve.
3 Disconnect the connector at the No. 1 control box, then lift the control box off its bracket and place it to one side.
4 Disconnect the purge control solenoid valve vacuum hose at the charcoal canister.
5 On California and high altitude vehicles remove the air jet controller. Also, where fitted, disconnect the No. 2 control box connector and remove the control box.
6 On carburettor engines proceed to paragraph 11. On fuel-injected engines proceed as follows.
7 Refer to Chapter 3 and depressurise the fuel system.
8 Disconnect the fuel feed and return hoses.
9 Disconnect the accelerator cable at the throttle body.
10 Disconnect the engine wiring sub-harness connectors.
11 On cars equipped with power-assisted steering, remove the pump mounting bolts, slip off the drivebelt and place the pump to one side without disturbing the fluid hoses.
12 On cars equipped with air conditioning remove the compressor drivebelt and the compressor as described in Chapter 11. Leave the refrigerant hoses connected and tie the compressor up out of the way.
13 For the remainder of the procedure refer to Section 18 and carry out the operations described in paragraphs 18 to 33 inclusive.

20 Engine – dismantling (general)

1 Stand the engine on a strong bench so as to be at a comfortable working height. Failing this it can be stripped down on the floor, but at least stand it on a sheet of hardboard.
2 During the dismantling process, the greatest care should be taken to keep the exposed parts free from dirt. As the engine is stripped, clean each part in a bath of paraffin.
3 Never immerse parts with oilways in paraffin, e.g. the crankshaft, but to clean, wipe down carefully with a paraffin dampened rag. Oilways can be cleaned out with a piece of wire. If an air line is available, all parts can be blown dry and the oilways blown through as an added precaution.
4 Re-use of old gaskets is false economy and can give rise to oil and water leaks, if nothing worse. To avoid to possibility of trouble after the engine has been reassembled always use new gaskets throughout.
5 Do not throw the old gaskets away as it sometimes happens that an immediate replacment cannot be found and the old gasket is then very

18.33 Separating the engine and manual transmission

useful as a template. Hang up the gaskets on a suitable nail or hook as they are removed.

6 To strip the engine, it is best to work form the top downwards. The engine oil sump provides a firm base on which the engine can be supported in an upright position. When the stage is reached where the pistons are to be removed, turn the engine on its side. Turn the block upside down to remove the crankshaft.

7 Wherever possible, replace nuts, bolts and washers finger-tight from where they were removed. This helps avoid later loss and muddle. If they cannot be replaced then lay them out in such a fashion that it is clear from where they came.

21 Engine ancillary components – removal

Before complete engine dismantling begins, remove the following ancillary components.

Distributor (Chapter 4)
Inlet manifold and carburettor or fuel-injection components (Chapter 3)
Fuel pump (Chapter 3)
Exhaust manifold and hot air collector (Chapter 3)
Alternator (Chapter 12)
Clutch (Chapter 5)
Oil filter cartridge and dipstick (Section 2)
Engine mounting brackets (Section 17)

22 Engine – complete dismantling

1 Remove the timing belt (Section 7).
2 Remove the rocker shafts (Section 10).
3 Remove the camshaft (Section 11)
4 Remove the cylinder head (Sections 12 or 13)
4 Refer to Chapter 2 and remove the water pump.
6 Remove the timing belt tensioner.
7 Lock the flywheel starter ring gear teeth and unbolt and remove the flywheel (or driveplate – automatic transmission). Renew the bolts and clean the threads in their holes.
8 Remove the crankcase breather.
9 Turn the engine upside down and remove the sump (Section 14) and the oil pump (Section 15).
10 Unbolt and remove the crankshaft rear oil seal retainer. Remove the dipstick guide tube.
11 Lay the engine on its side and remove the piston/connecting rods as described in Section 16.
12 Stand the engine on its block face and unbolt and remove the main bearing caps. These are in the form of a monobloc casting. Note the thrust washers located at No. 4 main bearing.
13 Lift the crankshaft from the crankcase. If the bearing shells are to be used again, identify them with their original crankcase or cap recesses.

23 Cylinder head – dismantling and decarbonising

1 With the cylinder head removed to the bench, dismantle in the following way.
2 Remove any applicable ancillary components as listed in Section 21 followed by the rocker shafts (Section 10), camshaft (Section 11), spark plugs and water outlet.
3 Using a valve spring compressor, compress the first valve spring and remove the split collets.
4 Gently release the compressor and remove it.
5 Take off the spring retainer, the spring and the spring seat.
6 Remove all the other valves in a similar way keeping them in their original fitted sequence together with their associated components. Remove and discard the valve stem oil seals.
7 On North American engines equipped with an auxiliary valve for each cylinder, remove these as follows.
8 Unscrew the valve holder nut using a box spanner, and withdraw the valve and holder assembly upwards from the cylinder head. Recover the holder gasket.
9 Using a valve spring compressor, compress the valve spring and remove the split collets.

10 Gently release the compressor and remove it.
11 Take off the spring retainer, spring, valve stem oil seal and spring seat.
12 Withdraw the valve from the valve holder, then remove and discard the valve holder O-ring.
13 Remove and dismantle the remaining auxiliary valves in the same way, keeping their associated components together.
14 Bearing in mind that the cylinder head is of light alloy construction and is easily damaged, use a blunt scraper or rotary wire brush to clean all traces of carbon deposits from the combustion spaces and the ports. The valve head stems and valve guides should also be freed from any carbon deposits. Wash the combustion spaces and ports down with paraffin and scrape the cylinder head surface free of any foreign matter with the side of a steel rule, or a similar article.
15 If the engine is installed in the car, clean the pistons and the top of the cylinder bores. If the pistons are still in the block, then it is essential that great care is taken to ensure that no carbon gets into the cylinder bores as this could scratch the cylinder walls or cause damage to the piston and rings. To ensure this does not happen, first turn the crankshaft so that two of the pistons are at the top of their bores. Stuff rag into the two other bores or seal them off with paper and masking tape to prevent particles of carbon entering the cooling system and damaging the coolant pump.
16 Press a little grease into the gap between the cylinder walls and the two pistons which are to be worked on. With a blunt scraper carefully scrape away the carbon from the piston crown, taking great care not to scratch the aluminium. Also scrape away the carbon from the surround lip of the cylinder wall. When all carbon has been removed, scrape away the grease which will now be contaminated with carbon particles, taking care not press any into the bores. To assist prevention of carbon build-up the piston crown can be polished with a metal polish. Remove the rags or masking tape from the other two cylinders and turn the crankshaft so that the two pistons which were at the bottom are now at the top. Place rag in the cylinders which have been decarbonised, and proceed as just described.
17 Examine the head of the valves for pitting and burning, especially the heads of the exhaust valves. The valve seatings should be examined at the same time. If the pitting on the valve and seat is very slight, the marks can be removed by grinding the seats and valves together with coarse, and then fine, valve grinding paste.
18 Where bad pitting has occurred to the valve seats it will be necessary to recut them and fit new valves. This latter job should be entrusted to the local agent or engineering works. In practice it is very seldom that the seats are so badly worn. Normally it is the valve that is too badly worn for refitting, and the owner can easily purchase a new set of valves and match them to the seats by valve grinding.
19 Valve grinding is carried out as follows. Smear a trace of coarse carborundum paste on the seat face and apply a suction grinder tool to the valve head. With a semi-rotary motion, grind the valve head to its seat, lifting the valve occasionally to redistribute the grinding paste. When a dull matt even surface is produced on both the valve seat and the valve, wipe off the paste and repeat the process with fine carborundum paste, lifting and turning the valve to redistribute the paste as before. A light spring placed under the valve head will greatly ease this operation. When a smooth unbroken ring of light grey matt finish is produced, on both valve and valve seat faces, the grinding operation is complete. Carefully clean away every trace of grinding compound, take great care to leave none in the ports or in the valve guides. Clean the valves and valve seats with paraffin soaked rag, then with a clean rag, and finally, if an air line is available, blow the valve, valve guides and valve ports clean.
20 Check that all valve springs are intact. If any one is broken, all should be renewed. Check the free length of the springs against new ones. If some springs are not within specifications, replace them all. Springs suffer from fatigue and it is a good idea to renew them even if they look serviceable.
21 The cylinder head can be checked for warping either by placing it on a piece of plate glass or using a straight-edge and feeler blades. If there is any doubt or if its block face is corroded, have it re-faced by your dealer or motor engineering works.
22 Test the valves in their guides for side to side rock. If this is any more than almost imperceptible new guides must be fitted, again a job for your dealer.
23 Examine the camshaft for wear or scoring of the journals or cam lobes. Any wear or scoring in the camshaft bearings will mean renewal of the cylinder head as the bearings are line-bored and cannot be

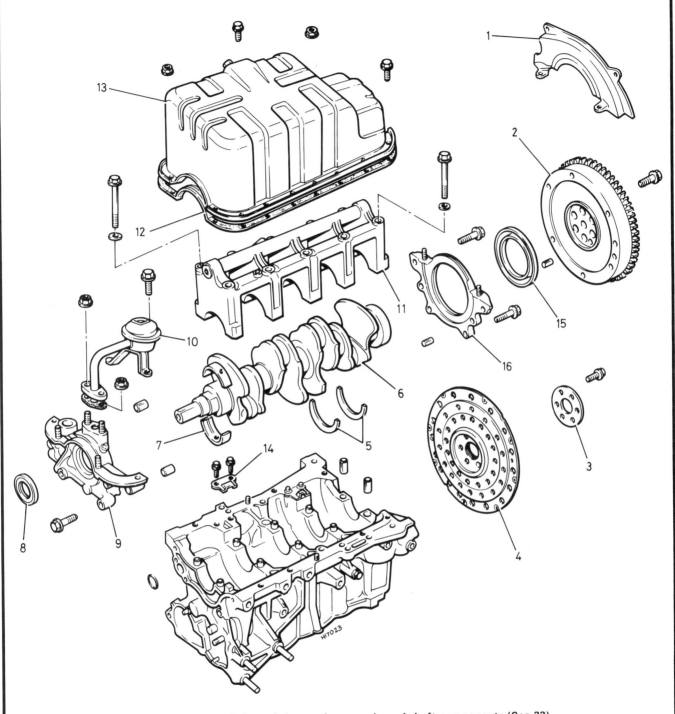

Fig. 1.13 Exploded view of the crankcase and crankshaft components (Sec 22)

1 Flywheel cover (manual transmission)
2 Flywheel (manual transmission)
3 Washer
4 Drive plate (automatic transmission)
5 Thrust washers
6 Crankshaft

7 Main bearings
8 Crankshaft front oil seal
9 Oil pump
10 Oil filter screen
11 Main bearing cap monobloc

12 Sump gasket
13 Sump
14 Oil deflector
15 Crankshaft rear oil seal
16 Oil seal retainer

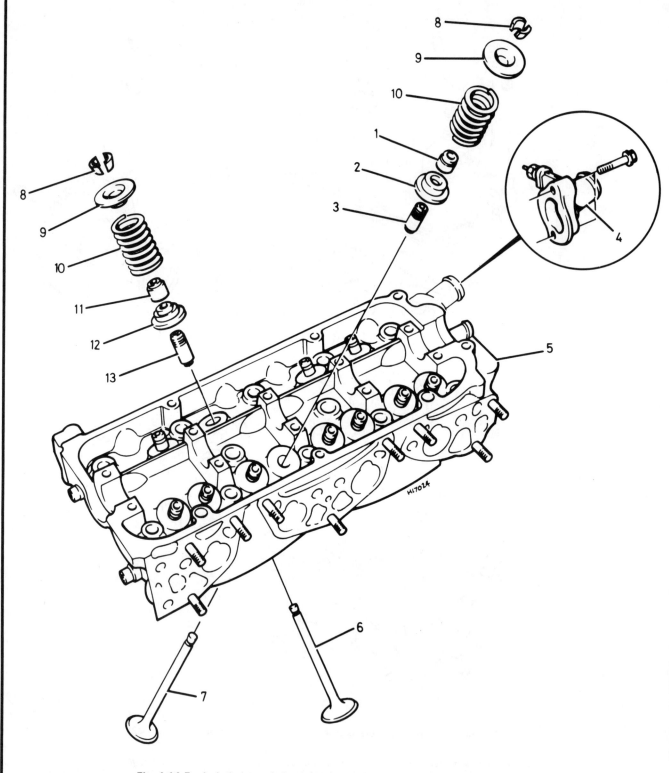

Fig. 1.14 Exploded view of the valve components – 12 valve engines (Sec 23)

1 Inlet valve stem seal	6 Exhaust valve	10 Valve springs
2 Inlet valve spring seat	7 Inlet valve	11 Exhaust valve stem seal
3 Inlet valve guide	8 Valve collets	12 Exhaust valve spring seat
4 Water outlet	9 Spring retainers	13 Exhaust valve guide
5 Cylinder head		

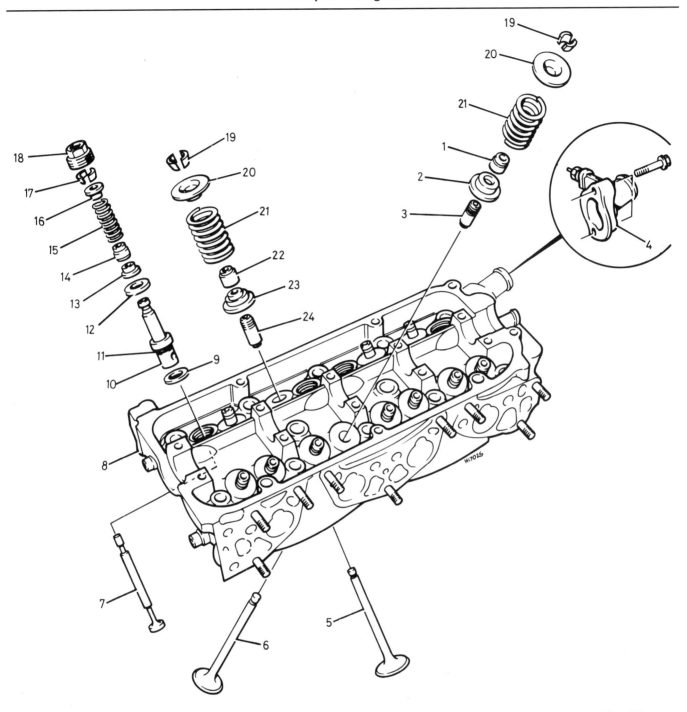

Fig. 1.15 Exploded view of the valve components – North American 12 valve engines with auxiliary valve (Sec 23)

1 Inlet valve stem seal	7 Auxiliary valve	13 Auxiliary valve spring seat	19 Valve collets
2 Inlet valve spring seat	8 Cylinder head	14 Auxiliary valve stem seal	20 Spring retainers
3 Inlet valve guide	9 Gasket	15 Auxiliary valve spring	21 Valve springs
4 Water outlet	10 Auxiliary valve holder	16 Spring retainer	22 Exhaust valve stem seal
5 Exhaust valve	11 O-ring	17 Valve collets	23 Exhaust valve spring seat
6 Inlet valve	12 Spring washer	18 Auxiliary valve holder nut	24 Exhaust valve guide

replaced independently. It may be possible to have worn cam lobes reprofiled by a specialist firm.

24 Check the rocker shafts and arms and renew any components which are worn.

25 Commence reassembly by oiling the stem of the first valve and pushing it into its guide which should be fitted with a new oil seal. The valve stem oil seals on the inlet valve guides have a bright metal clip while those for the exhaust valve guides have a black clip (photos).

26 Fit the spring seat, the valve spring so that the closer coils are towards the cylinder head, and then the spring retaining cap (photos).

27 Compress the valve spring and using a little grease locate the split collets in the valve stem cut-out (photo).

28 Gently release the compressor, checking to see that the collets are not displaced.

29 Fit the remaining valves in the same way.

30 Where auxiliary valves are fitted, reassemble the valves and valve

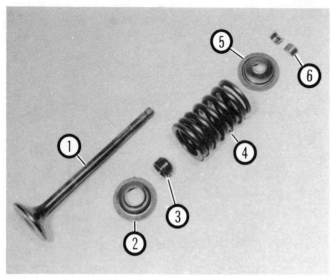

23.25A Valve components

1 Valve
2 Valve spring seat
3 Valve stem oil seal
4 Valve spring
5 Valve spring cap
6 Split collets

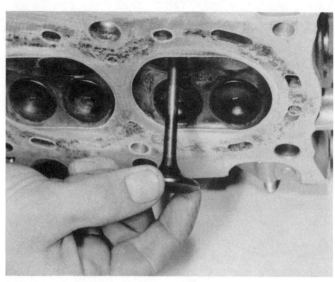

23.25B Insert the valve into its guide ...

holders using the same procedure as for the main valves and with reference to Fig. 1.15. Always use a new valve stem oil seal and new O-ring on the valve holder.

31 Using a new gasket, refit the auxiliary valve holders to the cylinder head and secure with the holder nut tightened to the specified torque.

32 With all the valves fitted, tap the end of each valve stem with a plastic or copper mallet to settle the components.

33 Refit all the components listed in paragraph 2 using the refitting procedures contained in the relevant Sections.

24 Engine components – examination and renovation

1 With the engine stripped down and all parts thoroughly clean, it is now time to examine everything for wear. The following items should be checked and where necessary renewed or renovated as described in the following Sections.

23.25C ... then fit the valve stem oil seal

23.26A Fit the valve spring seat ...

23.26B ... followed by the spring ...

23.26C ... and spring cap

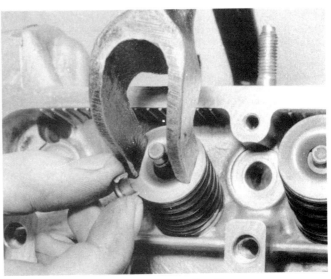

23.27 Compress the spring and fit the split collets

Cylinder block and crankcase

2   Clean away all old gasket material and then examine the casting for cracks particularly about bolt holes. If any are found, specialist welding or cold repair will be required.

3   Clean out the oilways and galleries with compressed air or wire.

4   If the cylinder bores are worn, this will be evident by the emission of exhaust smoke and general deterioration in engine performance together with increased oil consumption. A good way to test the condition of the engine is to have it at normal operating temperature with the spark plugs removed. Screw a compression tester (available from most modern accessory stores) into the first plug hole. Hold the accelerator pedal fully depressed and crank the engine on the starter motor for several revolutions. Record the reading. Zero the tester and check the remaining cylinders in the same way. All four compression figures should be approximately equal and within the tolerance given in the Specifications. If they are all low, suspect piston ring or cylinder bore wear. If only one reading is down, suspect a valve not seating.

5   The cylinder bores must be checked for taper, ovality, scoring and scratching. Start by examining the top of the cylinder bores. If they are at all worn, a ridge wil be felt on the thrust side. This ridge marks the limit of piston ring travel.

6   An internal micrometer or dial gauge can be used to check bore wear and taper against Specifications, but this is a pointless operation if the engine is obviously in need of reboring as indicated by excessive oil consumption.

Pistons and connecting rods

7   If the cylinders have been rebored, then the reconditioner will supply the oversize pistons, rings and the gudgeon pins. Give the job of fitting the new pistons to the connecting rods to him.

8   The gudgeon pin is an interference fit in the connecting rod small end and removal or refitting and changing a piston is a job best left to your dealer or engine reconditioner. This is owing to the need for a press and jig and careful heating of the connecting rod.

9   Removal and refitting of piston rings is described in Section 16.

Crankshaft

10 Examine the surfaces of the journals and crankpins; if scored or when measured with a micrometer they prove to be oval or tapered, then the manufacturer's recommendation is to renew the crankshaft and the colour-coded bearing shells. However, by consulting a specialist crankshaft grinder it may be possible for him to recondition the original crankshaft and supply undersize shells.

11 If the crankshaft is in good condition, but it is decided to renew the main and big-end bearing shells, use the following formula to select them.

Main bearings

12 Match the letter on the cylinder block with the number on the crankshaft web adjacent to each bearing (photo).

Big-end bearings

13 Match the number on the connecting rod with the letter on the crankshaft web adjacent to each bearing.

14 The resulting main bearing or big-end shell will be colour coded on its edge in accordance with the following table.

	A	B	C	D
1	Red	Pink	Yellow	Green
2	Pink	Yellow	Green	Brown
3	Yellow	Green	Brown	Black
4	Green	Brown	Black	Blue

Cylinder head, camshaft and rockers

15 Refer to Section 23.

24.12 Main and big-end bearing code number and letter

Timing belt, tensioner and sprockets

16 If the timing belt shows signs of cracking or tooth wear, renew it. If it has been in operation for 80 000 km (50 000 miles) or more, it should be renewed as a matter of routine.

17 If the sprockets have tooth wear, renew them.

18 The tensioner pulley should spin smoothly and quietly. If it is rough or worn on its spindle, renew it.

Flywheel (or driveplate)

19 Check the clutch mating surface of the flywheel. If it is deeply scored (due to failure to renew a worn driven plate), then it may be possible to have it surface ground provided the thickness of the flywheel is not reduced too much.

20 If lots of tiny cracks are visible on the surface of the flywheel then this will be due to overheating caused by slipping the clutch or 'riding' the clutch pedal.

21 With a pre-engaged type of starter motor it is rare to find the teeth of the flywheel ring gear damaged or worn, but if they are, then the ring gear will have to be renewed.

22 To remove the ring gear, drill a hole between the roots of two teeth taking care not to damage the flywheel and then split the ring with a sharp cold chisel.

23 The new ring gear must be heated to 350°C (662°F). If you do not have facilities for obtaining these temperatures, leave the job to your dealer or engine reconditioner.

24 Where such facilities are available, then the ring gear should be either pressed or lightly tapped gently onto its register and left to cool naturally, when the contraction of the metal on cooling will ensure that it is a secure and permanent fit. Great care must be taken not to overheat the ring gear, as if this happens its temper will be lost.

25 If the ring gear on the driveplate is worn, renew the plate complete.

Oil pump

26 Check that the oil relief valve slides freely in its housing.

27 If the pump has been in use for a long time carry out the following checks for wear outside the specified tolerance (see Specifications).

28 Extract the pump rear plate screws. An impact driver will probably be required for this (photo).

29 Remove the rear plate, remove the inner and outer rotors, identifying the faces which are in contact with the rear plate so that they can be refitted the same way round (photos).

30 Clean all components and reassemble the rotors.

31 Check the clearance between the outer rotor and the oil pump body using feeler gauges (photo).

32 Check the clearance between the inner rotor lobe tip and the outer rotor lobe tip (photo).

33 Place a straight-edge across the runs of the oil pump housing and insert feeler blades between the rotors and the straight-edge (photo).

34 If any clearance is outside that specified, renew the worn components or the pump complete.

24.28 Extracting the oil pump rear plate screws

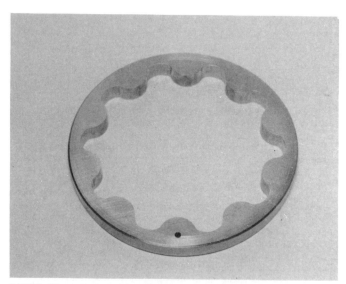

24.29A Oil pump outer rotor showing face 'up' dimple

24.29B Oil pump inner rotor showing face 'up' dimple

24.31 Checking oil pump outer rotor clearance

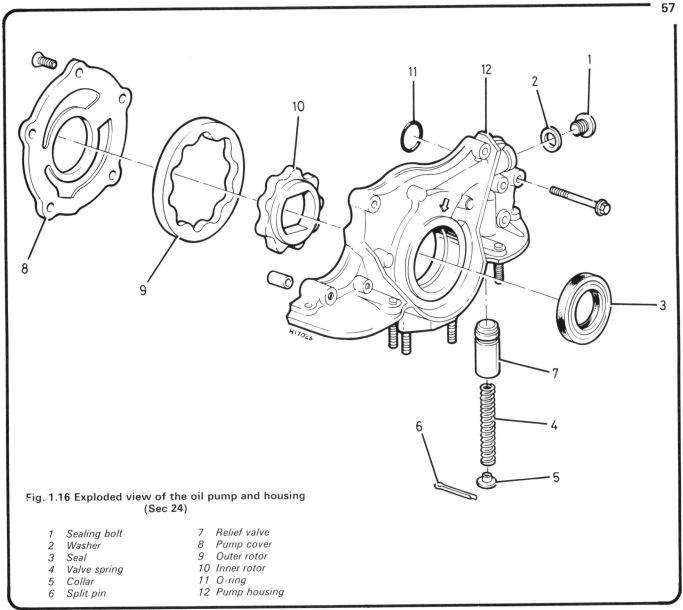

Fig. 1.16 Exploded view of the oil pump and housing
(Sec 24)

1	Sealing bolt	7	Relief valve
2	Washer	8	Pump cover
3	Seal	9	Outer rotor
4	Valve spring	10	Inner rotor
5	Collar	11	O-ring
6	Split pin	12	Pump housing

24.32 Checking oil pump rotor lobe tip clearance

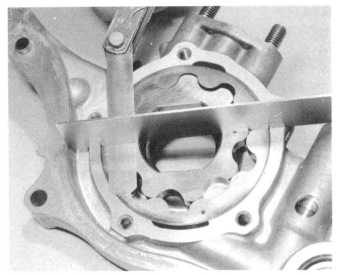

24.33 Checking oil pump rotor endfloat

Oil seals and gaskets

35 It is recommended that all gaskets and oil seals are renewed at major engine overhaul. Sockets are useful for removing or refitting oil seals. An arrow is moulded onto some seals to indicate the rotational direction of the component which it serves. Make sure that the seal is fitted the corect way round to comply with the arrow.

25 Engine – reassembly (general)

1 To ensure maximum life with minimum trouble from a rebuilt engine, not only must everything be correctly assembled, but it must also be spotlessly clean. All oilways must be clear, and locking washers and spring washers must be fitted where indicated. Oil all bearings and other working surfaces thoroughly with engine oil during assembly.
2 Before assembly begins, renew any bolts or studs with damaged threads.
3 Gather together a torque wrench, oil can, clean rags and a set of engine gaskets and oil seals, together with a new oil filter.

26 Engine – complete assembly

1 Set the cylinder block on the bench with the crankcase uppermost.
2 Wipe out the main bearing shell recesses in the crankcase and insert the selected shells or if the original ones are being used again, return them to their original locations (photo).
3 Oil the shells liberally and then stick the semi-circular thrust washers on either side of No. 4 main bearing in the crankcase using some thick grease. Make sure that the oil grooves on the thrust washers are visible when the thrust washers are fitted (photos).
4 Lower the crankshaft into the crankcase taking care not to displace the thrust washers (photo).
5 Wipe out the main bearing shell recesses in the main bearing cap monobloc and fit the selected shells or if the original ones are being used again, return them to their original locations (photo).
6 Oil the crankshaft journals and crankpins and fit the cap monobloc (photo).
7 Fit the cap bolts and tighten to the specified torque (photo).
8 Now check the crankshaft endfloat either using a dial gauge or by inserting a feeler blade between the machined shoulder of a crankshaft

26.2 Main bearing shell in crankcase

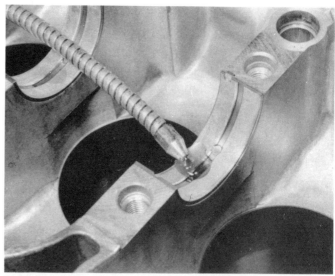

26.3A Ensure liberal lubrication of main bearing shells

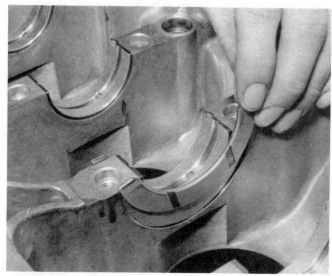

26.3B Fitting crankshaft thrust washer

26.4 Lowering the crankshaft into position

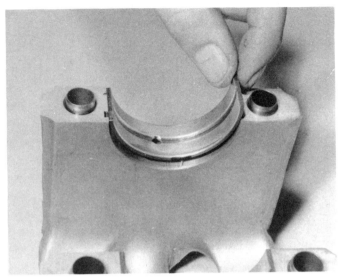

26.5 Main bearing shell location in monobloc

26.6 Fitting the monobloc to the crankcase

26.7 Tightening the main bearing monobloc bolts

26.8 Checking crankshaft endfloat

web and the thrust washers. If the endfloat is outside the specified tolerance then the thrust washer thickness must be incorrect (photo).

9   Lay the engine on its side and fit the piston/connecting rods as described in Section 16.

10 Fit the oil pump, having smeared its mounting face with jointing compound.

11 Fit the oil strainer using a new gasket at its mounting flange (photos).

12 Using a new gasket and seals, fit the sump as described in Section 14.

13 Tighten all bolts and nuts to the specified torque.

14 Bolt on the crankshaft rear oil seal retainer complete with new seal and having applied jointing compound to its mounting face (photo).

15 Fit the cylinder head complete with camshaft and rocker shafts as described in Section 12 or 13.

16 Refit the flywheel (or driveplate – automatic transmission), tightening new bolts to the specified torque and having applied locking fluid to their threads (photo).

17 Refer to Chapter 2 and fit the water pump. Bolt on the thermostat housing using a new gasket. Use a new O-ring and connect the coolant tube between the pump and thermostat housing (photos).

18 Fit the timing belt tensioner (photo).

26.11A Fit a new oil strainer gasket ...

26.11B ... then fit the strainer assembly

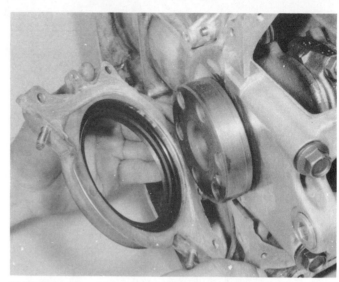

26.14 Fitting the crankshaft rear oil seal retainer

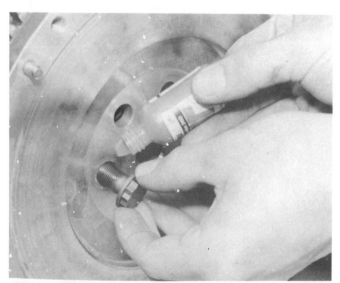

26.16 Applying thread locking fluid to the flywheel bolts

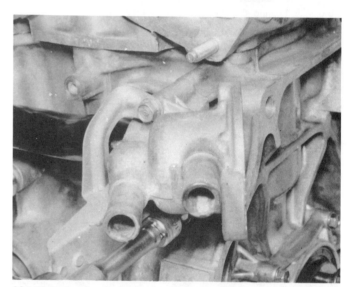

26.17A Fitting the thermostat housing ...

26.17B ... and coolant tube with new O-ring

26.18 Timing belt tensioner in position

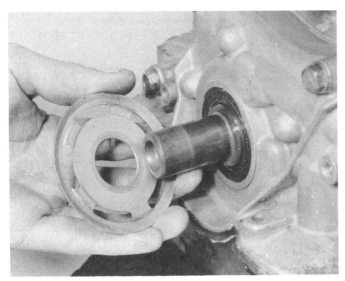

26.19A Fitting timing belt inner guide ...

26.19B ... and crankshaft sprocket

19 Fit the belt inner guide, the crankshaft sprocket, the timing belt and the belt outer guide, convex side to belt (photos).
20 Fit the belt lower cover, the crankshaft pulley and bolt. Set the crankshaft so that the pulley and cover timing marks are in alignment.
21 Fit the crankshaft breather and the oil dipstick guide tube (photo).
22 Connect the timing belt to the camshaft and coolant pump sprockets as described in Section 7 and tension the belt as described in Section 6.
23 Fit the timing belt upper cover triangular-shaped backing plate and then the upper cover (photo).
24 Check and adjust the valve clearances (Section 5).
25 Fit the rocker cover using a new gasket.
26 Tighten the domed nuts, but do not overtighten them.

27 Engine ancillary components – refitting

Refer to Section 21 and refit the listed components with reference to the Sections and Chapters specified where applicable.

28 Engine/transmission (UK models) – reconnection and refitting

1 Support the engine in an upright position.
2 On manual transmission models smear a trace of molybdenum disulphide grease on the transmission mainshaft splines. On automatic transmission models ensure that the torque converter is pushed fully into its transmission housing.
3 Offer the transmission squarely to the engine, push it fully home, then fit and tighten the retaining bolts.
4 On automatic transmission models refit the torque converter-to-driveplate bolts, turning the crankshaft as necessary to bring each bolt hole to an accessible position.
5 Refit the starter motor and flywheel housing cover plate.
6 Attach a crane or hoist to the engine using chains or rope slings as for removal. Lift the engine/transmission up and lower it into the engine compartment in its approximate fitted position.
7 Reconnect the engine/transmission mountings, but do not fully tighten the retaining nuts or bolts at this stage.
8 Check that none of the mountings are excessively strained or distorted and reposition the engine/transmission if necessary.
9 Tighten the mountings to the specified torque in the following sequence: *right-hand mounting, left-hand mounting, rear mounting.* Remove the crane or hoist.
10 Refit the alternator.
11 Reconnect the driveshafts to the transmission, ensuring that the

26.21 Crankshaft breather

26.23 Timing belt cover backing plate (arrowed)

inner joint retaining clip positively engages with the differential gears.

12 Reconnect the suspension lower arm balljoints to the steering knuckles. Tighten the balljoint nut to the specified torque and secure with a new split pin.

13 On automatic transmission models reconnect the transmission fluid cooler hoses.

14 Refit the exhaust front pipe with reference to Chapter 3.

15 On manual transmission models reconnect the gear change selector rod and torque rod, then refit and adjust the clutch cable as described in Chapter 5.

16 On automatic transmission models reconnect the selector cable, then check the cable adjustment as described in Chapter 7. Refit the centre console.

17 Refit the splash shields and undershield.

18 Refit the roadwheels and lower the car to the ground.

19 On fuel-injected engines reconnect the engine wiring sub-harness connectors and the fuel feed and return hoses.

20 Reconnect the accelerator cable and where applicable the choke cable, and check the cable adjustment as described in Chapter 3.

21 Reconnect the speedometer cable.

22 Refit the radiator top and bottom hoses and the heater hoses.

23 Refit the distributor as described in Chapter 4.

24 On carburettor engines refit the fuel pump as described in Chapter 3.

25 Reconnect the engine wiring connectors and multi-plugs.

26 Reconnect the brake servo vacuum hose.

27 Refit the air cleaner (carburettor engines) on air intake duct and vacuum hose (fuel-injected engines).

28 Refit the battery tray and the battery.

29 Refit the bonnet.

30 Fill the engine with oil with reference to Section 2.

31 Refill the cooling system (Chapter 2) and the transmission (Chapter 6 or 7).

29 Engine/transmission (North America models) – reconnection and refitting

1 Refer to Section 28 and carry out the operations described in paragraphs 1 to 18 inclusive.

2 On cars equipped with air conditioning, reft the compressor and drivebelt as described in Chapter 11 and adjust the drivebelt tension.

3 On cars equipped with power-assisted steering refit the pump and driveshaft as described in Chapter 10 and adjust the drivebelt tension.

4 On fuel-injected engines reconnect the engine wiring sub-harness connectors and the fuel feed and return hoses.

5 Reconnect the accelerator cable and check the adjustment as described in Chapter 3.

6 On California and high altitude models refit the air jet controller, and where applicable the No. 2 control box and connector.

7 Reconnect the purge control solenoid vacuum hose to the charcoal canister.

8 Refit the No. 1 control box and connector.

9 Refit the idle control solenoid valve on cars equipped with air conditioning.

10 For the remainder of the procedure refer to Section 28 and carry out the operations described in paragraphs 21 to 31 inclusive.

30 Fault diagnosis – engine

Symptom	Reason(s)
Engine fails to start	Discharged battery
	Loose battery connection
	Loose or broken ignition leads
	Moisture on spark plugs, distributor cap, or HT leads
	Incorrect spark plug gaps
	Cracked distributor cap or rotor
	Other ignition system fault
	Dirt or water in carburettor (where applicable)
	Empty fuel tank
	Faulty fuel pump
	Other fuel system fault
	Faulty starter motor
	Low cylinder compressions
Engine idles erratically	Inlet manifold air leak
	Leaking cylinder head gasket
	Worn camshaft lobes
	Faulty fuel pump
	Incorrect valve clearances
	Loose crankcase ventilation hoses
	Carburettor adjustment incorrect (where applicable)
	Uneven cylinder compressions
	Fuel-injection system fault (where applicable)
	Disconnected or faulty emission control component (where applicable)
Engine misfires	Spark plugs worn or incorrectly gapped
	Dirt or water in carburettor (where applicable)
	Carburettor adjustment incorrect (where applicable)
	Burnt out valve
	Leaking cylinder head gasket
	Distributor cap cracked
	Incorrect valve clearances
	Uneven cylinder compressions
	Worn carburettor or other fuel system fault
Engine stalls	Carburettor or fuel-injection system adjustment incorrect
	Inlet manifold air leak
	Ignition timing incorrect
Excessive oil consumption	Worn pistons, cylinder bores or piston rings
	Valve guides and valve stem seals worn
	Oil seal or gasket leakage
Engine backfires	Carburettor adjustment incorrect (where applicable)
	Ignition timing incorrect
	Incorrect valve clearances
	Inlet manifold air leak
	Sticking valve
	Emission control system fault (where applicable)

Chapter 2   Cooling system

Contents

Specifications

General
System type	Pressurized, water pump assisted thermo-syphon, with front mounted radiator and electric cooling fan
Pressure cap rating	0.75 to 1.0 bar (11 to 15 lbf/in²)

Thermostat
Start-to-open temperature	76 to 78°C (169 to 173°F)
Fully open temperature	91°C (196°F)
Valve lift height	8.0 mm (0.31 in)

Cooling fan thermo-switch
Cut-in temperature	88.5 to 91.5°C (191 to 197°F)
Cut-out temperature	85.5 to 86.5°C (186 to 188°F)

Torque wrench settings
	Nm	lbf ft
Cooling fan to radiator	10	7
Thermo-switch	23	17
Bleed bolt	10	7
Cylinder block drain plug	32	23
Thermostat housing cover	12	9
Thermostat housing to cylinder block	12	9
Temperature gauge sender	9	7
Water pump to cylinder block	12	9
Timing belt tensioner bolt	45	35
Crankshaft pulley bolt	115	83

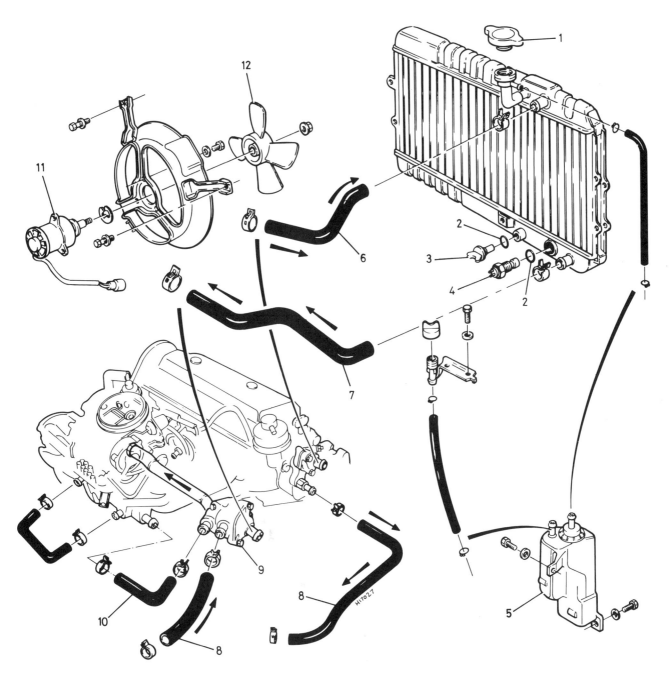

Fig. 2.1 Principal components of the cooling system – carburettor engine shown (Sec 1)

1 Radiator pressure cap	4 Thermo-switch	7 Lower radiator hose	10 Bypass inlet hose
2 O-rings	5 Coolant reservoir	8 Heater hoses	11 Fan motor
3 Drain plug	6 Upper radiator hose	9 Thermostat housing	12 Fan

Arrows on hoses indicate direction of flow

1 General description

The cooling system is of the pressurised, pump-assisted, thermo-syphon type. The system consists of the radiator, water pump, thermostat (unconventionally situated on the outlet side of the radiator), electric cooling fan, coolant reservoir and associated hoses.

The system functions as follows. When the engine is cold the coolant circulates around the engine and through the inlet manifold and the heater matrix. The thermostat remains closed until the coolant reaches a predetermined temperature, and so the coolant continues to circulate around the engine, manifold and heater. Once the predetermined temperature is reached, the thermostat opens and cold coolant from the bottom of the radiator enters through the thermostat housing. Coolant at a higher temperature leaves the engine through the cylinder head outlet and passes to the top of the radiator. As the coolant circulates through the radiator it is cooled by the inrush of air when the car is in forward motion, supplemented by the action of the electric cooling fan when necessary. As the coolant reaches the bottom of the radiator, having been cooled, the cycle is repeated.

When the engine is at normal operating temperature the coolant expands and some of it is displaced into the coolant reservoir. This coolant collects in the reservoir and is returned to the radiator when the system cools.

The electric cooling fan mounted behind the radiator is controlled by a thermo-switch located in the radiator bottom tank. At a predetermined coolant temperature the switch contacts close, thus actuating the fan.

Warning: *Take care when working in the vicinity of the electric cooling fan. The fan may start automatically and run for up to fifteen minutes even with the engine switched off.*

2 Maintenance and inspection

1   Check the coolant level in the system weekly, with the engine at normal operating temperature, ensuring that the level is up to the 'MAX' mark on the side of the coolant reservoir.
2   If topping-up is necessary, wait until the engine has cooled, then slowly turn the radiator cap anti-clockwise to its stop to release the pressure in the system.
3   Unscrew the filler cap at the top of the coolant reservoir extension hose and add a water and antifreeze mixture (see Section 6) to bring the level up to the mark. Refit the filler cap and the radiator cap (photo).
4   Wth a sealed cooling system, topping-up should only be necessary at very infrequent intervals. If this is not the case and frequent topping-up is required, it is likely there is a leak in the system. Check all hoses and joint faces for any staining or actual wetness, and rectify if necessary. If no leaks can be found it is advisable to have the system, and in particular the radiator cap, pressure tested. It is possible that the leak could be internal and it is a good idea to keep a check on the engine oil level, as a serious internal leak can often cause the level in the sump to rise, thus confirming suspicions.
5   At the service intervals given in 'Routine Maintenance' at the beginning of this Manual carefully inspect all the hoses, hose clips, and visible joint gaskets of the system for cracks, corrosion, deterioration and leakage. Renew any hoses or clips that are suspect, and also renew any gaskets or seals, if necessary.
6   At the intervals specified, drain, flush and refill the cooling system using fresh antifreeze, as described in Sections 3, 4, and 5 respectively.

3 Cooling system – draining

1   It is preferable to drain the cooling system when the engine is cold. If the engine is hot the pressure in the system must be released before attempting to drain the system. Place a cloth over the radiator cap and slowly turn the cap anti-clockwise until it reaches its stop.
2   Wait until the pressure has escaped, then press the cap downwards and turn it further in an anti-clockwise direction. Release the downward pressure on the cap very slowly and, after making sure that all the pressure in the system has been relieved, remove the cap.
3   Slide the heater temperature lever to the right (maximum heat position).
4   Place a suitable container beneath the radiator, unscrew the drain plug and allow the coolant to drain (photo).
5   When the radiator has drained, place the container under the engine, undo the drain plug on the front facing side of the cylinder block, and allow the coolant to drain from the engine.
6   Disconnect the hoses, undo the two bolts and remove the coolant reservoir. Empty out the old coolant, flush the reservoir with clean water, then refit and reconnect the hoses.
7   If the system is to be fluhed, refer to the next Section, otherwise refit the radiator drain plug using a new O-ring if necessary, and the cylinder block drain plug using a non-hardening sealant on its threads.

Fig. 2.2 'MAX' and 'MIN' level marks on coolant reservoir (Sec 2)

2.3 Topping-up the coolant reservoir   3.4 Radiator drain plug location

4 Cooling system – flushing

1 With time the cooling system may gradually lose its efficiency as the radiator core becomes choked with rust, scale deposits and other sediment, particularly if the specified concentration of antifreeze in the system has not been maintained.

2 To flush the system, first drain the coolant as described in the previous Section.

3 Insert a hose into the radiator filler neck and allow water to circulate through the system until it runs clear from the radiator and cylinder block drain holes.

4 In severe cases of contamination the radiator should be reverse flushed. To do this remove the radiator as described in Section 7, invert it and insert the hose into the bottom hose outlet. Allow water to circulate until it runs clear from the filler neck and top hose outlet.

5 The use of chemical cleaners should only be necessary as a last resort. The regular renewal of antifreeze should prevent the contamination of the system.

5 Cooling system – filling

1 Refit the radiator drain plug and cylinder block drain plug and ensure that the heater temperature lever is still in the maximum heat position.

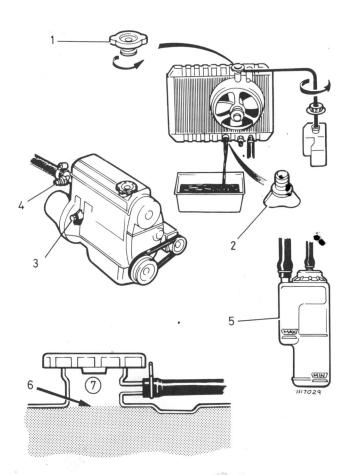

Fig. 2.3 Cooling system draining and filling details (Secs 3 and 5)

1 Radiator pressure cap
2 Radiator drain plug
3 Cylinder block drain plug
4 Bleed bolt
5 Coolant reservoir
6 Coolant level in radiator
7 Radiator filler neck

2 Pour the appropriate mixture of water and antifreeze into the coolant reservoir until the level is up to the 'MAX' mark, then refit the reservoir filler cap.

3 Slacken the bleed bolt on the cylinder head water outlet (Fig. 2.3).

4 Fill the radiator slowly using the appropriate mixture of water and antifreeze until the level is up to the base of the filler neck. Tighten the bleed bolt as soon as coolant flows out in a steady stream free from air bubbles (photo).

5 With the radiator cap off, start the engine and allow it to reach normal operating temperature (the electric cooling fan should operate at least twice).

6 Switch off, top up the radiator if necessary, then refit the radiator cap.

7 Run the engine again until the fan operates, then switch off and observe the level in the coolant reservoir. Top up the reservoir if necessary, after the engine has cooled, as described in Section 2.

6 Antifreeze mixture

1 The antifreeze should be renewed at regular intervals (see 'Routine Maintenance'). This is necessary not only to maintain the antifreeze properties, but also to prevent corrosion which would otherwise occur as the corrosion inhibitors become progressively less effective.

2 Always use an ethylene glycol based antifreeze which is suitable for use in mixed metal cooling systems.

3 Before adding antifreeze the cooling system should be completely drained and flushed and all hoses checked for condition and security.

4 The antifreeze concentration must be maintained all year round at 50% minimum but not exceeding 60%.

5 After filling with antifreeze a label should be attached to the radiator stating the type of antifreeze used and the date installed. Any subsequent topping-up should be done with a 50% concentration of the same type of antifreeze. Do not use additional rust inhibitors or anti-rust products as they may not be compatible with the antifreeze.

6 **Do not** use engine antifreeze in the screen washer system, as it will cause damage to the vehicle paintwork. Screen wash antifreeze is available from most accessory shops.

7 Radiator – removal, inspection and refitting

1 Remove the battery and battery tray as described in Chapter 12.

2 Drain the cooling system as described in Section 3.

3 Undo the two screws, lift off the distributor cap and place it to one side.

4 At the base of the radiator slide back the rubber cover and disconnect the thermo-switch wiring (photo).

5.4 Tighten the bleed bolt (arrowed) when coolant flows free from air bubbles

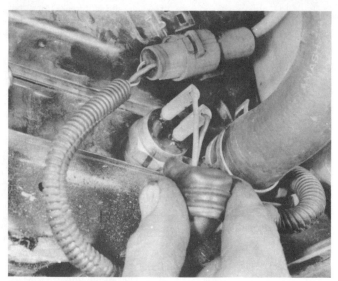

7.4 Disconnect the wiring at the thermo-switch

7.5 Detach the fan wiring plug from its tag ...

5   Detach the fan motor wiring plug from the tag on the side of the fan cowl (photo).
6   Using a screwdriver carefully release the retaining clip and separate the two halves of the wiring plug (photos).
7   Disconnect the coolant reservoir hose and radiator top and bottom at their radiator outlets (photos).
8   Undo the three upper bolts securing the bonnet lock platform to the front body panel, the two bolts securing the radiator to the platform, and the lower left-hand bonnet lock retaining bolt. Lift out the platform and place it to one side (photos).
9   Undo the vertical stay lower retaining bolt and remove the stay (photos).
10 Undo the three bolts securing the fan and cowl to the radiator, then carefully manipulate the fan and cowl out from between the radiator and engine. Clearance is extremely limited here and care must be taken to avoid damaging the radiator fins (photos).
11 Disengage the lower mountings and lift the radiator up and out of the engine compartment (photo).
12 Inspect the radiator carefully for damage or obvious signs of leaks. Should the radiator be suspect, repair must be left to a specialist. With the radiator removed clear the matrix of dead insects and small leaves with a soft brush or hose pipe. If necessary reverse flush the radiator as

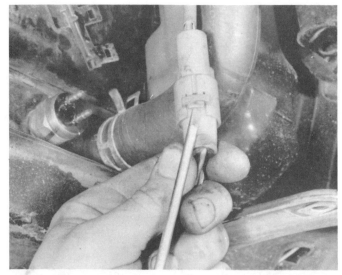

7.6A ... release the retaining clip ...

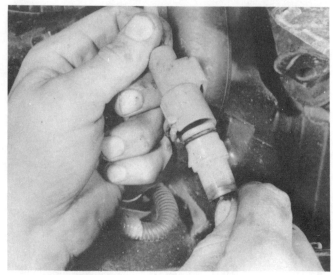

7.6B ... and separate the plug halves

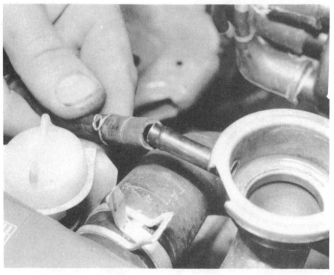

7.7A Disconnect the coolant reservoir hose ...

7.7B ... top hose ...

7.7C ... and the bottom hose at the radiator

7.8A Undo the bonnet lock platform and radiator mounting bolts ...

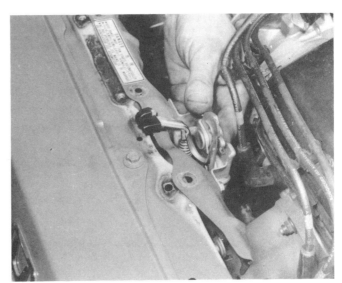

7.8B ... and remove the bonnet lock platform

7.9A Undo the vertical stay lower retaining bolt ...

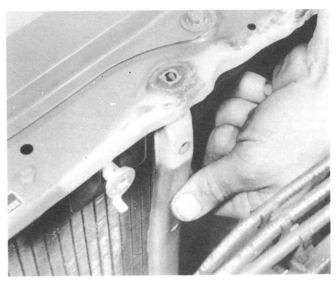

7.9B ... and remove the stay

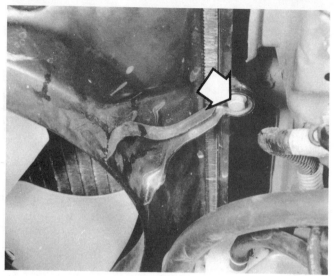

7.10A Cooling fan right-hand retaining bolt (arrowed) ...

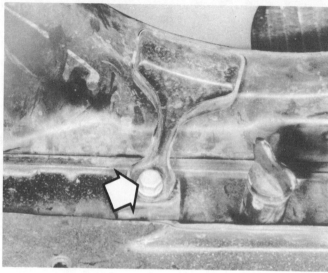

7.10B ... and lower retaining bolt (arrowed)

7.10C Removing the cooling fan

7.11 Removing the radiator

described in Section 4 and renew any hoses, clips or O-rings before refitting.

13 Refitting is the reverse sequence to removal, bearing in mind the following points:

(a) *Ensure that the radiator, fan and cowl, vertical stay and bonnet lock platform are all fitted and correctly positioned before tightening any of the retaining bolts*

(b) *Refill the cooling system as described in Section 5*

8 Cooling fan assembly – removal and refitting

1 Remove the battery and battery tray as described in Chapter 12.
2 Refer to Section 3 and drain the radiator, then remove the radiator top hose.
3 Undo the two screws, lift off the distributor cap and place it to one side.
4 Detach the fan motor wiring plug from the tag on the side of the fan cowl.

5 Using a screwdriver carefully release the retaining clip and separate the two halves of the wiring plug.
6 Undo the three upper bolts securing the bonnet lock platform to the front body panel, the two bolts securing the radiator to the platform, and the lower left-hand bonnet lock retaining bolt. Lift out the platform and place it to one side.
7 Undo the vertical stay lower retaining bolt and remove the stay.
8 Undo the three bolts securing the fan and cowl to the radiator, then carefully manipulate the fan and cowl out from between the radiator and engine. Clearance is extremely limited here and care must be taken to avoid damaging the radiator fins.
9 To remove the fan blades, unscrew the retaining nut and withdraw the fan blades from the motor spindle.
10 To remove the motor, undo the retaining bolts and withdraw the unit from the cowl.
11 Refitting is the reverse sequence to removal, bearing in mind the following points:

(a) *Ensure that the fan and cowl, vertical stay and bonnet lock platform are all fitted and correctly positioned before tightening any of the retaining bolts*

(b) *Refill the cooling system as described in Section 5*

9 Thermo-switch – testing, removal and refitting

1 The thermo-switch is located in the radiator bottom tank and controls the operation of the cooling fan according to coolant temperature. If there is any doubt about the operation of the cooling fan, test the thermo-switch as follows.

2 Slide back the rubber cover and disconnect the two wires at the thermo-switch.

3 Join the two wires together and switch on the ignition. If the fan operates then the thermo-switch is faulty and must be renewed. To do this drain the cooling system (Section 3) and unscrew the thermo-switch. Fit a new unit using a new O-ring seal. Refill the cooling system as described in Section 5, then reconnect the thermo-switch wires.

4 If as a result of the above test the motor still does not operate, first check for a blown fuse or wiring fault, otherwise the fault is likely to be in the fan motor and renewal will be necessary.

10 Thermostat – removal, testing and refitting

1 Drain the cooling system as described in Section 3.

2 Refer to Chapter 3 and remove the air cleaner to provide greater access if necessary.

3 Disconnect the radiator hose at the thermostat housing cover.

4 Undo the two bolts and lift off the thermostat housing cover and gasket (photo).

5 Withdraw the thermostat from the housing (photo).

6 To test the unit, suspend it on a string in a saucepan of cold water together with a thermometer. Heat the water and note the temperature at which the thermostat begins to open, and is fully open. Now remove the thermostat from the water and measure the lift height of the thermostat valve. Compare the readings obtained with the figures given in the Specifications. Allow the thermostat to cool and check that the valve closes fully.

7 If the thermostat does not perform as specified, a new unit must be

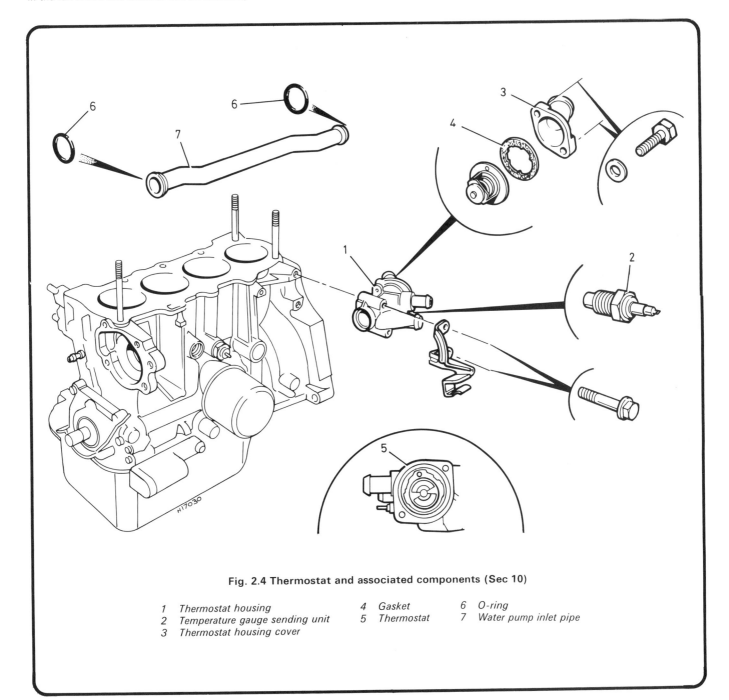

Fig. 2.4 Thermostat and associated components (Sec 10)

1 Thermostat housing
2 Temperature gauge sending unit
3 Thermostat housing cover
4 Gasket
5 Thermostat
6 O-ring
7 Water pump inlet pipe

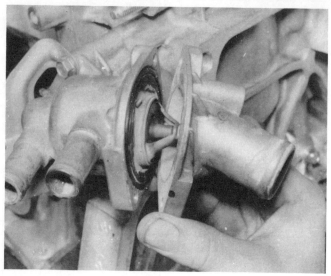

10.4 Remove the thermostat housing cover ...

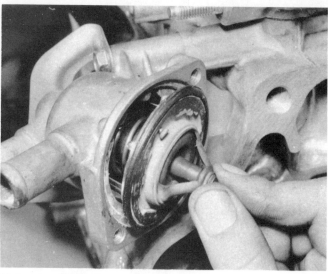

10.5 ... then lift out the thermostat

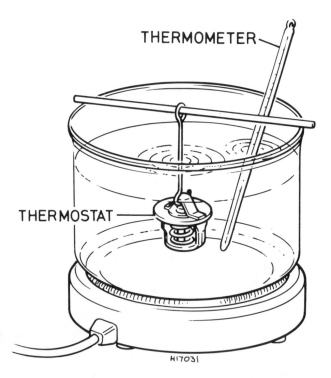

Fig. 2.5 Testing the thermostat (Sec 10)

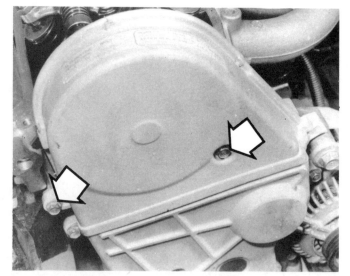

11.6 Timing belt upper cover retaining bolts (arrowed)

fitted. Under no circumstances should the car be used without a thermostat, as uneven cooling of the cylinder walls and head passages will occur, causing possible distortion and seizure of the engine internal components.

8   Clean off all traces of old gasket from the thermostat housing and cover prior to refitting.

9   Refitting is the reverse sequence to removal, but use a new cover gasket and ensure that the thermostat is fitted with the jiggle pin uppermost. Tighten the retaining bolts to the specified torque, and on completion fill the cooling system as described in Section 5.

11 Water pump – removal and refitting

1   Disconnect the battery negative terminal.
2   Drain the cooling system as described in Section 3.

3   If air conditioning is fitted remove the drivebelt as described in Chapter 11.
4   Remove the alternator drivebelt as described in Chapter 12.
5   Remove the air cleaner (Chapter 3) and the rocker cover (Chapter 1).
6   Undo the two bolts and lift off the timing belt upper cover (photo).
7   From under the left-hand wheel arch prise out the plug in the access panel and insert a socket and extension bar through the hole to engage the crankshaft pulley bolt.
8   Turn the crankshaft anti-clockwise to bring No. 1 piston to TDC on compression. In this position the 'UP' mark on the camshaft sprocket will be uppermost, with the marks on the sprocket edge aligned with the surface of the cylinder head (Fig. 2.6). The white painted TDC mark on the crankshaft pulley will be aligned with the pointer on the timing belt lower cover (photos).
9   Undo the crankshaft pulley retaining bolt and remove the pulley. To prevent the crankshaft rotating, engage a low gear and have an assistant firmly depress the footbrake. Alternatively remove the starter motor and lock the flywheel teeth using a stout screwdriver or flat bar.
10   Undo the retaining bolts and remove the timing belt lower cover.

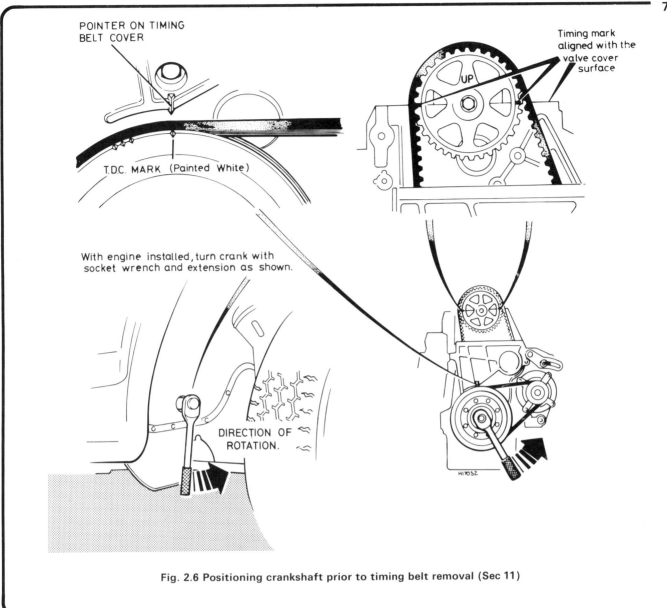

POINTER ON TIMING BELT COVER

Timing mark aligned with the valve cover surface

T.D.C. MARK (Painted White)

With engine installed, turn crank with socket wrench and extension as shown.

DIRECTION OF ROTATION.

Fig. 2.6 Positioning crankshaft prior to timing belt removal (Sec 11)

11.8A Camshaft sprocket timing mark positions with No. 1 piston at TDC on compression

11.8B Crankshaft pulley and timing belt cover timing marks aligned with No. 1 piston at TDC

11.12 Timing belt tensioner retaining bolt (arrowed)

11.15 Water pump retaining bolts (arrowed)

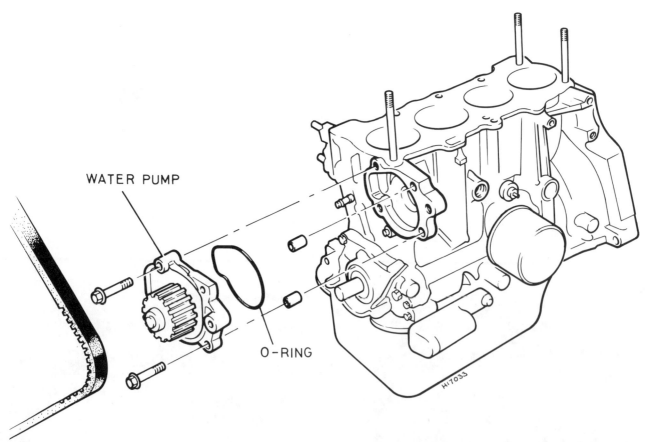

Fig. 2.7 Water pump mounting details (Sec 11)

11 Remove the outer belt guide and the Woodruff key from the end of the crankshaft.

12 Slacken the timing belt tensioner bolt, move the tensioner towards the alternator, then tighten the bolt (photo).

13 Mark the rotational direction of the belt, then slip it off the sprockets. **Do not** rotate the crankshaft or camshaft with the timing belt removed.

14 Undo the alternator adjustment arm bolt and pivot the arm clear of the engine.

15 Undo the four retaining bolts, ease the water pump off the locating dowels and remove it from the engine (photo). Recover the O-ring seal.

16 The water pump is a sealed unit and cannot be dismantled for repair. If the unit is leaking or faulty, the pump must be renewed.

17 Fit a new O-ring seal to the pump and bolt the unit in position, observing the specified torque for the retaining bolts.

18 Refit the alternator adjustment arm and bolt finger tight only at this stage.

19 Check that the crankshaft and camshaft are still correctly positioned as described in paragraph 8. Temporarily refit the timing belt lower cover and crankshaft pulley if necessary to check this.
20 Locate the timing belt over the sprockets and tensioner in its original rotational direction.
21 Refit the Woodruff key and outer belt guide with the convex side of the guide towards the belt.
22 Refit the timing belt lower cover.
23 Refit the crankshaft pulley and retaining bolt. Tighten the bolt to the specified torque, while preventing crankshaft rotation using the same method as for removal.
24 Using a screwdriver prise out the rubber plug in the timing belt lower cover located just above the crankshaft pulley.
25 Using a suitable socket inserted through the access hole slacken the tensioner retaining bolt. Rotate the crankshaft one quarter of a turn anti-clockwise, then tighten the tensioner bolt. The tensioner is spring loaded and will automatically adjust to the correct belt tension.
26 Refit the rubber plug to the lower cover.
27 Rotate the crankshaft through one complete cycle, then realign the pulley and lower cover TDC mark. Check that the camshaft sprocket timing marks are also correctly positioned as previously described. If the sprocket appears to be one tooth out either way, slacken the tensioner and reposition the belt on the sprocket as necessary. Retension the belt as described in paragraph 25.
28 Refit the plug to the access panel under the wheel arch.
29 Refit the timing belt upper cover and the rocker cover.
30 Refit and tension the alternator drivebelt as described in Chapter 12.
31 If air conditioning is fitted, refit and tension the drivebelt as described in Chapter 11.
32 Refit the air cleaner as described in Chapter 3.
33 Reconnect the battery, then fill the cooling system as described in Section 5.

12 Temperature gauge and sender unit – testing, removal and refitting

1 If the reading on the temperature gauge is suspect, the following tests can be used to determine the cause.
2 Disconnect the lead at the sender unit located in the thermostat housing and earth the lead.
3 Switch on the ignition. The gauge needle should move to 'Hot'. Do not leave the ignition on for more than five seconds. If the needle does not move as indicated, check the fuse and wiring and if these are satisfactory the gauge is faulty.
4 If the needle does move to 'Hot', then the sender is faulty.
5 If the fuel and temperature gauges indicate 'Full' and 'Hot' at the same time, then both are faulty.
6 To test the calibration of the sender unit, run the engine with the radiator cap removed until the coolant temperature reaches 50°C (122°F). Insert a thermometer in the radiator filler neck to check this.
7 Using an ohmmeter, measure the resistance between the terminal of the sender unit and earth. The resistance should be between 134 and 176 ohms.
8 Continue running the engine until the coolant temperature reaches 80°C (176°F). At this temperature the resistance should be between 47.6 and 56.9 ohms.
9 If the readings are not as specified renew the sender unit as follows.
10 Partially drain the radiator (approximately 1 litre/1.76 Imp pt/1.0 US qt) with reference to Section 3.
11 Disconnect the wiring, unscrew the sender unit and remove it from the thermostat housing.
12 Refitting is the reverse sequence to removal, but tighten the sender to the specified torque. Refill the cooling system as described in Section 5.
13 Removal and refitting of the fuel and temperature gauges is described in Chapter 12.

13 Fault diagnosis – cooling system

Symptom	Reason(s)
Overheating	Low coolant level (this may be the result of overheating for other reasons)
	Radiator blockage (internal or external) or grille restricted
	Thermostat defective
	Ignition timing incorrect or distributor defective (automatic advance inoperative)
	Faulty cooling fan thermo-switch
	Faulty cooling fan
	Blown cylinder head gasket
	Water pump defective
	Radiator pressure cap faulty
Overcooling	Thermostat missing, defective or wrong heat range
	Incorrect reading on gauge (faulty gauge or sender unit)
Water loss – external	Loose hose clips
	Perished or cracked hoses
	Radiator core or tank leaking
	Heater matrix leaking
	Radiator pressure cap faulty
	Boiling due to overheating
	Water pump or thermostat housing leaking
	Core plug leaking
Water loss – internal	Cylinder head gasket blown
	Cylinder head cracked or warped
	Cylinder block cracked
Corrosion	Infrequent draining and flushing
	Incorrect antifreeze mixture or incorrect type
	Combustion gases contaminating coolant

Chapter 3
Fuel, exhaust and emission control systems

Contents

Specifications

Part A Carburettor engines
Fuel pump
Type	Mechanical, driven off camshaft
Delivery pressure	0.19 to 0.26 bar (2.7 to 3.8 lbf/in²)

Carburettor (UK models)
Type	Keihin dual barrel fixed jet with manual choke
Accelerator pump stroke	18.5 to 19.5 mm (0.73 to 0.77 in)
Float level	35.4 to 37.4 mm (1.39 to 1.47 in) from flange gasket
Idle speed:	
Manual transmission	700 to 800 rpm
Automatic transmission	650 to 750 rpm (transmission in 'drive')
Fast idle speed	1500 to 2500 rpm
CO at idle	2.0% maximum

Carburettor (North American models)
Type	Keihin dual barrel fixed jet with automatic choke
Idle speed:	
1300	600 to 700 rpm*
1500 except CRX:	
Models for California	650 to 750 rpm
All other models:	
Manual transmission	650 to 750 rpm**
Automatic transmission	600 to 700 rpm**

1500 CRX:
    Models for California:
        Standard ....   650 to 750 rpm
        HF ....   550 to 650 rpm
        Si ....   700 to 800 rpm
    All other models:
        Standard:
            Manual transmission ....   650 to 750 rpm**
            Automatic transmission ....   600 to 700 rpm**
        HF ....   650 to 750 rpm**
        Si ....   700 to 800 rpm

* Increase by 100 rpm for high altitudes outside California
** Increase by 50 rpm for high altitudes outside California

Fast idle speed:
    1300 and 1500 except CRX ....   2500 to 3500 rpm
    1500 CRX:
        Standard and HF ....   2500 to 3500 rpm
        Si ....   1250 to 2250 rpm
CO at idle 0.1%

Fuel requirement
UK models ....   91 RON (two-star)
North American models ....   Unleaded

Part B Fuel-injected engines
Fuel pump
Type ....   Electric centrifugal
Delivery pressure ....   2.2 to 2.7 bar (33.0 to 39.0 lbf/in²)

Idle speed
UK models ....   800 to 900 rpm
North American models ....   700 to 800 rpm

Idle controller boosted speed .... 700 to 800 rpm

CO at idle
UK models ....   2.0% maximum
North American models 0.1%

Fuel requirements
UK models ....   97 RON (four-star)
North American models ....   Unleaded

Torque wrench settings	Nm	lbf ft
Carburettor engines		
Carburettor mounting nuts/bolts	24	17
Fuel pump nuts	24	17
Inlet manifold steady bracket:		
Upper bolt	22	16
Lower bolt	45	32
Inlet manifold to cylinder head	22	16
Air valve to manifold	11	8
EGR valve to manifold	22	16
Air suction valve to manifold	10	7
Air suction valve pipe to valve	10	7
Air suction valve pipe to connector	22	16
Fuel-injected engines		
Throttle body to manifold	22	16
Fuel filter service bolt	12	9
Injector fuel pipe nuts	12	9
Pressure regulator to fuel pipe	10	7
Fuel filter banjo unions	22	16
Fuel pump silencer	28	20
Inlet manifold to cylinder head	22	16
Inlet manifold steady bracket:		
Upper bolt	22	16
Lower bolt	45	33
Inlet manifold upper to lower parts:		
6 mm bolts	10	7
8 mm bolts	22	16

Torque wrench settings (continued)

All engines

	Nm	lbf ft
Fuel tank strap nuts	22	16
Fuel tank drain plug	50	36
Exhaust manifold to cylinder head	32	23
Exhaust downpipe to manifold	34	25
Catalytic converter nuts	34	25
Exhaust downpipe flexible joint nuts	22	16
Exhaust pipe joint flange nuts	22	16
Exhaust heat shield bolts	10	7

PART A CARBURETTOR ENGINES

1 General description

The fuel system consists of a fuel tank which is mounted forward of the rear suspension, a mechanically operated fuel pump, a dual barrel fixed jet carburettor and temperature controlled air cleaner.

The air cleaner contains a disposable paper filter element and incorporates an automatic air temperature control system. The system is controlled by an air control flap valve located at the junction of the air cleaner hot and cold air intakes. The control valve is operated by inlet manifold vacuum acting on a check valve in conjunction with a temperature sensitive air bleed valve. The system allows hot and cold air to be mixed to maintain a near constant air intake temperature.

Warning: *Many of the procedures in this Chapter entail the removal of fuel pipes and connections which may result in some fuel spillage. Before carrying out any operation on the fuel system refer to the precautions given in 'Safety First!' at the beginning of this manual and follow them implicitly. Petrol is a highly dangerous and volatile liquid and the precautions necessary when handling it cannot be over stressed.*

2 Maintenance and inspection

1   At the intervals given in 'Routine Maintenance' at the beginning of this Manual carry out the following operations on the fuel system components.
2   With the car over a pit, raised on a vehicle lift, or securely supported on axle stands, carefully inspect the fuel pipes, hoses and unions for chafing, leaks and corrosion. Renew any pipes that are severely pitted with corrosion or in any way damaged. Renew any hoses that show signs of cracking or other deterioration.

3   Examine the fuel tank for leaks, particularly around the fuel gauge sender unit, and for signs of corrosion or damage.
4   From within the engine compartment, check the security of all fuel hose attachments and inspect the fuel hoses and vacuum hoses for kinks, chafing or deterioration.
5   Renew the air cleaner element and check the operation of the air cleaner automatic temperature control, as described in Section 4.
6   Check the operation of the accelerator linkage and lubricate the linkage, cable and pedal pivot with a few drops of engine oil. On UK models, check the operation of the choke control and linkage, as described in Section 10.
7   Renew the fuel filter using the procedures described in Section 5.
8   Adjust the carburettor idle speed and mixture settings as described in Section 11.
9   Inspect the condition of all emission control components and hoses. Testing and component renewal should be carried out by a suitably equipped dealer (see Part C of this Chapter).
10   Check the condition of the security of the exhaust system as described in Section 34.

3 Air cleaner – servicing, removal and refitting

1   Unscrew the wing nut and where fitted the additional nuts, release the clips and lift off the cover (photo).
2   Remove the filter element and wipe clean the casing and cover.
3   Fit a new element and refit the cover.
4   To remove the complete air cleaner, unscrew the wing nut and where fitted the additional nuts.
5   Disconnect the hot and cold air intake ducts (photos).
6   Disconnect the crankcase ventilation hose from air cleaner to rocker cover (photo).
7   Disconnect the vacuum hose and remove the air cleaner from the carburettor (photo).
8   Refitting is the reverse sequence to removal.

3.1 Air cleaner cover wing nut and retaining clips (arrowed)

3.5A Air cleaner hot air intake duct (arrowed) ...

3.5B ... and cold air intake duct

3.6 Crankcase ventilation hose attachment

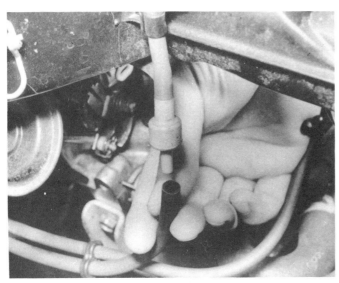

3.7 Disconnecting air cleaner vacuum hose

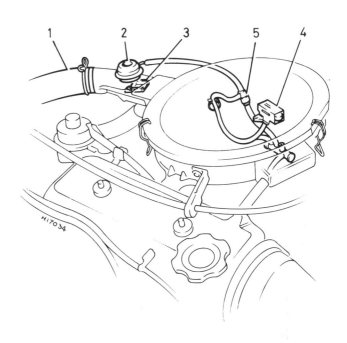

Fig. 3.1 Air cleaner air temperature control system (Sec 4)

1	Cold air intake duct	4	Air bleed valve
2	Air control diaphragm	5	Check valve
3	Flap valve		

4 Air cleaner air temperature control system – checking

1   The following checks should be carried out with the engine cold.

2   Remove the air cleaner cover and filter element.

3   Start the engine, allow it to idle for approximately five seconds, then switch off. The air control flap valve should rise when the engine is started and remain open for three seconds after the engine is switched off. If the valve operates correctly proceed to paragraph 10.

4   If the flap valve does not operate as described, check to see that it is free to move and not binding. If satisfactory, disconnect and plug the vacuum hose at the air bleed valve.

5   Start and run the engine as described in paragraph 3. If the flap valve now operates as described, the air bleed valve is faulty and should be renewed.

6   If the valve still does not open, disconnect the vacuum hose at the air control diaphragm and remove the deflector plate inside the air cleaner.

7   Block the air control diaphragm inlet using a finger, then reach inside the intake and manually raise the flap valve.

8   Release the flap valve. If it remains open the check valve is proved faulty and should be renewed. If the flap valve closes, the air control diaphragm is faulty and should be renewed.

9   Reconnect the vacuum hoses and air deflector plate, then refit the air filter element and air cleaner cover.

10 Start the engine and allow it to reach normal operating temperature.

11 With the engine hot and the cooling fan running, remove the air cleaner cover and filter, then immediately check the position of the flap valve.

12 The flap valve should be closed to fully shut off the hot air intake. If this is not the case, disconnect the vacuum hose at the air control diaphragm. If the flap now closes, the air bleed valve is proved faulty and should be renewed. If the flap still does not close and is free to move on its hinges, renew the air control diaphragm.

13 Switch off the engine, reconnect the vacuum hoses and refit the filter and air cleaner cover.

5 Fuel filter – renewal

Note: *For the following operations it is essential that the car is positioned in an open, well ventilated area.*

Front filter (North American models)
1 Disconnect the battery negative terminal and remove the air cleaner as described in Section 3.
2 Using suitable clamps, pinch the fuel lines to minimise spillage, then disconnect the fuel lines at the filter.
3 Remove the filter cover from the old filter and install it on the new filter.
4 Refit the fuel lines, remove the clamps and refit the air cleaner.
5 Reconnect the battery.

Rear filter (UK and North American models)
6 Disconnect the battery negative terminal.
7 Jack up the rear of the car and support it on stands.
8 Remove the fuel filter cover, then push in the tab on the filter to release the holder. Remove the filter from its bracket.
9 Using suitable clamps, pinch the fuel lines to minimise spillage, then disconnect the fuel lines at the filter.
10 Fit the new filter using the reverse sequence to removal.

6 Fuel pump – testing, removal and refitting

Note: *For the following tests it is essential that the car is positioned in an open, well ventilated area*

1 Disconnect the fuel supply hose from the carburettor and insert its open end in a suitable container.
2 Disconnect the HT lead from the ignition coil and then have an assistant turn the ignition key to actuate the starter motor.
3 Fuel should be ejected in regular well defined spurts from the fuel hose.
4 If this is not the case then the fuel pump must be renewed, as the pump is of sealed type and cannot be repaired or even cleaned.
5 To remove the pump, disconnect the battery negative terminal.
6 Disconnect the fuel lines from the pump and plug the ends to prevent loss of fuel (photo).
7 Unscrew the bolt which secures the coolant hose support bracket and fuel pump cover and remove the cover/drain tube complete.
8 Unscrew the pump fixing nuts and remove the pump, insulator block and gaskets.
9 Clean the old gasket from the flanges, locate a new gasket on each side of the insulator block and refit the pump.
10 Tighten the fixing nuts to the specified torque.
11 Fit the pump cover/support bracket and locate the drain hose in its clip.
12 Reconnect the fuel lines and the battery.

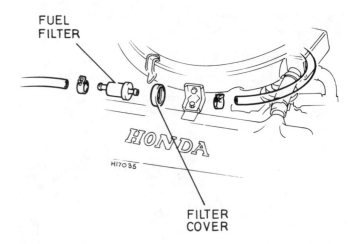

Fig. 3.2 Front fuel filter components – North American models (Sec 5)

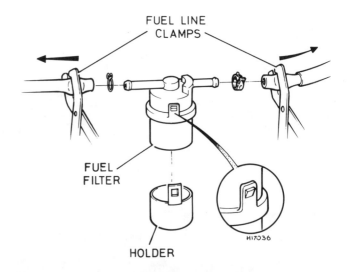

Fig. 3.3 Rear fuel filter renewal (Sec 5)

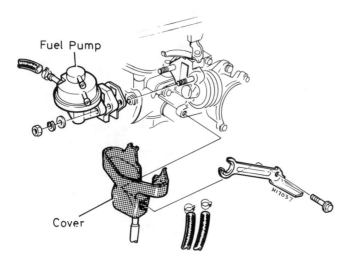

Fig. 3.4 Fuel pump removal and refitting details (Sec 6)

6.6 Fuel line attachments at fuel pump

7 Fuel tank – removal and refitting

Note: *For the following operations it is essential that the car is positioned in an open, well ventilated area.*

1 Disconnect the battery negative terminal.
2 Unscrew the tank drain plug and drain the fuel into a container which can be sealed.
3 Raise the rear of the car, support it securely on stands and remove the rear roadwheels.
4 Remove the fuel filter cover and release the fuel filler hose access panel.
5 Disconnect the filler and vent hoses from the neck of the fuel filler.
6 Disconnect the electrical leads from the fuel gauge sender unit.
7 Support the tank on a jack with a block of wood as an insulator. Slacken the mounting strap nuts and move the straps aside.
8 Lower the tank slowly until the hoses can be disconnected from the two way valve and fuel cut-off valve.
9 Lower the tank fully and remove it from under the car.
10 If the tank is leaking or damaged, have it repaired by specialists. Never attempt to weld or solder a fuel tank. Residual fuel vapour cannot be satisfactorily removed unless the tank is steamed or boiled out for several hours.
11 If the reason for tank removal was to remove sediment or water, remove the gauge sender unit as described in Section 8, the two way valve by undoing the screws, and the fuel cut-off valve by turning it through 90°.
12 Pour in some paraffin and shake the tank vigorously, then drain. Repeat as necessary, giving a final rinse with clean fuel.
13 Refitting of the tank components and tank is the reverse sequence to removal.

8 Fuel gauge sender unit – removal, testing and refitting

1 Remove the fuel tank as described in Section 7.
2 Unscrew the sender unit retaining ring using a suitable tool to engage with the ring lugs.
3 Carefully withdraw the sender unit taking care not to bend the float arm. Discard the sealing ring.
4 To test the sender unit use an ohmmeter connected across the two wire terminals and measure the resistance as follows:

Float in fully lowered (empty) position 105 to 110 ohms
Float in half full position 25.5 to 39.5 ohms
Float fully up (full) position 2.0 to 5.0 ohms

5 If the readings are not as indicated, renew the sender unit.
6 Refitting is the reverse sequence to removal, but use a new sealing ring.

9 Accelerator cable – adjustment and renewal

1 When correctly adjusted, the accelerator cable should have a slight slackness at the carburettor. Cable deflection should be between 4.0 and 10.0 mm (0.16 to 0.40 in).
2 To adjust the cable, remove the air cleaner (Section 3), and adjust

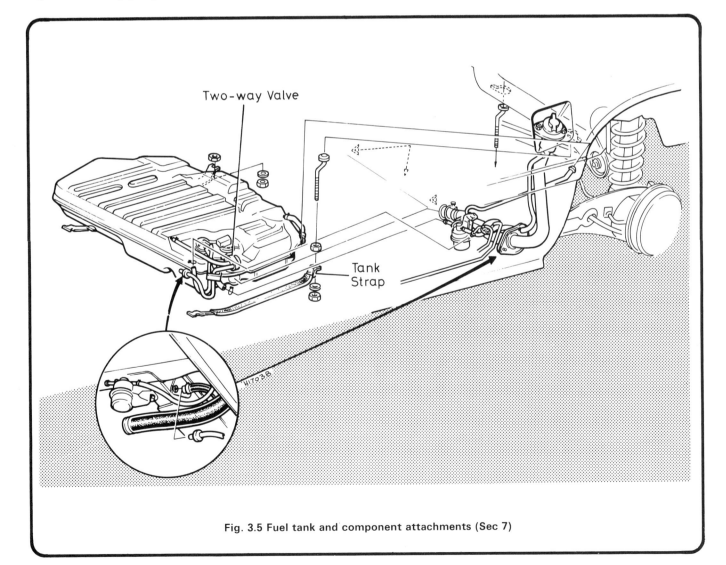

Two-way Valve

Tank Strap

Fig. 3.5 Fuel tank and component attachments (Sec 7)

9.2 Accelerator cable adjustment locknuts (arrowed)

the position of the two locknuts at the cable support bracket to give the desired cable deflection (photo).
3   With the aid of an assistant, check that the throttle opens and closes fully with the accelerator pedal depressed and released.
4   To renew the cable, release the cable bracket locknuts, slip the cable end fitting from the carburettor throttle quadrant and release the cable from the support bracket.
5   Working inside the car, disconnect the cable from the accelerator pedal by slipping the cable end fitting from the hole in the pedal arm.
6   Withdraw the cable assembly through the bulkhead by turning the grommet through 90°.
7   On automatic transmission models the accelerator cable is combined with the throttle control (kickdown) cable. Release this cable from the transmission control lever by slackening the two nuts and slipping out the end fitting.
8   Remove the cable assembly from the car.
9   Refitting is the reverse sequence to removal, but adjust the cable as previously described. On automatic transmission models, adjust the throttle control (kickdown) cable as described in Chapter 7.

10 Choke cable (UK models) – adjustment and renewal

1   Remove the air cleaner as described in Section 3.
2   With the choke control knob on the facia pushed fully in, check that the choke valve plate in the carburettor is fully open and that there is approximately 5.0 mm (0.20 in) deflection under finger pressure, of the cable.
3   If adjustment is necessary, alter the position of the cable locknuts at the support bracket (photo) until the adjustment is correct.
4   After adjustment check that with the choke knob pulled out, the choke valve plate is fully closed.
5   To remove the cable, unscrew the locknuts at the carburettor and release the cable end fitting from the linkage lever (photo).
6   Working inside the car, extract the choke knob retaining screw and pull off the knob.
7   Unscrew the bezel nut and release the cable from the facia panel.
8   Lower the cable slightly until the leads can be disconnected from the choke warning lamp switch.
9   Withdraw the choke cable through the bulkhead grommet.
10 Fitting the new cable is a reversal of removal. Adjust as previously described.

11 Carburettor – idle speed and mixture adjustment (UK models)

1   Before carrying out any adjustments ensure that the air cleaner filter element is clean (Section 3), that all ignition system adjustments are correct (Chapter 4) and that the valve clearances are properly set (Chapter 1).
2   If the tachometer is not fitted, connect a reliable instrument in accordance with the manufacturer's instructions.
3   Run the engine until normal operating temperature is obtained and the radiator cooling fan has cut in at least once.
4   Make sure that all electrical equipment is switched off.
5   Turn the throttle stop screw until the engine is idling at the specified speed (photo).
6   To adjust the idle mixture, hook out the tamperproof plug over the mixture screw and discard the plug. This may already have been done (Fig. 3.6).
7   Ideally the mixture should be adjusted using an exhaust gas analyser connected in accordance with the manufacturer's instructions. The mixture screw is then turned as necessary until the specified CO level in the exhaust gas is obtained.
8   If an exhaust gas analyser is not available, turn the mixture screw slowly in whichever direction is necessary to obtain the highest idle

10.3 Choke cable adjustment locknuts (arrowed)

10.5 Disconnecting choke cable from the linkage

11.5 Carburettor throttle stop screw (arrowed)

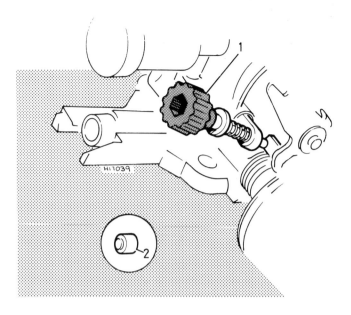

Fig. 3.6 Carburettor idle speed and mixture adjustment
points – UK models (Sec 11)

1 *Throttle stop screw*   2 *Mixture adjusting hole plug*

11.8 Carburettor mixture screw (arrowed)

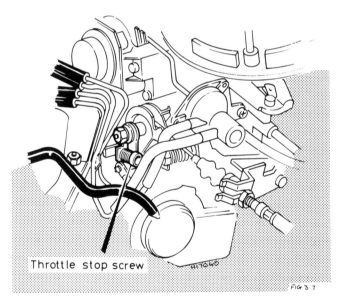

Fig. 3.7 Carburettor idle speed adjustment point – North
American models (Sec 11)

speed consistent with smooth even running (photo). Now turn the
screw in (clockwise) until the speed drops by 50 rpm.
9 Readjust the idle speed if necessary to the specified setting.
10 On completion switch off the engine and disconnect the
instruments.

North American models
11 Carry out the operations described in paragraphs 1 to 4.
12 On cars with power-assisted steering ensure that the steering is in
the straight ahead position, otherwise the idle boost solenoid valve will
be actuated.
13 Turn the throttle stop screw (Fig. 3.7) as necessary until the engine
is idling at the specified speed.
14 Except for automatic transmission models without air conditioning
or power steering, the idle controller boosted speed should be checked
as follows.
15 Switch on the headlights and set the heater blower to position III
(except 1500 models with automatic transmission and power
steering).
16 On 1500 models with automatic transmission and power steering,
turn the steering on full left- or right-hand lock.
17 Check that the idle controller compensates for the increased load

and maintains the engine at idling speed. If necessary adjust by means
of the idle control screw (Fig. 3.8).
18 On cars with air conditioning, turn the air conditioning on and
check that the engine speed increases by approximately 50 rpm over
the specified idle speed.
19 If adjustment is necessary, turn the adjusting screw on the idle
boost diaphragm as required (Fig. 3.9).
20 On completion switch off the accessories and engine, then
disconnect the instruments.
21 On North American models adjustment of the idle mixture can only
be carried out using a propane enrichment kit. Due to this requirement
and the risk of violating current emission control regulations, if the
manufacturer's procedure is not adhered to, mixture adjustment should
be undertaken by a suitably equipped dealer.

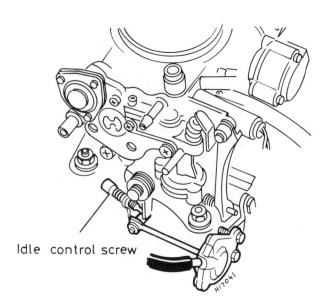

Fig. 3.8 Idle control screw for idle controller boosted speed – North American models (Sec 11)

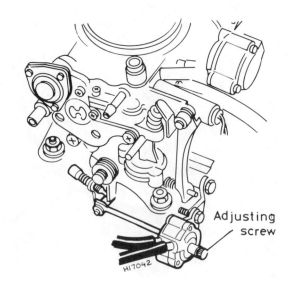

Fig. 3.9 Idle boost diaphragm adjusting screw – North American models with air conditioning (Sec 11)

12 Carburettor (UK models) – setting and adjustment of components

Choke relief valve

1 Under normal conditions the hook of the tension spring should be engaged in the rear notch as shown in Fig. 3.10.

2 In cold weather if difficult starting or hesitant cold running is experienced, the spring may be moved to the forward notch. Return it to its original position when milder conditions resume.

Fast idle speed

3 With the choke cable correctly adjusted, the notch on the choke linkage arm should be aligned with the reference boss on the carburettor body (photo) when the choke knob is pulled out to its first detent position (Fig. 3.11).

4 In this position the engine should run at a fast idle speed of between 1500 and 2500 rpm.

5 If the speed is not as specified, squeeze the slot in the fast idle adjusting link slightly using pliers to decrease the speed, or widen the slot using a screwdriver to increase the speed (Fig. 3.12).

12.3 Notch on choke linkage arm aligned with reference boss

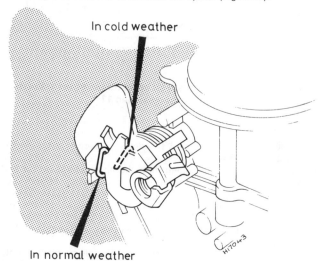

Fig. 3.10 Choke relief valve tension spring positions – UK models (Sec 12)

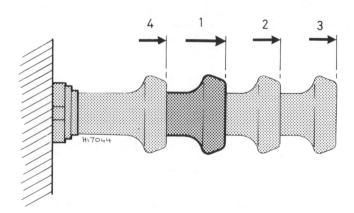

Fig. 3.11 Choke knob detent positions – UK models (Sec 12)

1   First detent position   3   Full choke
2   Second detent position   4   Choke return position

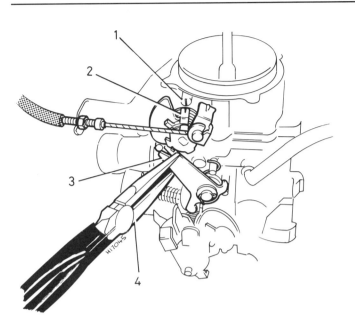

Fig. 3.12 Fast idle speed adjustment – UK models (Sec 12)

1	Reference boss	3	Fast idle adjusting link
2	Choke linkage arm	4	Long nose pliers

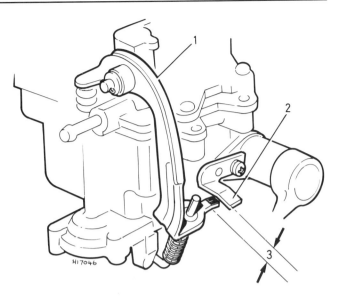

Fig. 3.13 Accelerator pump stroke adjustment – UK models (Sec 12)

1	Accelerator pump lever	3	Accelerator pump travel
2	Tang (bend to adjust stroke)		

12.7 Accelerator pump stroke adjustment tang (arrowed)

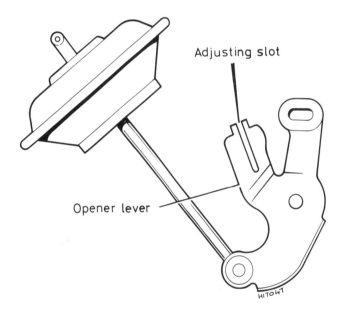

Fig. 3.14 Throttle damper adjustment point – UK models (Sec 12)

Accelerator pump stroke

6   Measure the accelerator pump lever travel between the stop on the pump lever and the tang on the carburettor body (Fig. 3.13). This is the accelerator pump stroke.

7   If the dimension is not as given in the Specifications, bend the tang slightly as necessary (photo).

Throttle damper

8   Have the engine running at 3500 rpm, holding it at this level by means of the carburettor throttle lever.

9   Release the throttle lever suddenly. The damper arm should fully extend during a period of between one and four seconds.

10   If the period is not as specified, small adjustments may be made to the fork slot on the opener lever (Fig. 3.14).

11   Failure to correct matters may be due to a leaking diaphragm hose or a faulty diaphragm unit.

Fuel cut-off solenoid valve

12   Place absorbent rags around the solenoid valve to collect any spilled fuel, then undo the screws and withdraw the solenoid.

13   Wipe up any spilled fuel, then discard the rags safely. Ensure adequate ventilation for the following operation.

14   Move the valve as far away from the carburettor as possible and earth the valve body.

15   Hold it in this position while an assistant switches on the ignition. The valve plunger should retract, then move out when the ignition is turned off. Take care during this test as there is a risk of sparks.

16   If the solenoid valve does not operate as described, check that there is voltage present at the valve and if so the valve is faulty and must be renewed.

17   Refit the valve using the reverse sequence to removal.

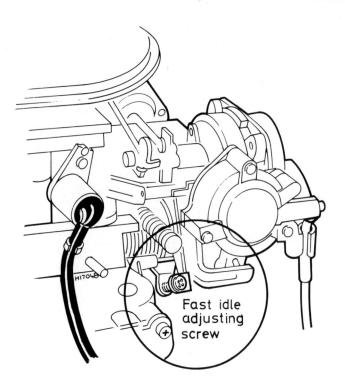

Fig. 3.15 Fast idle speed adjustment – North American models (Sec 13)

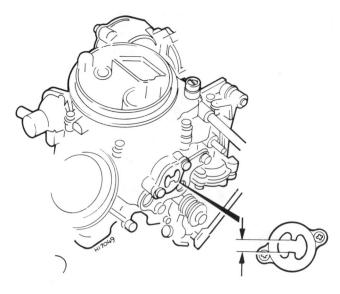

Fig. 3.16 Float level viewing window (level marks arrowed) – North American models (Sec 13)

13 Carburettor (North American models) – setting and adjustment of components

1   The carburettor fitted to North American models is equipped with an automatic choke, working in conjunction with a vacuum controlled choke opener system and fast idle unloader. Setting and adjustment of these components and their linkages is carried out in production and does not normally require attention in service. Should a fault develop, or adjustment become necessary due to component renewal, the work should be left to a dealer or service station, as a vacuum pump, compressed air, valves, and special gauges are required to carry out the work successfully. The contents of this Section are therefore limited to adjustments which can be carried out without the use of such equipment.

Fast idle speed
2   Connect a tachometer to the engine in accordance with the manufacturer's instructions, then start the engine and allow it to reach normal operating temperature.
3   Switch off the engine and disconnect the inner vacuum hose at the fast idle unloader.
4   Remove the air cleaner, then open and close the throttle fully while holding the choke valve closed.
5   Restart the engine and check that the fast idle speed is as given in the Specifications. If necessary turn the fast idle adjusting screw (Fig. 3.15) to obtain the specified speed.
6   Switch off, reconnect the hoses, refit the air cleaner and disconnect the tachometer.

Fuel cut-off solenoid valve
7   Refer to Section 12, paragraphs 12 to 16 inclusive.

Float level
8   Position the car on level ground, then start the engine and allow it to reach normal operating temperature.
9   Switch off and remove the air cleaner.
10 Start the engine again and quickly open the throttle to between idle and 3000 rpm and allow it to shut. Repeat this several times.

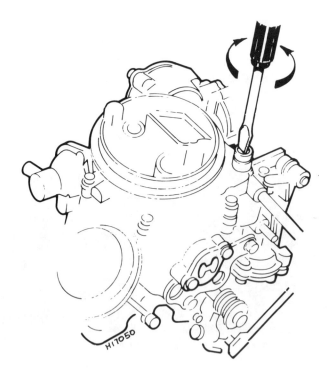

Fig. 3.17 Float level adjusting screw – North American models (Sec 13)

11 Observe the fuel level through the viewing window and check that the level is centred in the window (Fig. 3.16).
12 If necessary adjust by turning the adjusting screw (Fig. 3.17). Do not turn the screw more than one-eighth of a turn every fifteen seconds.
13 Switch off and refit the air cleaner after adjustment.

14 Carburettor – removal and refitting

1   Disconnect the battery negative terminal.
2   Remove the air cleaner as described in Section 3.

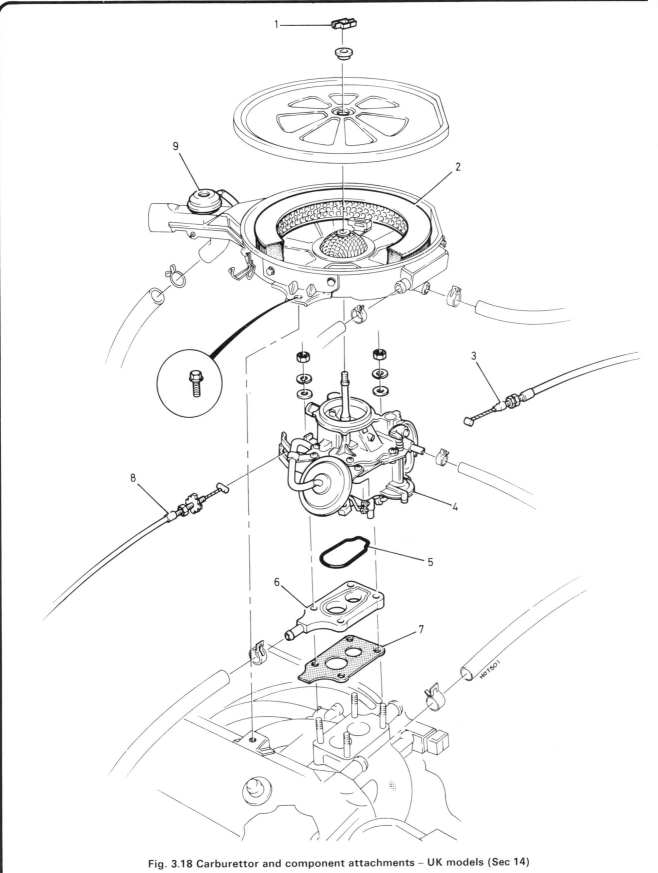

Fig. 3.18 Carburettor and component attachments – UK models (Sec 14)

1	Wing nut	3	Choke cable	5	O-ring	8	Accelerator cable
2	Air cleaner element	4	Carburettor	6	Insulator	9	Intake air control diaphragm
				7	Gasket		

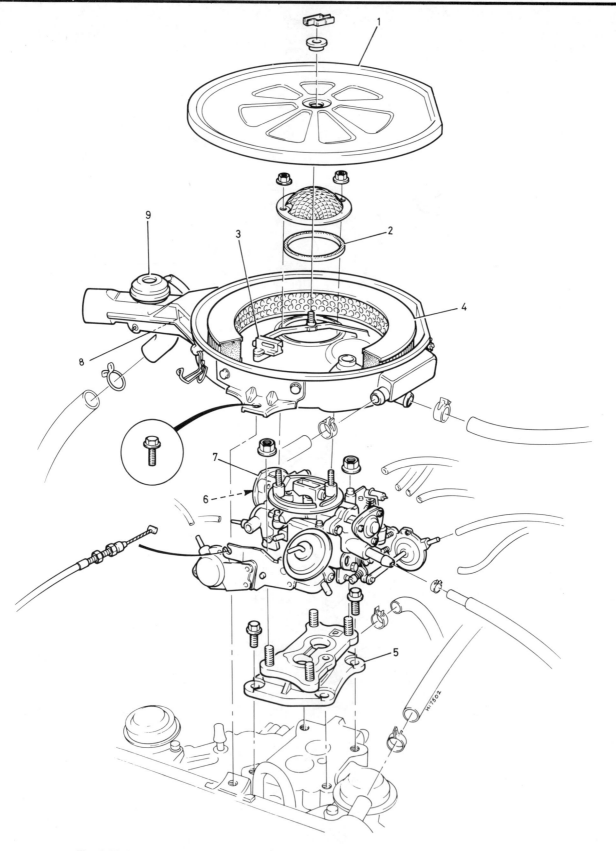

Fig. 3.19 Carburettor and component attachments – North American models (Sec 14)

1 Air cleaner cover	3 Air bleed valve	5 Insulator	7 Automatic choke
2 Air cleaner insulator	4 Air cleaner element	6 Fast idle unloader	8 Air temperature sensor
			9 Intake air control diaphragm

3   Disconnect the accelerator cable and, where fitted, the choke cable as described in Sections 9 and 10 of this Chapter.
4   Disconnect the electrical lead from the fuel cut-off solenoid valve and, where fitted, the automatic choke.
5   Disconnect the fuel supply hose (photo).
6   Make a note of all vacuum hose connections and disconnect them.
7   Undo the four nuts or four bolts and withdraw the carburettor from the inlet manifold.
8   Refitting is the reverse sequence to removal, but use a new gasket where necessary and adjust the cables as described in Sections 9 and 10.

15 Carburettor – overhaul

UK models

1   It is usually sufficient to overhaul a carburettor by removing the top cover, mopping out the fuel from the float chamber and extracting and cleaning the jets.
2   Obtain a gasket and seal set for use during reassembly.
3   If a carburettor has been in use for a long time and is obviously well worn, with slackness in the throttle valve spindle bores, it will probably be more economical to purchase a new or rebuilt unit.

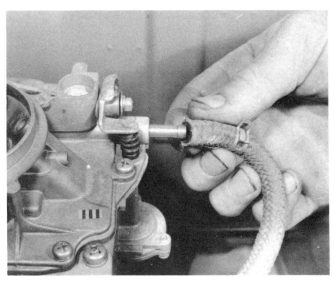

14.5 Disconnecting carburettor fuel supply hose

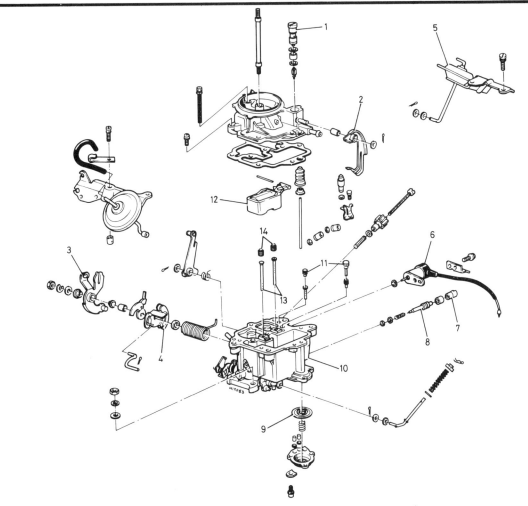

Fig. 3.20 Exploded view of the carburettor – UK models (Sec 15)

1 Float adjusting screw	5 Throttle opener	9 Accelerator pump diaphragm	12 Float
2 Accelerator pump lever	6 Fuel cut-off solenoid valve	10 Body	13 Emulsion tubes
3 Link lever	7 Limiter cap	11 Slow air jets	14 Air jets
4 Throttle lever	8 Adjusting screw		

90

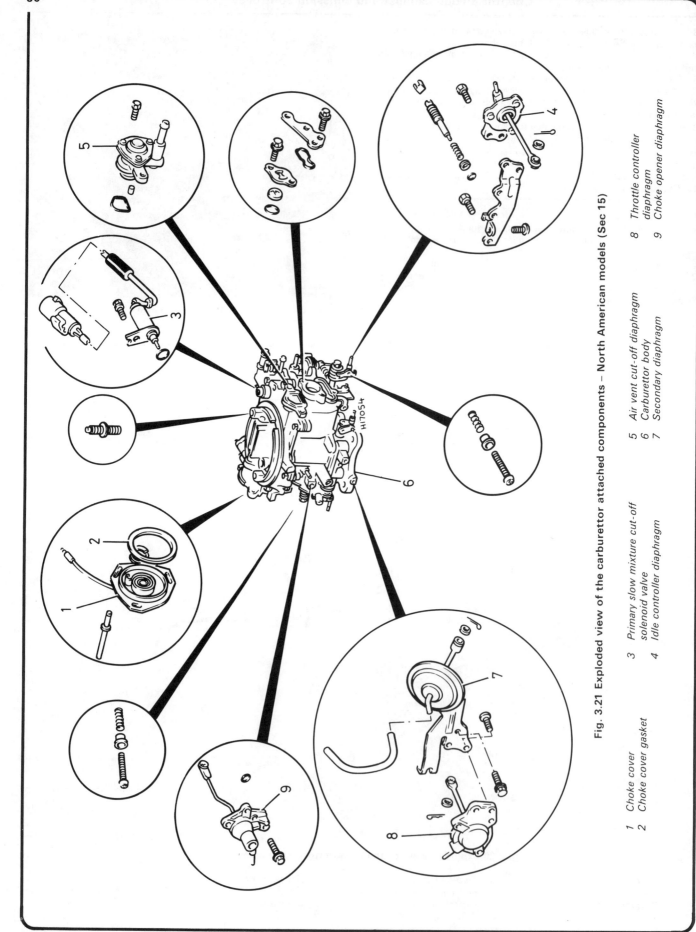

Fig. 3.21 Exploded view of the carburettor attached components – North American models (Sec 15)

1 Choke cover
2 Choke cover gasket
3 Primary slow mixture cut-off solenoid valve
4 Idle controller diaphragm
5 Air vent cut-off diaphragm
6 Carburettor body
7 Secondary diaphragm
8 Throttle controller diaphragm
9 Choke opener diaphragm

4   However, for those wishing to completely dismantle the carburettor, proceed in the following way.

5   With the unit removed from the car, clean away external dirt using paraffin and a brush.

6   Disconnect the accelerator pump arm from the top cover.

7   Extract the screws and remove the top cover and the gasket.

8   Carefully tap out the float pivot pin and remove the float.

9   Unscrew the float adjusting screw and take off the O-ring. Remove the filter gauze and the fuel inlet needle valve.

10 Remove the primary slow, main and secondary main air jets and emulsion tubes.

11 Remove the slow fuel jet plug, turn the carburettor upside down to eject the slow fuel jet.

12 Remove the main jet retainer, the power valve and the primary and secondary main jets. Take off the O-rings.

13 Remove the accelerator pump diaphragm cover, the diaphragm, spring and O-rings.

14 Clean all jets, passages and orifices with air from a tyre pump. On no account probe them with wire or this will ruin their calibration.

15 This should be the limit of dismantling.

16 Before reassembling, obtain the appropriate repair kit which will contain all the necessary seals and gaskets.

17 Reassembly is a reversal of dismantling, but adjust the float in the following way.

18 Locate the fuel inlet needle valve, O-rings and filter gauze, and screw in the float adjusting screw a turn or two.

19 Fit the float and its pivot pin.

20 Hold the top cover vertically so that the float hangs downwards under its own weight.

21 Position the float so that it is 35.4 to 37.4 mm (1.39 to 1.47 in) away from the top cover gasket. The clearance from the float arm to the needle valve should now be 0 to 0.1 mm (0 to 0.04 in). If necessary turn the adjusting screw in the top cover to adjust (photo).

North American models

22 No provision is made for overhaul on these carburettors and replacement parts are not available separately. If the unit has seen lengthy service it is advisable to obtain an exchange unit.

23 It is however possible to remove and refit the attached components and to remove the top cover for access to the jets (Fig. 3.21). Take care however not to disturb any sealed adjusting screws, as these are set in production.

---

16 Inlet manifold – removal and refitting

UK models

1   Disconnect the battery negative terminal.

2   Drain the cooling system as described in Chapter 2.

3   Remove the air cleaner as described in Section 3.

4   Disconnect the accelerator and choke cables at the carburettor as described in Sections 9 and 10.

5   Disconnect the fuel feed hose at the carburettor and plug its end.

6   Disconnect the brake servo vacuum hose (photo).

7   Disconnect the fuel cut-off valve solenoid electrical lead (photo).

8   Disconnect the heater hoses at the manifold (photo).

9   Disconnect the vacuum hoses and crankcase breather hose.

10 Unbolt and remove the manifold support bracket.

11 Undo the retaining nuts and remove the manifold complete with carburettor (photos). Remove the gasket.

12 Refitting is the reverse sequence to removal bearing in mind the following points:

(a) Use a new gasket and tighten all nuts and bolts to the specified torque

(b) Refit and adjust the accelerator and choke cables as described in Sections 9 and 10

(c) Refill the cooling system as described in Chapter 2

North American models

13 Disconnect the battery negative terminal.

14 Drain the cooling system as described in Chapter 2.

15.21 Float level adjusting screw (arrowed)

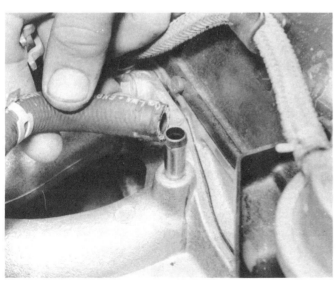

16.6 Disconnecting brake servo vacuum hose

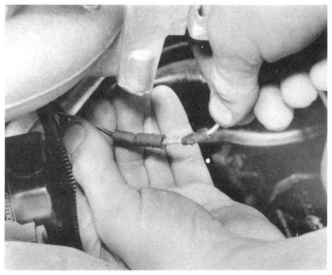

16.7 Disconnecting fuel cut-off solenoid wiring

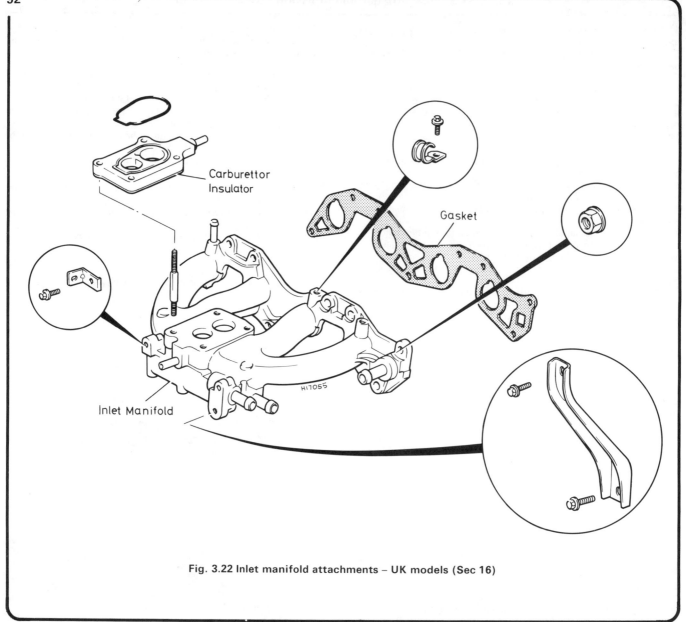

Carburettor Insulator

Gasket

Inlet Manifold

HI7055

Fig. 3.22 Inlet manifold attachments – UK models (Sec 16)

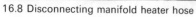

16.8 Disconnecting manifold heater hose

16.11A Undo the manifold retaining nuts ...

16.11B ... and remove the manifold with carburettor

15 Remove the air cleaner as described in Section 3.

16 Disconnect the accelerator cable as described in Section 9.

17 Disconnect the fuel feed hose at the carburettor and plug its end.

18 Disconnect the brake servo vacuum hose.

19 Disconnect the automatic choke and fuel cut-off solenoid electrical leads.

20 Disconnect the heater hoses at the manifold.

21 Remove the air valve, EGR valve, air suction valve and air suction pipe assembly with reference to Fig. 3.23.

22 Make a note of the vacuum hose locations and disconnect those affecting manifold removal.

23 Disconnect the crankcase breather hose.

24 Unbolt and remove the manifold support bracket.

25 Undo the retaining nuts and remove the manifold complete with carburettor.

26 Refitting is the reverse sequence to removal bearing in mind the following points:

(a) Use new gaskets on the manifold and components and tighten all nuts and bolts to the specified torque

(b) Refit the accelerator cable as described in Section 9

(c) Refill the cooling system as described in Chapter 2

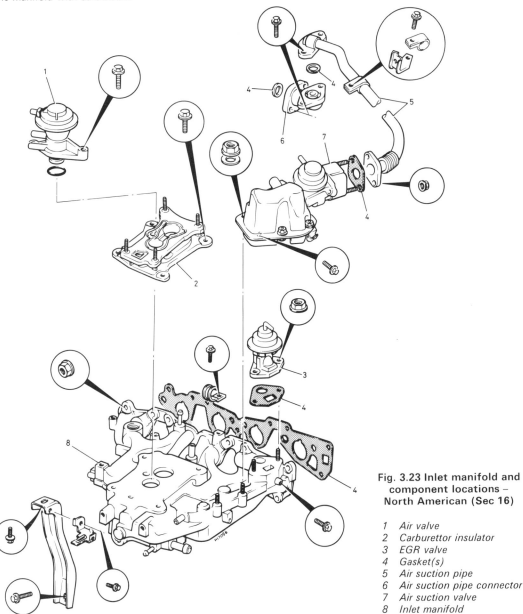

Fig. 3.23 Inlet manifold and component locations – North American (Sec 16)

1 Air valve
2 Carburettor insulator
3 EGR valve
4 Gasket(s)
5 Air suction pipe
6 Air suction pipe connector
7 Air suction valve
8 Inlet manifold

PART B FUEL-INJECTED ENGINES

17 Description and operation

1 The fuel system on fuel-injected engines consists of a fuel tank which is mounted forward of the rear suspension, an electrically-operated fuel pump, an air cleaner with disposable paper filter element and Honda PGM-F1 programmed fuel-injection system. A brief description of the fuel-injection components and their function is given in the following paragraphs.

Air intake system
2 The air intake system consists of the air cleaner, air intake pipe, throttle body, idle control system, fast idle mechanism and inlet manifold.
3 **Throttle body:** The throttle body is a twin barrel side draught unit with the primary throttle valve located in the upper part, and the secondary throttle valve located in the water heated lower part. A throttle angle sensor is attached to the primary throttle shaft to provide throttle angle information to the electronic control unit. A dashpot is used to progressively slow the throttle valve as it shuts.
4 **Idle control system:** Engine idling speed is controlled by the electronic control unit in conjunction with the idle control solenoid valve, fast idle control solenoid valve and the air conditioning idle boost solenoid valve. The valves open according to electrical or other loads, or when the engine is cold, to allow additional bypass air directly into the inlet manifold. This maintains a stabilised idle speed under normal conditions or a fast idle when the engine is cold. The air conditioning boost solenoid valve acts directly on the throttle valve to maintain the correct idle speed with the air conditioning running.
5 **Idle adjuster (bypass circuit):** This is an adjustable air passage designed to control the amount of air bypassing into the inlet manifold without changing the position of the throttle valve.
6 **Fast idle mechanism:** To allow increased engine speed for warm up conditions, an air bypass valve containing a wax element is used to control bypass air into the inlet manifold. When the engine is cold the valve is open, allowing the air to flow into the manifold. Engine coolant heats the wax which melts, and the valve closes progressively as the engine warms up.

Electronic control system
7 **Electronic control unit (ECU):** The control unit consists of an eight bit microcomputer with central processing unit, memory banks and input and output ports. The ECU contains basic data stored in its memory of fuel-injection opening duration and injected fuel quantity. This information can be amended according to information received from the various sensors. The ECU computes the information and provides injector discharge duration suitable for all conditions of engine temperature, speed and load. Various sub-routines within the ECU program cater for fuel enrichment for starting, fuel pump control and fuel overrun cut-off.
8 **Crank angle sensor (TDC/CYL sensors):** These are part of the ignition distributor and consist of two rotors attached to a common shaft and rotating in conjunction with the distributor shaft. The TDC rotor is used to determine TDC for each cylinder, and the CYL rotor is used to determine the position of No. 1 cylinder as a starting point for the injection sequence. Each rotor is equipped with a pick-up coil to determine rotor position.
9 **Manifold absolute pressure sensor (MAP sensor):** This sensor converts manifold pressure into an electrical voltage signal which is used by the ECU to determine engine load. Information from the MAP sensor and TDC/CYL sensors are used by the ECU to determine injector discharge duration initial values.
10 **Atmospheric pressure sensor (PA sensor):** This sensor performs in the same way as the MAP sensor and is used by the ECU to modify discharge duration according to changes in atmospheric pressure.
11 **Coolant temperature sensor (TW sensor):** This unit is a thermister used to monitor coolant temperature and signal the ECU to modify discharge duration accordingly.
12 **Intake air temperature sensor (TA sensor):** This unit is also a thermister located in the inlet manifold and used by the ECU in the same way as the TW sensor.
13 **Throttle angle sensor:** This sensor is a variable resistor attached to the throttle valve shaft. As the throttle valve moves, the resistance of

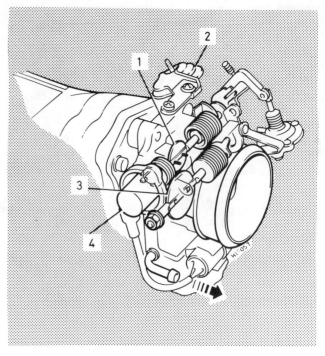

Fig. 3.24 Throttle body assembly (Sec 17)

1 Primary throttle valve	3 Secondary throttle valve
2 Dashpot diaphragm	4 Throttle angle sensor

Arrow indicates direction of coolant flow

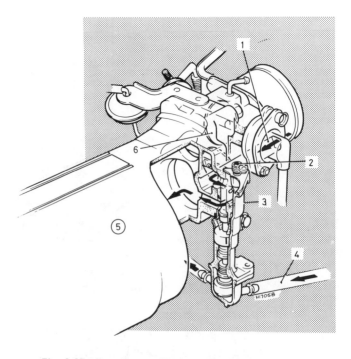

Fig. 3.25 Idle adjuster (bypass circuit) and fast idle mechanism (Sec 17)

1 Bypass	4 Coolant flow direction
2 Idle adjusting screw	5 Inlet manifold
3 Air bypass valve assembly	6 Primary throttle valve

the sensor varies, allowing the ECU to accurately determine throttle position.

14 **Oxygen sensor:** This device is fitted to the exhaust manifold and has its probe exposed to the hot gas flowing through. The unit probe is essentially a platinum electrode which can detect changes in the oxygen concentration of the exhaust gas and signal the ECU accordingly. This information is used by the ECU to further modify injector discharge duration.

15 **Idle mixture adjuster sensor (IMA sensor):** The main purpose of the IMA sensor is to maintain the correct air/fuel ratio when the engine is idling.

Fuel system

16 **Fuel pump:** The pump is a self-priming in-line direct drive unit, supplying fuel under pressure through an in-line filter to the injector fuel pipe and pressure regulator.

17 **Pressure regulator:** This is a mechanical device which controls fuel pressure to the injectors by means of manifold vacuum. The pressure regulator spring chamber is connected to the inlet manifold and maintains fuel pressure at 2.5 bar (36 lbf/in²) above manifold vacuum to ensure that the pressure difference across the injector nozzles remains constant. When the difference between fuel pressure and manifold vacuum exceeds 2.5 bar (36 lbf/in²), the diaphragm is

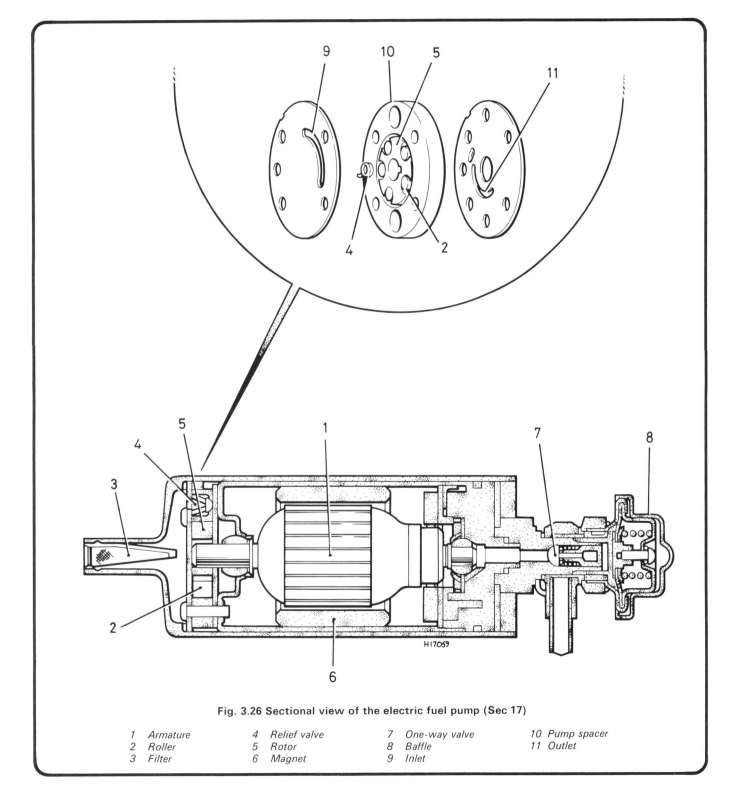

Fig. 3.26 Sectional view of the electric fuel pump (Sec 17)

1 Armature	4 Relief valve	7 One-way valve	10 Pump spacer
2 Roller	5 Rotor	8 Baffle	11 Outlet
3 Filter	6 Magnet	9 Inlet	

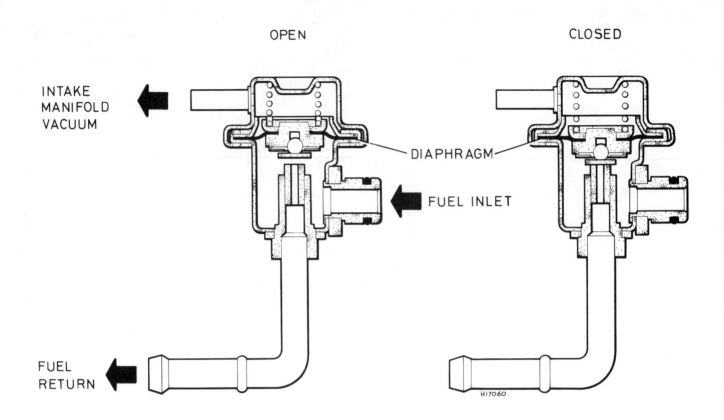

Fig. 3.27 Pressure regulator operating diagram (Sec 17)

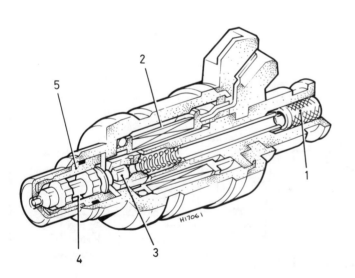

Fig. 3.28 Cutaway view of a fuel injector (Sec 17)

1	Filter	4	Plunger
2	Solenoid coil	5	Plunger housing
3	Core		

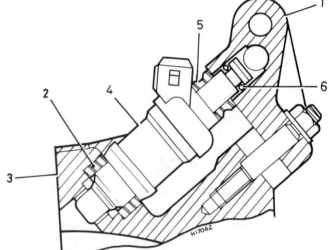

Fig. 3.29 Sectional view of the fuel injector location
(Sec 17)

1	Fuel pipe	4	Injector
2	Seal ring	5	Cushion ring
3	Manifold	6	O-ring

pushed up and excess fuel is passed back to the tank via the return line.
18 Injectors: The fuel injectors are of the solenoid-operated constant stroke pintle type, comprising a solenoid, plunger, needle valve and housing. When current is applied to the solenoid the valve lifts, fuel under pressure enters the injector housing and is injected into the inlet manifold. Because the valve lift and fuel pressure are constant,

injection quantity is determined by the duration that the valve remains open, which is controlled by the ECU.
19 Main relay: The main relay is a direct coupler type located at the rear of the fuse box and controlling the fuel pump and ECU supply voltages.

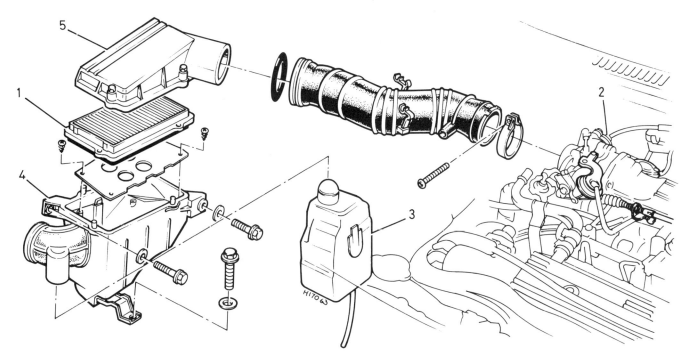

Fig. 3.30 Exploded view of the air cleaner components (Sec 19)

1 Air cleaner element	3 Resonator	5 Air cleaner cover
2 Throttle body	4 Air cleaner body	

18 Maintenance and inspection

1   At the intervals given in 'Routine Maintenance' at the beginning of this Manual, carry out the following service operations to the fuel system components.

2   With the car over a pit, raised on a vehicle lift, or securely supported on axle stands, carefully inspect the fuel pipes, hoses and unions for chafing, leaks and corrosion. Renew any pipes that are severely pitted with corrosion or in any way damaged. Renew any hoses that show signs of cracking or other deterioration.

3   Examine the fuel tanks for leaks, particularly around the fuel gauge sender unit, and for signs of corrosion or damage.

4   From within the engine compartment, check the security of all fuel hose attachments and inspect the fuel hoses and vacuum hoses for kinks, chafing or deterioration.

5   Renew the air cleaner element and clean the air cleaner body and cover.

6   Check the operation of the accelerator linkage and lubricate the linkage, cable and pedal pivot with a few drops of engine oil.

7   Check the fuel-injection system idle speed and mixture settings, as described in Section 27, where necessary.

8   Renew the fuel filter as described in Section 21.

9   Inspect the condition of all emission control components and hoses. Testing and component renewal should be carried out by a suitably equipped dealer (see Part C of this Chapter).

10 Check the condition and security of the exhaust system as described in Section 34.

19 Air cleaner – servicing, removal and refitting

1   Disconnect the air intake hose, then undo the screws and lift off the air cleaner cover.

2   Remove the filter element and wipe clean the casing and cover.

3   Fit a new element and refit the cover.

4   To remove the complete air cleaner, first remove the battery as described in Chapter 12.

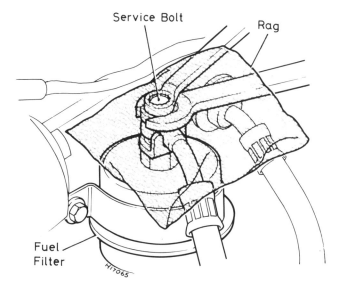

Fig. 3.31 Depressurising the fuel system (Sec 20)

5   Undo the bolts securing the air cleaner body to the wing valance, disconnect the intake and resonator, then remove the unit from the car.

6   Refitting is the reverse sequence to removal.

20 Fuel system – depressurising

1   The fuel system must be depressurised as follows before any of the pipes or hoses between the fuel pump and the pressure regulator are disconnected.

2   With the car positioned in a well ventilated area first disconnect the battery negative terminal.

3   Using an open ended spanner hold the fuel line banjo union bolt on top of the fuel filter, and using a second spanner slowly unscrew the service bolt one turn. Place an absorbent rag over the union, as this is done, to collect ejected fuel (Fig. 3.31).

4   When the pressure is relieved, remove the rag, unscrew the service bolt completely and check the condition of the sealing washer. Renew the washer if necessary, then screw in and tighten the service bolt.

5   Reconnect the battery.

21 Fuel filter – renewal

Note: *For the following operations it is essential that the car is positioned in an open, well ventilated area.*

1   Disconnect the battery negative terminal.

2   Refer to Section 20 and depressurise the fuel system.

3   Place suitable quantities of rag on and under the filter to collect spilled fuel.

4   Undo the fuel line upper and lower banjo unions and recover the sealing washers.

5   Undo the clamp mounting bolt and remove the filter.

6   Refitting is the reverse sequence to removal, but use new sealing washers at the banjo unions.

22 Fuel pump – testing

Note: *For the following test it is essential that the car is positioned in an open, well ventilated area.*

1   With the ignition turned off, disconnect the wiring plug from the main relay at the rear of the fuse box.

2   Using a bridging wire, connect the black/yellow and the yellow wires in the plug together (Fig. 3.33).

3   Refer to Section 20 and depressurise the fuel system.

4   Disconnect the fuel return hose at the pressure regulator. Connect a suitable hose to the return hose outlet on the pressure regulator and place the other end of the hose in a graduated beaker.

5   Switch on the ignition and allow fuel to flow for exactly ten seconds, then switch off. The amount of fuel collected in the beaker should be in excess of 230 cc (7.8 oz).

6   If the flow is less than this amount check for a clogged fuel filter or fuel line or possible faulty pressure regulator. If these items are satisfactory renew the pump.

7   Reconnect the fuel return hose and the main relay connector.

8   If during the above test no fuel was delivered, or if it is suspected that the pump is not operating, jack up the rear of the car and support it on stands.

9   Switch the ignition on and check whether the pump can be heard operating.

10   If not, switch off the ignition, and remove the left-hand rear roadwheel and the fuel pump cover.

11   Disconnect the yellow and black wires and connect a voltmeter positive probe to the yellow wire and negative probe to the black wire.

12   Switch on the ignition and check that battery voltage is present at the pump. If it is, the pump is faulty. If no voltage is recorded, check the main relay and the wiring harness.

13   Reconnect the wires with the ignition switched off, refit the fuel pump cover and roadwheel and lower the car.

23 Fuel pump – removal and refitting

Note: *For the following operation it is essential that the car is positioned in an open, well ventilated area*

1   Disconnect the battery negative terminal.

2   Jack up the rear of the car and support it on stands.

3   Remove the left-hand rear roadwheel and the fuel pump cover.

4   Undo the three bolts and withdraw the pump and its mounting.

5   Disconnect the electrical wiring and the fuel hoses.

6   Remove the clamp and withdraw the pump.

7   If necessary remove the fuel line and silencer from the front of the

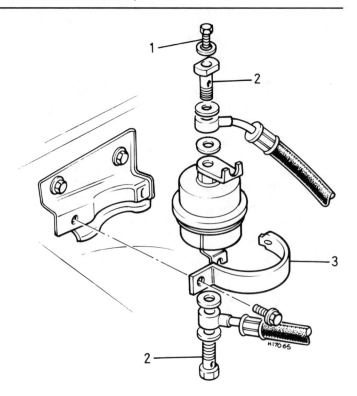

Fig. 3.32 Fuel filter renewal details (Sec 21)

1   Service bolt   *3   Clamp*
2   Banjo bolt

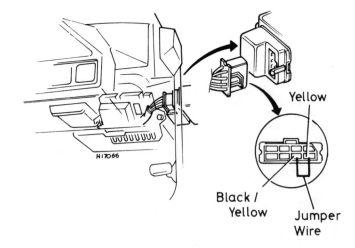

Fig. 3.33 Fuel pump testing (Sec 22)

pump. The remainder of the pump is sealed and no attempt should be made to dismantle it.

8   Refitting is the reverse sequence to removal. Before refitting the fuel pump cover, reconnect the battery, switch on the ignition and check for leaks at the fuel lines.

24 Fuel tank – removal and refitting

1   Refer to Part A, Section 7.

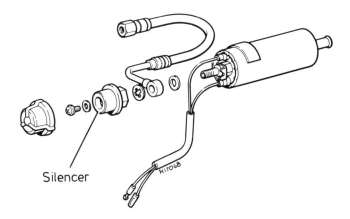

Fig. 3.35 Fuel pump silencer and fuel line connection
(Sec 23)

Fig. 3.34 Fuel pump attachments and mountings (Sec 23)

25 Fuel gauge sender unit – removal, testing and refitting

1   Refer to Part A, Section 8.

26 Accelerator cable – adjustment and renewal

1   The procedure is the same as for carburettor engines described in
Part A, Section 9, except that the cable end is attached to the throttle
valve linkage on the throttle body and the free play should be 10.0 to
12.0 mm (0.39 to 0.47 in).

27 Idle speed and mixture – adjustment

UK models
1   Before carrying out any adjustments ensure that the air cleaner filter
element is clean (Section 3), that all ignition system adjustments are
correct (Chapter 4) and that the valve clearances are properly set
(Chapter 1).
2   If a tachometer is not fitted, connect a reliable instrument in
accordance with the manufacturer's instructions.
3   Run the engine until normal operating temperature is obtained and
the radiator cooling fan has cut in at least once.
4   Make sure that all electrical equipment is switched off.
5   Check that the engine is idling at the specified speed. If necessary
adjust by turning the idle adjusting screw located on the air bypass
valve assembly on the side of the throttle body (Fig. 3.36).
6   To adjust the idle mixture, connect an exhaust gas analyser in
accordance with the manufacturer's instructions, but do not insert the
tail pipe probe at this stage.
7   With the engine at normal operating temperature, run it for a further
two or three minutes at 3000 rpm, then let it idle.
8   Insert the tail pipe probe, then check that the CO level is as given in
the Specifications.
9   If adjustment is necessary remove the rubber cap on the control box
and remove the hole plug on the IMA sensor (Fig. 3.37). Turn the
adjusting screw as necessary to obtain the specified CO reading.

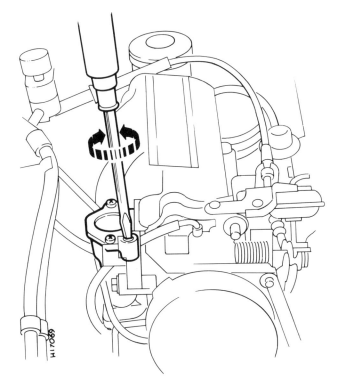

Fig. 3.36 Idle speed adjustment (Sec 27)

10 On completion, switch off the engine, disconnect the instruments
and refit the cap and plug.

North American models
11 Carry out the operations described in paragraphs 1 to 4 inclusive.
12 Using a suitable clamp, pinch the No. 10 vacuum hose (Fig. 3.38)
to prevent the idle control system from operating.
13 Check that the engine is idling at the specified speed. If necessary
adjust by turning the idle adjusting screw located on the air bypass
valve assembly on the throttle body (Fig. 3.36).
14 On cars equipped with air conditioning, turn the air conditioning
on and remove the clamp from the vacuum hose.
15 Check that the engine speed is now in accordance with the idle
controller boosted speed setting given in the Specifications.

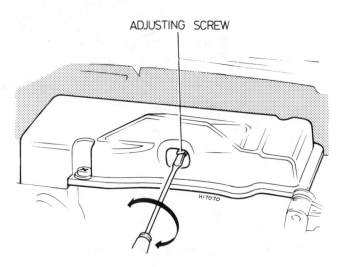

Fig. 3.37 Idle mixture adjustment point at the control box –
UK models (Sec 27)

16 If necessary turn the adjusting screw B (Fig. 3.39) on the idle boost diaphragm linkage to give the specified speed.

17 On North American models the idle mixture is controlled by the oxygen sensor and is not adjustable.

18 On completion switch off the engine and disconnect the instruments.

Fig. 3.38 Fuel-injection control box showing component locations and No. 10 vacuum hose outlet – North American models (Sec 27)

A   Cold advance solenoid valve
B   Purge cut-off solenoid valve
C   Idle control solenoid valve
D   Fast idle control solenoid valve
E   Air filter
F   Dashpot check valve
G   Air chamber
H   Air filter
J   Check valve
K   IMA sensor

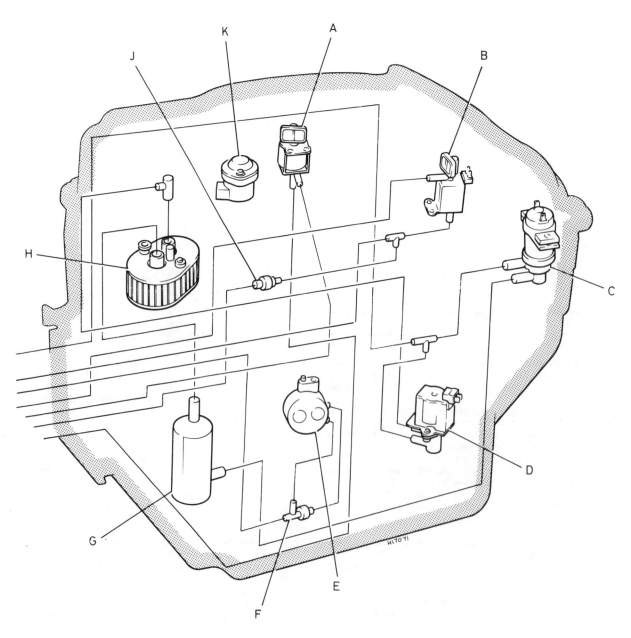

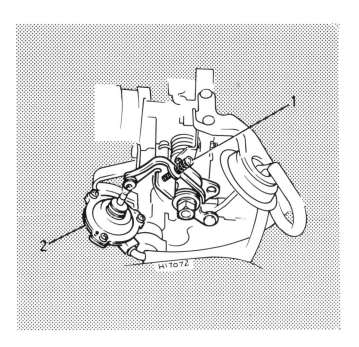

**Fig. 3.39 Idle controller boosted speed adjustment point –
North American models with air conditioning (Sec 27)**

1   Adjusting screw B   *2   Idle boost diaphragm*

28 Fuel-injection system components – testing (general)

1   Testing of the fuel-injection system components entails the use of Honda dedicated electronic test equipment in conjunction with a systematic test procedure. Apart from the basic checks and tests described in the relevant Sections of this Chapter all other testing should be carried out by a dealer suitably equipped to undertake the work.

29 Fuel-injection system components – removal and refitting

Throttle body
1   Disconnect the battery negative terminal.
2   Drain the cooling system as described in Chapter 2.
3   Remove the air cleaner as described in Section 19.
4   Disconnect the accelerator cable as described in Section 26.
5   Make a note of their locations, then disconnect the water hose, vacuum and electrical connections at the throttle body.
6   Unbolt and remove the steady bracket.
7   Undo the nuts and remove the throttle body from the manifold. Recover the gasket.
8   Refitting is the reverse sequence to removal, but use a new gasket and tighten the nuts to the specified torque.

Pressure regulator
9   Depressurise the fuel system as described in Section 20.
10 Disconnect the vacuum hose and fuel return line at the regulator.
11 Undo the bolts and remove the regulator. Recover the O-ring seal.
12 Refitting is the reverse sequence to removal, but use a new O-ring lubricated with engine oil. Tighten the bolts to the specified torque.

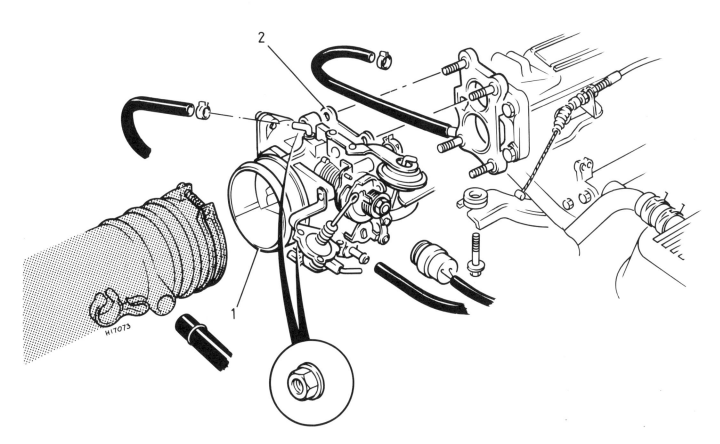

Fig. 3.40 Throttle body and component attachments (Sec 29)

1   Throttle body   *2   Gasket*

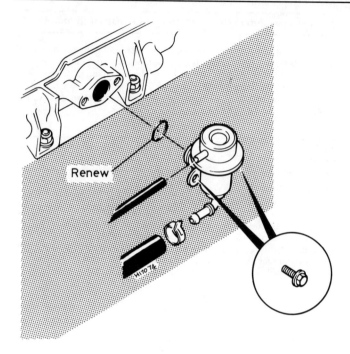

Fig. 3.41 Pressure regulator attachments (Sec 29)

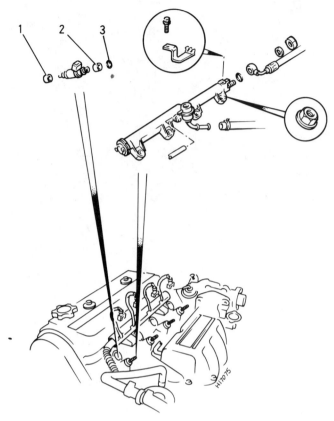

Fig. 3.42 Fuel injector and fuel pipe components (Sec 29)

1 *Seal ring*   3 *O-ring*
2 *Cushion ring*

Fuel injectors

13 If the operation of a fuel injector is suspect it can be tested in the following way.

14 Ensure that the ignition timing (Chapter 4), valve clearances (Chapter 1) and idle speed and mixture (Section 27) are all correctly adjusted.

15 Connect a tachometer in accordance with the manufacturer's instructions.

16 With the engine idling, disconnect then reconnect each injector wiring connector in turn and note the change in engine speed.

17 If the speed change is approximately the same each time, the injectors are satisfactory. If the engine speed remains the same when a particular injector is disconnected, check the voltage at the wiring plug. If this fluctuates between 0 and 2.0 volts, then the injector is faulty. If there is no voltage at the connector, check for a wiring fault.

18 To remove the injectors, disconnect the battery negative terminal, then depressurise the fuel system as described in Section 20.

19 Disconnect the injector wiring connectors.

20 Disconnect the fuel return hose and vacuum hose at the pressure regulator.

21 Undo the retaining nuts and lift off the injector fuel pipe.

22 Withdraw the injectors from the manifold and remove the O-ring, cushion ring and seal ring.

23 To refit, slide new cushion rings onto each injector.

24 Lubricate new O-rings with engine oil and place them on the injectors.

25 Fit the injectors into the fuel pipe.

26 Lubricate new seal rings with engine oil and insert them into the manifold.

27 Place the injectors and fuel pipe in position, then fit and tighten the retaining nuts to the specified torque.

28 Reconnect the fuel and vacuum hose to the pressure regulator and the injector wiring connectors.

29 Switch on the ignition after reconnecting the battery and check for fuel leaks.

TDC/CYL sensors

30 The sensors are located in a housing attached to the distributor body. Removal and refitting procedures are covered in Chapter 4.

TA and TW sensors

31 The TA and TW sensors are secured by two bolts to the inlet manifold and cylinder head respectively. Removal and refitting consists of disconnecting the wiring plug and unbolting the sensor from its location. With the TW sensor, partially drain the cooling system first and top up after refitting (Chapter 2).

Oxygen sensor

32 Disconnect the wiring connector and unscrew the sensor from the exhaust manifold.

33 Refit in the reverse sequence.

MAP sensor

34 Disconnect the vacuum hose and wiring plug and remove the sensor from its location on the bulkhead behind the engine.

35 Refit in the reverse sequence.

Idle control solenoid, fast idle control solenoid, IMA sensor, PA sensor

36 These sensors are all located in the control box and are rivetted to their respective brackets.

37 Renewal entails drilling out the rivets and securing with new rivets and is best undertaken by a dealer.

ECU

38 The electronic contro unit is located under the right-hand front seat.

39 To remove the unit disconnect the battery negative terminal, disconnect the wiring connector and remove the unit.

40 Refitting is the reverse sequence to removal.

30 Inlet manifold – removal and refitting

1 Remove the throttle body, pressure regulator and fuel injectors as described in Section 29.

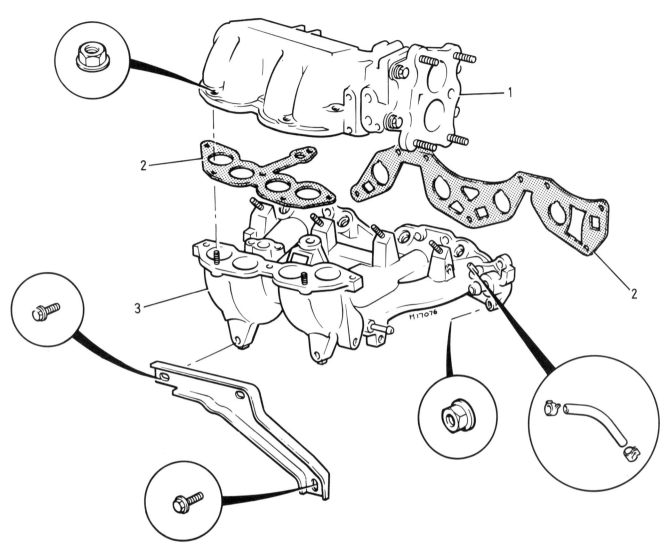

Fig. 3.43 Inlet manifold components (Sec 30)

1 Inlet manifold upper part   2 Gasket   3 Inlet manifold lower part

2   Disconnect the coolant hoses and brake servo vacuum hose at the manifold.
3   Remove the crankcase breather pipe bracket and disconnect the hose.
4   Unbolt and remove the steady bracket.
5   Undo the retaining nuts and withdraw the manifold from the cylinder head. Recover the gasket.
6   If required, the manifold upper and lower parts can be separated after undoing the nuts and retaining bolts.
7   Refitting is the reverse sequence to removal, but use new gaskets and tighten all nuts and bolts to the specified torque.

PART C EMISSION CONTROL SYSTEMS AND EXHAUST SYSTEM

31 Emission control systems – general

1   The emission control systems can be divided into three groups, crankcase ventilation, fuel evaporative emission control and exhaust emission control.
2   The crankcase ventilation system is described in Chapter 1 and the air intake control, which is part of the exhaust emission control system, is described in Part A of this Chapter. The crankcase ventilation system and air intake control are fitted to UK and North American models. In general, the remaining systems and components are fitted to North American models only.
3   The complexity of the systems and the need for special test equipment renders checking, servicing and repair beyond the scope of the home mechanic. Apart from a periodic inspection of the components and hose attachments, all other operations should be undertaken by a suitably equipped dealer or service station. The contents of the following Sections are therefore limited to descriptions of the systems and their components. Note that not all the components described will be found on each model.

32 Evaporative emission control system – description and operation

Carburettor engines
Fuel tank venting
1   A two-way valve is fitted between the fuel tank and charcoal canister to regulate the pressure or vacuum in the tank due to temperature and fuel level.

2   As pressure increases with temperature the valve opens to allow the vapour to escape to the charcoal canister.

3   As temperature decreases or fuel level falls the valve opens to the atmosphere to relieve the vacuum being created in the tank.

Air vent cut-off diaphragm

4   With the engine stopped, the main and auxiliary air vent passages in the carburettor are cut off by the valve attached to the air vent cut-off diaphragm. This allows fuel vapour to be diverted to the charcoal canister.

5   With the engine running, manifold vacuum supplied through a holding solenoid valve causes the diaphragm to open.

Thermo-valve

6   When engine coolant temperature exceeds the preset value of the thermo-valve, the valve closes allowing the purge control diaphragm valve on the charcoal canister to be opened by manifold vacuum. The depression in the carburettor venturi draws the fuel vapour from the charcoal canister, through the purge control diaphragm valve and into the carburettor intake air stream.

Fuel filler cap

7   The fuel filler cap incorporates a two-way valve to act as a safety valve for fuel tank venting in the event of an evaporative control system malfunction.

Carburettor fuel cut-off

8   When the engine is switched off, the slow primary fuel metering passages in the carburettor are shut off by the fuel cut-off solenoid valve, thus preventing fuel in the float chamber from entering the carburettor venturi.

Fuel-injected engines

Fuel tank venting

9   The system operates in the same way as for carburettor engine models with a two-way valve also fitted to the fuel filler cap as a safety device.

Purge cut-off solenoid valve

10   This valve opens under signals from the fuel system ECU and allows fuel vapour collected in the charcoal canister to be drawn through the purge control diaphragm valve to the inlet manifold.

33 Exhaust emission control system – description and operation

Carburettor engines

1   Exhaust emissions are controlled primarily by the efficiency of the CVCC engine cylinder head combustion chamber and by ten interrelated sub-systems, which are:

Intake air temperature control
Ignition timing controls
Dashpot system
Mixture control system
Air jet controller
Exhaust gas recirculation
Catalytic converter
Air injection system
Feedback control system
Auxiliary carburettor air supply system

CVCC engine

2   The CVCC designation is used to describe the cylinder head type which incorporates two combustion chambers for each cylinder. On each intake stroke a rich fuel/air mixture enters the pre-combustion chamber via a small inlet port and auxiliary valve. At the same time a weak mixture enters the main combustion chamber through the main inlet valves. Under compression the two mixtures partially merge forming a moderate mixture adjacent to the pre-combustion chamber opening in the main chamber. The spark plug ignites the rich mixture which in turn ignites the moderate and weak main charges. This arrangement provides improved control of the combustion process, more complete burning of the fuel air mixture and reduced noxious emissions.

Intake air temperature control

3   The system maintains uniform air temperature inside the air cleaner irrespective of outside temperature by mixing hot and cold intake air in the air cleaner intake spout.

Ignition timing controls

4   In addition to the normal distributor centrifugal and vacuum advance operation, an additional vacuum diaphragm operating in conjunction with a thermo-valve is used. This allows further control of distributor advance characteristics according to engine temperature.

Dashpot system

5   The throttle controller or throttle damper functions as a dashpot to prevent rapid closure of the throttle.

6   The throttle is allowed to close when vacuum in the throttle controller diaphragm overcomes the pressure of the diaphragm spring.

7   In this way the diaphragm slowly pulls the diaphragm rod against spring pressure and the throttle closes.

Mixture control system

8   The purpose of the mixture control system is to allow fresh air into the inlet manifold under conditions of increased manifold vacuum such as when decelerating.

9   The system consists of an anti-afterburn valve and air valve and their respective control solenoids.

Air jet controller

10   The air jet controller senses atmospheric pressure and controls the amount of air flow into the carburettor primary slow and main air jets and the secondary slow air jet.

11   The unit is used to increase the air flow to the jets when the car is operating under conditions of high altitude, thus maintaining an accurate air/fuel ratio.

Exhaust gas recirculation

12   The EGR system is provided to reduce oxides of nitrogen (NOx) emission by recirculating exhaust gases back through the inlet manifold and combustion chamber via the EGR valve.

13   Operation of the EGR valve is controlled by vacuum from the carburettor port via two control valves. The volume of recirculated gas is proportional to inlet air volume and is therefore porportional to engine load. In this way gas is only recirculated when accelerating or cruising, which are the two conditions creating the largest proportion of NOx emission.

14   Control valves and solenoids cut off recirculation during idle, deceleration, and cold running.

Catalytic converter

15   The catalytic converter is incorporated in the exhaust system to convert hyrocarbons (HC), carbon monoxide (CO) and oxides of nitrogen (NOx) in the exhaust gas into carbon dioxide (CO_2), dinitrogen (N_2) and water vapour by catalytic reaction.

Air injection system

16   The air injection system utilizes vacuum pulses in the exhaust manifold to draw air from the air cleaner into the exhaust manifold to promote oxidation of hydrocarbons.

17   A control unit energises the air suction control solenoid valve to apply manifold vacuum to the air suction cut-off diaphragm valve which opens a secondary air passage.

18   When negative pressure created by the exhaust pulses opens the air suction reed valve, fresh air is allowed to enter the exhaust manifold. An air bleed valve is used to cut off manifold vacuum at the air suction cut-off diaphragm and control the operation of the system.

Feedback control system

19   The feedback control system maintains the correct air/fuel ratio by allowing air into the inlet manifold in cases of a temporarily over rich mixture.

20   The system utilizes an oxygen sensor in the exhaust manifold to signal the system control unit when excessively rich mixtures are detected.

21   A system of air valves and control solenoids is activated by the control unit, air is supplied directly into the inlet manifold to modify the air/fuel mixture ratio.

Auxiliary carburettor air supply system

22   This system works in conjunction with the mixture control system to compensate for excessively rich mixtures in the auxiliary inlet manifold ports and in the CVCC pre-combustion chambers.

23   The system is operated by a thermo-valve which is activated when engine coolant is below a preset value.

Fuel-injected engines

24   Due to the efficiency of the fuel-injection system and the ability of the ECU to accurately control injector duration and therefore the combustion process, the only exhaust emission components used are the catalytic converter and ignition timing controls. Both these systems function as described for carburettor engines.

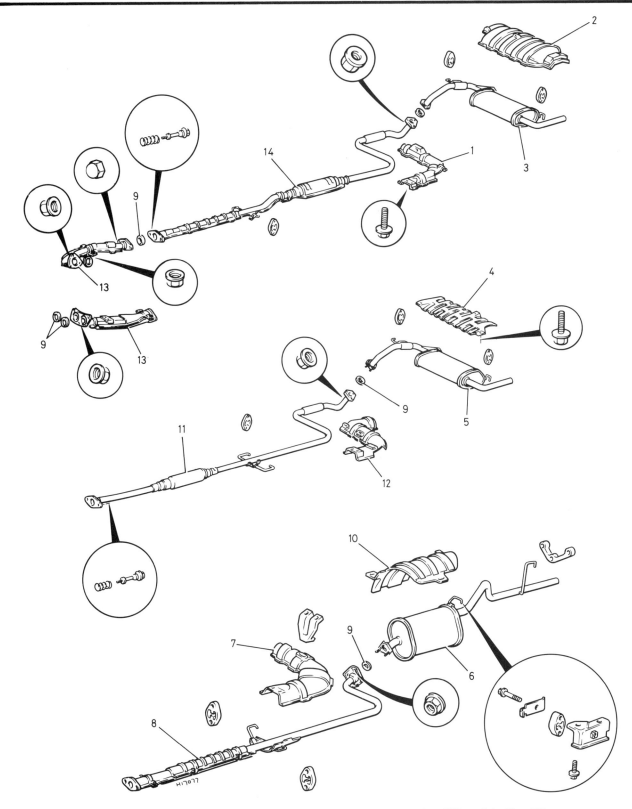

Fig. 3.44 General arrangement of the exhaust system fitted to UK models (Sec 34)

1	Heat shield (Hatchback)	4	Fuel tank heat shield (CRX)	8 Exhaust pipe (Shuttle)
2	Fuel tank heat shield (Hatchback)	5	Silencer (CRX)	9 Gasket
3	Silencer (Hatchback)	6	Silencer (Shuttle)	10 Fuel tank heat shield (Shuttle)
		7	Heat shield (Shuttle)	

11 Exhaust pipe (CRX)
12 Heat shield (CRX)
13 Downpipe
14 Exhaust pipe (Hatchback)

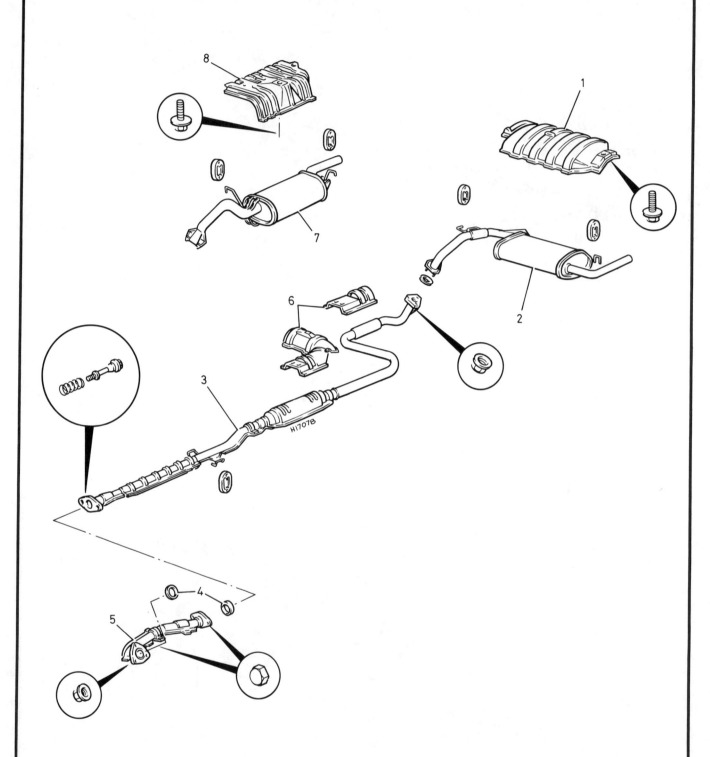

Fig. 3.45 General arrangement of the exhaust system fitted to North American models except CRX and Hatchback Si models (Sec 34)

1	Fuel tank heat shield (Hatchback)	3	Exhaust pipe	6	Heat shield	8	Fuel tank heat shield (Sedan and Wagon)
2	Silencer (Hatchback)	4	Gasket	7	Silencer (Sedan and Wagon)		
		5	Downpipe				

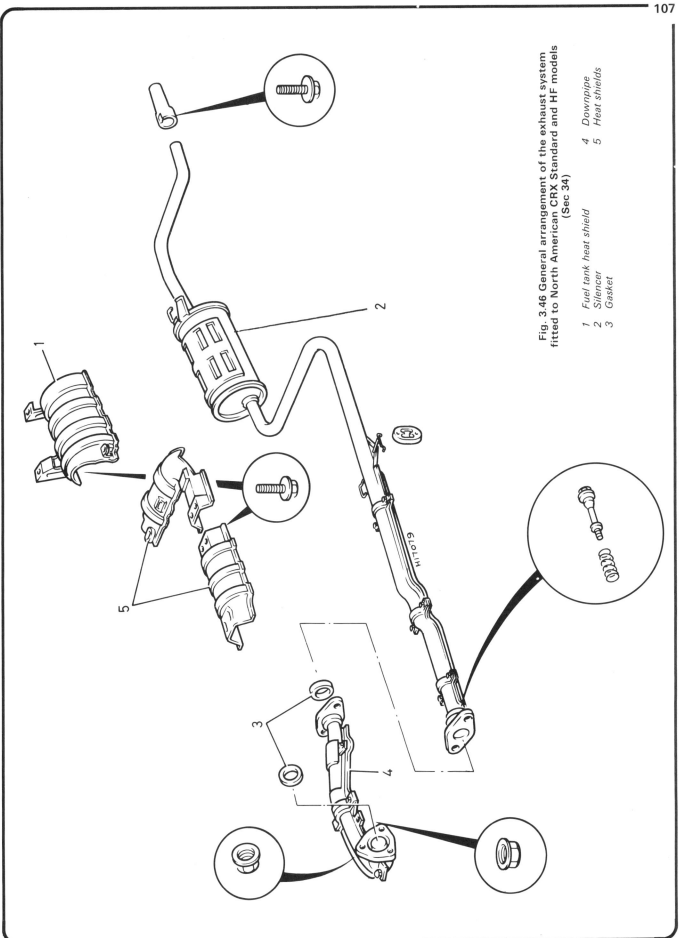

Fig. 3.46 General arrangement of the exhaust system fitted to North American CRX Standard and HF models (Sec 34)

1 Fuel tank heat shield
2 Silencer
3 Gasket
4 Downpipe
5 Heat shields

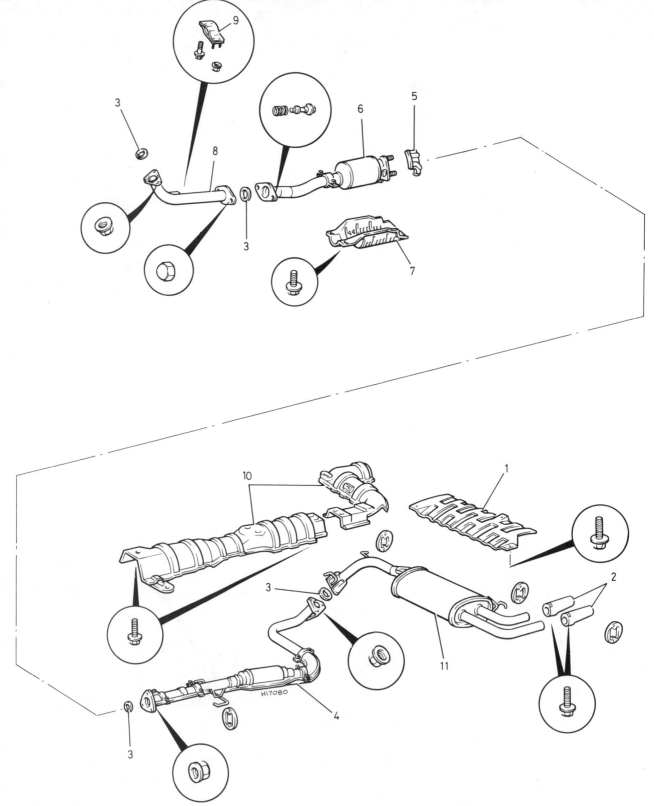

Fig. 3.47 General arrangement of the exhaust system fitted to North American CRX Si and Hatchback Si models (Sec 34)

1 Fuel tank heat shield	4 Exhaust pipe	7 Lower converter cover	9 Downpipe bracket
2 Exhaust tailpipes	5 Converter upper cover	8 Downpipe	10 Heat shields
3 Gasket	6 Catalytic converter		11 Silencer

34 Exhaust system – inspection, removal and refitting

1 The exhaust system should be examined for leaks, damage and security at regular intervals (see 'Routine Maintenance'). To do this, apply the handbrake and in a well ventilated area, allow the engine to idle. Lie down on each side of the car in turn, and check the full length of the exhaust system for leaks while an assistant temporarily places a wad of cloth over the end of the tailpipe. If a leak is evident, stop the engine and use a proprietary repair kit to seal. If the leak is excessive, or damage is evident, renew the section. Check the rubber mountings for deterioration, and renew them, if necessary.

2 All systems are of three or four section type, using a flexible joint with bolts and coil springs to absorb the flexing of the engine on its mountings (photo). The accompanying illustrations show the various types according to model.

3 If only one section of the system requires renewal, it is recommended that the complete exhaust is withdrawn from under the car to make separation easier. Do this by disconnecting the downpipe from the manifold and releasing the flexible mountings (photos).

4 When reassembling the system, do not tighten the clamps until the exhaust has been attached to the car. Once the pipe and silencer have been correctly aligned and they are likely to knock against any adjacent suspension or body components, fully tighten the clamps.

34.2 Exhaust system flexible joint

35 Exhaust manifold – removal and refitting

1 The exhaust manifold is of cast iron construction and incorporates a hot air collecting shroud.

2 To remove the manifold, disconnect the battery negative terminal, then jack up the front of the car and support it on stands.

3 Remove the engine undershield.

4 Disconnect the exhaust downpipe, or where applicable on North American models, the catalytic converter. Recover the gasket.

5 Undo the bolts and remove the hot air collecting shrouds.

6 On North American models remove the oxygen sensor.

7 Undo the nuts and support bracket bolts and remove the manifold from the cylinder head. Recover the gasket.

8 Refitting is the reverse sequence to removal. Use new gaskets and tighten all nuts and bolts to the specified torque.

34.3A Exhaust manifold-to-downpipe support bracket

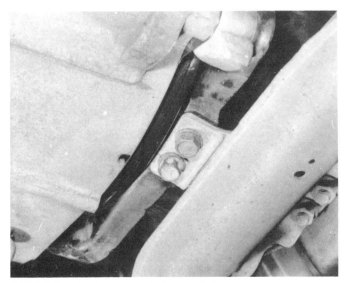

34.3B Exhaust system support at transmission

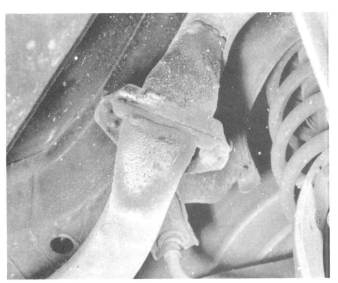

34.3C Exhaust section rear flange joint

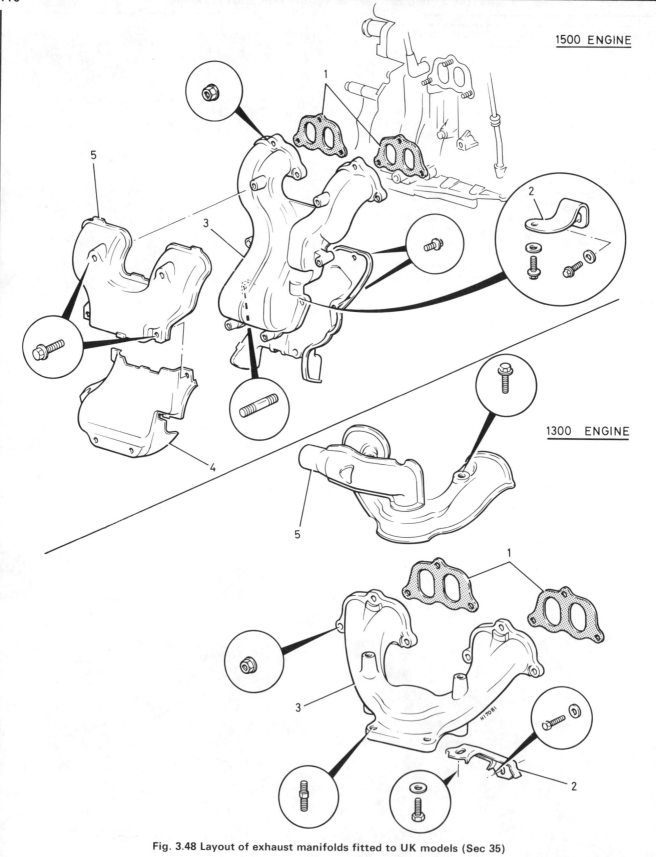

1500 ENGINE

1300 ENGINE

Fig. 3.48 Layout of exhaust manifolds fitted to UK models (Sec 35)

1 Gasket
2 Exhaust pipe bracket
3 Exhaust manifold
4 Lower manifold shroud
5 Upper manifold shroud

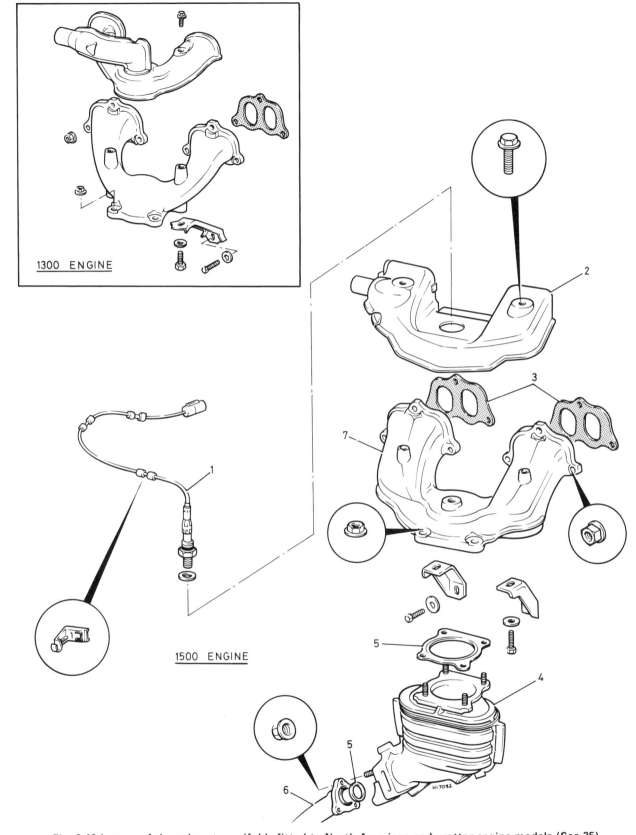

Fig. 3.49 Layout of the exhaust manifolds fitted to North American carburettor engine models (Sec 35)

1 Oxygen sensor
2 Exhaust manifold shroud
3 Gaskets
4 Catalytic converter
5 Gasket
6 Downpipe
7 Exhaust manifold

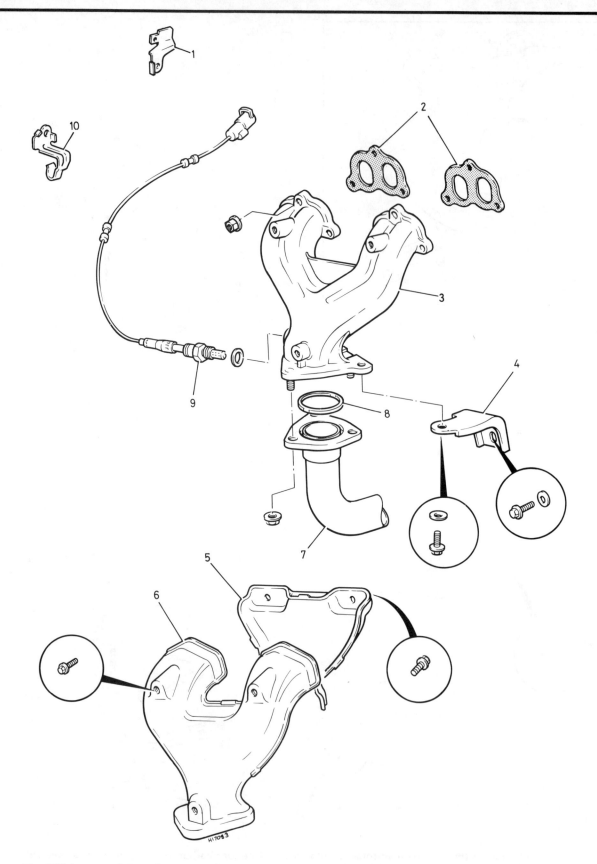

Fig. 3.50 Layout of the exhaust manifolds fitted to North American fuel-injected engine models (Sec 35)

1 Oxygen sensor clamp
2 Gaskets
3 Exhaust manifold
4 Exhaust manifold bracket
5 Exhaust manifold lower shroud
6 Exhaust manifold upper shroud
7 Downpipe
8 Gasket
9 Oxygen sensor
10 Oxygen sensor clamp

PART D FAULT DIAGNOSIS

36 Fault diagnosis – fuel, exhaust and emission control systems

Unsatisfactory engine performance, poor starting and excessive fuel consumption are not necessarily the fault of the fuel system. In fact they more commonly occur as a result of ignition system faults. Before acting on the following, it is necessary to check the ignition system first. Even though a fault may lie in the fuel system it will be difficult to trace unless the ignition is correct. With the information below, therefore, it is assumed that this has been attended to first.

Accurate diagnosis of faults in fuel-injection and emission control equipment entails the use of equipment not normally available to the home mechanic. Suspected faults in these systems should therefore be referred to a Honda dealer.

Symptom	Reason(s)
Difficult starting when cold	Choke cable incorrectly adjusted (where applicable)
	Faulty or maladjusted automatic choke (where applicable)
	Choke valve not closing
	Choke linkage binding
	Insufficient fuel in float chamber
	Fuel tank empty or pump defective
	Blocked fuel filter
	Idle cut-off solenoid valve faulty
	Vacuum hoses damaged or insecure
	Air leak at carburettor or manifold
Difficult starting when hot	Choke cable incorrectly adjusted (where applicable)
	Faulty or maladjusted automatic choke (where applicable)
	Choke valve sticking or linkage binding
	Float chamber flooding
	Fuel tank empty or pump defective
	Blocked fuel filter
	Air cleaner element dirty or choked
Excessive fuel consumption	Leakage from tank, pipes, pump or carburettor
	Air cleaner choked
	Float chamber flooding
	Excessively worn carburettor
Fuel starvation	Faulty fuel pump
	Fuel tank vents restricted
	Fuel pipes or hoses restricted
	Incorrect float level
	Blocked carburettor jets
	Blocked fuel filter
Poor performance, hesitation or erratic running	Carburettor idle settings incorrect
	Carburettor component settings correct
	Faulty carburettor accelerator pump
	Air cleaner air temperature control inoperative
	Leaking carburettor or manifold gasket
	Blocked carburettor jets
	Fuel starvation

Chapter 4 Ignition system

Contents

Specifications

General
System type .... Electronic breakerless, inductive type

Ignition coil
UK models:
   Primary winding resistance .... 1.24 to 1.46 ohms at 20°C (70°F)
   Secondary winding resistance .... 8000 to 12000 ohms at 20°C (70°F)
North American models:
   1984 models:
      Primary winding resistance .... 1.24 to 1.46 ohms at 20°C (70°F)
      Secondary winding resistance .... 8000 to 12000 ohms at 20°C (70°F)
   1985 models:
      Primary winding resistance .... 1.06 to 1.24 ohms at 20°C (70°F)
      Secondary winding resistance .... 7400 to 11000 ohms at 20°C (70°F)
   1986 models:
      Primary winding resistance .... 1.215 to 1.485 ohms at 20°C (70°F)
      Secondary winding resistance .... 11.074 to 11.526 ohms at 20°C (70°F)
      B and D terminal resistance .... 2200 ohms at 20°C (70°F)

Interference suppression condenser
Capacitance .... 0.38 to 0.56 microfarads

Distributor
Direction of rotation .... Clockwise
Firing order .... 1-3-4-2 (No.1 cylinder at crankshaft pulley end)
Reluctor air gap .... Equal both sides of stator

Spark plugs
Type:
  UK models .... NGK BPR6EY-11, Nippon-Denso W20EXR-U11, Champion RN9YC or equivalent

North American models except CRX*:
  1984 .... NGK BUR5EB-11, Nippon-Denso W16EKR-S11 or equivalent
  1985 and 1986 carburettor engine .... NGK BUR5EB-11, Nippon-Denso W16EKR-S11 or equivalent
  1986 fuel-injected engine .... NGK BUR6EY-11, Nippon-Denso W20EXR-U11 or equivalent
North American CRX models*
  1985:
    Standard .... NGK BUR5EB-11, Nippon-Denso W16EKR-S11 or equivalent
    HF .... NGK BUR4EB-11, Nippon-Denso W14EKR-S11 or equivalent
    Si .... NGK BUR6EY-11, Nippon-Denso W20EXR-U11 or equivalent
  1986:
    Standard and HF .... NGK BUR4EB-11, Nippon-Denso W14EKR-S11 or equivalent
    Si .... NGK BPR6EY-11, Nippon-Denso W20EXR-U11 or equivalent

*For further information consult the vehicle handbook

Electrode gap:
  NGK and Nippon-Denso plugs .... 1.0 to 1.1 mm (0.039 to 0.043 in)
  Champion plugs .... 0.7 mm (0.025 in)

HT leads
Resistance .... 25 000 ohms (maximum)

Ignition timing
Stroboscopic at idling speed with vacuum connected (UK models)/disconnected (North American models)
Setting (all models) .... Red notch on crankshaft pulley aligned with projection on timing belt cover – engine idling

Actual value:

	USA except California	California
UK models:		
1300 cc	10° to 14° BTDC	
1500 cc carburettor engine	12° to 16° BTDC	
1500 cc fuel-injected engine	14° to 18° BTDC	
North American models except CRX:		
1984:		
1300 cc	19° to 23° BTDC	14° to 18° BTDC
1500 cc:		
Manual transmission	18° to 22° BTDC	18° to 22° BTDC
Automatic transmission	13° to 17° BTDC	13° to 17° BTDC
1985:		
1300 cc	19° to 23° BTDC	14° to 18° BTDC
1500 cc:		
Manual transmission	18° to 22° BTDC	18° to 22° BTDC
Automatic transmission:		
With manual steering	13° to 17° BTDC	13° to 17° BTDC
With power-assisted steering	15° to 19° BTDC	15° to 19° BTDC
1986:		
1300 cc	19° to 23° BTDC	14° to 18° BTDC
1500 cc carburettor engine:		
Manual transmission	18° to 22° BTDC	18° to 22° BTDC
Automatic transmission:		
With manual steering	13° to 17° BTDC	13° to 17° BTDC
With power-assisted steering	15° to 19° BTDC	15° to 19° BTDC
1500 cc fuel-injected engine	14° to 18° BTDC	10° to 14° BTDC
North American CRX models:		
Standard:		
Manual transmission	18° to 22° BTDC	18° to 22° BTDC
Automatic transmission	13° to 17° BTDC	13° to 17° BTDC
HF	19° to 23° BTDC	14° to 18° BTDC
Si	14° to 18° BTDC	10° to 14° BTDC

Torque wrench settings

	Nm	lbf ft
Spark plugs	18	13
Distributor hold down bolts	24	18

1 General description

A breakerless inductive type electronic ignition system is fitted to all models. The system comprises the battery, main harness fuse, ignition switch, ignition coil, distributor, igniter and spark plugs, together with the associated leads and wiring. The distributor is mounted on the right-hand end of the cylinder head and is driven directly from the rear of the camshaft.

The ignition system is divided into two circuits, the low tension circuit and the high tension circuit. The low tension circuit consists of the battery, lead to the ignition switch, lead from the ignition switch to the low tension coil windings, and leads from the coil windings to the igniter and pick-up coil assembly in the distributor. The high tension circuit consists of the high tension coil windings, the heavy lead from the coil to the distribtor cap, the rotor arm, spark plug leads and spark plugs.

The system functions in the following manner. Low tension voltage is changed in the coil into high tension voltage by the action of the igniter in conjunction with the pick-up coil assembly. As each of the reluctor teeth pass through the magnetic field around the stator, an electrical signal is sent via the pick-up coil to the igniter, which triggers the ignition coil in the same way as the opening of the contact breaker

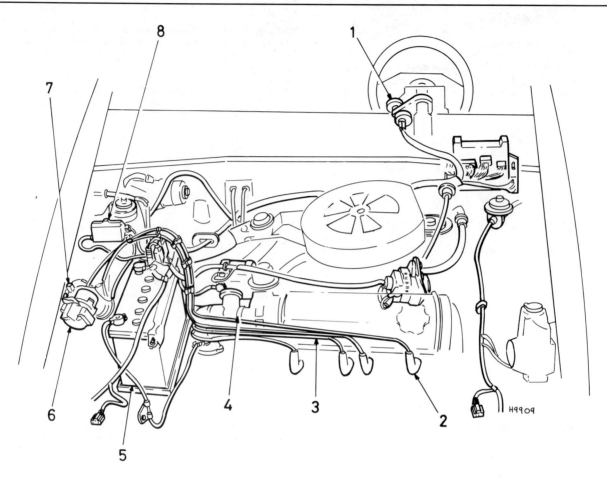

Fig. 4.1 General layout of the ignition system components (Sec 1)

1	Ignition switch	3	HT leads	5	Battery	7	Radio suppressor
2	Spark plug	4	Distributor	6	Ignition coil	8	Main fuse

points in a conventional system. High tension voltage is then fed via the carbon brush in the centre of the distributor cap to the distributor rotor arm. The voltage passes across to the appropriate metal segment in the distributor cap and via the spark plug lead to the spark plug, where it finally jumps the spark plug gap to earth. The ignition is advanced and retarded automatically to ensure that the spark occurs at just the right instant for the particular load at the prevailing engine speed.

The ignition advance is controlled both mechanically and by a vacuum operated system. The mechanical governor mechanism consists of two weights, which move out from the distributor shaft as the engine speed rises, due to centrifugal force. As they move outward, they rotate the rotor shaft relative to the distributor shaft and so advance the spark. The weights are held in position by two light springs and it is the tension of these springs which is largely responsible for correct spark advancement.

The vacuum control consists of a diaphragm, one side of which is connected via a small bore hose to the inlet manifold and the other side to the distributor breaker plate. Depression in the inlet manifold and carburettor, which varies with engine speed and throttle opening, causes the diaphragm to move, so moving the breaker plate, with igniter and pick-up coil attached, and thus advancing or retarding the spark.

2 Maintenance and inspection

1 At the service intervals given in 'Routine Maintenance' at the beginning of this Manual carry out the following operations on the ignition system.

2 Remove the distributor cap and thoroughly clean it inside and out with a clean lint free rag. Examine the four HT lead segments inside the cap. If the segments appear badly burned or pitted, renew the cap. Make sure that the carbon brush in the centre of the cap is free to move and that it stands proud of its holder.

3 Wipe clean all the ignition system wiring, paying particular attention to the HT leads, then check the security of all connections.

4 Remove, clean and reset the spark plugs using the procedure described in Section 8. If the plugs have exceeded their service life or if their condition is suspect, renew all four spark plugs as a set.

5 Check and if necessary adjust the distributor reluctor air gap and the ignition timing, as described in Section 4 and 5 respectively.

3 Distributor – removal and refitting

1 Disconnect the battery negative terminal or, on models where clearance is limited, remove the battery completely (Chapter 12).

2 Undo the two screws, lift off the distributor cap and place it to one side (photos).

3 Disconnect the hose(s) from the distributor vacuum advance unit, noting their locations (photo).

4 Disconnect the low tension leads by pulling off the coil rubber cap and removing the terminal nuts and/or plug-in connectors (photo).

5 On fuel-injected models release the TDC sensor wiring plug from the clip on the side of the distributor and disconnect the plug.

6 Scribe a line across the joint between the distributor mounting flange and drive housing or cylinder head as an aid to refitting.

7 Undo the hold down bolts and remove the distributor (photos).

3.2A Undo the distributor cap retaining screws ...

3.2B ... and lift off the cap

3.3 Disconnect the vacuum hose(s)

3.4 Pull off the coil rubber cover and disconnect the LT leads

3.7A Undo the distributor hold down bolts ...

3.7B ... and remove the distributor

8 Before refitting the distributor renew the O-ring seal if it is at all damaged.

9 Push the distributor into its location and turn the rotor arm until the drive dog coupling positively engages with the camshaft. Note that the lug on the coupling and slot on the camshaft are offset so that the distributor shaft can only be fitted in one position.

10 Align the scribed marks on the flange and housing, then fit and tighten the hold down bolts.

11 Reconnect the wiring and vacuum hose(s), then refit the distributor cap and battery or lead.

12 Check, and if necessary reset, the ignition timing as described in Section 5.

4 Distributor – overhaul

Note: *Before attempting distributor overhaul, check that spare parts are available separately for the unit concerned. If this is not the case, it will be necessary to renew the complete distributor if any of the internal parts are found to be worn or damaged.*

UK models and North American fuel-injected models

1 Remove the distributor as described in Section 3.

2 Remove the O-ring from the base of the distributor housing.

3 Withdraw the rotor arm from the rotor shaft.

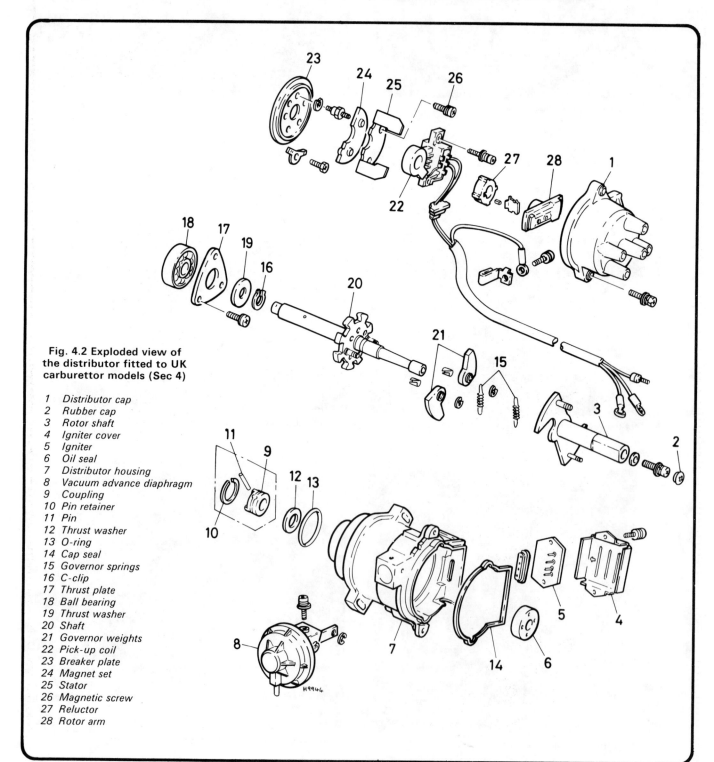

Fig. 4.2 Exploded view of the distributor fitted to UK carburettor models (Sec 4)

1   Distributor cap
2   Rubber cap
3   Rotor shaft
4   Igniter cover
5   Igniter
6   Oil seal
7   Distributor housing
8   Vacuum advance diaphragm
9   Coupling
10   Pin retainer
11   Pin
12   Thrust washer
13   O-ring
14   Cap seal
15   Governor springs
16   C-clip
17   Thrust plate
18   Ball bearing
19   Thrust washer
20   Shaft
21   Governor weights
22   Pick-up coil
23   Breaker plate
24   Magnet set
25   Stator
26   Magnetic screw
27   Reluctor
28   Rotor arm

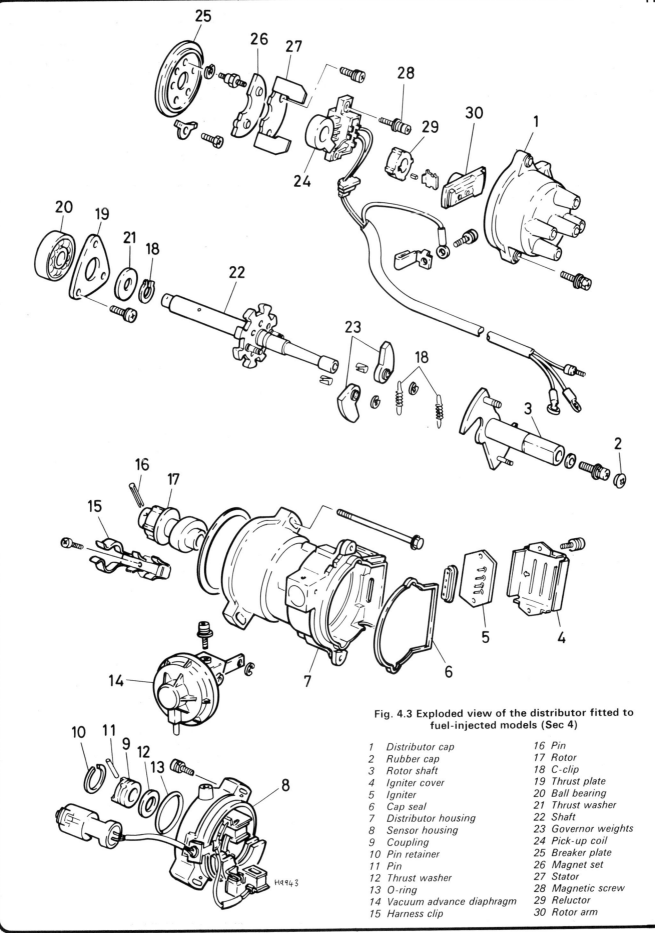

Fig. 4.3 Exploded view of the distributor fitted to
fuel-injected models (Sec 4)

1	Distributor cap	16	Pin
2	Rubber cap	17	Rotor
3	Rotor shaft	18	C-clip
4	Igniter cover	19	Thrust plate
5	Igniter	20	Ball bearing
6	Cap seal	21	Thrust washer
7	Distributor housing	22	Shaft
8	Sensor housing	23	Governor weights
9	Coupling	24	Pick-up coil
10	Pin retainer	25	Breaker plate
11	Pin	26	Magnet set
12	Thrust washer	27	Stator
13	O-ring	28	Magnetic screw
14	Vacuum advance diaphragm	29	Reluctor
15	Harness clip	30	Rotor arm

H9943

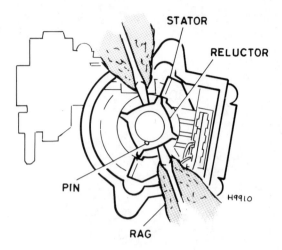

Fig. 4.4 Distributor reluctor removal (Sec 4)

4   Using two screwdrivers held at opposite points, carefully prise the reluctor off the rotor shaft and recover the roll pin.
5   Undo the two igniter cover retaining screws, noting the position of the earth lead, and remove the cover (photo).
6   Pull the igniter squarely off the distributor housing (photo).
7   Undo the two pick-up coil assembly retaining screws and remove the unit.
8   Extract the C-clip which secures the vacuum advance diaphragm link rod and release the rod from the stud.
9   Undo the retaining screws and remove the vacuum advance diaphragm from the distributor housing.
10 Undo the breaker plate clamp screw, withdraw the clamp and remove the breaker plate assembly.
11 Withdraw the pin retainer, then top out the drive dog coupling roll pin using a punch. Remove the coupling and thrust washer.
12 On fuel-injected models undo the three screws and withdraw the sensor housing and O-ring from the distributor housing. Scribe an alignment mark on the rotor and distributor shaft, tap out the roll pin and remove the rotor.
13 Remove the springs and governor weights from the distributor shaft and rotor shaft.
14 Hook out the rubber cap, then undo the screw in the centre of the rotor shaft. Withdraw the rotor shaft from the distributor shaft.
15 Withdraw the distributor shaft from the distributor housing and retrieve the thrust washer.
16 Undo the screws and remove the thrust plate, bearing and, where fitted, the oil seal.
17 With the distributor dismantled, renew any parts that show signs of wear, or damage, and any that are known to be faulty. Pay close attention to the centrifugal advance mechanism, checking for loose or broken springs, wear in the governor weight pivots and play or roughness in the distributor shaft bearing. Check the operation of the vacuum advance diaphragm by sucking on the outlet connection and checking for movement of the link rod. No movement indicates a punctured diaphragm necessitating renewal. Before reassembly, renew all O-rings and seals as a matter of course.
18 Begin reassembly by installing the oil seal (where fitted), bearing and thrust plate in the distributor housing.
19 Fit the governor weights to the distributor shaft, lubricate the shaft with molybdenum disulphide grease and fit the shaft and thrust washer.
20 Lubricate the bore of the rotor shaft and locate the shaft in position. Fit the retaining screw and rubber plug, then attach the governor springs to the shaft posts.
21 On fuel-injected models, refit the rotor to the distributor shaft, align the previously made marks and secure with a new roll pin. Refit the sensor housing and O-ring.
22 On all models, temporarily refit the rotor arm and position the rotor shaft as shown in Fig. 4.9. Invert the distributor and fit the thrust washer and drive dog coupling. Check that the rotor shaft is still positioned correctly, then align the index mark on the coupling with

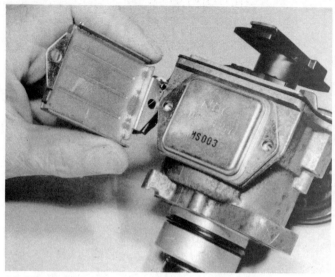

4.5 Remove the igniter cover ...

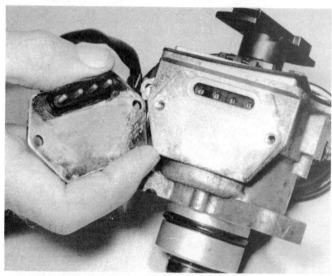

4.6 ... followed by the igniter

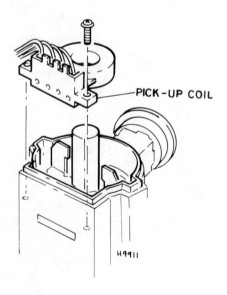

Fig. 4.5 Pick-up coil attachments (Sec 4)

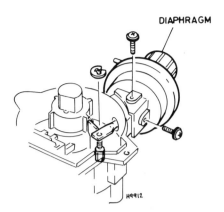

Fig. 4.6 Vacuum advance diaphragm removal (Sec 4)

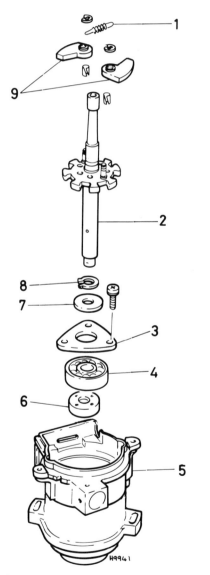

Fig. 4.8 Exploded view of the distributor shaft components
(Sec 4)

1   Governor spring   6   Oil seal (carburettor engines
2   Shaft   only)
3   Thrust plate   7   Thrust washer
4   Ball bearing   8   C-clip
5   Distributor housing   9   Governor weights

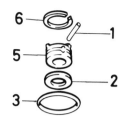

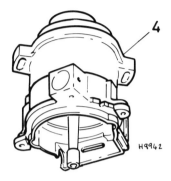

Fig. 4.7 Distributor shaft drive dog coupling details (Sec 4)

1   Roll pin   4   Distributor housing
2   Thrust washer   5   Coupling
3   O-ring   6   Pin retainer

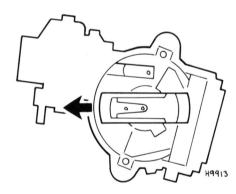

Fig. 4.9 Rotor arm position for drive dog coupling fitment –
UK models and North American fuel-injected models
(Sec 4)

the mark on the base of the distributor (Figs. 4.10 and 4.11). Tap in a
new roll pin and secure with the pin retainer.
23 Refit the breaker plate assembly and secure with the clamp.
24 Refit the vacuum advance diaphragm and engage the link rod with
the stud. Secure with the C-clip.
25 Refit the igniter unit and pick-up coil assembly and secure with the
two screws.
26 Refit the igniter unit and cover, ensuring that the earth lead is
secured with the cover screw.
27 Fit the reluctor to the rotor shaft, then push in the roll pin ensuring
that its gap faces away from the rotor shaft.
28 Position the reluctor so that its teeth are aligned with the stator
arms. Using feeler gauges check that the air gaps on both sides are
equal (Fig. 4.12). Slacken the stator retaining screws and reposition
the stator if necessary to achieve this. Tighten the screws securely
when the gaps are equal.
29 Refit the rotor arm and the O-ring seal to the base of the distributor
housing.

CARBURETTOR ENGINE

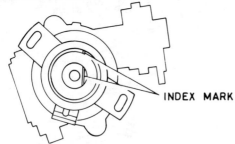

INDEX MARK

FUEL-INJECTED ENGINE

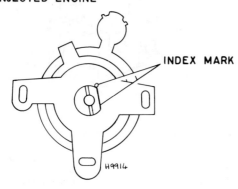

INDEX MARK

Fig. 4.10 Drive dog coupling index mark alignment – UK models (Sec 4)

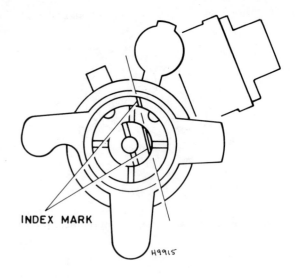

INDEX MARK

Fig. 4.11 Drive dog coupling index mark alignment – North American fuel-injected models (Sec 4)

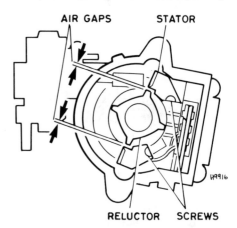

AIR GAPS   STATOR

RELUCTOR   SCREWS

Fig. 4.12 Reluctor air gap checking points (Sec 4)

North American carburettor models

30 Carry out the previously described procedure, but with reference to Fig. 4.13 and note the following differences.
31 An externally mounted igniter unit is not fitted. The pick-up coil and igniter unit are a combined assembly mounted on the breaker plate.
32 The vacuum advance diaphragm link rod is secured to the breaker plate with a screw.
33 The breaker plate is secured by two 'hold down screws. When refitting ensure that the plate is positioned as shown in Fig. 4.14, paying particular attention to the position of the upper plate in relation to the lower plate.
34 When refitting the drive dog coupling, position the rotor arm as shown in Fig. 4.15 and note the coupling index mark position as shown in Fig. 4.16.

5   Ignition timing – adjustment

Note: *Before checking the ignition timing, ensure that the carburettor or fuel-injection system adjustments are correct and that the valve clearances and spark plug gaps are correctly set. A stroboscopic timing light will be required for the following operations.*

1 Turn the crankshaft, using a socket on the pulley bolt, until the timing marks on the pulley are uppermost.
2 Identify the timing marks as follows. The single notch on its own is the TDC mark for No.1 piston. To the left of this is a group of three notches and the centre notch of this group is coloured red. This red notch is the mark used for ignition timing on all models (photo). To make identification easier with the timing light it may be beneficial to highlight the mark, and also the raised projection on the timing belt lower cover, with white chalk.
3 Connect the timing light to the engine in accordance with the manufacturer's instructions (usually between No.1 spark plug and its HT lead).

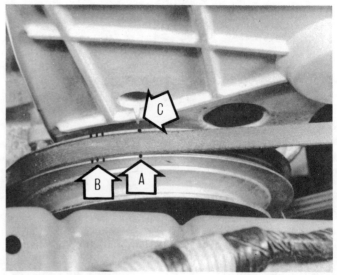

5.2 Timing mark identification

A   *TDC mark*
B   *Red coloured timing notch*
C   *Raised projection on timing belt lower cover*

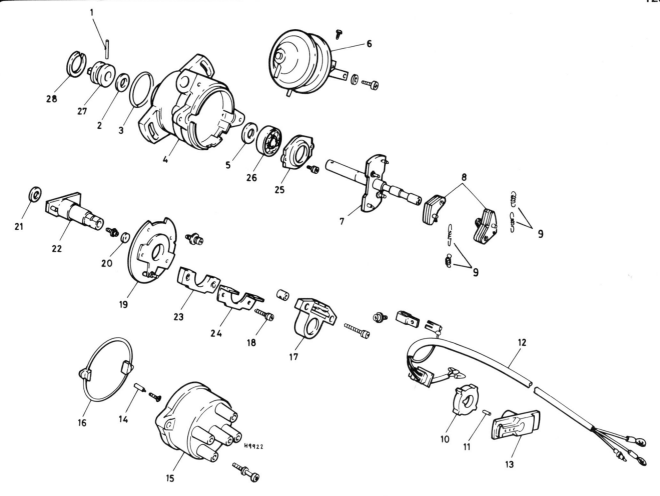

Fig. 4.13 Exploded view of the distributor fitted to North American carburettor engines (Sec 4)

1	Pin	8	Governor weights	15 Distributor cap
2	Thrust washer	9	Governor springs	16 O-ring
3	O-ring	10	Reluctor	17 Igniter/pick-up coil
4	Distributor housing	11	Pin	18 Magnetic screw
5	Oil seal	12	Primary lead	19 Breaker plate
6	Vacuum advance diaphragm	13	Rotor arm	20 Rubber cap
7	Shaft	14	Carbon contact	21 Thrust washer

22 Rotor shaft
23 Magnet set
24 Stator
25 Thrust plate
26 Ball bearing
27 Coupling
28 Pin retainer

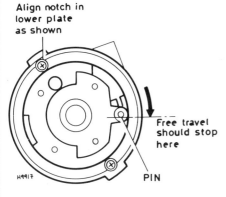

Fig. 4.14 Correct positioning of breaker plate upper and lower parts – North American carburettor engines (Sec 4)

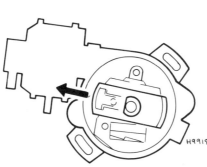

Fig. 4.15 Rotor arm position for drive dog coupling fitment – North American carburettor engines (Sec 4)

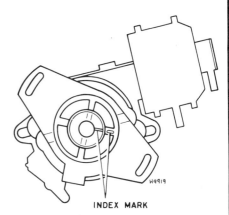

Fig. 4.16 Drive dog coupling index mark alignment – North American carburettor engines (Sec 4)

4   Start the engine and allow it to warm up until the radiator cooling fan has cut in at least once.

5   On North American models disconnect the hoses at the vacuum advance diaphragm and plug their ends. On UK models leave the vacuum hose connected.

6   On automatic transmission models ensure that the handbrake is securely applied, then place the transmission in 'D' (Drive).

7   With the engine idling at the specified speed (see Chapter 3), point the timing light at the timing marks. The red notch on the pulley should appear stationary and in alignment with the raised projection on the timing belt lower cover.

8   If adjustment is necessary, slacken the distributor hold down bolts, turn the distributor as necessary until the marks are aligned, then tighten the bolts.

9   To check the operation of the centrifugal advance mechanism, gradually increase the engine speed while still pointing the timing light at the marks (on automatic transmission models return the transmission to 'Park' or 'Neutral' before doing this). As the engine speed increases, the pulley notch should move away from the projection on the timing belt cover, indicating that the advance is operating. If the marks remain stationary, or if the movement is erratic or jerky, then the distributor should be dismantled for inspection as described in Section 4.

10 To check the operation of the vacuum advance unit, a vacuum pump and gauge are required. If in doubt about the vacuum unit operation, have this checked by a Honda dealer or suitably equipped workshop.

11 After carrying out the adjustments, switch off the engine and disconnect the timing light. On North American models reconnect the vacuum hoses.

6   Ignition coil – description and testing

1   Three different types of ignition coil are used on Civic models according to year of manufacture and model type. All are mounted in the engine compartment either on the right-hand valance behind the battery or on the left-hand side of the engine compartment bulkhead.

2   To ensure correct HT polarity at the spark plugs, and to avoid the risk of damage to the electronic ignition components, the coil LT leads must always be connected correctly as follows. Black/yellow lead to the coil positive terminal, blue lead to the coil negative terminal.

3   To test the coil the primary and secondary winding resistance can be checked with an ohmmeter as follows.

4   With the ignition switched off, pull off the rubber cover and disconnect the LT wiring and the HT lead in the centre of the coil.

5   Two of the coil types fitted have stud and nut terminals to secure the LT wiring. If working on this type, measure the primary resistance

by connecting the ohmmeter across the positive and negative terminals. The resistance should be as given in the Specifications. Now measure the secondary resistance by connecting the ohmmeter across the positive primary terminal and the HT lead centre terminal. Again the resistance should be as specified. If any of the values obtained are not as specified, the coil must be renewed.

6   The third type of coil fitted has push fit connectors for the primary leads with two terminals in each connector. To check the primary winding resistance, connect the ohmmeter across coil terminals A and D (Fig. 4.21). Check the secondary winding resistance between terminal A and the HT lead centre terminal. Also check the resistance between terminals B and D. Compare the values obtained with the figures in the Specifications and renew the coil if any are outside the limits given. Additionally, check for continuity between terminals A and C. Renew the coil if there is no continuity.

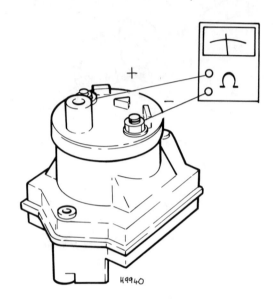

Fig. 4.17 Checking ignition coil primary winding resistance – UK models and 1984 North American models (Sec 6)

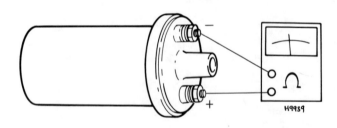

Fig. 4.18 Checking ignition coil primary winding resistance – 1985 North American models (Sec 6)

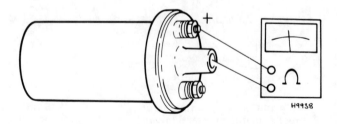

Fig. 4.20 Checking ignition coil secondary winding resistance – 1985 North American models (Sec 6)

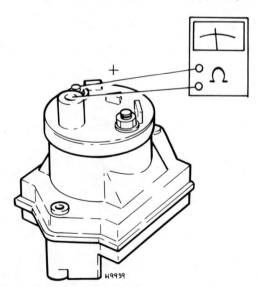

Fig. 4.19 Checking ignition coil secondary winding resistance – UK models and 1984 North American models (Sec 6)

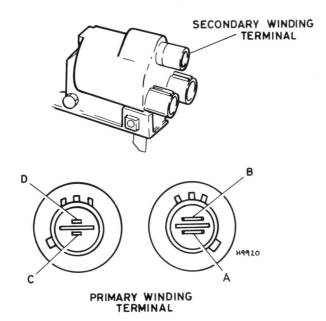

Fig. 4.21 Ignition coil primary and secondary winding terminal identification – 1986 North American models (Sec 6)

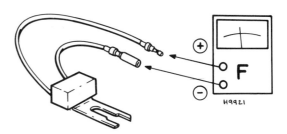

Fig. 4.22 Checking noise suppression condenser capacitance (Sec 6)

7 Reconnect the coil winding on completion of the checks.
8 All models are equipped with a radio interference suppression condenser mounted alongside the coil. Although this is intended purely for igniton noise suppression, if it fails it can cause engine misfire or even stop the engine. To test the condenser, a commercially available condenser tester is required and is connected across the condenser leads (Fig. 4.22). Renew the condenser if the reading is not as specified.

7 Igniter unit and pick-up coil assembly – testing

UK models and North American fuel-injected models
1 Undo the two screws, lift off the distributor cap and place it to one side.
2 Undo the two screws securing the igniter cover to the side of the distributor and remove the cover. Note the location of the harness clip and earth lead.
3 Carefully pull the igniter squarely out of its location on the distributor.
4 Using an ohmmeter and voltmeter, test the pick-up coil as follows.
5 Connect the voltmeter across the blue and green wire terminals, and check that the measured resistance is approximately 750 ohms at 20°C (70°F) (Fig. 4.23).
6 Disconnect the black/yellow wire and the blue wire from the pick-up coil terminals inside the distributor. With the ignition switched on, connect the voltmeter between the blue wire and earth, then the black/yellow wire and earth (Fig. 4.24). Battery voltage should be indicated at each check. Switch off the ignition and reconnect the two wires.
7 Using an ohmmeter test the igniter unit as follows.
8 Check that there is continuity indicated with the ohmmeter positive probe connected to the igniter blue pin, and the negative probe to the black/yellow pin (Fig. 4.25). Now check that there is no continuity indicated with the ohmmeter positive probe connected to the black/yellow pin, and the negative probe connected to the blue pin.

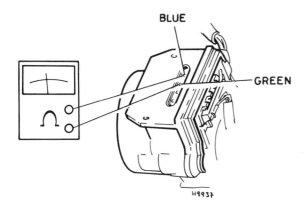

Fig. 4.23 Checking pick-up coil resistance – UK models and North American fuel-injected models (Sec 7)

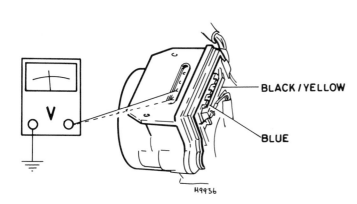

Fig. 4.24 Checking pick-up coil voltage – UK models and North American fuel-injected models (Sec 7)

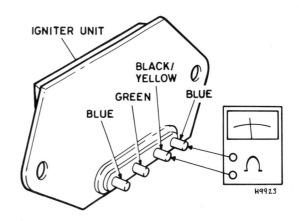

Fig. 4.25 Checking igniter unit continuity – UK models and North American fuel-injected models (Sec 7)

9 If the stated values are not obtained during these tests, either the pick-up coil or the igniter unit should be renewed accordingly.
10 On completion refit the igniter unit and cover and the distributor cap.

North American carburettor models
11 Undo the two screws, lift off the distributor cap and place it to one side.
12 Using an ohmmeter and voltmeter, test the combined pick-up coil and igniter unit as follows.
13 Disconnect the two wires at the pick-up coil assembly inside the distributor. With the ignition switched on, connect the voltmeter between the blue wire and earth, then the black/yellow wire and earth (Fig. 4.26). Battery voltage should be indicated at each check.
14 Switch off the ignition, but leave the two wires disconnected.
15 Using an ohmmeter, check that there is continuity indicated with the ohmmeter positive probe connected to the pick-up coil/igniter unit blue terminal, and the negative probe connected to the black/yellow terminal (Fig. 4.27). Now check that there is no continuty indicated with the ohmmeter positive probe connected to the black/yellow terminal and the negative probe connected to the blue terminal.
16 If the stated values are not obtained, the pick-up coil/igniter unit should be renewed.
17 On completion, reconnect the two wires and refit the distributor cap.

8 Spark plugs and HT leads – general

1 The correct functioning of the spark plugs is vital for the proper running and efficiency of the engine. The spark plugs should be renewed at the intervals given in 'Routine Maintenance' at the beginning of this Manual. If misfiring or bad starting is experienced within the service period, they must be removed, cleaned and regapped.
2 To remove the plugs, first mark the HT leads to ensure correct refitment, and then pull them off the plugs. Using a spark plug spanner, or suitable deep socket and extension bar, unscrew the plugs and remove them from the engine.
3 The condition of the spark plugs will also tell much about the overall condition of the engine.
4 If the insulator nose of the spark plug is clean and white, with no deposits, this is indicative of a weak mixture, or too hot a plug. (A hot plug transfers heat away from the electrode slowly – a cold plug transfers it away quickly).
5 If the tip and insulator nose are covered with hard black-looking deposits, then this is indicative that the mixture is too rich. Should the plug be black and oily, then it is likely that the engine is fairly worn, as well as the mixture being too rich. Note that on North American models equipped with the CVCC engine, the spark plugs may have more carbon build up on the electrodes than would normally be expected. This is due to the characteristics of the combustion chamber on these engines and is a normal condition.
6 If the insulator nose is covered with light tan to greyish brown deposits, then the mixture is correct and it is likely that the engine is in good condition.
7 If there are any traces of long brown tapering stains on the outside of the white portion of the plug, then the plug will have to be renewed, as this shows that there is a faulty joint between the plug body and the insulator, and compression is being lost.
8 The shape of the two electrodes should also be carefully inspected. Spark erosion can cause the centre electrode to become rounded with a corresponding depression on the outer electrode. If this condition is evident the plugs should be renewed.
9 Plugs should be cleaned by a sand blasting machine, which will free them from carbon more thoroughly then cleaning by hand. The machine will also test the condition of the plugs under compression. Any plug that fails to spark at the recommended pressure should be renewed.
10 The spark plug gap is of considerable importance, as, if it is too large or too small, the size of the spark and its efficiency will be seriously impaired. The spark plug gap should be set to the figure given in the Specifications at the beginning of this Chapter.
11 To set it, measure the gap with a feeler gauge, and then bend open,

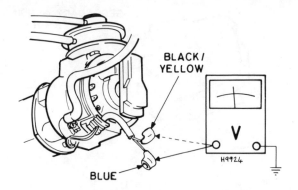

Fig. 4.26 Checking pick-up coil/igniter unit voltage – North American carburettor models (Sec 7)

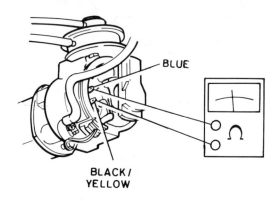

Fig. 4.27 Checking pick-up coil/igniter unit continuity – North American carburettor models (Sec 7)

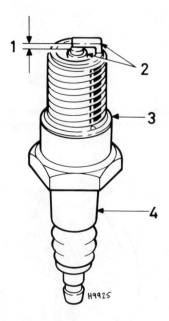

Fig. 4.28 Spark plug checking points (Sec 8)

1 Incorrect gap, oil fouling, carbon deposits or cracked centre electrode insulator
2 Worn or deformed electrodes
3 Damaged gasket
4 Cracked insulator

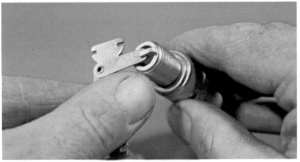

Measuring plug gap. A feeler gauge of the correct size (see ignition system specifications) should have a slight 'drag' when slid between the electrodes. Adjust gap if necessary

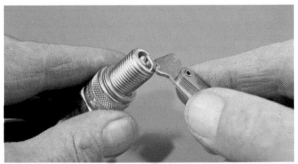

Adjusting plug gap. The plug gap is adjusted by bending the earth electrode inwards, or outwards, as necessary until the correct clearance is obtained. Note the use of the correct tool

Normal. Grey-brown deposits, lightly coated core nose. Gap increasing by around 0.001 in (0.025 mm) per 1000 miles (1600 km). Plugs ideally suited to engine, and engine in good condition

Carbon fouling. Dry, black, sooty deposits. Will cause weak spark and eventually misfire. Fault: over-rich fuel mixture. Check: carburettor mixture settings, float level and jet sizes; choke operation and cleanliness of air filter. Plugs can be re-used after cleaning

Oil fouling. Wet, oily deposits. Will cause weak spark and eventually misfire. Fault: worn bores/piston rings or valve guides; sometimes occurs (temporarily) during running-in period. Plugs can be re-used after thorough cleaning

Overheating. Electrodes have glazed appearance, core nose very white – few deposits. Fault: plug overheating. Check: plug value, ignition timing, fuel octane rating (too low) and fuel mixture (too weak). Discard plugs and cure fault immediately

Electrode damage. Electrodes burned away; core nose has burned, glazed appearance. Fault: pre-ignition. Check: as for 'Overheating' but may be more severe. Discard plugs and remedy fault before piston or valve damage occurs

Split core nose (may appear initially as a crack). Damage is self-evident, but cracks will only show after cleaning. Fault: pre-ignition or wrong gap-setting technique. Check: ignition timing, cooling system, fuel octane rating (too low) and fuel mixture (too weak). Discard plugs, rectify fault immediately

or close, the *outer* plug electrode until the correct gap is achieved. The centre electrode should *never* be bent as this may crack the insulation and cause plug failure, if nothing worse.

12 To refit the plugs, screw them in by hand initially and then fully tighten to the specified torque. The use of a little anti-seize compound on the plug threads is recommended. If a torque wrench is not available, tighten the plugs until initial resistance is felt as the sealing washer contacts its seat, and then tighten by a futher quarter of a turn. Refit the HT leads in the correct order, ensuring that they are a tight fit over the plug ends. Periodically wipe the leads clean to reduce the risk of HT leakage by arcing.

13 If the condition of the HT leads is suspect, remove them one at a time from their locations and check for signs of cracking or deterioration of the insulation and for broken, corroded or bent terminals. Renew the leads as a complete set if any are suspect. Using an ohmmeter, measure the resistance of each lead and compare the readings with the figure given in the Specifications. Renew all the leads if any are faulty.

9 Fault diagnosis – ignition system

Symptom	Reason(s)
Engine turns over normally but fails to start	Dampness or condensation on distributor cap or HT leads No current reaching spark plugs Spark plugs fouled or incorrectly adjusted Faulty HT leads or loose connections Distributor cap cracked or tracking between segments Rotor arm cracked or making poor contact with centre electrode Fault in igniter unit or pick-up coil assembly Faulty ignition coil Reluctor air gap incorrect Faulty suppression condenser Broken or loose wiring connections in ignition circuit
Engine misfires	Worn, dirty or incorrectly adjusted spark plugs Faulty HT leads or loose connections Distributor cap cracked or tracking between segments Incorrect ignition timing Faulty ignition coil Faulty suppression condenser Fault in igniter unit or pick-up coil assembly
Engine performance unsatisfactory	Incorrect ignition timing Distributor centrifugal advance not functioning Distributor vacuum advance not functioning

Chapter 5 Clutch

Contents

Specifications

General

Type	Single dry plate, diaphragm spring, cable actuation
Clutch pedal free play:	
All models except CRX	16.0 to 21.0 mm (0.63 to 0.83 in)
CRX models	10.0 to 30.0 mm (0.39 to 1.18 in)
Release arm free play	4.0 to 5.0 mm (0.15 to 0.19 in)

Clutch driven plate

Minimum lining thickness	0.2 mm (0.008 in) above rivet heads
Maximum allowable run-out	1.0 mm (0.04 in)
Maximum allowable radial play in hub splines	0.5 mm (0.02 in)
Minimum plate thickness	5.7 mm (0.22 in)

Clutch cover assembly

Maximum allowable pressure plate warpage	0.15 mm (0.006 in)

Torque wrench settings

	Nm	lbf ft
Clutch cover assembly to flywheel	26	19
Release fork special bolt	30	22

1 General description

The clutch is of conventional diaphragm spring type, mechanically operated by means of a cable.

The clutch components comprise a steel cover assembly, clutch driven plate, release bearing and release mechanism. The cover assembly which is bolted and dowelled to the rear face of the flywheel contains the pressure plate and diaphragm spring.

The driven plate is free to slide along the transmission mainshaft splines and is held in position between the flywheel and pressure plate by the pressure of the diaphragm spring.

Friction material is rivetted to the driven plate which has a rubber cushioned hub to absorb transmission shocks and to help ensure a smooth take-up of the drive.

Depressing the clutch pedal moves the release arm on the transmission by means of the clutch cable. This movement is transmitted to the release bearing which moves inwards against the fingers of the diaphragm spring. The spring is sandwiched between two annular rings which act as fulcrum points. As the release bearing pushes the spring fingers in, the outer circumference pivots out, so moving the pressure plate away from the flywheel and releasing its grip on the driven plate.

When the pedal is released, the diaphragm spring forces the pressure plate into contact with the driven plate friction linings. The driven plate is now firmly sandwiched between the pressure plate and the flywheel, thus delivering engine power to the transmission.

To compensate for wear of the friction linings, adjustment of the clutch cable as described in Section 2 should be carried out at the intervals given in 'Routine Maintenance' at the beginning of this Manual.

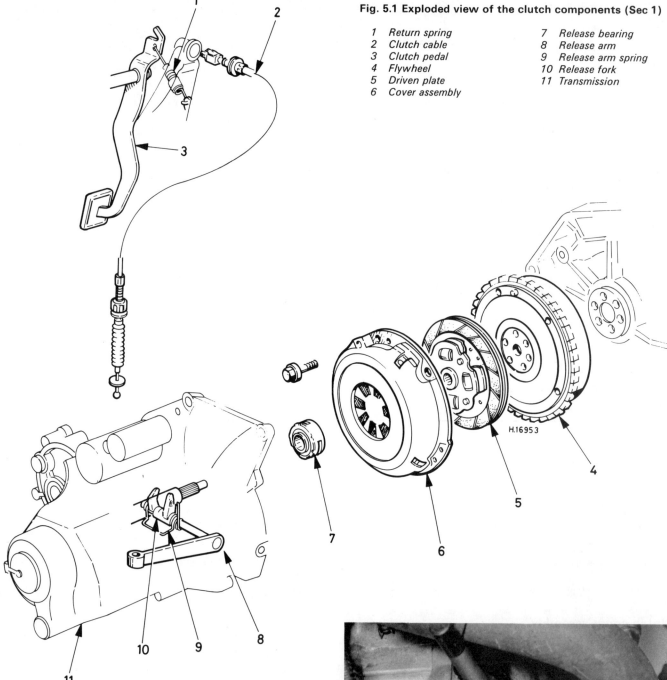

Fig. 5.1 Exploded view of the clutch components (Sec 1)

1 Return spring
2 Clutch cable
3 Clutch pedal
4 Flywheel
5 Driven plate
6 Cover assembly
7 Release bearing
8 Release arm
9 Release arm spring
10 Release fork
11 Transmission

H.16953

2 Clutch cable – adjustment

1   The clutch adjustment should be checked at the intervals given in 'Routine Maintenance' using the following procedure.

2   Measure the free play at the clutch pedal, by depressing the pedal by hand from the fully released position to the point where diaphragm spring pressure can be felt.

3   If the free play is not as given in the Specifications, turn the cable adjusting nut at the transmission support bracket as necessary until the specified free play is obtained. When viewed from above, turning the adjusting nut clockwise decreases the free play, turning it anti-clockwise increases the free play (photo).

4   After adjustment, ensure that there is 4.0 to 5.0 mm (0.15 to 0.19 in) of free movement at the clutch release arm on the side of the transmission.

2.3 Clutch cable adjusting nut location

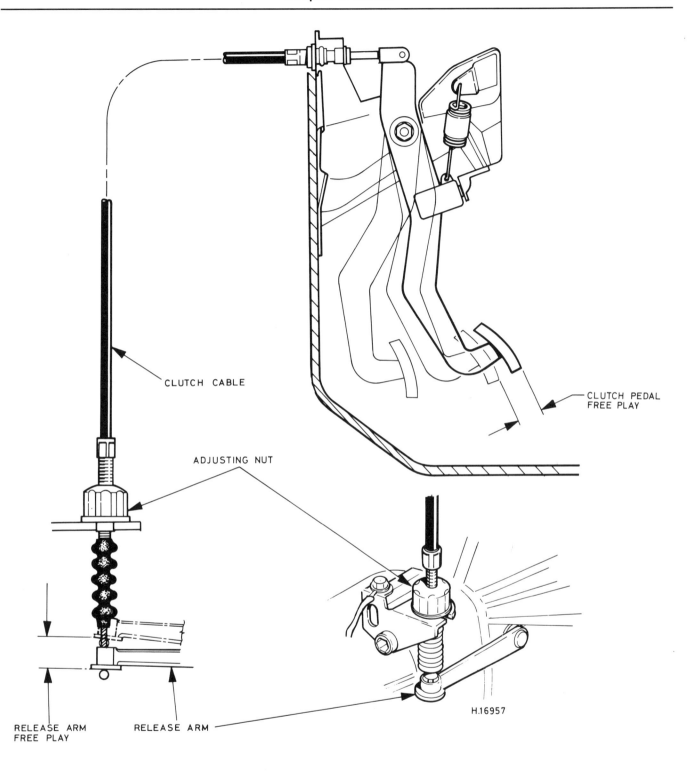

CLUTCH CABLE

CLUTCH PEDAL
FREE PLAY

ADJUSTING NUT

RELEASE ARM
FREE PLAY

RELEASE ARM

H.16957

Fig. 5.2 Clutch cable adjustment details (Sec 2)

3 Clutch cable – removal and refitting

1   Disconnect the battery negative terminal.
2   Slacken the cable adjusting nut right off, then disconnect the inner cable end from the transmission release arm (photo).
3   Withdraw the cable from the support bracket and release any cable clips within the engine compartment.

4   From under the facia disconnect the other end of the inner cable from the clutch pedal.
5   Withdraw the clutch cable assembly into the engine compartment and remove it from the car.
6   Refitting is the reverse sequence to removal. Lubricate the clutch pedal end of the inner cable with molybdenum disulphide grease and adjust the cable free play as described in Section 2.

3.2 Inner cable attachment at release arm (arrowed)

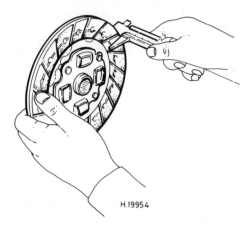

Fig. 5.3 Checking driven plate thickness (Sec 5)

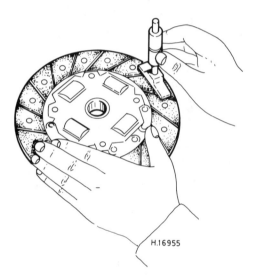

Fig. 5.4 Checking friction lining thickness (Sec 5)

4 Clutch pedal – removal and refitting

1   Disconnect the battery negative terminal.
2   Where applicable remove the facia lower panel.
3   Slacken the cable adjusting nut at the transmission, then disconnect the inner clutch cable at the pedal.
4   Disconnect the pedal return spring.
5   Unscrew the nut from the brake and clutch pedal pivot bolt, then withdraw the bolt sufficiently to allow pedal removal.
6   If necessary renew the pedal bushes before refitting.
7   Refitting is the reverse sequence to removal. Lubricate the pivot bolt with molybdenum disulphide grease and adjust the clutch cable as described in Section 2.

5 Clutch assembly – removal, inspection and refitting

1   Remove the transmission as described in Chapter 6.
2   In a diagonal sequence, half a turn at a time, slacken the bolts securing the clutch cover assembly to the flywheel.
3   When all the bolts are slack, remove them and then ease the cover assembly off the locating dowels. Collect the driven plate which will drop out when the cover assembly is removed.
4   With the clutch assembly removed, clean off all traces of asbestos dust using a dry cloth. This is best done outside or in a well ventilated area; asbestos dust is harmful, and must not be inhaled.
5   Examine the linings of the driven plate for wear and loose rivets, and for rim distortion, cracks and worn splines. The surface of the friction linings may be highly glazed, but, as long as the friction material pattern can be clearly seen, this is satisfactory. If there is any sign of oil contamination, indicated by a continuous, or patchy, shiny black discolouration, the plate must be renewed and the source of the contamination traced and rectified. This will be either a leaking crankshaft oil seal or mainshaft oil seal – or both. Renewal procedures are given in Chapter 1 and Chapter 6 respectively. The driven plate must also be renewed if the lining thickness has worn down to the minimum specified height above the rivet heads.
6   Check the machined faces of the flywheel and pressure plate. If either is grooved, or heavily scored, renewal is necessary. The pressure plate must also be renewed if warped; if any cracks are apparent, or if the diaphragm spring is damaged or its pressure suspect.
7   With the transmission removed it is advisable to check the condition of the release bearing, as described in the following Section.
8   To refit the clutch assembly, place the driven plate in position with the raised portion of the hub facing away from the flywheel.
9   Hold the plate in place and refit the cover assembly loosely on the dowels (photo). Refit the retaining bolts and tighten them finger tight so that the driven plate is gripped, but can still be moved.

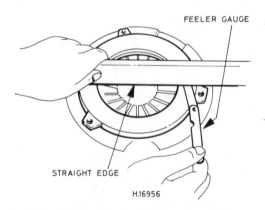

Fig. 5.5 Checking pressure plate warpage (Sec 5)

10 The driven plate must now be centralised so that when the engine and transmission are mated, the mainshaft splines will pass through the splines in the centre of the plate.
11 Centralisation can be carried out quite easily by inserting a round bar or long screwdriver through the hole in the centre of the driven plate, so that the end of the bar rests in the hole in the centre of the crankshaft. Moving the bar sideways or up and down will move the driven plate in whichever direction is necessary to achieve centralisation. With the bar removed, view the driven plate hub in relation to

5.9 Fitting the driven plate and cover assembly

5.11 Using a round bar to centralise the driven plate

the hole in the end of the crankshaft and the circle created by the ends of the diaphragm spring fingers. When the hub appears exactly in the centre, all is correct. Alternatively, if a clutch aligning tool can be obtained this will eliminate all the guesswork, obviating the need for visual alignment (photo).

12 Tighten the cover retaining bolts gradually, in a diagonal sequence to the specified torque wrench setting.

13 Refit the transmission as described in Chapter 6.

6 Clutch release mechanism – removal and refitting

1 Remove the transmission as described in Chapter 6.

2 Undo the special bolt securing the release fork to the release arm (photo).

3 Withdraw the release arm from the transmission and remove the release fork, bearing and spring. Separate the bearing from the spring and fork (photo).

4 Check the bearing for smoothness of operation and renew it if there is any roughness or harshness as the bearing is spun.

5 Refitting is the reverse sequence to removal (photo). Lubricate the release arm bushes, spring and bearing inner contact surface with molybdenum disulphide grease. Tighten the release fork special bolt to the specified torque.

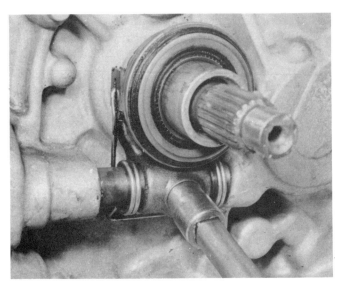

6.2 Undoing the release fork special bolt

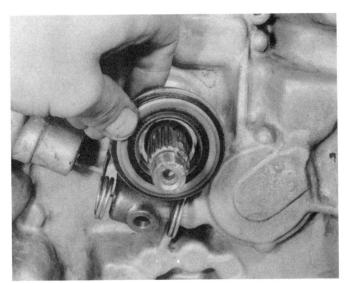

6.3 Removing the release bearing, fork and spring

6.5 Correct arrangement of release bearing spring

7   Fault diagnosis – clutch

Symptom	Reason(s)
Judder when taking up drive	Loose or worn engine/transmission mountings Driven plate linings contaminated with oil or excessively worn Clutch cable sticking or defective Excessive driven plate run-out Driven plate sticking on mainshaft splines Faulty pressure plate or diaphragm assembly
Clutch fails to disengage	Clutch cable sticking or defective Incorrect clutch adjustment Driven plate linings contaminated Driven plate sticking on mainshaft splines
Clutch slips	Incorrect clutch adjustment Release mechanism sticking or partially seized Faulty pressure plate or diaphragm assembly Driven plate linings worn or contaminated with oil
Noise when depressing clutch pedal	Worn release bearing Defective release mechanism Faulty pressure plate or diaphragm assembly
Noise when releasing clutch pedal	Faulty pressure plate or diaphragm assembly Defective driven plate Transmission internal wear

Chapter 6 Manual transmission

Contents

Specifications

General

Type .... Four or five forward speeds (all synchromesh) and reverse. Final drive differential integral with transmission

Gear ratios

UK models 1984-on:
All models except Shuttle:

1st	2.916 : 1
2nd	1.764 : 1
3rd	1.181 : 1
4th	0.846 : 1
5th (where applicable)	0.714 : 1
Reverse	2.916 : 1

Shuttle models:

1st	3.181 : 1
2nd	1.823 : 1
3rd	1.181 : 1
4th	0.846 : 1
5th	0.714 : 1
Reverse	2.916 : 1

North American 1984 and 1985 models:

	Four-speed	Five-speed
Hatchback and Sedan:		
1st	3.272 : 1	2.916 : 1
2nd	1.666 : 1	1.764 : 1
3rd	1.041 : 1	1.181 : 1
4th	0.777 : 1	0.846 : 1
5th	–	0.714 : 1
Reverse	2.916 : 1	2.916 : 1
Wagon:		
1st		3.181 : 1
2nd		1.823 : 1
3rd		1.181 : 1
4th		0.846 : 1
5th		0.714 : 1
Reverse		2.916 : 1

Gear ratios (continued)

	Four-speed	Five-speed
CRX:		
1300:		
1st		2.916 : 1
2nd		1.526 : 1
3rd		0.960 : 1
4th		0.750 : 1
5th		0.655 : 1
Reverse		2.916 : 1
1500 except HF:		
1st		2.916 : 1
2nd		1.764 : 1
3rd		1.181 : 1
4th		0.846 : 1
5th		0.714 : 1
Reverse		2.916 : 1
1500 HF except California:		
1st		3.272 : 1
2nd		1.666 : 1
3rd		1.041 : 1
4th		0.807 : 1
5th		0.714 : 1
Reverse		2.916 : 1
1500 HF for California:		
1st		2.916 : 1
2nd		1.526 : 1
3rd		0.960 : 1
4th		0.750 : 1
5th		0.655 : 1
Reverse		2.916 : 1
North American 1986 models:		
Hatchback and Sedan:		
1st	3.272 : 1	2.916 : 1
2nd	1.666 : 1	1.764 : 1
3rd	1.041 : 1	1.192 : 1
4th	0.777 : 1	0.866 : 1
5th	–	0.718 : 1
Reverse	2.916 : 1	2.916 : 1
Wagon:		
1st		3.181 : 1
2nd		1.823 : 1
3rd		1.192 : 1
4th		0.866 : 1
5th		0.718 : 1
Reverse		2.916 : 1
CRX except HF:		
1st		2.916 : 1
2nd		1.764 : 1
3rd		1.181 : 1
4th		0.846 : 1
5th		0.714 : 1
Reverse		2.916 : 1
CRX HF except California:		
1st		3.272 : 1
2nd		1.666 : 1
3rd		1.041 : 1
4th		0.807 : 1
5th		0.714 : 1
Reverse		2.916 : 1
CRX HF for California:		
1st		2.916 : 1
2nd		1.526 : 1
3rd		0.960 : 1
4th		0.750 : 1
5th		0.655 : 1
Reverse		2.916 : 1

Final drive ratios

UK models 1984-on	4.266 : 1
North American models:	
1984:	
Hatchback	3.272 : 1, 4.066 : 1 or 4.266 : 1
Sedan and Wagon	4.266 : 1
CRX:	
1300	3.473 : 1
1500	4.266 : 1

1985:
    Hatchback .... 3.272 : 1, 4.066 : 1, 4.266 : 1
    Sedan and Wagon .... 4.266 : 1
    CRX except HF .... 4.266 : 1 or 4.428 : 1
    CRX HF .... 2.954 : 1, 3.576 : 1 or 4.066 : 1
1986:
    Hatchback:
        Four-speed .... 4.062 : 1 or 4.400 : 1
        Five-speed .... 3.578 : 1, 3.722 : 1 or 4.266 : 1
    Sedan and Wagon .... 4.250 : 1
    CRX except HF .... 4.266 : 1 or 4.428 : 1
    CRX HF .... 2.954 : 1, 3.576 : 1 or 4.066 : 1

Transmission overhaul data

1st speed gear endfloat .... 0.03 to 0.18 mm (0.001 to 0.007 in)
    Endfloat adjustment .... Selective thrust washers
    Thrust washer thickness .... 1.89 to 1.92 mm (0.074 to 0.076 in), 1.92 to 1.95 mm (0.076 to 0.077 in), 1.95 to 1.98 mm (0.077 to 0.078 in)

2nd, 3rd and 4th speed gear endfloat .... 0.05 to 0.18 mm (0.002 to 0.007 in)
    Endfloat adjustment .... Selective spacer collars
    Spacer collar thickness .... 28.01 to 28.04 mm (1.103 to 1.104 in), 28.04 to 28.07 mm (1.104 to 1.105 in), 28.07 to 28.10 mm (1.105 to 1.106 in), 28.10 to 28.13 mm (1.106 to 1.107 in)

5th speed gear or end cover circlip thickness .... 0.500 to 1.575 mm (0.019 to 0.062 in), in 0.025 mm (0.001 in) increments
5th speed gear endfloat on mainshaft .... 0.05 to 0.4 mm (0.002 to 0.016 in)
Selector fork-to-synchro sleeve groove clearance .... 0.45 to 1.0 mm (0.018 to 0.039 in)
Baulk ring-to-gear clearance .... 0.40 mm (0.016 in) minimum
Differential pinion gear backlash .... 0.05 to 0.15 mm (0.002 to 0.006 in)
    Backlash adjustment .... Selective thrust washer
    Thrust washer thicknesses .... 0.7 to 1.0 mm (0.028 to 0.039 in) in 0.05 mm (0.002 in) increments
Differential side clearance .... 0.10 to 0.15 mm (0.004 to 0.006 in)
    Side clearance adjustment .... Selective circlips
    Circlip thickness .... 2.45 to 2.95 mm (0.096 to 0.116 in) in 0.10 mm (0.004 in) increments

Torque wrench settings

	Nm	lbf ft
Oil filler/level plug	45	33
Oil drain plug	40	29
Transmission-to-engine bolts	68	50
Transmission rear mounting-to-transmission bolts	65	47
Transmission right-hand mounting-to-transmission bolts	45	33
Engine-to-transmission connecting bracket:		
M10 bolt	45	33
M8 bolt	24	18
Lower suspension arm balljoint nuts	44	32
Tie-rod balljoint nuts	44	32
Gear lever pivot bolt	22	16
Gear selector torque rod to transmission	9	7
Torque rod mounting bracket bolts	22	16
Countershaft locknut	90	65
End cover bolts	12	9
Selector detent plugs	22	16
Transmission casing-to-flywheel housing bolts	27	20
Selector fork lock bolts	17	12
Reverse gear selector arm nut	24	17
Selector arm holder bolts	12	9
Selector arm-to-rod retaining bolt	22	18
Crownwheel retaining bolts	103	74

1 General description

The transmission is equipped with either four forward and one reverse gear or five forward and one reverse gear, according to model and country of export. The transmission is mounted transversely on the right-hand side of the engine, in line with the crankshaft.

The final drive (differential) unit is integral with the transmission and is located between the transmission and clutch housings. The transmission and differential both share the same lubricating oil.

The 1st, 2nd, 3rd, 4th and reverse gears are integral with the mainshaft and cannot be detached from the shaft. On five-speed transmissions the 5th speed synchro unit is splined to the mainshaft, while the 5th speed driven gear is free on the shaft.

The countershaft incorporates the final drive pinion and carries the 5th speed driving gear (where applicable), 1st/2nd and 3rd/4th synchro units. The 1st, 2nd, 3rd and 4th speed gears are free on the shaft.

Except for reverse gear, all gears are in constant mesh. The transmission operates by transmitting engine torque through the mainshaft and selected gear to the countershaft pinion, and then to the final drive (crownwheel), driveshafts and roadwheels.

If the transmission overhaul is necessary, due consideration should be given to the costs involved, since it is often more economical to obtain a service exchange or good secondhand transmission, rather than fit new parts to the existing unit.

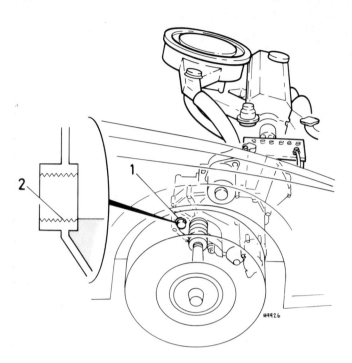

Fig. 6.1 Transmission oil level/filler plug location (1) and correct oil level (2) (Sec 2)

2 Maintenance and inspection

1   Periodically check the transmission oil level using the following procedure.
2   Have the car standing on level ground, then wipe clean the area around the filler/level plug located on the right-hand side of the transmission adjacent to the driveshaft (photo).
3   Unscrew the filler/level plug and check that the oil is up to the plug orifice (the oil should run out). If the level is low, top up with the specified oil type (photo). With the level correct refit and tighten the filler/level plug.
4   At the intervals given in 'Routine Maintenance' at the beginning of this Manual, the oil should be drained when hot and the transmission refilled with fresh oil as described above. The drain plug is located on the right-hand side of the transmission below the filler/level plug, and can be unscrewed using the square end of a $^3/_8$ in drive socket bar or ratchet (photo). After draining check the condition of the drain plug washer and renew it if at all damaged or deformed.
5   At the same service intervals inspect the transmission joint faces and oil seals for any signs of damage, deterioration or oil leakage.

3 Gearchange lever – removal and refitting

1   Working under the car, remove the pivot bolt and disconnect the gear lever from the selector remote control rod (photo).
2   Remove the gear lever washers, bushes and the spacer collar and the O-rings.
3   Remove the gear lever knob and the centre console (chapter 11).
4   Remove the rubber gaiter, extract the circlip and withdraw the gear lever (photo).
5   Remove the gear lever ball seat, retainer, O-rings and dust cover.
6   Renew any worn or deformed components.
7   Refitting is a reversal of removal. Apply grease to the spacer collar and tighten the pivot bolt to the specified torque.

2.2 Transmission oil level/filler plug location (arrowed)

2.3 Topping-up the transmission

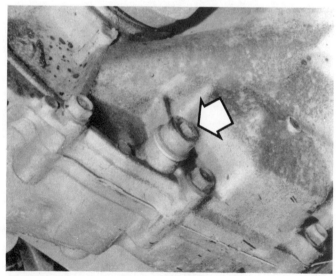

2.4 Transmission oil drain plug location (arrowed)

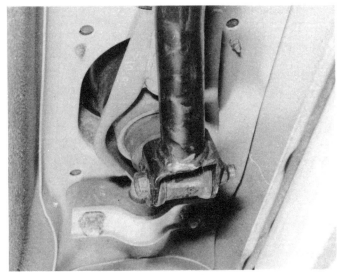

3.1 Gearchange lever connection to remote control rod

3.4 Gearchange lever retaining circlip (arrowed)

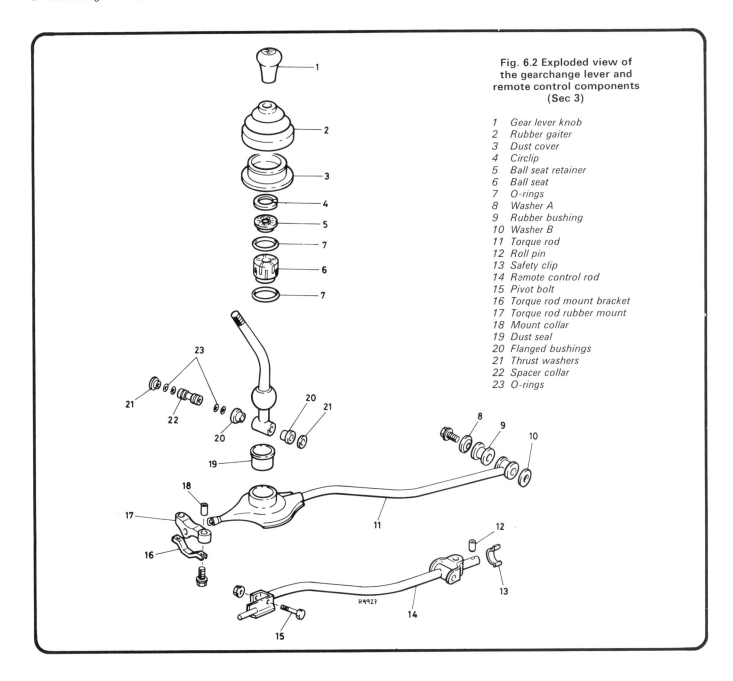

Fig. 6.2 Exploded view of
the gearchange lever and
remote control components
(Sec 3)

1   Gear lever knob
2   Rubber gaiter
3   Dust cover
4   Circlip
5   Ball seat retainer
6   Ball seat
7   O-rings
8   Washer A
9   Rubber bushing
10 Washer B
11 Torque rod
12 Roll pin
13 Safety clip
14 Remote control rod
15 Pivot bolt
16 Torque rod mount bracket
17 Torque rod rubber mount
18 Mount collar
19 Dust seal
20 Flanged bushings
21 Thrust washers
22 Spacer collar
23 O-rings

4 Selector shaft oil seal – renewal

1 Disconnect the torque rod from the transmission.
2 Slide the selector shaft safety clip aside and drive out the roll pin which secures the remote control rod to the selector shaft (photos).
3 Disconnect the remote control rod from the selector shaft.
4 Pull back the gaiter from the selector shaft at the transmission casing and prise out the shaft oil seal (photo).
5 Grease the lips of the new seal and drive it into position.
6 When refitting the gaiter make sure that the drain hole is at the bottom.
7 Reconnect the remote control rod, drive in the roll pin and fit the clip. Smear the joint with grease to prevent corrosion.
8 Reconnect the torque rod to the transmission.

5 Differential oil seals – renewal

1 The differential oil seals located behind each driveshaft inner constant velocity joint may be renewed without having to remove the transmission from the car.
2 Disconnect the battery negative terminal and drain the oil from the transmission.
3 Refer to Chapter 8 and remove the relevant driveshaft.
4 Using a large screwdriver or other suitable tool as a lever, carefully prise the oil seal out of the housing.
5 Apply grease to the lips of a new seal and drive it squarely into place using a hammer and block of wood. Ensure that the open side of the seal is towards the transmission.
6 Refit the driveshaft as described in Chapter 8.
7 Reconnect the battery, then fill the transmission as described in Section 2.

6 Transmission – removal and refitting

1 Refer to Chapter 12 if necessary and remove the battery and battery tray.
2 Disconnect the transmission casing earth cable.
3 Disconnect the reverse lamp switch leads.
4 Disconnect the speedometer drive cable from the transmission. Do this by pulling up the rubber cover and extracting the clip. *Do not unbolt the retaining plate or the speedo pinion will drop into the gearbox.*
5 Unbolt and move the starter motor aside.
6 Refer to Chapter 5 and disconnect the clutch cable at the transmission and release arm.

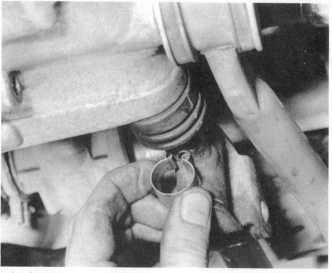
4.2A Selector shaft safety clip

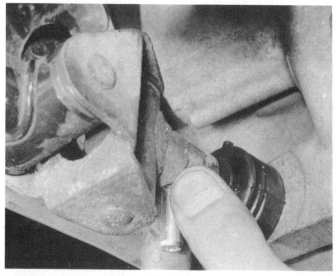
4.2B Removing the selector shaft roll pin

4.4 Selector shaft gaiter and oil seal

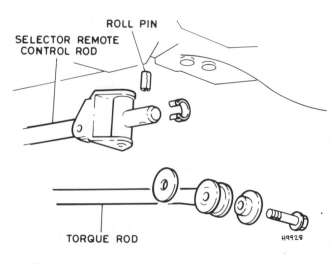
Fig. 6.3 Selector remote control rod and torque rod attachments at transmission (Sec 4)

7 Raise the front of the car and support it securely on axle stands.
8 Remove the front roadwheels.
9 Drain the transmission oil.
10 Remove the engine compartment undershield and right-hand splash shield.
11 Disconnect the gear selector and torque rods from the transmission as described in Section 4 (photo).
12 Support the lower suspension arms on jacks and unscrew the nuts from their balljoints.
13 Using a suitable splitter tool disconnect the balljoints from the steering knuckles. Make sure that the car is well supported when the balljoint is released, as the torque at the suspension arm is considerable (see Fig. 6.4).
14 Disconnect both steering tie-rod balljoints using the same tool as

for the suspension arm balljoints.
15 Prise both driveshafts from the transmission and lower them to the floor. Do this by inserting a lever between the transmission casing and the driveshaft inboard joint and prising against the tension of the shaft locking clip. The front suspension struts can now be pulled outwards within the limit of flexibility of their upper mountings and the driveshafts disconnected from the transmission. The left-hand brake pipe bracket may have to be released to prevent strain on the pipe.
16 Unbolt and remove the exhaust downpipe from the manifold and the rest of the exhaust system.
17 Support the engine using a hoist, or by placing a block of wood and jack under the sump.
18 Disconnect and remove the rear and right-hand transmission mountings.

6.11 Removing the torque rod from the transmission

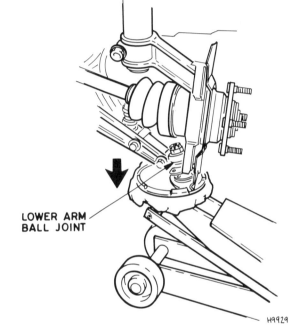

Fig. 6.4 Suspension lower arm correctly supported prior to disconnecting the balljoints (Sec 6)

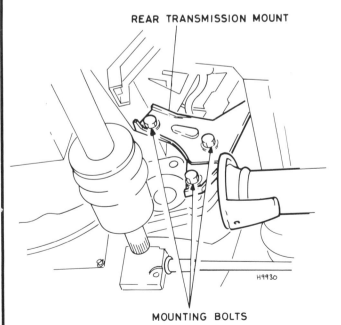

Fig. 6.5 Rear transmission mounting details (Sec 6)

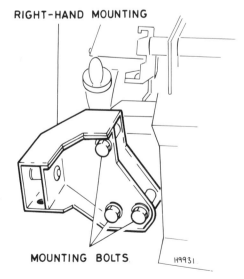

Fig. 6.6 Right-hand transmission mounting details (Sec 6)

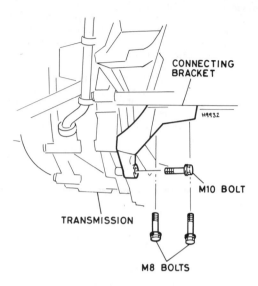

**Fig. 6.7 Engine-to-transmission connecting bracket bolt
locations (Sec 6)**

19 Using a second hoist or workshop jack, take the weight of the
transmission and then unscrew the engine-to-transmission connecting bolts and connecting bracket.
20 Unscrew and remove the cover plate bolts from the front face of the
clutch housing.
21 Withdraw the transmission until it comes off its positioning
dowels, then lower the unit to the floor and remove it from under the
car.
22 Refitting is the reverse sequence to removal, bearing in mind the
following points:

(a) *Smear a trace of molybdenum disulphide grease on the
transmission mainshaft splines*
(b) *Tighten all retaining nuts and bolts to the specified torque*
(c) *Fill the transmission with oil as described in Section 2*

7 Transmission overhaul – general

Transmission overhaul is a viable proposition only if minor items
require renewal such as a synchroniser assembly or worn bearing.
Where the transmission has covered a high mileage and is in a poor
condition, generally, major overhaul can be an expensive proposition.
In this case an exchange reconditioned unit is often the best solution.
Before starting any repair work, thoroughly clean the exterior of the
casings using paraffin or a suitable solvent. Dry the unit with a lint-free
rag. Make sure that an uncluttered working area is available with some
small containers and trays handy to store the various parts. Label
everything as it is removed.
Before starting reassembly all the components must be spotlessly
clean and should be liberally lubricated with the recommended grade
of gear oil during assembly.
Apart from the additional 5th speed gear and slight differences in
the selector mechanism, the four- and five-speed transmissions are
virtually identical, and the following Sections are applicable to both
types. Where any significant differences occur, these will be described
in the text.
After dismantling, all roll pins, circlips and staked nuts must be
renewed, regardless of condition, before reassembling.

8 Transmission – dismantling into major components

Five-speed transmission

1 With the transmission removed from the car, drain the oil if not
already done then, after cleaning the unit externally, place it on the
work bench.

2 Unbolt and remove the end cover from the end of the transmission
casing.
3 Extract the circlip and remove the dished spring washer or oil guide
plate (later models) from the end cover.
4 Draw off the mainshaft bearing.
5 Drive out 5th speed gear selector fork roll pin.
6 Push down the 5th gear synchro sleeve to lock the gears. Relieve
the staking on the nut on the end of the countershaft and unscrew the
nut.
7 Pull off the selector fork and 5th speed gear synchro sleeve
together as an assembly.
8 Remove 5th speed gear synchro hub, then the baulk ring and
spring.
9 Remove 5th speed gear.
10 Remove the needle roller bearing.
11 Remove the thrust washer.
12 Remove 5th speed gear, noting the boss is downwards. Remove
the dished washer, noting its concave side is downwards. Use a puller
if the gear is tight.
13 Unscrew the three selector detent plugs and extract the coil springs
and balls, using a pencil magnet if necessary.
14 Unbolt the clutch cable bracket.
15 Unscrew the connecting bolts and separate the transmission
casing from the flywheel housing. Do this by lifting the casing evenly
from the housing.
16 Drive out the differential oil seal and remove the circlip from the
transmission casing.
17 Expand the circlips and tap the mainshaft and countershaft
bearings from the transmission casing.
18 Withdraw the reverse idler gear shaft and the gear.
19 Unscrew the reverse gear selector arm nut, take off the special
washer and then remove the selector arm, the detent ball, and detent
spring. Note that the ball is of larger diameter than the other three
detent balls.
20 Bend up the lock tabs on the three selector fork lock bolts, unscrew
and remove the bolts.
21 Remove the 5th/reverse selector shaft and dog. The shaft chamfer
should be at the top.
22 Remove 1st/2nd selector shaft and then the 3rd/4th selector shaft
and dog.
23 Move the sleeve of the 1st/2nd synchro sleeve upwards into 2nd
gear position and withdraw the 1st/2nd gear selector fork.
24 Lift the mainshaft and countershaft from the flywheel housing as
an assembly meshed together.
25 Slide the selector arm from side to side to obtain access to the
selector arm holder bolts. Unscrew the bolts and remove the holder.
Remove the selector rod, detent ball and spring.
26 Lift the differential/final drive from the flywheel housing.
27 Remove the differential oil seal.
28 Remove the selector rod gaiter and oil seal.
29 Unbolt the retaining plate and withdraw the speedometer drivegear
pinion assembly.
30 Extract the countershaft bearing retainer plate screws. An impact
screwdriver will be required for this.
31 Remove the countershaft bearings from the flywheel housing.
32 Lift out the oil guide plate.
33 Remove the breather baffle plate from the flywheel housing.
34 Remove the mainshaft bearing and oil seal from the flywheel
housing.

Four-speed transmission

35 With the transmission removed from the car, drain the oil, if not
already done, then after cleaning the unit externally, place it on the
workbench.
36 Unbolt and remove the end cover from the end of the transmission
casing.
37 Extract the circlip and withdraw the dished washer (early models),
or oil guide plate (later models) from the end cover.
38 Draw off the bearing from the end of the mainshaft.
39 Relieve the staking on the countershaft nut then unscrew the nut.
To prevent the countershaft turning, either grip the mainshaft splines at
the flywheel housing end using a self-locking wrench and with the
transmission in gear (use rags to protect the splines), or use mainshaft
holder tool 07923 – 6890101.
40 The remainder of the procedure is identical to the five-speed
transmission described in paragraphs 13 to 34 inclusive.

Fig. 6.8 Exploded view of the transmission components
(Sec 8)

1 End cover
2 Washer
3 Reverse lamp switch
4 Countershaft locknut
5 Dished washer
6 5th speed driving gear
7 Circlip
8 Oil level/filler plug
9 Washer
10 Differential oil seal
11 Countershaft bearing
12 Oil guide plate (dished washer on early models)
13 Circlip

14 Mainshaft bearing
15 5th speed gear selector fork
16 Roll pin
17 5th gear synchro sleeve
18 5th gear synchro hub
19 Synchro spring
20 Baulk ring
21 5th speed driven gear
22 Needle roller bearing
23 Thrust washer
24 Detent plug
25 Washer
26 Detent spring
27 Detent ball

28 Transmission casing
29 Circlip
30 Clutch cable bracket
31 Breather assembly
32 Circlip
33 Mainshaft bearing
34 Oil drain plug
35 Sealing washer
36 Reverse idler gear shaft
37 Reverse idler gear
38 5th/reverse selector dog
39 5th/reverse selector shaft
40 3rd/4th selector dog
41 3rd/4th selector fork

42 3rd/4th selector shaft
43 1st/2nd selector fork
44 1st/2nd selector shaft
45 Countershaft assembly
46 Differential
47 Magnet holder
48 Magnet
49 Bearing retainer plate
50 Countershaft bearing
51 Oil guide plate
52 Selector arm holder
53 Lock plate
54 Mainshaft
55 Selector shaft arm

56 Dowel
57 Selector shaft oil seal
58 Selector shaft gaiter
59 Selector shaft
60 Flywheel housing
61 Differential oil seal
62 Dust seal
63 Detent spring
64 Detent ball
65 Screw
66 Speedometer pinion assembly

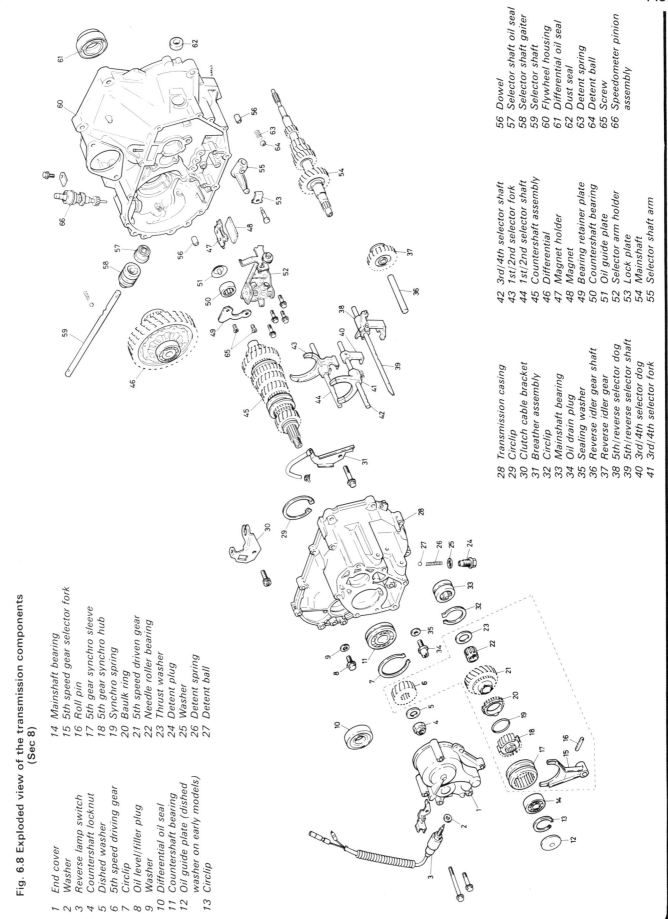

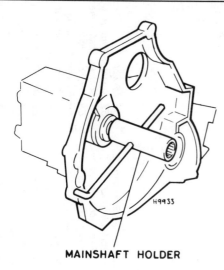

MAINSHAFT HOLDER

Fig. 6.9 Mainshaft holder tool – four-speed transmission (Sec 8)

9 Countershaft – dismantling and reassembly

1 Remove the flanged spacer collar.
2 Remove the 4th speed gear.
3 Remove the baulk ring and synchro ring.
4 Remove the 4th gear needle bearing.
5 Remove 3rd/4th synchro unit.
6 Remove 3rd speed gear baulk ring and spring.
7 Take off 3rd speed gear.
8 Remove the needle bearing and spacer collar.
9 Remove the spacer washer and 2nd speed gear.
10 Remove 1st/2nd synchro baulk ring and spring.
11 Remove the needle bearing and spacer collar.
12 Remove 1st/2nd synchro unit. The synchro sleeve incorporates reverse gear.
13 Take off 1st speed gear complete with baulk ring and spring.
14 Remove the needle bearing and thrust washer.
15 Clean and renew components as necessary (see Section 10), lightly oil and reassemble them as described in the following paragraphs.
16 Fit the thrust washer and needle bearing (photos).
17 Fit 1st speed gear complete with baulk ring (photos).
18 Fit 1st/2nd synchro unit with reverse followed by the baulk ring and spring, spacer sleeve and needle bearing (photos).

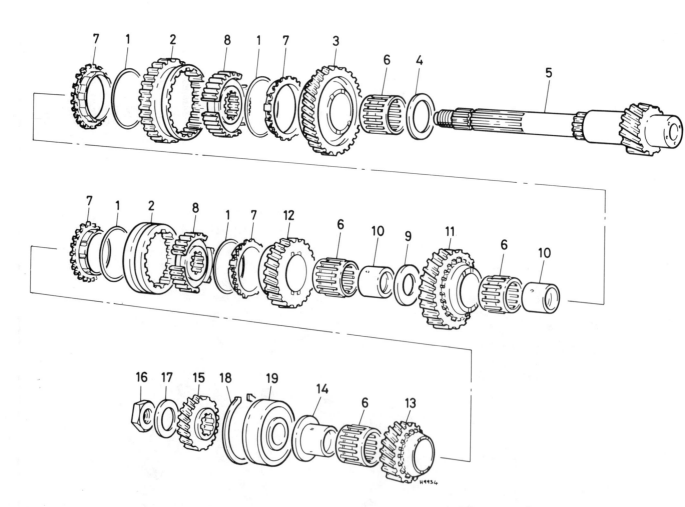

Fig. 6.10 Exploded view of the countershaft assembly (Sec 9)

1	Synchro spring	
2	Synchro sleeve	
3	1st gear	
4	1st gear 32 mm thrust washer	
5	Countershaft	
6	Needle bearing	
7	Baulk ring	
8	Synchro hub	
9	Spacer washer	
10	28 mm spacer collar	
11	2nd gear	
12	3rd gear	
13	4th gear	
14	Flanged spacer collar	
15	5th gear	
16	Locknut	
17	Dished washer	
18	65 mm circlip	
19	Ball bearing	

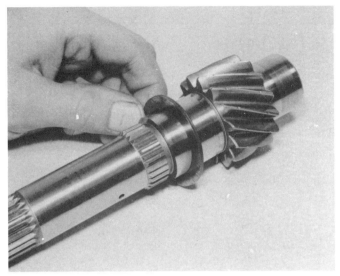

9.16A Fitting the thrust washer to the countershaft

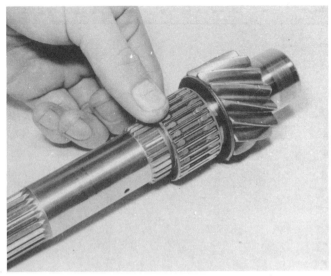

9.16B Fitting the needle roller bearing to the countershaft

9.17A Fitting 1st speed gear ...

9.17B ... and baulk ring

9.18A Fitting the 1st/2nd synchro unit, baulk ring and spring ...

9.18B ... followed by the spacer sleeve ...

9.18C ... and 2nd speed gear needle roller bearing

9.19 Fitting the 2nd speed gear ...

19 Fit 2nd speed gear (photo).
20 Fit the spacer washer (photo).
21 Fit the spacer collar and needle bearing (photos).
22 Fit 3rd speed gear (photo).
23 Fit the baulk ring and spring (photo).
24 Fit 3rd/4th speed synchro unit (photo).
25 Fit the needle bearing (photo).
26 Fit the baulk ring and spring.
27 Fit 4th speed gear (photo).
28 Fit the flanged spacer collar (photo).
29 Apply light pressure to the flanged spacer collar, measure and record the endfloat of all gears. Check against the specified tolerances and if outside the limit, change 1st speed gear thrust washer, 2nd or 3rd speed gear spacer collars or 4th speed gear flanged spacer collar as necessary to rectify matters.
30 Spacer thickness availability is given in the Specifications at the beginning of this Chapter.
31 If working on the five-speed transmission, place the 5th speed gear thrust washer on the mainshaft, followed by 5th speed gear, needle roller bearing and synchro unit. Apply pressure to the synchro hub and check the 5th speed gear endfloat. If not as specified, renew the thrust washer.

9.20 ... followed by the spacer washer

9.21A Fitting the 3rd speed gear spacer collar ...

9.21B ... followed by the needle roller bearing ...

9.22 ... the 3rd speed gear ...

9.23 ... and the baulk ring and spring

9.24 Fitting the 3rd/4th speed synchro unit

9.25 Fitting the needle roller bearing ...

9.27 ... 4th speed gear, baulk ring and spring ...

9.28 ... followed by the flanged spacer collar

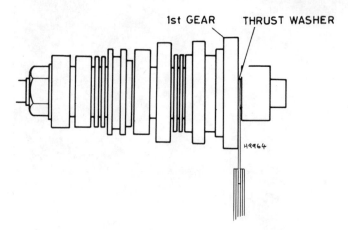

Fig. 6.11 Checking 1st speed gear endfloat (Sec 9)

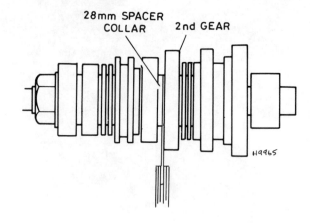

Fig. 6.12 Checking 2nd speed gear endfloat (Sec 9)

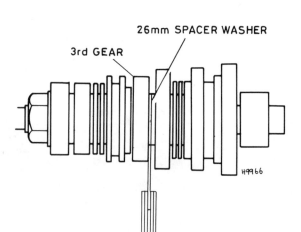

Fig. 6.13 Checking 3rd speed gear endfloat (Sec 9)

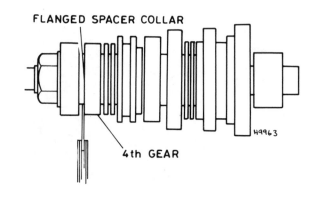

Fig. 6.14 Checking 4th speed gear endfloat (Sec 9)

10 Examination of components

1   Check the transmission casing and flywheel housing for cracks, especially around the bolt holes. Clean and refit the magnet.
2   Inspect all shafts for grooving or scoring and the gear teeth for chipping or wear.
3   Test the shaft bearings. If they are obviously shaky or rattle when spun, renew them. Always renew the bearings in the flywheel housing once they have been removed.
4   Check the clearance of the selector forks in their respective synchro sleeve grooves. If the clearance exceeds that specified, renew the fork.
5   Press each synchro baulk ring onto its gear cone at the same time applying a twisting motion. If the ring sticks firmly and has a minimum ring to gear clearance of 0.40 mm (0.016 in) then the parts are in good condition. If not, renew the baulk ring.
6   Wear in a synchroniser assembly will already be evident from noisy gear changing and by the fact that the synchro could be easily beaten when changing gear. In this case, renew the synchro unit complete.
7   If a synchroniser unit is dismantled, note the hub can only be fitted into the sleeve in one of three positions as there are master splines. Always mark which way round the hub is located in its sleeve before separating the components. No sliding keys are used with this type of synchromesh.
8   To dismantle the countershaft refer to the previous Section. The mainshaft cannot be dismantled as the gears are integral with the shaft. Any wear will therefore mean renewal of the mainshaft complete.
9   All oil seals and O-rings should be renewed as a matter of course and a new countershaft retaining nut should be used.

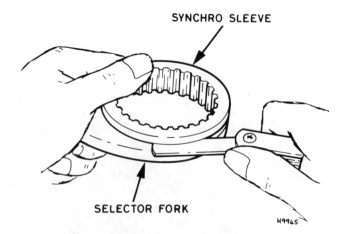

Fig. 6.15 Checking selector fork-to-synchro sleeve groove clearance (Sec 10)

11 Final drive differential – overhaul

1   Access to the differential is obtained by dismantling the transmission as described in Section 8.
2   It is rare for wear to occur in the differential or final drive components, but check visually for damaged teeth on the crownwheel, pinion and side gear teeth.

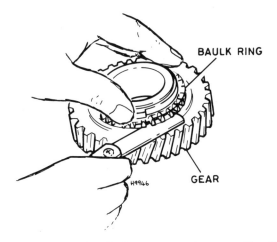

Fig. 6.16 Checking baulk ring-to-gear clearance (Sec 10)

BAULK RING

GEAR

DEEPER GROOVES

LONGER TEETH

SYNCHRO SLEEVE

SYNCHRO HUB

Fig. 6.17 Synchroniser sleeve-to-hub orientation (Sec 10)

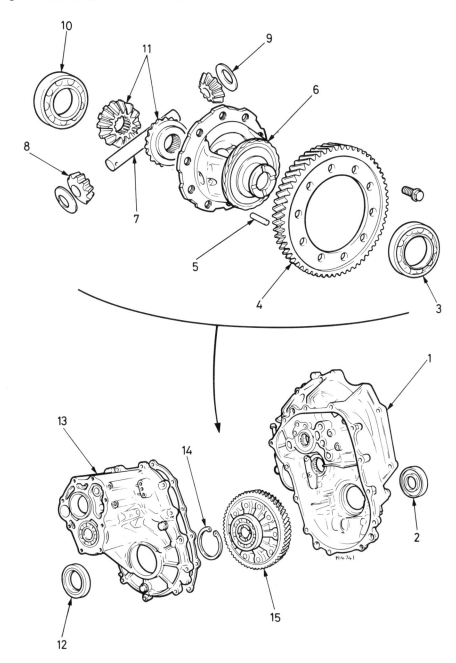

Fig. 6.18 Exploded view of the final drive differential (Sec 11)

1 Clutch housing
2 Seal
3 Ball bearing
4 Crownwheel
5 Roll pin
6 Carrier
7 Pinion shaft
8 Pinion gear
9 Thrust washer
10 Ball bearing
11 Side gears
12 Seal
13 Transmission casing
14 Snap ring
15 Differential assembly

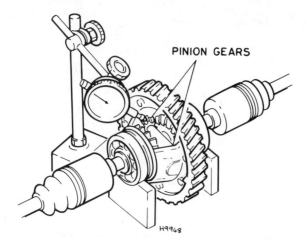

Fig. 6.19 Checking differential pinion gear backlash using a dial gauge (Sec 11)

3   To dismantle, first mark the relationship of the crownwheel to the differential carrier, and then unscrew the crownwheel bolts. *These bolts have a left-hand thread.*
4   Drive out the differential pinion shaft roll pin.
5   Tap the pinion shaft from the carrier.
6   Remove the pinion gears, thrust washers and side gears.
7   Using a suitable puller, draw off the differential carrier bearings.
8   Reassembly is a reversal of dismantling. Apply pressure only to the bearing inner tracks.
9   When refitting the crownwheel the chamfer on the flange should be towards the differential carrier and the positioning marks aligned. Use pinion thrust washers of identical thickness.
10   To check the backlash of both pinion gears the differential carrier should be supported on Vee blocks located under the bearings.
11   Temporarily connect the driveshafts and then check the pinion gear backlash with a dial gauge. If outside the specified limit, change the thrust washers. Thickness availability of these washers is given in the Specifications.

12 Transmission – reassembly

Five-speed transmission

1   Fit the mainshaft bearing and the new oil seal into the flywheel housing.
2   Fit the breather baffle into the flywheel housing.
3   Fit the oil guide plate.
4   Fit the countershaft bearing, its retainer plate and tighten the screws securely to the flywheel housing. Stake the screw heads (photos).
5   Fit the speedometer drivegear pinion assembly and secure it with the plate and screw (photo).
6   Fit the selector rod seal and gaiter.
7   If the differential bearings are being renewed, lightly drive the new bearing into the transmission casing to seat the circlip, then drive the differential into the flywheel housing until it is seated.
8   Mate the flywheel housing and transmission casing and check the clearance between the circlip and the differential bearing outer track (see Fig. 6.20). If this is not as specified, change the circlip for one of different thickness from the selection available (see Specifications) (photo).
9   Remove the transmission casing and have the differrntial located in the flywheel housing (photo).
10   Insert the larger spring and ball in the hole in the flywheel housing, depress the ball and insert the selector rod. Fit the selector arm to the rod, tighten the lock bolt and bend up the lockplate tab (photos).
11   Fit the selector arm holder with the selector arm corrctly located. Tighten the holder bolts to the specified torque.
12   Fit the mainshaft and countershaft simultaneously with their gears meshed together, into the flywheel housing (photos).
13   Move the 1st/2nd synchro sliding sleeve into 2nd gear position and locate the 1st/2nd selector fork in the sleeve groove (photo).
14   Fit 3rd/4th selector shaft and fork (photo).
15   Fit the 1st/2nd gear selector shaft (photo).
16   Locate the 5th/reverse selector dog and insert the selector shaft through it (photo).
17   Check that the detent grooves on the selector shafts are furthest from the flywheel housing and are also facing towards the outside of the transmission casing.
18   Tighten the three selector shaft fork lock bolts using new lockplates and bend up their tabs (photos).
19   Fit the reverse detent spring and ball followed by reverse selector arm, special washer and the nut (photos).
20   Fit reverse idler gear and shaft (photo).

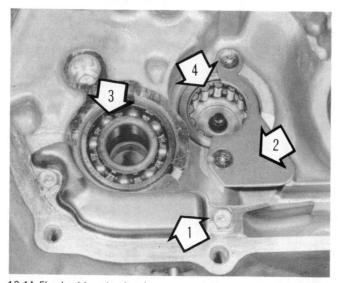

12.4A Flywheel housing bearing components

12.4B Securing the countershaft bearing retainer plate

1   *Breather baffle*   3   *Mainshaft bearing*
2   *Bearing retainer plate*   4   *Countershaft bearing*

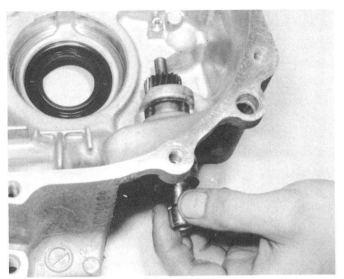

12.5A Fitting the speedometer drive gear pinion ...

12.5B ... and retaining plate

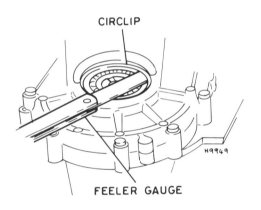

Fig. 6.20 Checking differential side clearance (Sec 12)

12.8 Differential bearing and circlip

12.9 Fitting the differential to the flywheel housing

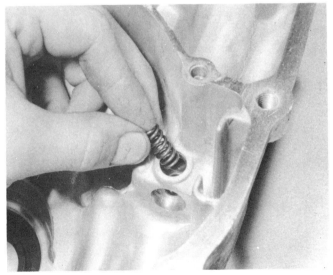

12.10A Fitting the selector rod detent spring ...

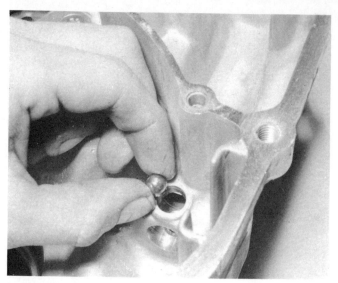

12.10B ... followed by the detent ball

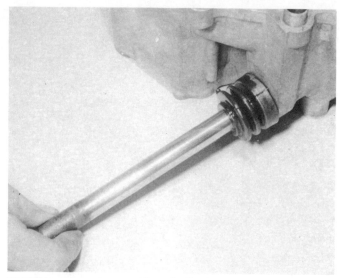

12.10C Inserting selector rod into the flywheel housing

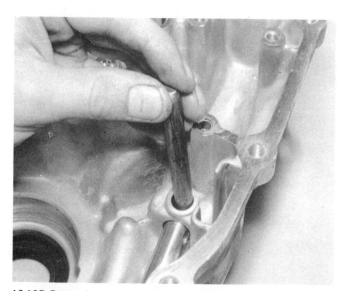

12.10D Depressing selector rod detent ball

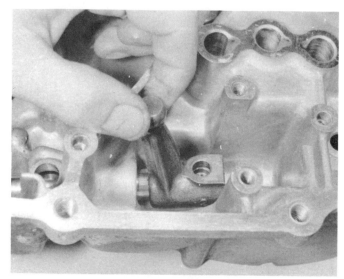

12.10E Fitting the selector arm to the rod

12.10F Selector arm secured with bolt and lockplate

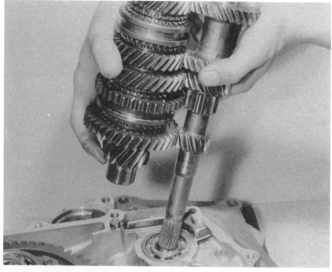

12.12A Geartrains held in mesh ...

12.12B ... and fitted into flywheel housing

12.13 1st/2nd selector fork engaged with synchro sleeve and selector arm holder

12.14 Fitting 3rd/4th selector shaft and fork

12.15 Fitting 1st/2nd selector shaft

12.16 Fitting 5th/reverse selector shaft

12.18A Tightening selector shaft fork lockbolts

12.18B Securing lockbolts with the lockplate tabs

12.19A Fitting reverse detent spring ...

12.19B ... followed by the detent ball

12.19C Fitting reverse selector arm

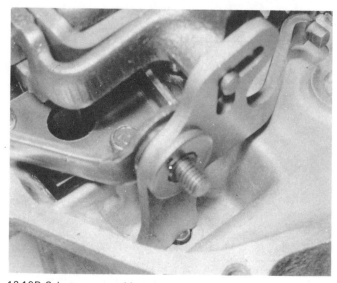

12.19D Selector arm positioned correctly over detent ball

12.19E Fitting the selector arm special washer ...

12.19F ... and the retaining nut

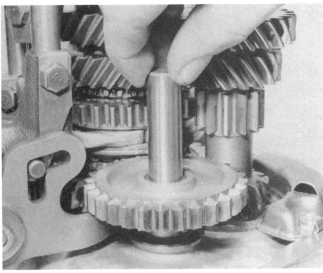

12.20 Locating reverse idler gear and shaft in position

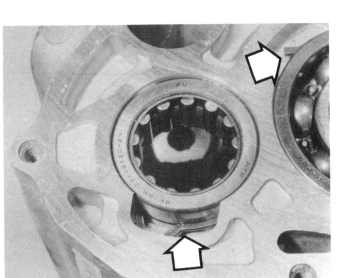

12.21 Transmission casing bearing circlips (arrowed)

12.22A Applying transmission casing sealant

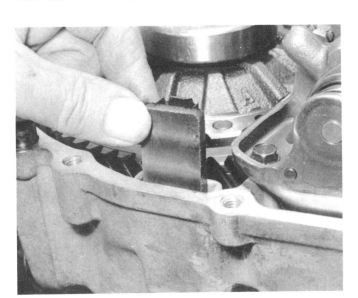

12.22B Fitting the magnet

21 Expand the mainshaft and countershaft bearing circlips using strong circlip pliers and fit the bearings into the transmission casing (photo).
22 Check that the positioning dowels are in place in the transmission casing flange and apply a thin bead of RTV sealant to the joint face. Fit the magnet (photos).
23 Lightly oil the shaft ends and differential bearing to facilitate the connection of the transmission casing and the flywheel housing.
24 Fit the casing to the housing and insert and tighten the connecting bolts to the specified torque and in the sequence shown (Fig. 6.21) (photos).
25 Fit the clutch cable bracket (photo).
26 Fit the detent balls, springs and plugs (photos).
27 Fit 5th speed gear to the countershaft so that its boss is towards the bearing (photo).
28 Fit the dished washer (concave side to the gear) (photo).
29 Fit 5th speed synchro hub and bearing onto the mainshaft. Using a depth gauge, measure the height 'A' in Fig. 6.22. Take the average of three measurements around the bearing.
30 Remove the bearing and synchro hub from the mainshaft. Extract the circlip and remove the dished washer or oil guide plate from the end cover if not already done (photo).

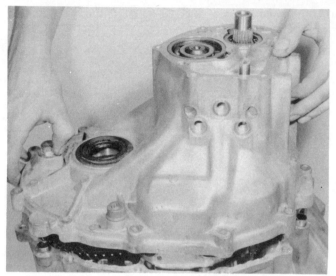

12.24A Mating transmission casing to flywheel housing ...

12.24B ... and securing with retaining bolts

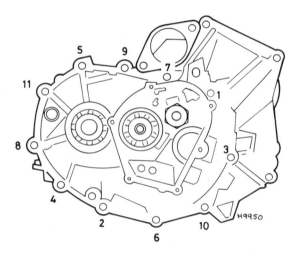

Fig. 6.21 Transmission casing bolt tightening sequence
(Sec 12)

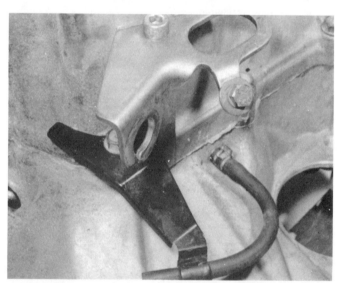

12.25 Clutch cable bracket and breather hose location

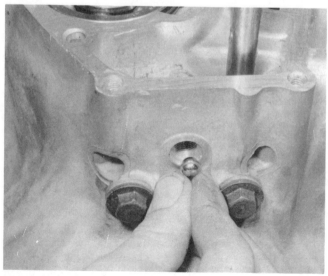

12.26A Installing selector shaft detent ball ...

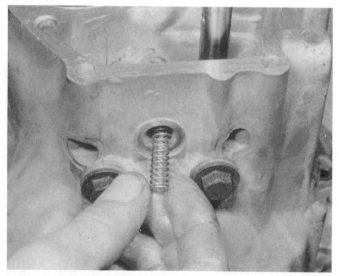

12.26B ... detent spring ...

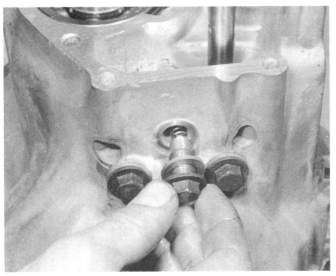

12.26C ... and detent plug

12.27 Fitting 5th speed gear to the countershaft ...

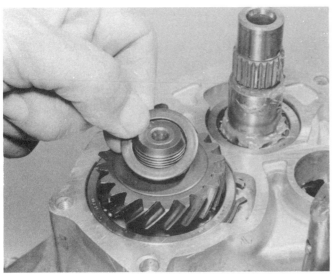

12.28 ... followed by the dished washer

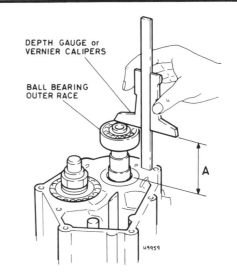

Fig. 6.22 Measuring 5th speed bearing height (Sec 12)

A = Height above casing

DEPTH GAUGE or
VERNIER CALIPERS

BALL BEARING
OUTER RACE

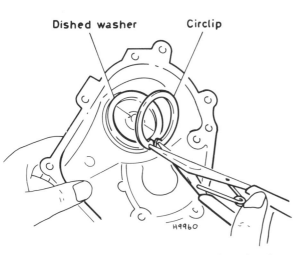

Dished washer   Circlip

Fig. 6.23 Removing the circlip and dished washer from
the end cover – early models (Sec 12)

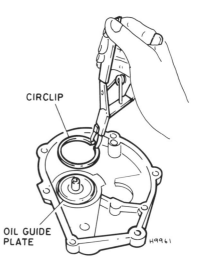

CIRCLIP

OIL GUIDE
PLATE

Fig. 6.24 Removing the circlip and oil guide plate from
the end cover – later models (Sec 12)

12.30 Oil guide plate and selective circlip in end cover

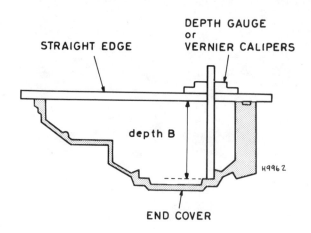

Fig. 6.25 Measuring the end cover internal depth 'B'
(Sec 12)

31 Place a straight edge across the mounting flange of the end cover
and using the depth gauge, measure the dimension 'B' (Fig. 6.25).
Take the average of three measurements into the circlip seat at
equidistant points and subtract the thickness of the straight edge from
the measurements.
32 To calculate the thickness of the 5th speed gear circlip use the
following formula:

Early models with dished washer behind circlip:
*B – A – 0.85 mm (thickness of dished washer) = thickness of
circlip required*
Later models with oil guide plate behind circlip:
*B – A – 0.11 to 0.18 mm (standard clearance) = thickness of
circlip required*

33 Fit the dished washer or oil guide plate to the end cover followed
by the circlip. Note that it is permissible to use two circlips if necessary
to obtain the required thickness.
34 Fit 5th speed gear thrust washer, 5th speed gear and needle roller
bearing to the mainshaft (photos).

12.34A Fitting the mainshaft 5th gear thrust washer ...

12.34B ... needle roller bearing ...

12.34C ... and 5th speed gear

35 Fit the synchro baulk ring and spring.
36 Fit the synchro hub with its recessed side towards 5th speed gear (photo).
37 Engage the selector fork in the groove of the 5th speed gear synchro sleeve (chamfered side of sleeve furthest from gear) and fit the sleeve and fork to the shaft as an assembly. Remember that the sleeve will only slide onto the hub on one of three positions due to the location of the master splines. Lock up the geartrains by pushing 5th speed gear synchro sleeve downwards (photo).
38 Tighten the new countershaft locknut to the specified torque. Slacken the nut and then tighten to the specified torque for the second time. Stake the nut into the shaft groove (photos).
39 Drive in 5th gear selector fork roll pin (photo).
40 Fit the mainshaft ball bearing so that the engraved numbers are visible when fitted (photo).
41 Apply RTV sealant to the flange joint, check that the positioning dowels are in place and bolt on the end cover, complete with selected circlip and dished washer or oil guide plate (photo).
42 Screw in the reverse lamp switch (photo).
43 Check the selection of all gears by moving the selector shaft.
44 Fit the clutch release shaft and bearing (if removed).

12.36 Fitting 5th speed synchro hub

12.37 5th speed synchro sleeve and selector fork fitted as an assembly

12.38A Tightening the countershaft nut

12.38B Using hammer and punch to stake the countershaft nut

12.39 Fitting 5th speed selector fork roll pin

12.40 Fitting mainshaft bearing

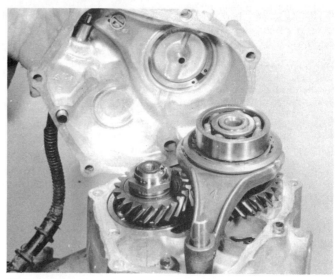

12.41 Locating the end cover onto the casing

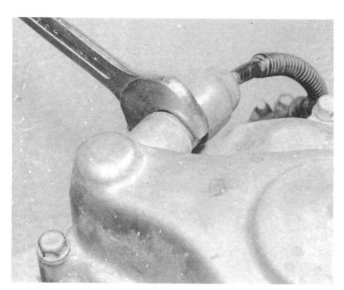

12.42 Fitting the reverse lamp switch

Four-speed transmission

45 Carry out the operations described in paragraphs 1 to 26 inclusive.
46 Fit the mainshaft bearing onto the mainshaft, and using a depth gauge measure the height 'A' (fig. 6.26). Take the average of three measurements around the bearing.
47 Remove the bearing from the mainshaft. Extract the circlip and remove the dished washer or oil guide plate from the end cover if not already done.
48 Calculate the thickness of end cover circlip required, using the same procedure as for the 5th speed gear circlip described in paragraphs 31 to 33 inclusive.
49 Lock the countershaft using the same method used during dismantling and screw on a new countershaft locknut. Tighten the nut to the specified torque, slacken it off then tighten once more. Stake the nut into the shaft groove.

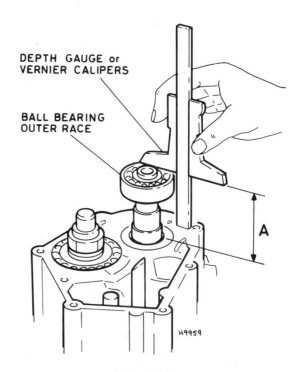

DEPTH GAUGE or
VERNIER CALIPERS

BALL BEARING
OUTER RACE

A

H9959

Fig. 6.26 Measuring mainshaft bearing height – four-speed transmission (Sec 12)

A = Height above casing

50 Apply RTV sealant to the flange joint, check that the positioning dowels are in place and bolt on the end cover.
51 Screw in the reverse lamp switch.
52 Check the selection of all gears by moving the selector shaft.
53 Fit the clutch release shaft and bearing (if removed).

13 Fault diagnosis – manual transmission

Symptom	Reason(s)
Gearbox noisy in neutral	Mainshaft bearings worn
Gearbox noisy only when moving (in all gears)	Countershaft bearings worn Differential bearings worn Differential final drive gear or countershaft pinion chipped or worn
Gearbox noisy in only one gear	Worn, damaged or chipped gear teeth Worn needle roller bearings
Gearbox jumps out of gear	Worn synchro hubs or synchro sleeves Weak or broken selector shaft detent spring Weak or broken gearchange shaft detent spring Worn shaft detent grooves Worn selector forks
Ineffective synchromesh	Worn baulk rings or synchro hubs
Difficulty in engaging gears	Clutch fault Ineffective synchromesh Worn gear lever bushes and linkage

Chapter 7 Automatic transmission

Contents

Specifications

General

Type .... Hydraulically-controlled dual-shaft, constant mesh geartrain. Three element torque converter with top gear lock-up

Gear ratios

UK models:	1300 cc	1500 cc
1st	1.782 : 1	1.782 : 1
2nd	1.206 : 1	1.133 : 1
3rd	0.828 : 1	0.777 : 1
Reverse	1.954 : 1	1.954 : 1

North American models:

Three-speed transmission up to 1986:		
1st	2.380 : 1	
2nd	1.560 : 1	
3rd	0.911 : 1	
Reverse	1.954 : 1	

Four-speed transmission – 1986-on:	All models except CRX	CRX models
1st	2.500 : 1	2.500 : 1
2nd	1.560 : 1	1.500 : 1
3rd	1.031 : 1	0.969 : 1
4th	0.777 : 1	0.729 : 1
Reverse	1.954 : 1	1.954 : 1

Final drive ratios

UK models	3.588 : 1
North American models:	
1984 (three-speed transmission):	
Hatchback and CRX	3.588 : 1
Sedan and Wagon	3.875 : 1
1985 (three-speed transmission):	
Hatchback, and CRX for California	3.588 : 1
Sedan, Wagon, and CRX except California	3.875 : 1
1986 (four-speed transmission):	
All models	3.933 : 1

Throttle control (kickdown) cable adjusting dimension

UK models	84.0 to 84.5 mm (3.307 to 3.327 in)
North American models	85.5 mm (3.366 in)

Torque wrench settings

	Nm	lbf ft
Fluid drain plug	40	29
Transmission-to-engine bolts	68	50
Transmission rear mounting-to-transmission bolts	65	47
Transmission right-hand mounting-to-transmission bolts	45	33
Engine to transmission connecting bracket:		
M10 bolt	45	33
M8 bolt	24	18
Lower arm balljoint nuts	44	32
Tie-rod balljoint nuts	44	32

1 General description

The Hondamatic automatic transmission consists of a torque converter, dual shaft constant mesh geartrain, and hydraulically operated clutches and shift mechanism. The transmission incorporates the final drive differential and is mounted in line with the engine crankshaft at the front of the car. Two different types of transmission are fitted to models covered by this manual. UK models and North American models up to 1986 are fitted with a three-speed transmission, whereas North American models from 1986 onwards utilize a four-speed unit.

The torque converter provides a fluid coupling between engine and transmission which acts as an automatic clutch and also provides a degree of torque multiplication when accelerating. The torque converter also incorporates an overdrive lock-up facility for improved fuel economy during sustained high speed cruising.

The geartrain provides one of three forward (or four forward on later North American models) or one reverse gear ratio, according to which combination of gears is engaged by the clutches and shift mechanism. The clutches and shift mechanism are activated by hydraulic valves, with hydraulic pressure being supplied by an oil pump within the transmission.

Due to the complexity of modern automatic transmissions and the need for professional facilities and equipment for repair and overhaul, the contents of this Chapter are limited to operations which can be carried out by the diy mechanic without recourse to special tools or equipment.

2 Maintenance and inspection

1   Periodically check the transmission fluid level using the following procedure.
2   Run the engine until normal operating temperature is reached, or preferably take the car on a short journey.
3   With the car standing on level ground, wipe clean the area around the transmission fluid dipstick at the right-hand end of the transmission casing.
4   Switch off the engine, and within one minute of doing this unscrew the dipstick, wipe it on a clean lint free rag, reinsert it (without screwing it down), withdraw it once more and note the fluid level. This should be between the full and low marks on the dipstick.
5   If topping-up is necessary, do this through the dipstick hole using the specified type of fluid. Take care not to overfill the transmission.
6   On completion refit the dipstick and screw it into place.
7   At intervals given in Routine Maintenance at the beginning of this Manual drain and refill the transmission using the procedure described in the following Section.
8   At the same service intervals carefully inspect the transmission joint faces and oil seals for any signs of damage, deterioration or oil leakage.

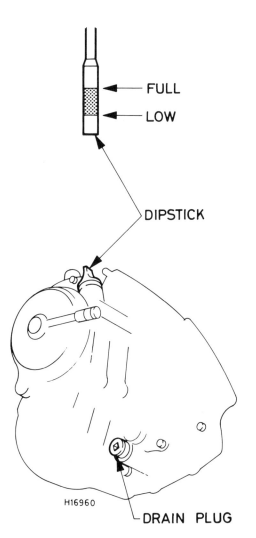

Fig. 7.1 Transmission fluid dipstick and drain plug locations – three-speed transmission (Secs 2 and 3)

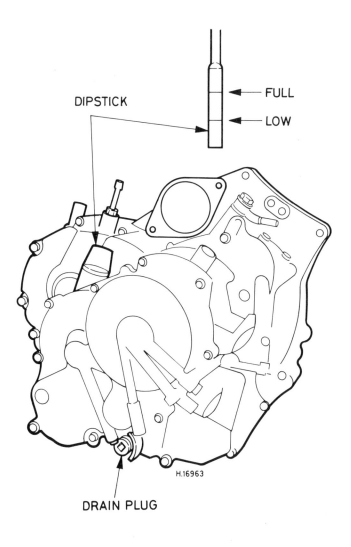

Fig. 7.2 Transmission fluid dipstick and drain plug locations – four-speed transmission (Secs 2 and 3)

3 Transmission fluid – draining and refilling

1   It is preferable to drain the fluid when the transmission is warm, such as after a short journey.
2   With the car on level ground place a suitable container beneath the transmission, unscrew the drain plug and allow the fluid to drain.
3   Refit the drain plug when all the fluid has drained, but renew the drain plug washer if it is at all damaged or deformed.
4   Wipe the area around the dipstick at the right-hand end of the casing, unscrew the dipstick and fill the transmission, using the specified type and quantity of fluid, through the dipstick hole. While filling, periodically insert the dipstick (without screwing it down) and check the level. Continue adding fluid until the level reaches the full mark on the dipstick. Take care not to overfill the transmission.
5   On completion, refit the dipstick and screw it into place. Take the car on a short trip to warm up the fluid, then recheck the level as described in Section 2.

4 Selector cable – adjustment

1   Refer to Chapter 11 and remove the centre console.
2   Place the selector lever in the D3, D4 or * position according to model and transmission type.
3   Prise off the lock pin from the selector cable adjuster (Fig. 7.3).
4   Check that the hole in the selector cable and cable adjuster are in exact alignment. If this is not the case, slacken the locknut and turn the adjuster a quarter of a turn in whichever direction is necessary to achieve alignment. Note that there are two holes in the adjuster at 90° to each other for this purpose.
5   When the holes are aligned, tighten the locknut, then refit the lock pin and centre console.

5 Selector cable – removal and refitting

1   Place the transmission in neutral, then jack up the front of the car and support it on stands.
2   Remove the engine compartment undershield.
3   Refer to Chapter 3 and remove the exhaust front pipe.
4   Remove the torque converter cover plate.
5   Extract the split pin from the selector cable retaining pin, then withdraw the pin.
6   Remove the cable holder and carefully withdraw the cable assembly from the transmission. Take care not to lose the selector cable bush.
7   Remove the centre console as described in Chapter 11.
8   Refer to Fig. 7.3 and prise off the selector cable lock pin. Withdraw the cable from the selector lever housing and remove it from under the car.
9   Refitting is the reverse sequence to removal, but adjust the cable as described in Section 4.

6 Selector lever assembly – removal, overhaul and refitting

1   Remove the centre console as described in Chapter 11.
2   Disconnect the starter inhibitor/reverse lamp switch connector plug, also the selector index illumination lead.
3   Extract the screws which retain the index plate.
4   Select R and remove the selector cable lock pin.
5   Unscrew the selector lever retaining nuts and remove the lever assembly.
6   To dismantle the assembly, extract the securing screws and withdraw the handle from the lever. Remove the push-button and spring.
7   Select N and remove the starter inhibitor/reverse lamp switch.
8   Remove the index panel and twist the lamp through 90° to remove it.
9   Release the spring and remove the detent lever. Withdraw the pivot bolt and withdraw the selector lever.
10 Reassembly and refitting are reversals of removal and dismantling.

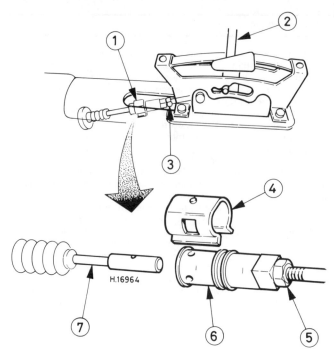

Fig. 7.3 Selector cable adjustment details (Sec 4)

1   Lock pin
2   Selector lever
3   Locknut
4   Lock pin
5   Lock nut
6   Adjuster
7   Selector cable

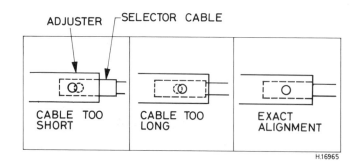

Fig. 7.4 Selector cable and cable adjuster adjustment conditions (Sec 4)

Smear the pivots and rubbing surfaces with grease and check operation after installation.

7 Throttle control (kickdown) cable – adjustment

1   Start the engine and allow it to reach normal operating temperature; the radiator cooling fan should operate at least twice.
2   Refer to Chapter 3 and ensure that the engine is idling at the specified speed and that the accelerator cable free play is correct.
3   Switch off the engine.
4   Disconnect the throttle control cable from the control lever and bracket on the transmission.
5   On UK models, lay the disconnected cable across the radiator cap (Fig. 7.7). On North American models lay the cable across the battery (Fig. 7.8).
6   Attach a 1.3 kg (1.6 lb) weight to the accelerator pedal, lift the pedal, then release it and allow the weight to take up the free play.
7   On North American models disconnect the vacuum hose from the carburettor throttle controller diaphragm. Connect a suitable length of

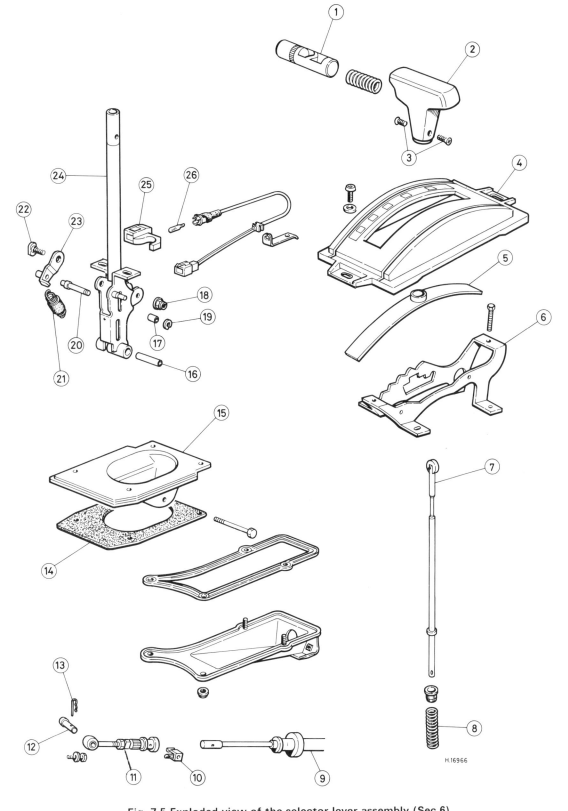

Fig. 7.5 Exploded view of the selector lever assembly (Sec 6)

1	Push button	8	Detent spring	15	Selector lever bracket	21 Stop spring
2	Handle	9	Shift cable	16	Collar	22 Stop bolt
3	Screw	10	Lock pin	17	Collar	23 Stop
4	Indicator panel	11	Adjuster	18	Nut	24 Selector lever
5	Lever cover	12	Control rod pin	19	Clip	25 Bulb housing
6	Selector mount bracket	13	Lock pin	20	Lock	26 Bulb
7	Detent lever	14	Seat			

tube to the diaphragm outlet and apply suction, either by mouth or using a vacuum pump, to simulate the action of the diaphragm under normal driving conditions.

8 Measure the distance between the end of the disconnected cable and the first locknut (locknut 'A' – Fig. 7.10). Compare the dimension obtained with the adjusting dimension given in the Specifications according to transmission type and model year.

9 Turn locknut 'A' to achieve the specified dimension, then ensure that the locknut remains undisturbed for the remainder of the procedure.

10 Reconnect the cable end and outer cable, and secure the cable by turning locknut 'B' only.

11 Depress the accelerator pedal and make sure that the cable moves freely.

12 Remove the weight on the pedal and check that there is 2.0 to 4.0 mm (0.078 to 0.157 in) of free play at the throttle control lever with the pedal at rest.

13 Start the engine and check that the throttle control lever just starts to move as the engine speed is increased off the idle. If the lever starts to move before the engine speed rises, move locknut 'A' anti-clockwise slightly. If the speed rises before the lever moves, turn locknut 'A' slightly clockwise.

14 On completion switch off the engine, ensure that the two locknuts are securely tightened and, where applicable, reconnect the diaphragm vacuum hose.

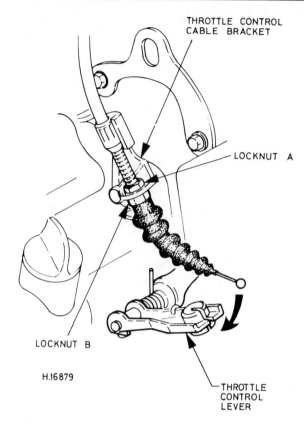

Fig. 7.6 Throttle control cable attachments at the transmission (Sec 7)

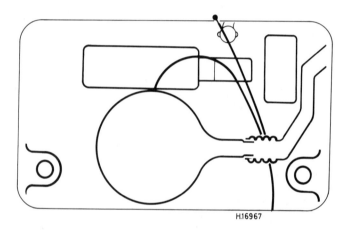

Fig. 7.7 Throttle cable position for adjustment – UK models (Sec 7)

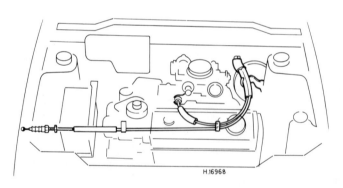

Fig. 7.8 Throttle control cable position for adjustment – North American models (Sec 7)

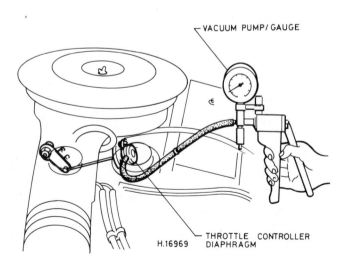

Fig. 7.9 Using a vacuum pump to actuate the throttle controller diaphragm – North American models (Sec 7)

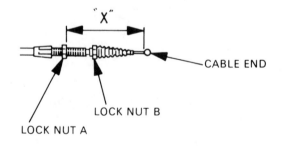

Fig. 7.10 Throttle control cable adjustment points (Sec 7)

'X' = adjusting dimension

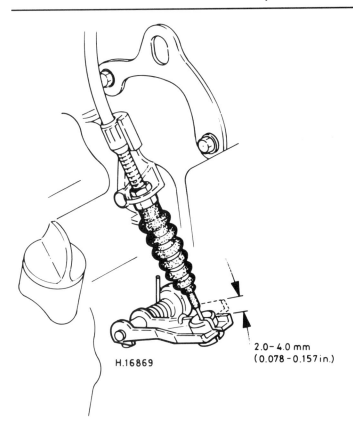

Fig. 7.11 Throttle control lever specified free play (Sec 7)

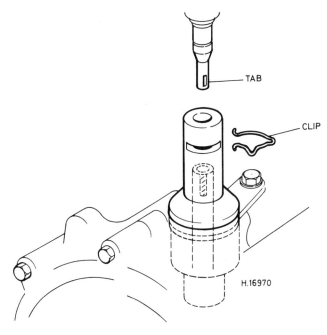

Fig. 7.12 Speedometer cable attachment details (Sec 9)

8 Throttle control (kickdown) cable – removal and refitting

On automatic transmission models the throttle control cable is removed in conjunction with the accelerator cable and reference should be made to Chapter 3, Section 9.

9 Automatic transmission – removal and refitting

In the event of a fault occurring on the transmission, it is first necessary to determine whether it is of a mechanical or hydraulic nature and to do this the transmission must be in the car. Special test equipment is necessary for this purpose, together with a systematic test procedure, and the work should be entrusted to a suitably equipped Honda dealer or automatic transmission specialist.

Do not remove the transmission from the car for repair or overhaul until professional fault diagnosis has been carried out.
1   Disconnect and remove the battery and remove its tray.
2   Disconnect the speedometer cable from the transmission by pulling up the rubber cover and extracting the retaining clip.
3   Disconnect the transmission earth cable.
4   Disconnect the leads from the starter motor, then unbolt and remove the starter motor.
5   Disconnect the transmission fluid cooler hoses and plug them.
6   Drain the transmission fluid.
7   Raise the front of the car and support it securely, then remove the front roadwheels.
8   Remove the engine compartment undershield and right-hand splash shield.
9   Support the lower suspension arms on jacks and unscrew the nuts from their balljoints.
10 Using a suitable splitter tool, disconnect the balljoints from the steering knuckles. Make sure that the car is well supported when the

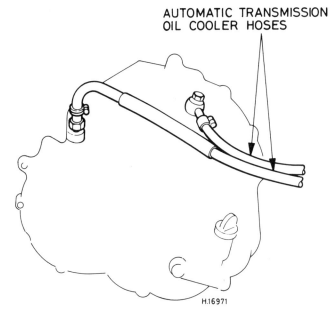

Fig. 7.13 Transmission fluid cooler hoses and connections (Sec 9)

balljoint is released as the torque at the suspension arm is considerable (see Fig. 7.14).
11 Disconnect both steering tie-rod balljoints using the same tool as for the suspension arm balljoint.
12 Prise both driveshafts from the transmission and lower them to the floor. Do this by inserting a lever between the transmission casing and the driveshaft inboard joint and prising against the tension of the shaft locking clip. The front suspension struts can now be pulled outwards within the limit of flexibility of their upper mountings, and the driveshafts disconnected from the transmission. The left-hand brake-pipe bracket may have to be released to prevent strain on the pipe.

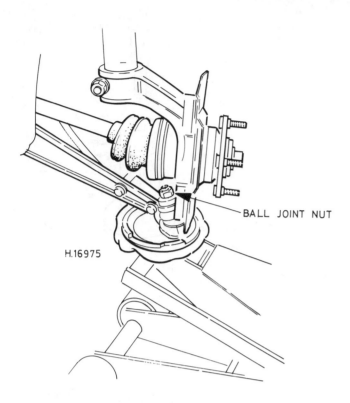

Fig. 7.14 Suspension lower arm correctly supported prior to disconnecting the balljoint (Sec 9)

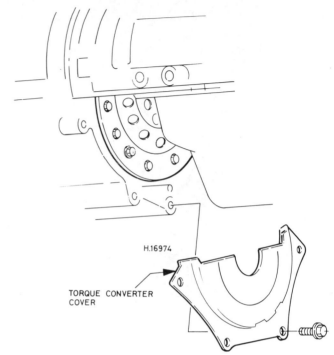

Fig. 7.15 Torque converter cover plate details (Sec 9)

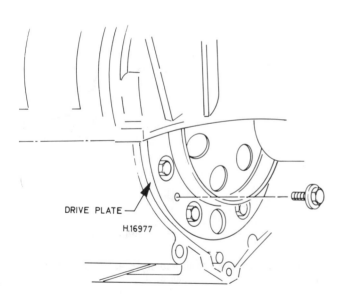

Fig. 7.16 Torque converter-to-drive plate retaining bolt locations (Sec 9)

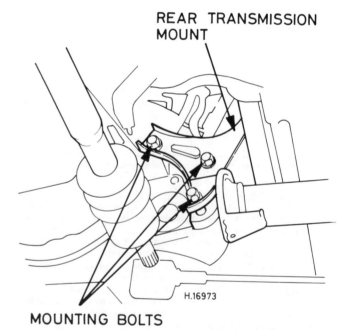

Fig. 7.17 Rear transmission mounting details (Sec 9)

13 Unbolt and remove the exhaust downpipe from the manifold and the rest of the exhaust system.

14 Unbolt and remove the torque converter cover plate.

15 Disconnect the selector cable and the kickdown cable from the transmission.

16 Working through the aperture left by removal of the torque converter cover plate, unscrew the bolts which hold the driveplate to

the torque converter. The crankshaft will have to be turned by means of its pulley bolt to bring the bolts into view.

17 Support the weight of the engine either on a hoist or by locating a jack and block of wood as an insulator under the sump.

18 Disconnect and remove the rear and right-hand transmission mountings.

19 Using a second hoist or workshop jack, take the weight of the

RIGHT-HAND MOUNTING

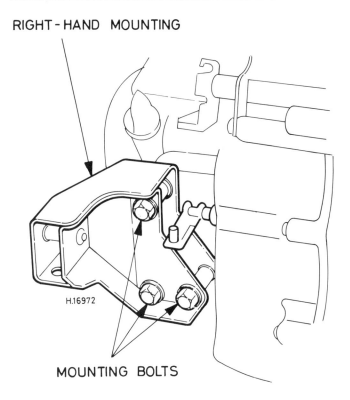

H.16972

MOUNTING BOLTS

Fig. 7.18 Right-hand transmission mounting details (Sec 9)

CONNECTING BRACKET

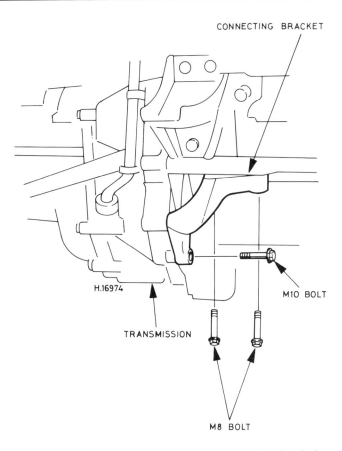

H.16974

TRANSMISSION

M10 BOLT

M8 BOLT

Fig. 7.19 Engine-to-transmission connecting bracket bolt locations (Sec 9)

transmission and then unscrew the engine-to-transmission connecting bolts and connecting bracket.

20 Withdraw the transmission until it comes off its positioning dowels, then lower it to the floor and remove it from under the car. During the removal operations, have an assistant keep the torque converter pushed fully into the bellhousing and retain it afterwards using a plate bolted to the bellhousing flange. Failure to do this may damage the fluid seal and will cause loss of fluid.

21 If the transmission is being changed for a new or reconditioned unit, make sure that you take off any items which are not supplied with the new unit. Check with your supplier.

22 Refitting is a reversal of removal. Tighten all bolts and nuts to the specified torque, adjust the control cables as previously described. Refill the transmission with fluid.

10 Fault diagnosis – automatic transmission

Faults in these units are nearly always the result of incorrect adjustment of the selector cable or throttle control cable, or low fluid level. Should a fault still persist after attention to these items, then the car should be taken to a Honda dealer or transmission specialist for professional fault diagnosis.

Chapter 8   Driveshafts

Contents

Specifications

General

| Type .... | Unequal length driveshafts splined to inner and outer constant velocity joints |

Torque wrench settings

	Nm	lbf ft
Driveshaft retaining nut	185	134
Roadwheel nuts	110	80
Lower arm balljoint nut	44	32

1   General description

Drive is transmitted from the differential to the front wheels by means of two unequal length driveshafts. To overcome torque reaction during acceleration, the shorter left-hand driveshaft is of solid steel construction, whereas the right-hand shaft is tubular.

Both driveshafts are fitted with constant velocity joints at each end. The outer joints are of the ball and cage type and are splined to accept the driveshaft and front hub. The inner joints may be of either the ball and cage type or tripode roller type, and are splined to accept the driveshaft and differential sun gears.

Driveshaft repair procedures are limited, as only the inner and outer rubber boots and complete inner constant velocity joints are available separately. The outer joints and driveshafts are supplied as complete assemblies.

2   Maintenance and inspection

1   At the intervals given in Routine Maintenance at the beginning of this Manual, carry out a thorough inspection of the driveshafts and joints as follows.
2   Jack up the front of the car and support it securely on axle stands.
3   Slowly rotate the roadwheel and inspect the condition of the outer joint rubber boots. Check for signs of cracking, splits or deterioration of the rubber which may allow the grease to escape and lead to water and grit entry into the joint. Also check the securiy and condition of the retaining clips. Repeat these checks on the inner constant velocity joints. If any damage or deterioration is found, the boots should be renewed as described in Section 4.

4   Continue rotating the roadwheel and check for any distortion or damage to the driveshaft. Check for any free play in the joints by first holding the driveshaft and attempting to rotate the wheel. Repeat this check by holding the inner joint and attempting to rotate the driveshaft. Any appreciable movement indicates wear in the joints, wear in the driveshaft splines or loose driveshaft retaining nut.
5   Road test the car and listen for a metallic clicking from the front as the car is driven slowly in a circle with the steering on full lock. If a clicking noise is heard, this indicates wear in the outer constant velocity joint caused by excessive clearance between the balls in the joint and the recesses in which they operate. Remove the driveshaft and inspect the joint, as described in Section 7.
6   If vibration, consistent with road speed, is felt through the car when accelerating, there is a possibility of wear in the inner constant velocity joint. Again the joint should be inspected as described in Sections 5 or 6 according to type.

3   Driveshaft – removal and refitting

1   While the vehicle is standing on its wheels, remove the wheel trim and slacken the driveshaft retaining nut, using a 32 mm socket, while an assistant firmly depresses the footbrake.
2   Jack up the front of the car and support it on stands. Remove the front roadwheel and driveshaft retaining nut.
3   Refer to Chapter 6 or 7 as appropriate and drain the transmission oil/fluid.
4   Position a suitable jack beneath the front suspension lower arm balljoint. The jack will take the full torque reaction of the torsion bar when the balljoint is released, so ensure that the jack head is centrally and securely located.

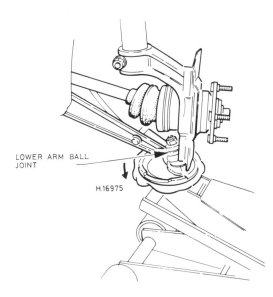

Fig. 8.1 Location of support jack prior to releasing lower
arm balljoint (Sec 3)

3.5 Lower arm balljoint retaining nut

5   Extract the split pin, then undo the lower arm balljoint retaining nut
(photo).
6   Using a suitable balljoint separator tool, release the balljoint from
the steering knuckle.
7   Lower the jack to provide clearance between the driveshaft and
lower suspension arm.
8   Pull the steering knuckle and front hub outwards as far as possible,
push the driveshaft inwards and manoeuvre the outer constant velocity
joint from the hub (photo).
9   Insert a large screwdriver or similar tool between the driveshaft
inner constant velocity joint and the transmission casing, and release
the inner joint (photo).
10 Remove the driveshaft from under the car.
11 Refitting is the reverse sequence to removal bearing in mind the
following points:

(a) Renew the spring clip on the inner joint if it is at all damaged
    or deformed, then push the inner joint firmly home so that the
    spring clip engages the differential gears
(b) Tighten all nuts to the specified torque and use a new split pin
    to secure the balljoint nut
(c) Use a new driveshaft retaining nut and tighten it fully with the
    car standing on its wheels. Stake the nut into the groove in
    the outer constant velocity joint
(d) Refill the transmission as described in Chapter 6 or 7 as
    applicable

3.8 Withdrawing the driveshaft from the front hub

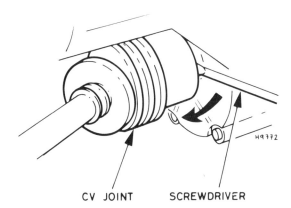

Fig. 8.2 Using a screwdriver to release the inner constant
velocity joint (Sec 3)

3.9 Withdrawing the driveshaft from the transmission

4 Constant velocity joint rubber boots – removal and refitting

1 Remove the driveshaft from the car as described in Section 3.
2 Remove the inner constant velocity joint from the driveshaft according to type as follows.

Roller type

3 Remove the two rubber boot retaining clips and peel the boot back to expose the joint.
4 Mark the relationship of the joint body to the spider and roller so that all parts can be reassembled in their original positions.
5 Withdraw the joint body from the spider and rollers.
6 Extract the two snap rings, and withdraw the spider and roller assembly from the driveshaft.

Ball and cage type

7 Remove the two rubber boot retaining clips and peel the boot back to expose the joint.
8 Remove the retaining ring and withdraw the joint body from the ball cage assembly.
9 Extract the snap rings and withdraw the ball cage assembly from the driveshaft.

All types

10 Slide the inner joint rubber boot off the driveshaft.
11 If the outer joint rubber boot is to be renewed, remove the retaining clips and slide off this boot also.
12 Wipe away as much of the old grease as possible using old rags, then repack the joint(s) with molybdenum disulphide grease.
13 If the outer joint boot is being renewed, slide the new boot onto the shaft and secure the small diameter end only with a new retaining clip. Ensure that the clip is positioned between the raised portions on the driveshaft.
14 Slide on the new inner joint rubber boot and secure the small diameter end as previously described.
15 Refit the inner joint components using the reverse sequence to removal and ensuring that, on the roller type joint, the parts are assembled in their original positions.
16 **Locate** the large diameter end of the rubber boot(s) over the joint(s), then expand and compress them until they return to their normal shape and length.
17 Adjust the length of the driveshaft by moving the inner joint until the dimension as given in Fig. 8.4. Hold the joint in this position and fit the new clip(s) to the rubber boot large diameter end.
18 When fitting the rubber boot retaining clips, ensure that both sets of locking tabs are bent over and that the boot is secured tightly.

5 Inner constant velocity joint (roller type) – dismantling, inspection and reassembly

1 Remove the driveshaft from the car as described in Section 3.
2 Remove the two inner joint rubber boot retaining clips and peel the boot back to expose the joint.
3 Mark the relationship of the joint body to the spider and rollers so that all parts can be reassembled in their original positions.
4 Withdraw the joint body from the spider, then remove the three rollers, marking their positions on the spider.
5 Extract the two snap rings and withdraw the spider from the driveshaft. Remove the rubber boot.
6 With the joint dismantled, wipe away all the old grease and carefully inspect the components for wear or damage. Pay particular attention to the roller grooves and splines of the joint body, the splines and arms of the spider and the rollers themselves. If there is any sign of scoring, wear ridges or other damage, the joint will have to be renewed as parts are not available separately.
7 If the joint is in a satisfactory condition, obtain a new rubber boot and retaining clips, then begin reassembly by thoroughly lubricating all the parts with molybdenum disulphide grease.
8 Fit the new rubber boot to the driveshaft and secure the small diameter end with the retaining clip. Ensure that the clip is positioned between the raised portions on the driveshaft.
9 Refit the spider and snap rings followed by the three rollers. Make

sure that the rollers are fitted in their original locations and positioned as shown in Fig. 8.5.
10 Locate the joint body over the rollers in its original position and slip the rubber boot onto the shoulder. Expand and compress the rubber boot until it returns to its normal shape and length.
11 Adjust the length of the driveshaft by moving the inner joint until the dimension is as given in Fig. 8.4. Hold the joint in this position and fit the large retaining clip. When fitting the clips ensure that both sets of locking tabs are bent over and that the boot is secured tightly.

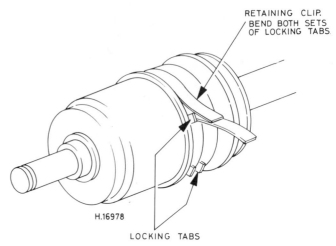

Fig. 8.3 Rubber boot retaining clip fitting details
(Secs 4, 5 and 6)

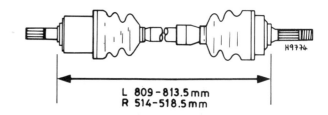

Fig. 8.4 Driveshaft length setting dimension
(Secs 4, 5 and 6)

6 Inner constant velocity joint (ball and cage type) – dismantling, inspection and reassembly

1 Remove the driveshaft from the car as described in Section 3.
2 Remove the two inner joint rubber boot retaining clips and peel the boot back to expose the joint.
3 Remove the retaining ring and withdraw the joint body from the ball cage assembly.
4 Extract the snap ring and withdraw the ball cage assembly from the driveshaft. Remove the rubber boot.
5 Using a blunt screwdriver prise out each of the balls, then separate the ball cage from the inner member.
6 Thoroughly clean all the components, removing all traces of old grease.
7 Carefully inspect all the parts for wear or damage, paying particular attention to the balls and ball tracks in the joint body and inner member. If there is any sign of scoring, wear ridges or other damage, the joint will have to be renewed as parts are not available separately.
8 If the joint is in a satisfactory condition, obtain a new rubber boot and retaining clips, then reassemble the joint as follows.
9 Place the inner member in the ball cage with the chamfered end of the inner member towards the small end of the ball cage.
10 Press each ball into place until firmly seated.

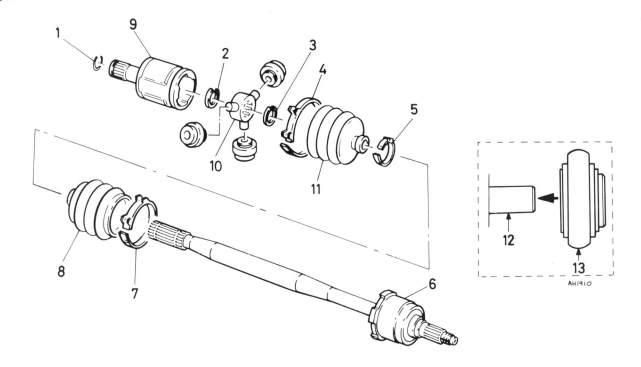

Fig. 8.5 Exploded view of the driveshaft and roller type inner constant velocity joint (Sec 5)

1 Spring clip
2 Snap ring
3 Snap ring
4 Retaining clip

5 Retaining clip
6 Outboard CV joint
7 Retaining clip

8 Outboard joint boot
9 Inboard CV joint
10 Spider assembly

11 Inboard joint boot
12 Spider
13 Roller

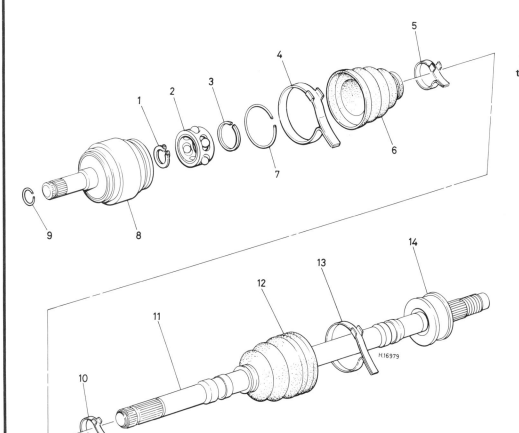

Fig. 8.6 Exploded view of
the driveshaft and ball and
cage type inner constant
velocity joint (Sec 6)

1 Snap ring
2 Ball cage assembly
3 Snap ring
4 Retaining clip
5 Retaining clip
6 Inboard joint boot
7 Retaining ring
8 Inboard CV joint
9 Spring clip
10 Retaining clip
11 Driveshaft
12 Outboard joint boot
13 Retaining clip
14 Outboard CV joint

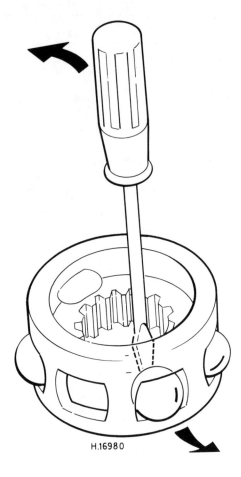

Fig. 8.7 Releasing the balls from the ball cage (Sec 6)

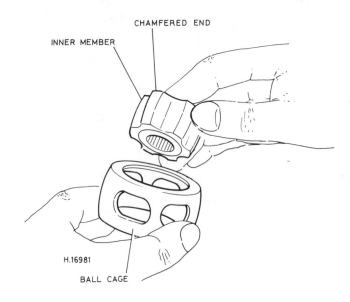

Fig. 8.8 Correct orientation of the ball cage and inner member (Sec 6)

11 Fit a new rubber boot to the driveshaft and secure the small diameter end with the retaining clip. Ensure that the clip is positioned between the raised portions on the driveshaft.
12 Refit the ball cage assembly to the driveshaft and secure with the snap ring.
13 Thoroughly lubricate all the parts with molybdenum disulphide grease.
14 Slide the joint body over the ball cage and refit the retaining ring.
15 Slip the rubber boot over the joint body shoulder, then expand and compress the boot until it returns to its normal shape and length.
16 Adjust the length of the driveshaft by moving the inner joint until the dimension is as given in Fig. 8.4. Hold the joint in this position and fit the large retaining clip. When fitting the clips ensure that both sets of locking tabs are bent over and that the boot is secured tightly.

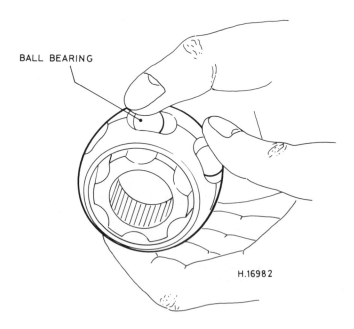

Fig. 8.9 Refitting the balls to the ball cage (Sec 6)

---

7 Outer constant velocity joint – inspection

1 Remove the driveshaft from the car as described in Section 3.
2 Remove the two rubber boot retaining clips and peel back the boot to expose the joint.
3 Wipe away as much of the grease as possible, then inspect the joint for wear, damage and roughness as it is moved from side to side.

4 If the joint is worn, it will be necessary to obtain a new driveshaft assembly as the outer joint is not available separately.
5 If the joint is satisfactory lubricate it thoroughly with molybdenum disulphide grease, then refit the rubber boot. Secure the boot with new retaining clips, ensuring that the clip at the small diameter end is positioned between the raised portions on the driveshaft.

8 Fault diagnosis – driveshafts

Symptom	Reason(s)
Vibration and/or noise on turns	Worn constant velocity outer joint(s)
Vibration when accelerating	Worn constant velocity inner joint(s) Bent or distorted driveshaft
Noise on taking up drive	Worn driveshaft or constant velocity joint splines Loose driveshaft retaining nut Worn constant velocity joints

See also Fault diagnosis – suspension and steering

Chapter 9 Braking system

Contents

Specifications

General

System type .... Diagonally split, dual circuit hydraulic, with pressure regulating valve in rear hydraulic circuit. Cable-operated handbrake on rear wheels. Servo assistance on all models

Front brakes

Type	Disc with single piston sliding calipers
Disc diameter	190.0 mm (7.5 in)
Disc thickness:	
Solid disc	12.0 mm (0.47 in)
Ventilated disc	17.0 mm (0.67 in)
Disc regrind limit:	
Solid disc	10.0 mm (0.39 in)
Ventilated disc	15.0 mm (0.59 in)
Maximum disc runout	0.10 mm (0.0039 in)
Maximum thickness variation	0.015 mm (0.0006 in)
Disc pad minimum thickness	3.0 mm (0.12 in)

Rear brakes

Type	Self-adjusting single leading shoe drum
Drum diameter:	
All models except 4 door Hatchback (UK) and Wagon (North America)	180.0 mm (7.09 in)
4 door Hatchback (UK) and wagon (North America)	200.00 mm (7.87 in)
Drum regrind limit:	
180.0 mm (7.09 in) diameter drum	181.0 mm (7.13 in)
200.00 mm (7.87 in) diameter drum	201.0 mm (7.91 in)
Brake lining minimum thickness	2.0 mm (0.08 in)

Adjustment data

Brake pedal height:	
All models except 4 door Hatchback (UK) and Wagon (North America)	174.0 mm (6.8 in)
4 door Hatchback (UK) and Wagon (North America)	168.0 mm (6.6 in)
Brake pedal free play	1.0 to 5.0 mm (0.04 to 0.2 in)
Servo pushrod-to-master cylinder piston clearance	0 to 0.4 mm (0 to 0.016 in)

Torque wrench settings

	Nm	lbf ft
Brake caliper guide pin bolts:		
Tokico caliper	27	20
Nissin caliper	18	13
Sumitomo caliper	50	36
Caliper bracket to steering knuckle	78	56
Brake hose banjo union	35	25
Pressure regulating valve to bracket	10	7
Brake pipe union nuts	15	11
Master cylinder to servo	7	5
Servo to bulkhead	13	9
Bleed screws:		
Front calipers	9	7
Rear wheel clyinders	7	5
Master cylinder stop bolt	9	7
Wheel cylinder to backplate	8	6

1 General description

The braking system is of the servo-assisted, dual circuit hydraulic type with disc brakes at the front and drum brakes at the rear. A diagonally split dual circuit hydraulic system is employed in which each circuit operates one front and one diagonally opposite rear brake from a tandem master cylinder. Under normal conditions both circuits operate in unison; however, in the event of hydraulic failure in one circuit, full braking force will still be available at two wheels. A pressure regulating valve is incorporated in the rear brake hydraulic circuit. This valve regulates the pressure applied to each rear brake and reduces the possibility of the rear wheels locking under heavy braking.

The front disc brakes are operated by single piston sliding type calipers. At the rear leading and trailing brake shoes are operated by twin piston wheel cylinders and are self-adjusting by footbrake application.

A cable-operated handbrake provides an independent mechanical means of rear brake actuation.

2 Maintenance and inspection

1   The brake hydraulic fluid should be checked weekly and, if necessary, topped up with the specified fluid to the 'MAX' mark on the reservoir (photo).

2   At the intervals given in 'Routine Maintenance' at the beginning of this Manual, the hydraulic pipes, hoses and unions should be carefully inspected for chafing, cracks, leaks and corrosion. Details will be found in Section 12. The condition of the front and rear brake assemblies should be checked and the thickness of the disc pads and brake shoes inspected as described in Sections 3 and 6.

3   At the less frequent intervals specified renew the brake hydraulic fluid by draining the system and refilling with fresh fluid, as described in Section 13.

2.1 Master cylinder reservoir 'MAX' and 'MIN' markings (arrowed)

3 Front disc pads – inspection and renewal

Note: *Three different types of brake calipers are used on Civic models covered by this manual, and reference should be made to the accompanying illustrations to identify the type being worked on. The photographs applicable to this Section depict the more common Tokico type unit.*

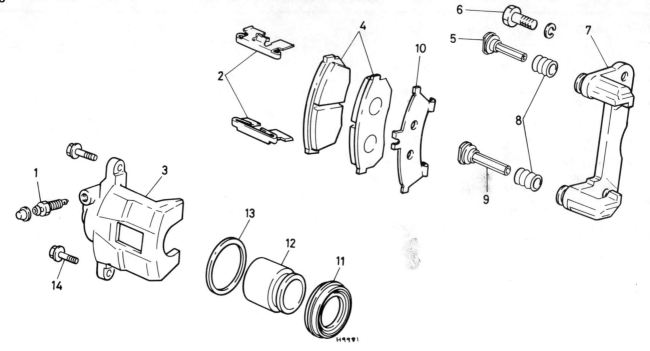

Fig. 9.1 Exploded view of the Tokico type front brake assembly (Secs 3 and 4)

1	Bleed screw	5	Guide pin	8	Dust cover	12	Piston
2	Pad spring	6	Caliper bracket retaining	9	Guide pin	13	Piston seal
3	Caliper body		bolt	10	Disc pad shim	14	Guide pin bolt
4	Disc pad	7	Caliper bracket	11	Dust boot		

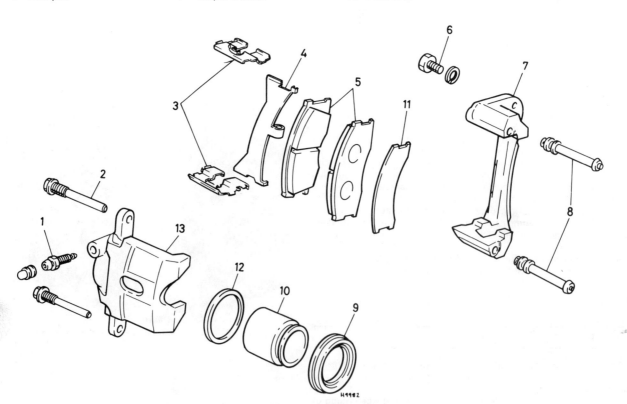

Fig. 9.2 Exploded view of the Sumitomo type front brake assembly (Secs 3 and 4)

1	Bleed screw	5	Disc pad	8	Guide pin bush	11	Disc pad shim
2	Guide pin bolt	6	Caliper bracket retaining	9	Dust boot	12	Piston seal
3	Pad spring		bolt	10	Piston	13	Caliper body
4	Spring plate	7	Caliper bracket				

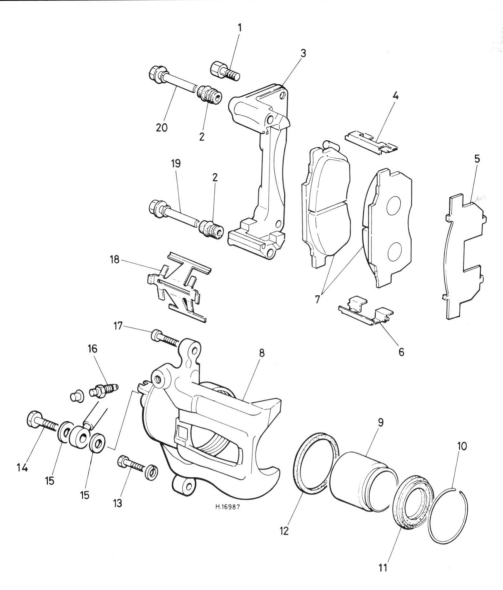

Fig. 9.3 Exploded view of the Nissin type front brake assembly (Secs 3 and 4)

1 Caliper bracket retaining bolt	6 Pad retainer	11 Dust boot	16 Bleed screw
2 Dust cover	7 Disc pad	12 Piston seal	17 Guide pin bolt
3 Caliper bracket	8 Caliper body	13 Guide pin bolt	18 Pad spring
4 Pad retainer	9 Piston	14 Banjo union bolt	19 Guide pin
5 Disc pad shim	10 Boot clip	15 Caliper washer	20 Guide pin

1 Jack up the front of the car and securely support it on stands. Remove the front roadwheels.

2 Check the thickness of the disc pad friction material by viewing through the inspection hole in the front of the caliper (photo). If the friction material on any of the pads is at, or below, the minimum specified thickness, all four pads must be renewed as a complete set.

3 To remove the pads, unscrew the caliper lower guide pin bolt and pivot the caliper body upwards (photo). If a pad wear warning light is fitted, disconnect the wiring at the connector before lifting the caliper.

4 Where fitted, remove the pad spring plate, then withdraw the pads and shim from the caliper bracket. Note that the shim is only fitted to the outer pad (photos).

5 Withdraw the pad retainers from the caliper bracket (photo).

6 Brush the dust and dirt from the caliper piston, disc and pads, but do not inhale it as it is injurious to health.

7 Check for weakness, distortion or damage to the spring plate

(where fitted), the pad retainers and the shim, and renew these parts if necessary. Check the condition of the disc as described in Section 5.

8 The caliper piston must now be pushed fully back into its cylinder in order to accommodate the new, thicker pads. This will cause the fluid level to rise in the master cylinder. Anticipate this by drawing off some of the fluid using a suitable clean syringe.

9 Locate the pad retainers into the caliper bracket.

10 Apply a thin coat of high temperature brake grease between the shim and the metal backing of the outer pad, then fit the pad and shim.

11 Fit the inner pad and, where applicable the spring plate.

12 Pivot the caliper downwards and refit the lower guide pin bolt, tightened to the specified torque. Where fitted, reconnect the pad wear warning light wiring.

13 Depress the brake pedal several times to bring the piston into contact with the pads.

14 If the pads are being renewed as a set, repeat the procedure on the

3.2 Disc pad thickness viewed through inspection hole

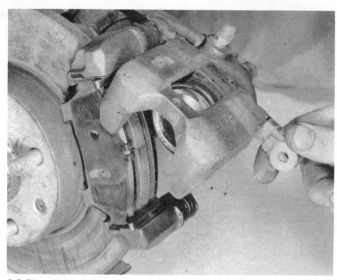

3.3 Pivot the caliper upwards for access to the pads

3.4A Withdraw the outer pad shim ...

3.4B ... and outer pad

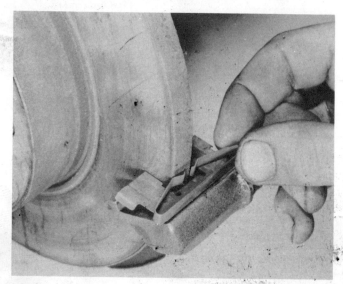

3.5 Disc pad retainers

opposite brake, then refit the roadwheels and lower the car to the ground.

15 Check and if necessary, top up the fluid in the master cylinder reservoir.

4 Front brake caliper – removal, overhaul and refitting

1 Jack up the front of the car and securely support it on stands. Remove the front roadwheel.

2 Clamp the flexible brake hose using a brake hose clamp or self-locking wrench with protected jaws. Unscrew the hose-to-caliper banjo union bolt and recover the two copper washers.

3 Remove the disc pads as described in Section 3.

4 Unscrew the upper guide pin bolt and remove the caliper from the caliper bracket.

5 Clean away dust and dirt, taking care not to inhale it as it is injurious to health.

6 Remove the dust excluding boot.

7 Remove the piston. Do this by applying air pressure to the fluid union hole. Only a low air pressure is required such as is generated from a hand or foot-operated type pump.

8   Examine the surfaces of the piston and cylinder bore. If they are scored or there is any sign of rust or corrosion, then a new caliper must be obtained. If the components are in good condition, then extract the piston seal from its groove in the cylinder. Take great care not to scratch the bore surfaces when doing this. Discard the seal.

9   Obtain a repair kit which will contain all the necessary seals and other renewable items.

10   Clean the piston and cylinder in clean hydraulic fluid or methylated spirit – nothing else, and observe absolute cleanliness during the reassembly operations.

11   Fit the new piston seal, manipulating it into the cylinder groove using the fingers.

12   Smear the cylinder bore with clean hydraulic fluid and push the piston squarely into it. Do not push the piston fully home until the dust excluding boot has been engaged in its groove.

13   Refit the disc pads, spring plate and shim as described in Section 3.

14   Fit the caliper over the disc and screw in the guide pin bolts. Tighten them to the specified torque.

15   Use new sealing washers and reconnect the hydraulic hose to the caliper.

16   Bleed the hydraulic system as described in Section 13, then refit the roadwheel and lower the car.

5   Front brake disc – inspection, removal and refitting

1   Jack up the front of the car and securely support it on stands. Remove the roadwheel.

2   Remove the disc pads as described in Section 3.

3   Rotate the disc by hand and examine it for deep scoring, grooving or cracks. Light scoring is normal, but if excessive the disc must be renewed. Any loose rust and scale around the outer edge of the disc can be removed by lightly tapping it with a small hammer while rotating the disc.

4   If severe scoring has occurred it may be possible to have the disc re-ground provided the finished thickness is not less than the specified minimum (see Specifications).

5   Using a dial gauge with its probe positioned approximately 10 mm (0.4 in) in from the outer edge, check the disc run-out. Using a micrometer check the disc thickness at various points around the disc, but at the same distance in from the edge. If the run-out or thickness variation is greater than specified, it may be possible to have the disc re-ground, but renewal will probably be necessary.

6   To remove the disc, undo the two caliper bracket retaining bolts and lift off the caliper and bracket assembly (photo). Avoid stretching the brake hose.

7   Undo the two retaining screws and remove the disc from the hub. If tight, use two 8.0 mm bolts screwed into the holes provided to push the disc off.

8   Before fitting a new disc, clean away any protective grease using a suitable solvent, and make sure that the disc and hub mating faces are perfectly clean and smooth.

9   Fit the disc and secure with the two screws.

10   Fit the caliper bracket and caliper assembly and tighten the bolts to the specified torque.

11   Refit the disc pads as described in Section 3 then lower the car.

6   Rear brake shoes – inspection and renewal

1   Jack up the rear of the car and securely support it on stands. Remove the rear roadwheels.

2   Remove the brake drums. If the drums will not come off, tap them carefully with a plastic-faced mallet, or screw two 8.0 mm bolts into the tapped holes provided. If they still refuse to move, then the shoes are probably locked into wear grooves inside the drums. To release them, extract the rubber plug from the backplate, insert a screwdriver and turn the star wheel adjuster on the self-adjuster strut. Pivot the point of the screwdriver downwards (photo).

3   With the drums removed, brush away dust, taking care not to inhale it as it is dangerous to health. Inspect the shoe linings. If they are worn down to their minimum thickness then the shoes must be renewed as an axle set (photo).

4   The brake shoes can be removed with the rear hub in place, but for easier access the hub can be removed if necessary as described in Chapter 10.

5   To remove the shoes, release the shoe hold-down spring pins by gripping them with a pair of pliers and then turn them through 90° (photo).

6   Pull the upper ends of the shoes outwards off the wheel cylinder pistons, pull the shoes slightly forward and gently release them, taking care that the shoes do not damage the wheel cylinder rubber boots.

7   Prise the lower ends of the shoes apart and remove them from the anchor block.

8   Pull the shoes outwards against the tension of their return springs and remove them from around the hub.

9   Disconnect the handbrake cable from the shoe lever and withdraw the complete shoe assembly together with return springs, and adjuster mechanism (photo).

10   Lay the assembly on the bench, noting the relative position of the leading and trailing shoes and the holes in the shoe webs in which the springs engage. Make a sketch if necessary (photo).

11   Transfer the handbrake lever from the old trailing shoe to the new one. This will require removal of the circlip and washer. When refitting, make sure that the head of the retaining pin will be towards the hub when the shoe is on the backplate.

12   Reassemble the shoes and return springs. Fit the adjuster strut, having fully retracted it after having cleaned and lightly greased its threads. Engage the spring with the self-adjuster lever.

13   Apply a smear of high melting-point grease to the shoe rubbing

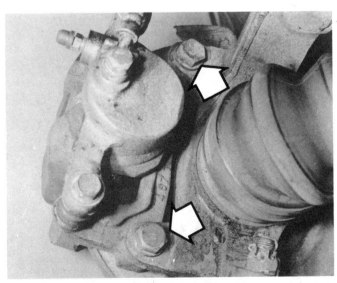

5.6 Caliper bracket retaining bolts (arrowed)

6.2 Using two bolts to draw off the brake drum

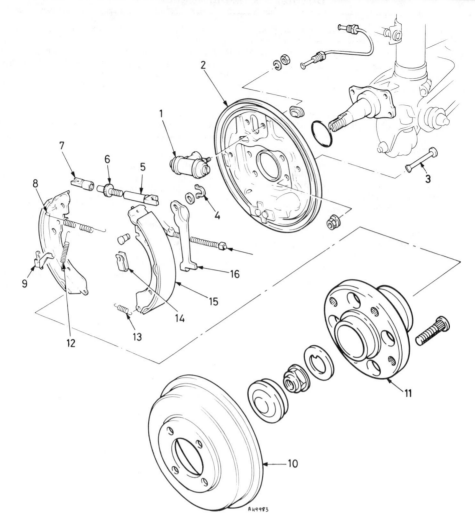

Fig. 9.4 Exploded view of the rear brake components (Sec 6)

1 Wheel cylinder	5 Clevis A	9 Self-adjuster lever	13 Lower return spring
2 Backing plate	6 Starwheel adjuster	10 Rear brake drum	14 Hold-down spring
3 Hold-down pin	7 Clevis B	11 Rear hub	15 Brake shoe
4 Circlip	8 Upper return spring	12 Self-adjuster spring	16 Handbrake lever

6.3 Rear brake component arrangement – right-hand side

6.5 Releasing the brake shoe hold down spring pins

6.9 Disconnecting the handbrake cable from the brake shoe lever

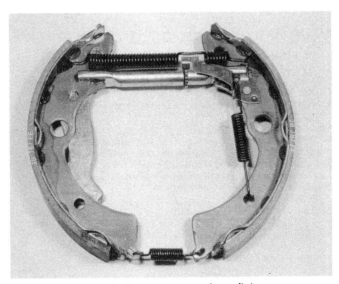

6.10 Right-hand side brake components prior to fitting

high spots on the backplate and to the slots in the wheel cylinder pistons and anchor block.

14 Fit the shoe assembly over the hub, and engage the shoe ends with the wheel cylinder and anchor block. Fit the shoe hold-down spring clip pins.

15 Refit the hub as described in Chapter 10, if previously removed.

16 Centralise the shoes in the backplate and then rotate the star wheel adjuster until the brake drum will just slide over the shoes. Fit the brake drum and the roadwheel.

17 Renew the shoes on the opposite wheel.

18 Lower the car to the ground and apply the footbrake several times to set the shoes to give minimum clearance from the drum.

7 Rear wheel cylinder – removal, overhaul and refitting

1 Remove the brake shoes as described in the preceding Section.

2 Disconnect the brake pipe from the rear wheel cylinder and cap the

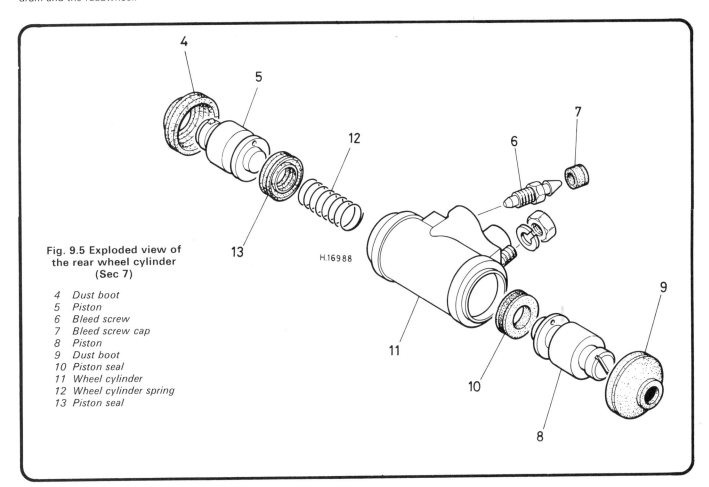

Fig. 9.5 Exploded view of
the rear wheel cylinder
(Sec 7)

H.16988

4 Dust boot
5 Piston
6 Bleed screw
7 Bleed screw cap
8 Piston
9 Dust boot
10 Piston seal
11 Wheel cylinder
12 Wheel cylinder spring
13 Piston seal

pipe to prevent loss of fluid. A bleed screw dust cap is useful for this purpose.

3 Unscrew the nuts and remove the wheel cylinder from the brake backplate.

4 Clean away external dirt, remove the dust excluding boots and take out the pistons and spring. The pistons may be ejected by shaking the cylinder or by applying low air pressure to the fluid entry port on the cylinder body (photo).

5 Inspect the surfaces of the cylinder bore and pistons. If there is any sign of scoring, rust or corrosion, then the cylinder must be renewed complete.

6 If the components are in good condition, clean away external dirt, discard the seals and obtain a repair kit which will contain all the necessary seals and other renewable components.

7 Observe strict cleanliness during reassembly and manipulate the new seals into position using the fingers only.

8 Dip the pistons in clean hydraulic fluid and insert them into the cylinder with the spring between them. Fit the dust excluding boots.

9 Fit the cylinder to the backplate, tighten the retaining nuts and reconnect the brake pipe.

10 Refit the shoes and drum.

11 Bleed the hydraulic system as described in Section 13, then refit the roadwheel and lower the car.

8 Rear brake drum – inspection and renovation

1 Whenever the brake drum is removed, take the opportunity to clean all dust and dirt and inspect it for scoring, grooving or cracks.

2 If any of these problems is evident, or if as a result of reference to the Fault Diagnosis Section the drum is suspected of being out-of-round, it may be possible to refinish it provided the finished internal diameter does not exceed the maximum specified.

3 If it does, then a new drum must be fitted.

9 Master cylinder – removal and refitting

1 Drain the master cylinder reservoir. Do this by either drawing off the fluid with a suitable syringe, or by opening the front brake caliper bleed screws and slowly pumping the brake pedal. On completion discard the expelled fluid.

2 Disconnect the fluid level sensor wiring plug and remove the reservoir cap.

3 Unscrew the brake pipe unions at the master cylinder and carefully ease out the pipes. Cap the pipe open ends to prevent dirt entry (photo).

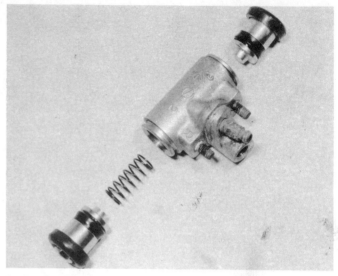

7.4 Rear wheel cylinder dismantled

4 Unscrew the retaining nuts and remove the master cylinder from the servo unit (photo).

5 Refitting is the reverse sequence to removal. Bleed the complete hydraulic system as described in Section 13, and adjust the pedal height as described in Section 19.

10 Master cylinder – overhaul

1 With the master cylinder removed from the car, clean away external dirt and prepare a clean working area.

2 Referring to Fig. 9.6 extract the primary piston end circlip.

3 Shake the primary piston from the cylinder.

4 Insert a rod to depress the secondary piston, then unscrew and remove the stop bolt.

5 Shake out the secondary piston assembly. If it is difficult to remove, apply low pressure air to the secondary fluid entry port.

6 Examine the surfaces of the cylinder bore and the pistons. If there is any sign of corrosion, scoring or wear ridges, renew the cylinder complete. If the parts appear satisfactory, obtain a repair kit which will contain all the necessary seals for overhaul.

9.3 Master cylinder pipe union locations (arrowed)

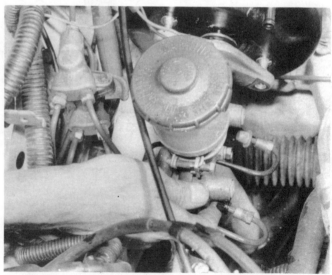

9.4 Removing the master cylinder from the servo

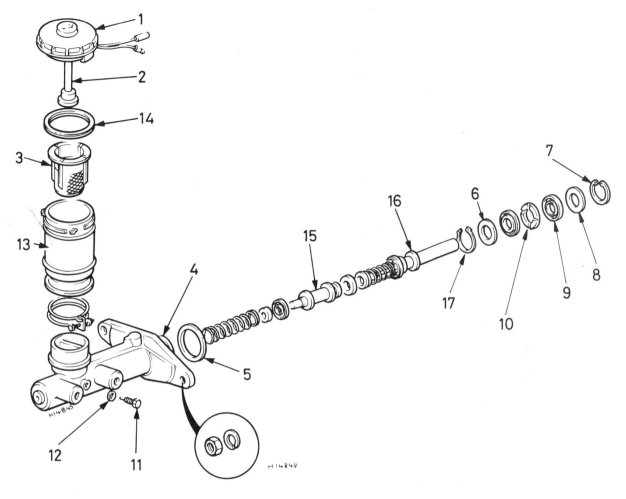

Fig. 9.6 Exploded view of the master cylinder (Sec 10)

1 Reservoir cap	6 Primary seal	10 Bushing	14 Reservoir seal
2 Fluid level sensor	7 Circlip	11 Stop bolt	15 Secondary piston
3 Filter	8 Washer	12 Metal gasket	16 Primary piston
4 Master cylinder	9 Primary seal	13 Reservoir	17 Circlip
5 Seal			

7 Remove the old seals from the pistons, then clean all the components in methylated spirit or clean hydraulic fluid – nothing else.

8 Lubricate all the parts in hydraulic fluid before fitting. Using the fingers only, manipulate the new seals into position with reference to Figs. 9.6 and 9.7.

9 Insert the secondary piston into the cylinder bore using a twisting motion to prevent trapping of the seal lips. Depress the piston using a rod and screw in the stop bolt.

10 Fit the primary piston and the circlip.

11 Fit the new mounting flange seal.

11 Pressure regulating valve – removal and refitting

1 The valve cannot be overhauled or repaired and in the event of a fault, it must be renewed.

2 Unscrew the filler cap from the master cylinder reservoir, and seal the reservoir with a piece of polythene secured by an elastic band. This will minimise fluid loss when the valve is removed.

3 Place some rags under the valve, then unscrew the brake pipe union nuts. Carefully ease the pipes out of the valve body, noting their

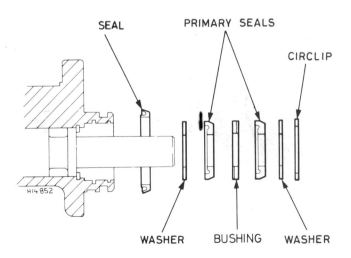

Fig. 9.7 Master cylinder primary piston seal orientation (Sec 10)

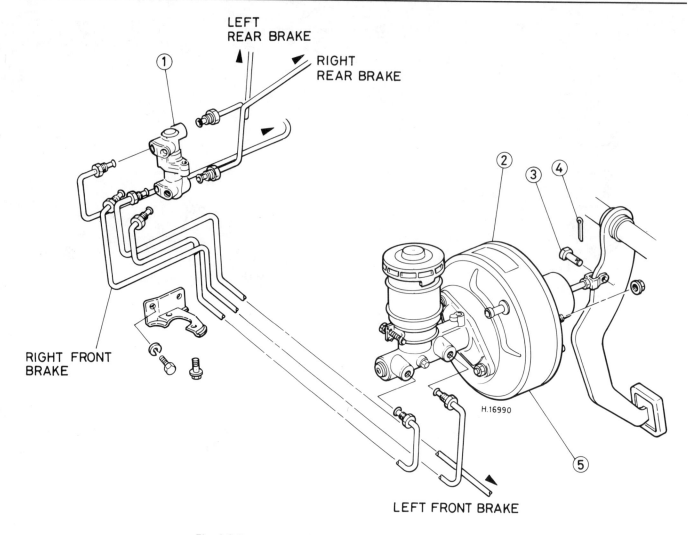

Fig. 9.8 Pressure regulating valve pipe locations (Sec 11)

1   *Dual proportioning valve*   3   *Clevis pin*   5   *Servo unit*
2   *Master cylinder*   4   *Split pin*

locations and with reference to Fig. 9.8. Cap the pipes after removal to prevent further loss of fluid.

4   Undo the retaining bolts and remove the valve from its mounting bracket.

5   Refitting is the reverse sequence to removal. Remove the polythene from the master cylinder reservoir, then bleed the complete hydraulic system as described in Section 13.

12 Hydraulic pipes and hoses – inspection, removal and refitting

1   At the intervals given in 'Routine Maintenance' carefully examine all brake pipes, hoses, hose connections and pipe unions.

2   First check for signs of leakage at the pipe unions, then examine the flexible hoses for signs of cracking, chafing and fraying.

3   The brake pipes must be examined carefully and methodically. They must be cleaned off and checked for signs of dents, corrosion or other damage. Corrosion should be scraped off and, if the depth of pitting is significant, the pipes renewed. This is particularly likely in those areas underneath the vehicle body where the pipes are exposed and unprotected.

4   If any section of pipe or hose is to be removed, first unscrew the master cylinder reservoir filler cap and place a piece of polythene over the filler neck. Secure the polythene with an elastic band, ensuring that

an airtight seal is obtained. This will minimise brake fluid loss when the pipe or hose is removed.

5   Brake pipe removal is usually quite straightforward. The union nuts at each end are undone, the pipe and union pulled out and the centre section of the pipe removed from the body clips. Where the union nuts are exposed to the full force of the weather they can sometimes be quite tight. As only an open ended spanner can be used, burring of the flats on the nuts is not uncommon when attempting to undo them. For this reason a self-locking wrench is often the only way to separate a stubborn union. Some of the pipes run through the interior of the car and access to these is gained by lifting up the carpets and removing the appropriate interior trim panels (photo).

6   To remove a flexible hose, wipe the unions and brackets free of dirt and undo the union nut from the brake pipe end(s) (photo).

7   Next extract the hose retaining clip, or unscrew the nut, and lift the end of the hose out of its bracket. If a front hose is being removed, it can now be unscrewed from the brake caliper.

8   Brake pipes can be obtained individually, or in sets, from most accessory shops or garages with the end flares and union nuts in place. The pipe is then bent to shape, using the old pipe as a guide, and is ready for fitting to the car.

9   Refitting the pipes and hoses is the reversal of the removal procedure. Make sure that the hoses are not kinked when in position and also make sure that the brake pipes are securely supported in their clips. After refitting, remove the polythene from the reservoir and bleed the brake hydraulic system, as described in Section 13.

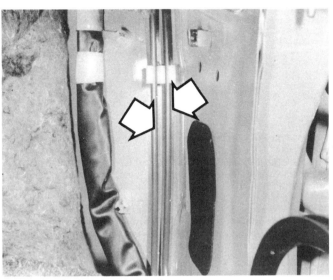

12.5 Brake pipe locations inside the car

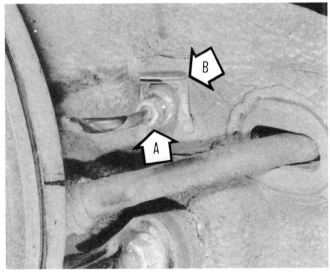

12.6 Brake pipe union nut (A) and hose retaining clip (B)

13 Hydraulic system – bleeding

1   The correct functioning of the brake hydraulic system is only possible after removal of all air from the components and circuit; this is achieved by bleeding the system. Note that only clean unused brake fluid, which has remained unshaken for at least 24 hours, must be used.

2   If there is any possibility of incorrect fluid being used in the system, the brake lines and components must be completely flushed with uncontaminated fluid and new seals fitted to the components.

3   *Never reuse* brake fluid which has been bled from the system.

4   During the procedure, do not allow the level of brake fluid to drop more than halfway down the reservoir.

5   Before starting work, cleck that all pipes and hoses are secure, unions tight and bleed screws closed. Take great care not to allow brake fluid to come into contact with the car paintwork, otherwise the finish will be seriously damaged. Wash off any spilled fluid immediately with cold water.

6   There are a number of one-man, do-it-yourself, brake bleeding kits currently available from motor accessory shops. Always follow the instructions supplied with the kit. It is recommended that one of these kits is used wherever possible, as they greatly simplify the bleeding operation and also reduce the risk of expelled air and fluid being drawn back into the system. If one of these kits is not available, it will be necessary to gather together a clean jar and a suitable length of clear plastic tubing which is a tight fit over the bleed screw, and also to engage the help of an assistant.

7   If brake fluid has been lost from the master cylinder due to a leak in the system, ensure that the cause is traced and rectified before proceeding further.

8   If the hydraulic system has only been partially disconnected and suitable precautions were taken to prevent further loss of fluid it should only be necessary to bleed the part of the system being worked on (i.e. at the brake caliper or wheel cylinder nearest to the disconnected pipe or hose).

9   If the complete system is to be bled, then it should be done in the following sequence:

Secondary circuit: Left-hand front then right-hand rear
Primary circuit: Right-hand front then left-hand rear

10 To bleed the system, first clean the area around the bleed screw and fit the bleed tube (photo). If necessary top up the master cylinder reservoir with brake fluid.

11 The system incorporates a vacuum servo, destroy the vacuum by giving several applications of the brake pedal in quick succession.

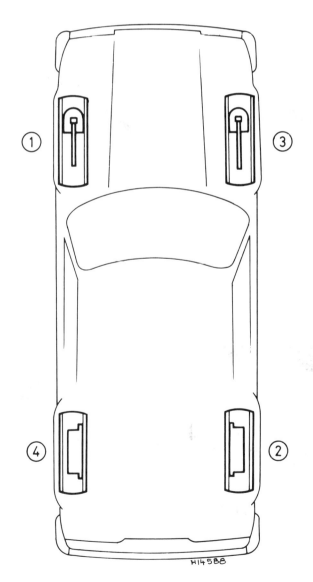

H14588

Fig. 9.9 Hydraulic system bleeding sequence (Sec 13)

13.10 Front brake caliper bleed screw location

Bleeding – two man method

12 Gather together a clean jar and a length of rubber or plastic tubing which will be a tight fit on the brake bleed screws.
13 Engage the help of an assistant.
14 Push one end of the bleed tube onto the first bleed screw and immerse the other end in the jar which should contain enough hydraulic fluid to cover the end of the tube.
15 Open the bleed screew one half a turn and have your assistant depress the brake pedal fully when slowly release it. Tighten the bleed screw at the end of each pedal downstroke to obviate any chance of air or fluid being drawn back into the system.
16 Repeat this operation until clean brake fluid, free from air bubbles, can be seen coming through into the jar.
17 Tighten the bleed screw at the end of a pedal downstroke and remove the bleed tube. Bleed the remaining screws in a similar way.

Bleeding – using one-way valve kit

18 It is recommended that one of these kits is used wherever possible as it will greatly simplify the bleeding operation and also reduce the risk of air or fluid being drawn back into the system, quite apart from being able to do the work without the help of an assistant.
19 To use the kit, connect the tube to the bleed screw and open the screw one half turn.
20 Depress the brake pedal fully then slowly release it. The one-way valve in the kit will prevent expelled air from returning at the end of each pedal downstroke. Repeat this operation several times to be sure of ejecting all air from the system. Some kits include a translucent container which can be positioned so that the air bubbles can actually be seen being ejected from the system.
21 Tighten the bleed screw, remove the tube and repeat the operations on the remaining brakes.
22 On completion, depress the brake pedal. If it is still feels spongy, repeat the bleeding operations, as air must still be trapped in the system.

Bleeding – using a pressure bleeding kit

23 These kits are available from motor accessory shops and are usually operated by air pressure from the spare tyre.
24 By connecting a pressurised container to the master cylinder fluid reservoir, bleeding is then carried out simply by opening each bleed screw in turn and allowing the fluid to run out, rather like turning on a tap, until no air is visible in the expelled fluid.

25 By using this method, the large reserve of brake fluid provides a safeguard action against air being drawn into the master cylinder during bleeding which may occur if the fluid level in the reservoir is not maintained.
26 Pressure bleeding is particularly effective when bleeding 'difficult' systems or when bleeding the complete system at the time of routine fluid renewal.

All methods

27 When bleeding is completed, check and top up the fluid level in the master cylinder reservoir.
28 Check the feel of the brake pedal. If it feels at all spongy, air must still be present in the system and the need for further bleeding is indicated. Failure to bleed satisfactorily after a reasonable repetition of the bleeding operations may be due to worn master cylinder seals.
29 Discard brake fluid which has been expelled. It is almost certain to be contaminated with moisture, air and dirt making it unsuitable for further use. Clean fluid should always be stored in an airtight container as it is hygroscopic (absorbs moisture readily) which lowers its boiling point and could affect braking performance under severe conditions.

14 Vacuum servo unit – description

1 A vacuum servo unit is fitted into the brake hydraulic circuit in series with the master cylinder, to provide assistance to the driver when the brake pedal is depressed. This reduces the effort required by the driver to operate the brakes under all braking conditions.
2 The unit operates by vacuum obtained from the inlet manifold and comprises basically a booster diaphragm, control valve, and a non-return valve.
3 The servo unit and hydraulic master cylinder are connected together so that the servo unit piston rod acts as the master cylinder pushrod. The driver's braking effort is transmitted through another pushrod to the servo unit piston and its built-in control system. The servo unit piston does not fit tightly into the cylinder, but has a strong diaphragm to keep its edges in constant contact with the cylinder wall,

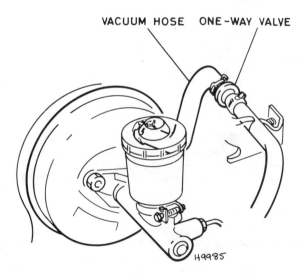

Fig. 9.10 Servo unit vacuum hose and one-way valve details (Sec 14)

so ensuring an airtight seal between the two parts. The forward chamber is held under vacuum conditions created in the inlet manifold of the engine and, during periods when the brake pedal is not in use, the controls open a passage to the rear chamber so placing it under vacuum conditions as well. When the brake pedal is depressed, the vacuum passage to the rear chamber is cut off and the chamber opened to atmospheric pressure. The consequent rush of air pushes the servo piston forward in the vacuum chamber and operates the main pushrod to the master cylinder.

4   In the event of failure of the servo unit, the hydraulic circuit remains unaffected except that increased pedal pressure will be required.

5   If a servo unit is suspected of being faulty, carry out the following test.

6   Depress the footbrake and then start the engine. As the engine starts there should be a noticeable 'give' in the brake pedal. Allow the engine to run for at least two minutes, then switch it off. If the brake pedal is depressed again it should be possible to detect an audible hiss from the unit when the pedal is depressed. After about four or five applications no further hissing will be heard and the pedal will feel considerably firmer. If the servo does not function as described, check the condition of the vacuum hose, connections, and one-way valve. If these are satisfactory the servo is faulty.

15 Vacuum servo unit – removal and refitting

1   Refer to Section 9 and remove the master cylinder.
2   Disconnect the vacuum hose at the servo unit.
3   Remove the facia lower panel (where applicable) and disconnect the servo pushrod from the brake pedal.
4   Undo the retaining nuts and withdraw the servo from the engine compartment bulkhead. Retrieve the seal.
5   If the servo has been renewed, or if a reconditioned unit is being fitted, the servo pushrod-to-master cylinder piston clearance must be checked and if necessary adjusted before fitting. A special gauge and vacuum pump are required for this, and it is recommended that the servo unit and master cylinder are taken to a dealer who will have the necessary special tools for adjustment.
6   After adjustment, refit the servo unit using the reverse sequence to removal, followed by the master cylinder (Section 9).

16 Handbrake – adjustment

1   The handbrake is normally kept in constant adjustment by the action of the shoe automatic adjusters. However, if the handbrake lever has to be pulled through more than eight notches (clicks) of the ratchet quadrant to fully apply the brake, this will be due to cable stretch and must be rectified in the following way.
2   Raise the rear of the car so that the rear wheels are clear of the floor. Support the car securely.
3   Pull the handbrake lever over one notch only.
4   Remove the cover from the rear of the centre console and turn the cable adjuster nut until the rear wheels drag very slightly when the roadwheels are turned (photo).
5   Release the handbrake and check that the rear wheels rotate freely.
6   The handbrake should be fully applied when the lever has been pulled through between four and eight notches.
7   Lower the car to the floor.

17 Handbrake cable – removal and refitting

1   Jack up the rear of the car and support it on stands. Remove the appropriate rear roadwheel.
2   Remove the brake drum and brake shoes on the side being worked on as described in Section 6.
3   Refer to Chapter 11 and remove the centre console.
4   Fit a cranked 12.0 mm ring spanner over the cable retainer in the backplate, compress the retainer and release it. Withdraw the cable from the backplate.

5   Unscrew the handbrake cable adjuster and disconnect the cable from the equaliser.
6   From under the car remove the heat shield and unscrew the cable guide retaining bolts. Withdraw the cable assembly and remove it from under the car.
7   Refit the cable using the reverse sequence to removal. Refit the brake shoes and drum as described in Section 6, then apply the footbrake several times to fully operate the automatic adjusters. Adjust the handbrake as described in Section 16, refit the roadwheel and lower the car.

18 Handbrake lever – removal and refitting

1   Refer to Chapter 11 and remove the centre console.
2   Unscrew the handbrake cable adjuster and withdraw the lever threaded rod from the equaliser. Recover the tension spring.
3   Disconnect the warning light switch wiring, undo the retaining bolts and remove the lever from the car (photo).
4   Refitting is the reverse sequence to removal. Adjust the handbrake cable as described in Section 16.

19 Brake pedal height – adjustment

1   The brake pedal height should be checked periodically or, after removal and refitting of the brake pedal or vacuum servo unit.
2   To check the pedal height, remove the carpets so that the bare floor pan is exposed beneath the pedal.
3   Slacken the locknut on the brake light switch and back off the switch until it is clear of the pedal.
4   Measure the distance from the floor to the underside of the pedal pad and compare this figure with the brake pedal height dimension given in the Specifications.
5   If adjustment is necessary, slacken the pedal pushrod locknut and turn the pushrod as necessary to achieve the specified dimension. Check that 1.0 to 5.0 mm (0.04 to 0.02 in) of free play exists when the pedal is pushed by hand, then tighten the pushrod locknut.
6   Screw in the brake light switch until the switch plunger is fully depressed, then unscrew the switch half a turn. Tighten the locknut.
7   Refit the carpets.

20 Brake pedal – removal and refitting

1   From inside the car remove the facia lower panel (where applicable).

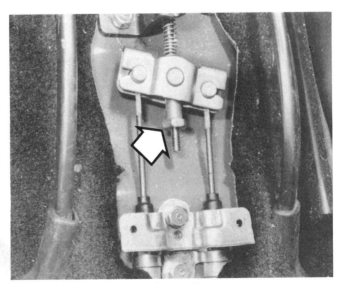

16.4 Handbrake cable adjuster (arrowed)

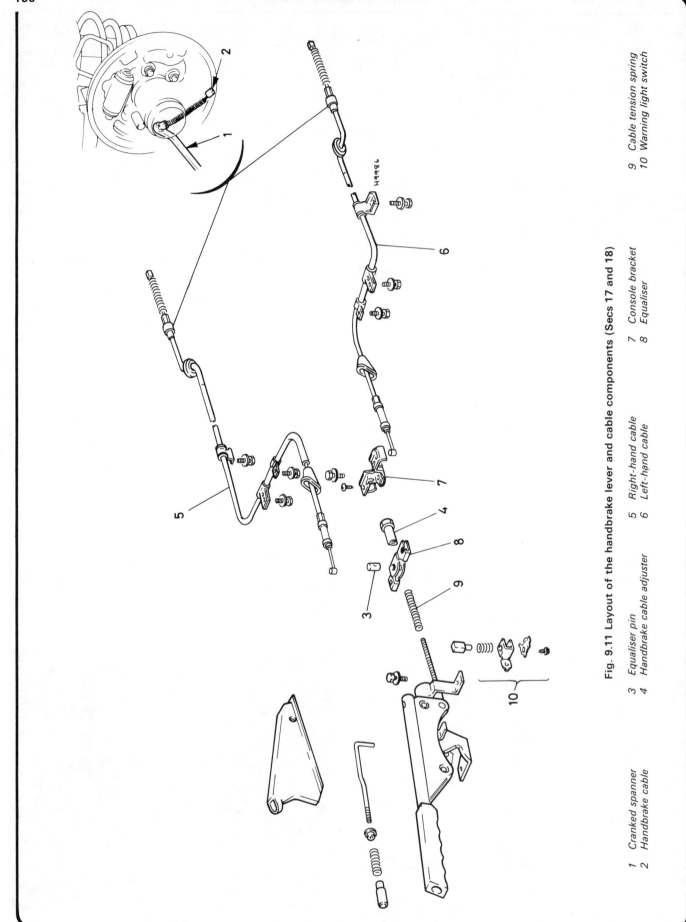

Fig. 9.11 Layout of the handbrake lever and cable components (Secs 17 and 18)

1 Cranked spanner
2 Handbrake cable

3 Equaliser pin
4 Handbrake cable adjuster

5 Right-hand cable
6 Left-hand cable

7 Console bracket
8 Equaliser.

9 Cable tension spring
10 Warning light switch

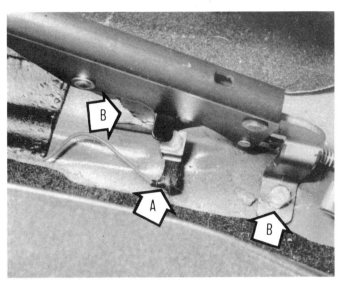

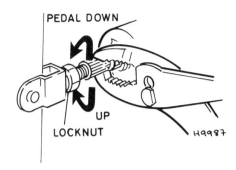

Fig. 9.12 Brake pedal height adjustment details (Sec 19)

18.3 Handbrake warning light switch wiring (A) and lever retaining bolts (B)

2 Disconnect the pad return spring and the pushrod clevis fork from the pedal arm.
3 Unscrew the pivot cross-shaft nut and withdraw the shaft until the brake pedal can be removed. The clutch and brake pedals pivot on a common cross-shaft (see Chapter 5).
4 On cars with automatic transmission, the brake pedal pivots on a shorter cross-shaft, otherwise the arrangement is similar.
5 Refitting is the reverse sequence to removal, but check the pedal height as described in Section 19 after fitting.

21 Fault diagnosis – braking system

Symptom	Reason(s)
Excessive pedal travel	Rear brake self-adjust mechanism inoperative Air in hydraulic system Faulty master cylinder
Brake pedal feels spongy	Air in hydraulic system Faulty master cylinder
Judder felt through brake pedal or steering wheel when braking	Excessive run-out or distortion of front discs or rear drums Disc pads or brake linings worn Brake backplate or disc caliper loose Wear in suspension or steering components or mountings – see Chapter 10
Excessive pedal pressure required to stop car	Faulty servo unit, disconnected, damaged or insecure vacuum hose Wheel cylinder(s) or caliper piston seized Disc pads or brake shoe linings worn or contaminated Brake shoes incorrectly fitted Incorrect grade of pads or linings fitted Primary or secondary hydraulic circuit failure
Brakes pull to one side	Disc pads or linings worn or contaminated Wheel cylinder or caliper piston seized Seized rear brake self-adjust mechanism Disc pads or linings renewed on one side only Faulty pressure regulating valve Tyre, steering or suspension defect – see Chapter 10
Brakes binding	Wheel cylinder or caliper piston seized Handbrake incorrectly adjusted Faulty master cylinder
Rear wheels locking under normal braking	Rear brake shoe linings contaminated Faulty pressure regulating valve

Chapter 10 Suspension and steering

Contents

Specifications

Front suspension

Type .... Independent strut type with torsion bars, telescopic shock absorbers and anti-roll bar

Vehicle ride height (measured from the ground to the edge of the front wheel arch):

UK models:

Hatchback .... 631 to 661 mm (24.8 to 26.0 in)
Shuttle .... 634 to 664 mm (24.9 to 26.1 in)
CRX .... 629 to 659 mm (24.7 to 25.9 in)

North American models:

Hatchback .... 631 to 661 mm (24.8 to 26.0 in)
Wagon .... 634 to 664 mm (24.9 to 26.1 in)
Sedan .... 636 to 666 mm (25.0 to 26.2 in)
CRX .... 629 to 659 mm (24.7 to 25.9 in)

Rear suspension

Type .... Rigid beam axle with trailing arm and Panhard rod location. Coil springs and telescopic shock absorbers, anti-roll stabilizer

Vehicle ride height (measured from the ground to the edge of the rear wheel arch):

UK models:

Hatchback .... 637 to 652 mm (25.0 to 25.6 in)
Shuttle .... 641 to 656 mm (25.2 to 25.8 in)
CRX .... 626 to 641 mm (24.6 to 25.2 in)

North American models:

Hatchback .... 637 to 652 mm (25.0 to 25.6 in)
Wagon .... 641 to 656 mm (25.2 to 25.8 in)
Sedan .... 629 to 644 mm (24.7 to 25.3 in)
CRX .... 626 to 641 mm (24.6 to 25.2 in)

Rear wheel toe setting .... 0 to 4 mm (0 to 0.15 in) toe-in
Rear wheel camber angle .... 0°30′ to 1° negative

Steering

Type	Rack and pinion with power assistance available on certain models
Camber angle:	
Hatchback, Sedan and CRX	1° negative to 1° positive
Shuttle and Wagon	1°20′ negative to 1°20′ positive
Castor angle:	
Manual steering:	
Hatchback and Sedan	1°20′ to 3°20′
Shuttle and Wagon	1°05′ to 3°05′
CRX	1°25′ to 3°25′
Power-assisted steering:	
All models	2° to 4°
Steering axis inclination:	
Hatchback and Sedan	12°20′ to 13°20′
Shuttle and Wagon	11°30′ to 12°30′
CRX	12°25′ to 13°25′
Toe setting	3.0 mm (0.11 in) toe-in to 3.0 mm (0.11 in) toe-out

Tyres

Tyre size and pressures	Refer to data label on edge of door or door pillar

Torque wrench settings

	Nm	lbf ft
Front suspension		
Anti-roll bar clamp bolts	22	16
Anti-roll bar to lower arm	22	16
Lower arm balljoint nut	44	32
Driveshaft retaining nut	185	134
Lower arm to radius arm	39	28
Suspension strut-to-steering knuckle pinch bolt	65	47
Strut top mounting nuts	39	28
Strut spindle nut	44	32
Radius arm bushing nut	83	60
Torque tube holder bolts	22	16
Front crossmember bolts	65	47
Rear suspension		
Panhard rod to body bracket	55	40
Panhard rod to axle beam	75	54
Trailing arm to body	65	47
Hub retaining nut	185	134
Shock absorber upper mounting nut	22	16
Shock absorber lower mounting nut	55	40
Control arm nuts	40	29
Stub axle nuts	45	33
Swing bearing nuts	45	33
Anti-roll stabilizer to axle beam	75	54
Steering		
Tie-rod balljoint nut	44	32
Steering wheel nut	50	36
Intermediate shaft universal joint pinch bolts	30	22
Column lower bracket bolts	22	16
Bending plate nuts	13	9
Bending plate guide bolts	22	16
Steering tie-rod to rack	75	54
Rack damper locknut	25	18
Steering gear mounting brackets	40	29
Power-assisted steering pump bolts	45	33
Roadwheel nuts	110	80

1 General description

The independent front suspension is of the torsion bar type in conjunction with strut type telescopic shock absorbers. Lateral and longitudinal location of each front strut unit is by a lower suspension arm and radius arm assembly splined to the torsion bar at its inner end, and incorporating a balljoint at its outer end. Both radius arms are interconnected by an anti-roll bar. The steering knuckles which carry the hub bearings, brake calipers and the hub/disc assemblies are clamped to the front struts and connected to the radius arms via the balljoints.

The rear suspension is of the trailing arm type incorporating a beam axle. Lateral location of the axle is by a Panhard rod, while longitudinal location is controlled by the trailing arms. Suspension and damping is by strut assemblies containing coil springs and integral telescopic shock absorbers. An anti-roll stabilizer assembly is fitted to the right-hand side of the beam axle and operates in conjunction with a swing bearing unit and control arm.

The steering gear is of the conventional rack and pinion type located behind the front wheels. Movement of the steering wheel is transmitted to the steering gear by means of a steering shaft and intermediate shaft containing two universal joints. The front steering knuckles are connected to the steering gear by tie-rods, each having an inner and outer balljoint. Certain models are available with power-assisted steering operated by a hydraulic pump, belt driven from the crankshaft pulley.

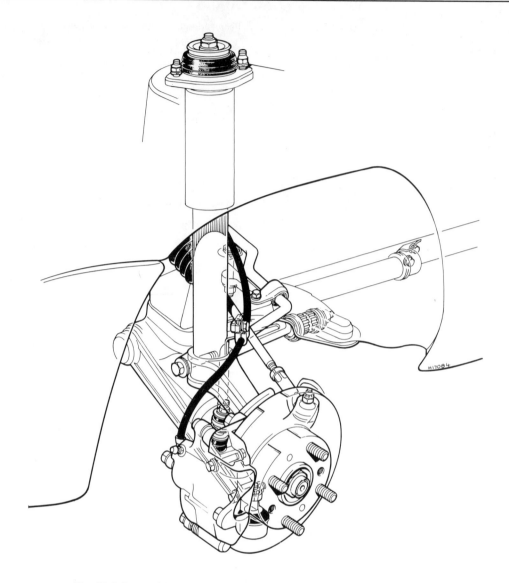

Fig. 10.1 General layout of the front suspension components (Sec 1)

2 Maintenance and inspection

1   At the intervals specified in 'Routine Maintenance' at the beginning of this Manual a thorough inspection of all suspension and steering components should be carried out using the following procedure as a guide.

Front suspension and steering gear

2   Jack up the front of the car and securely support it on stands.

3   Visually inspect the lower balljoint dust covers and the steering rack and pinion gaiters for splits, chafing, or deterioration. Renew the rubber gaiters or the balljoint dust cover, as described in the appropriate Sections of this Chapter, if any damage is apparent.

4   On vehicles equipped with power-assisted steering, check the fluid hoses for chafing or deterioration, and the pipe and hose unions for fluid leaks. Also check for any signs of fluid leakage from the rubber gaiters which would indicate failed fluid seals within the steering gear.

5   Check and if necessary top up the fluid in the power-assisted steering pump reservoir, as described in Section 33. Check the condition of the pump drivebelt, adjust the tension or if worn renew the belt using the procedure described in Section 35.

6   Grasp the roadwheel at the 12 o'clock and 6 o'clock positions and try to rock it. Very slight free play may be felt, but if the movement is

appreciable further investigation is necessary to determine the source. Continue rocking the wheel while an assistant depresses the footbrake. If the movement is now eliminated or significantly reduced, it is likely that the hub bearings are at fault. If the free play is still evident with the footbrake depressed, then there is wear in the suspension joints or mountings. Renew any worn components, as described in the appropriate Sections of this Chapter.

7   Now grasp the wheel at the 9 o'clock and 3 o'clock positions and try to rock it as before. Any movement felt now may again be caused by wear in the hub bearings or the steering tie-rod inner or outer balljoints. If the outer balljoint is worn the visual movement will be obvious. If the inner joint is suspect it can be felt by placing a hand over the rack and pinion rubber gaiter and gripping the tie-rod. If the wheel is now rocked, movement will be felt at the inner joint if wear has taken place. Repair procedures are described in Section 23 or 21 respectively.

8   With the car standing on its wheels have an assistant turn the steering wheel back and forth about one eighth of a turn each way. There should be no lost movement whatever between the steering wheel and roadwheels. If this is not the case, closely observe the joints and mountings previously described, but in addition check the intermediate shaft universal joints for wear and the steering rack damper adjustment (Sec 29). Any wear should be visually apparent and must be rectified, as described in the appropriate Sections of this Chapter.

Rear suspension

9 Chock the front wheels, jack up the rear of the car and support it securely on axle stands.

10 Visually inspect the rear suspension components, attachments and linkages for any visible signs of wear or damage.

11 Grasp the roadwheel at the 12 o'clock and 6 o'clock positions and try to rock it. Any excess movement here indicates wear in the hub bearings which may also be accompanied by a rumbling sound when the wheel is spun. Repair procedures are described in Section 13.

Wheels and tyres

12 Carefully inspect each tyre, including the spare, for signs of uneven wear, lumps or damage to the sidewalls or tread face. Refer to Section 39 for further details.

13 Check the condition of the wheel rims for distortion, damage and excessive run-out. Also make sure that the balance weights are secure with no obvious signs that any are missing. Check the torque of the wheel nuts and check the tyre pressures.

Shock absorbers

14 Check for any signs of fluid leakage around the shock absorber body. Should any fluid be noticed the shock absorber is defective internally and renewal is necessary.

15 The efficiency of the shock absorber may be checked by bouncing the car at each corner. Generally speaking the body will return to its normal position and stop after being depressed. If it rises and returns on a rebound, the shock absorber is probably suspect. Examine also the shock absorber mountings for any sign of wear. Renewal procedures are contained in Sections 5 and 14.

3 Steering knuckle – removal and refitting

1 While the vehicle is standing on its wheels, remove the wheel trim and slacken the driveshaft retaining nut, using a 32 mm socket, while an assistant firmly depresses the footbrake.

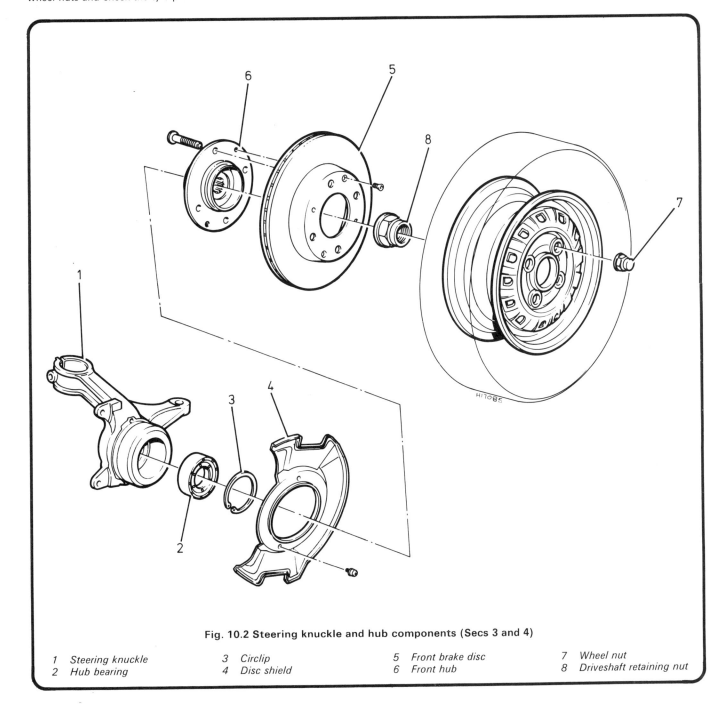

Fig. 10.2 Steering knuckle and hub components (Secs 3 and 4)

1 Steering knuckle	3 Circlip	5 Front brake disc	7 Wheel nut
2 Hub bearing	4 Disc shield	6 Front hub	8 Driveshaft retaining nut

2   Jack up the front of the car and support it on stands. Remove the front roadwheel and driveshaft retaining nut.

3   Undo the two bolts securing the brake caliper bracket to the steering knuckle. Slide the caliper assembly complete with pads off the disc and suspend it using string or wire from a convenient place under the wheel arch. Take care not to strain the brake hose.

4   Undo the two screws and withdraw the disc from the hub. If necessary two 8.0 mm diameter bolts may be screwed into the holes provided to draw the disc off.

5   Position a suitable jack beneath the suspension lower arm balljoint. The jack will take the full torque reaction of the torsion bar when the balljoint is released, so ensure that the jack head is centrally and securely located.

6   Extract the split pin, then undo the lower arm balljoint retaining nut.

7   Using a suitable balljoint separator tool, release the balljoint from the steering knuckle (photo).

8   Undo the retaining nut and release the tie-rod outer balljoint using the same procedure (photo).

9   Undo the pinch bolt from the steering knuckle clamp and tap the knuckle down off the suspension strut using a mallet.

10 Withdraw the steering knuckle from the driveshaft and remove it from the car.

11 Refitting is the reverse sequence to removal bearing in mind the following points:

   (a) Renew the clamp pinch bolt if a nut can easily be screwed past the nylon locking insert
   (b) Tighten all nuts and bolts to the specified torque and use new split pins where applicable
   (c) Use a new driveshaft retaining nut and tighten it fully with the car standing on its wheels. Stake the nut into the groove in the driveshaft outer constant velocity joint

4   Front hub bearing – renewal

1   Remove the steering knuckle as described in Section 3.

2   Undo the three screws securing the disc shield to the steering knuckle.

3   Securely support the steering knuckle and remove the hub using a press or harness and suitable mandrels. It is likely that the bearing will come apart during this operation and the inner race will remain in position on the hub. If so, draw the inner race off the hub using a two or three legged puller. To facilitate removal, use the U-shaped piece from an exhaust clamp located in the ball track of the inner race and locate the puller legs behind this (photos).

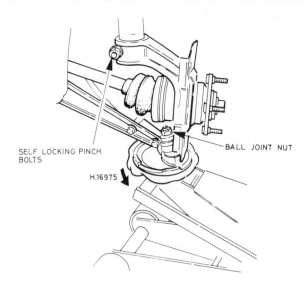

Fig. 10.3 Suspension lower arm correctly supported prior to disconnecting the balljoint (Sec 3)

SELF LOCKING PINCH BOLTS

BALL JOINT NUT

H.16975

3.7 Releasing lower arm balljoint from steering knuckle

3.8 Releasing tie-rod outer balljoint from steering knuckle

4.3A Removing the front hub

4.3B Removing the bearing inner race from the hub

4   Remove the disc shield.
5   Extract the circlip and remove the bearing from the steering knuckle using the same procedure as for removal of the hub.
6   Clean the steering knuckle thoroughly and remove any burrs that may have been caused during bearing removal.
7   Fit the new bearing using the same procedure as for removal. Ensure that the bearing enters the knuckle squarely and that the mandrel locates against the outer race only. •
8   Refit the bearing retaining circlip, then place the disc shield in position on the knuckle.
9   Support the bearing inner race and press or drive in the hub.
10 Refit the disc shield retaining screws.
11 Refit the steering knuckle as described in Section 3.

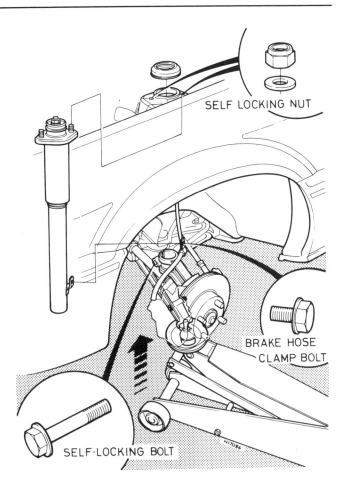

Fig. 10.4 Front suspension strut removal (Sec 5)

5   Front suspension strut – removal and refitting

1   Jack up the front of the car and support it on stands. Remove the roadwheel.
2   Support the suspension lower arm on a jack and disconnect the brake hydraulic hose from the support bracket on the suspension strut.
3   Working within the engine compartment, unscrew the strut top mounting nuts and then lower the jack under the suspension lower arm to separate the strut from the wing valance.
4   Unscrew the clamp pinch-bolt from the base of the strut and slide the steering knuckle off the strut. Be prepared for reaction from the torsion bar, so make sure that the car and the suspension is well supported. Withdraw the strut from the car.
5   Unscrew the self-locking spindle nut and remove the top mounting, tubular shield and bump stop. The spindle can be held against rotation using an Allen key in its socket.
6   Fully extend and retract the strut piston rod. If it is jerky, noisy, or offers little or no resistance, the strut must be renewed. It is a sealed unit and cannot be dismantled.
7   To refit the strut, first assemble the top mounting, shield and bump stop. Screw on the self-locking nut, again holding the spindle from turning using an Allen key.
8   Offer the strut up under the wing and tighten the nuts holding it to the valance.
9   Connect the lower end of the strut to the steering knuckle, making sure that the tab on the strut locates in the clamp slot. Tighten the pinch-bolt to the specified torque.
10 Connect the brake hose to the strut bracket.
11 Fit the roadwheel and lower the car to the floor.

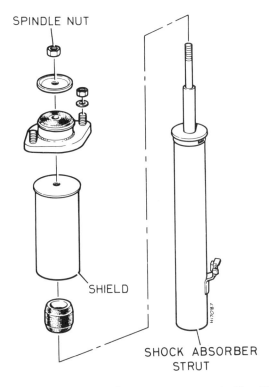

Fig. 10.5 Front suspension strut components (Sec 5)

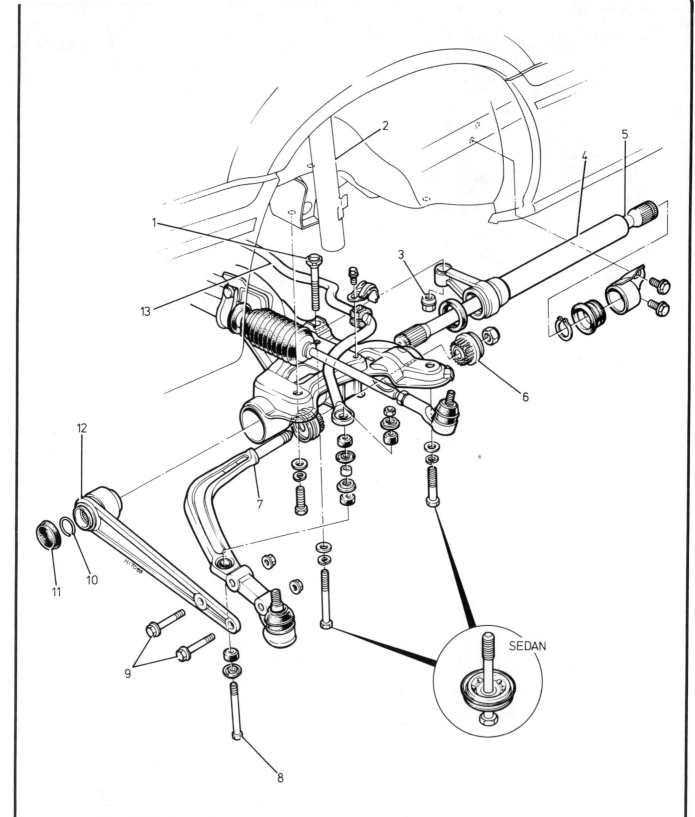

Fig. 10.6 Exploded view of the radius arm, lower arm and torsion bar assemblies (Secs 6 to 10)

1 Height adjusting bolt	5 Torsion bar	8 Anti-roll bar mounting bolt	11 Torsion bar cap
2 Strut unit	6 Radius arm bushing	9 Lower arm bolt	12 Lower arm
3 Height adjusting nut	7 Radius arm	10 Torsion bar clip	13 Anti-roll bar
4 Torque tube			

6 Front radius arm – removal and refitting

1 Jack up the front of the car and support it on stands. Remove the roadwheel.
2 Position a suitable jack beneath the front suspension lower arm. The jack will take the full torque reaction of the torsion bar during subsequent operations so ensure that the jack head is centrally and securely located (see Fig. 10.3).
3 Extract the split pin, then undo the lower arm balljoint retaining nut (photo).
4 Using a suitable balljoint separator tool, release the balljoint from the steering knuckle.
5 Unbolt the radius arm from the lower arm, and then unscrew the bolt which secures the anti-roll bar to the radius arm.
6 Unscrew the radius arm bushing self-locking nut (photo).
7 Lower the jack to relieve the tension on the torsion bar and to provide clearance for radius arm removal.
8 Lower the radius arm, move it forward and remove it from under the car.

9 If necessary the radius arm bushes can be renewed, but wear in the balljoint can only be rectified by purchase of a new arm complete.
10 Refitting is the reverse sequence to removal, bearing in mind the following points:

   (a) Renew any self-locking nuts that are not a tight fit on their respective bolt threads
   (b) Tighten all nuts and bolts to the specified torque
   (c) Tighten the radius arm bushing nut fully when the weight of the car is standing on its wheels

7 Front suspension lower arm – removal and refitting

The front suspension lower arm is fitted with a rubber bonded steel-backed bush which is a press fit on the arm and in the front crossmember. Due to the large number of Honda special tools required for removal, which are not generally available outside the trade, it is considered advisable to have this work carried out by a suitably equipped dealer.

8 Front crossmember – removal and refitting

1 Refer to Section 30 (manual steering) or Section 37 (power-assisted steering) and remove the rack and pinion steering gear.
2 Position a suitable jack beneath the left-hand lower arm balljoint. The jack will take the full torque reaction of the torsion bar when the balljoint is released, so ensure that the jack head is centrally and securely located (see Fig. 10.3).
3 Extract the split pin, unscrew the nut and release the lower arm balljoint from the steering knuckle using a balljoint extractor tool.
4 Lower the jack under the lower arm until the arm is free of tension.
5 Repeat paragraphs 2, 3 and 4 on the right-hand side.
6 Undo the two bolts each side securing the torque tube holders at the rear of the torsion bars to the underbody.
7 Support the engine using a crane and slings or by using an additional jack.
8 Undo the nuts and bolts securing the engine/transmission rear mounting to the crossmember.
9 Support the crossmember at its centre using a jack and undo the six mounting bolts.
10 Carefully lower the crossmember to the ground and remove it from under the car.
11 If necessary the crossmember can be further dismantled with reference to the relevant Sections of this Chapter.
12 Refitting is the reverse sequence to removal, but tighten all nuts and bolts to the specified torque.

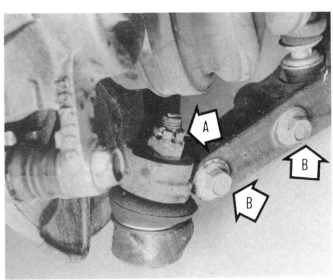

6.3 Balljoint retaining nut (A) and radius arm retaining bolts (B)

9 Front anti-roll bar – removal and refitting

1 Remove the front crossmember as described in Section 8.
2 Undo the two bolts securing the anti-roll bar clamps to the crossmember and remove the clamps.
3 Undo the two nuts securing the anti-roll bar to the suspension lower arms. Withdraw the washers and bushes, noting their arrangement, then remove the anti-roll bar.
4 Refitting is the reverse sequence to removal. Lubricate the bushes with silicone grease and tighten all nuts and bolts to the specified torque.

10 Front torsion bar – removal and refitting

1 Jack up the front of the car and support it on stands. Remove the roadwheel.
2 Undo and remove the height adjusting nut.
3 Undo the two bolts and remove the torque tube holder from the rear of the torsion bar (photos).
4 Withdraw the cap bushing and extract the 30 mm circlip from the rear of the torsion baar (photo).

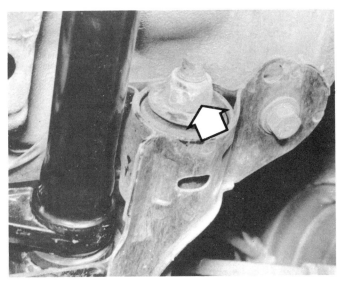

6.6 Radius arm bushing retaining nut (arrowed)

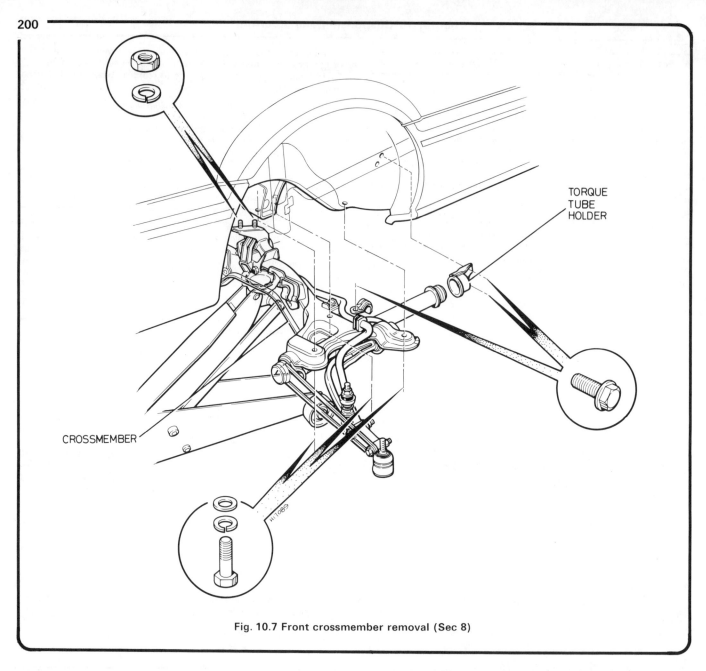

TORQUE
TUBE
HOLDER

CROSSMEMBER

Fig. 10.7 Front crossmember removal (Sec 8)

10.3A Undo the torque tube holder retaining bolts ...

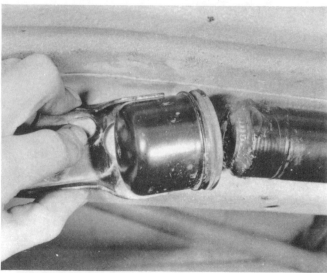

10.3B ... and withdraw the holder and cap bushing

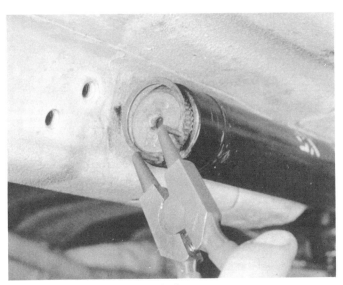

10.4 Extracting torsion bar rear circlip

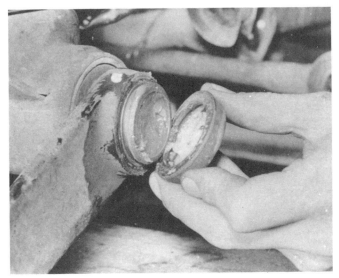

10.5A Remove the torsion bar front cap ...

10.5B ... and extract the circlip

5   At the front of the torsion bar remove the cap, then tap the bar forward slightly until clearance exists to enable the front torsion bar circlip to be removed. Move the lower arm up and down slightly if the torsion bar is tight (photos).
6   Tap the torsion bar rearward and remove it from the torque tube.
7   Remove the torque tube.
8   Remove the torque tube seal.
9   Examine the torsion bar for cracks or wear of the splines and renew if necessary.
10 Liberally lubricate the torque tube sliding surfaces and new seal with grease, then position the seal and torque tube on the crossmember.
11 Lubricate the torsion bar splines with grease and insert the bar into the torque tube from the rear.
12 Align the projection or punch mark on the torque tube splines with the cut-out or paint mark on the torsion bar splines.
13 Engage the torsion bar with the lower arm so that the cut-out in the torsion bar splines engages with the projection on the lower arm splines.
14 Push the torsion bar through the lower arm until the front circlip can be fitted, then tap the cap into place.
15 Fit the 30 mm circlip to the rear of the torsion bar.
16 Lubricate the cap bushing with grease, then fit the cap bushing followed by the torque tube holder.
17 Lubricate the height adjusting nut with grease and screw it on just over finger tight.
18 Refit the roadwheel then lower the car to the ground.
19 Adjust the vehicle side height as described in Section 11.

11 Vehicle side height – adjustment

1   Have the car on a level surface with the tyre pressures correct and the front wheels in the straight ahead position.
2   The car should have a full fuel tank but otherwise be unladen.
3   Bounce the car up and down several times to settle the suspension.
4   Measure between the floor vertically to the highest point of the front wheel arch edge (fig. 10.8) on both sides of the car and record the measurements.
5   Compare the dimensions obtained with the figures given in the Specifications. If adjustment is necessary, proceed as follows.
6   Jack up and support the side of the car to be adjusted.
7   Turn the torsion bar height adjusting nut clockwise (as viewed from below) to increase the height, or anti-clockwise to decrease it (photo). Note that one complete turn of the nut will alter the vehicle height by 5.0 mm (0.20 in).
8   After making an approximate adjustment, lower the car, move it

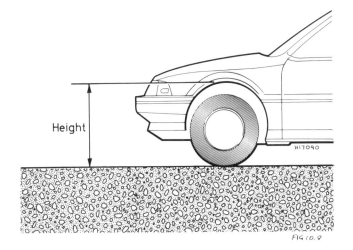

Fig. 10.8 Vehicle ride height front measuring point (Sec 11)

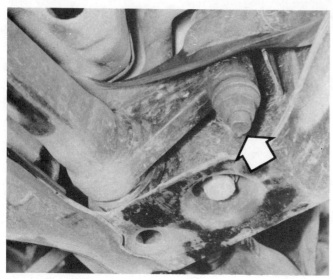

11.7 Torsion bar height adjusting nut (arrowed)

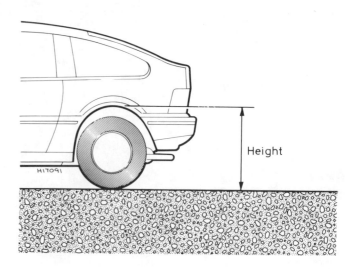

Fig. 10.9 Vehicle ride height rear measuring point (Sec 11)

forwards and backwards over half a car's length, then bounce the suspension as before. Take further measurements and repeat the procedure until the side height is as specified.

9   Check the side height at the rear in the same way as at the front by measuring from the floor to the wheel arch edge. The rear side height is not adjustable and any deviation from the specified value can only be rectified by renewal of the rear coil springs.

12 Front suspension balljoint dust covers – renewal

1   The rubber dust covers on the suspension lower arm balljoint and steering tie-rod outer balljoint can be renewed separately using the following procedures. It must be stressed however that if the joint is excessively worn due to water or grit entry from a damaged dust cover, the balljoint should be renewed complete.

Suspension lower arm balljoint

2   Jack up the front of the car and support it on stands. Remove the front roadwheel.

3   Position a suitable jack beneath the front suspension lower arm. The jack will take the full torque reaction of the torsion bar when the balljoint is released, so ensure that the jack head is centrally and securely located (see Fig. 10.3).

4   Extract the split pin, then undo the lower arm balljoint retaining nut.

5   Using a suitable balljoint separator tool, release the balljoint from the steering knuckle.

6   Extract the retaining clip at the base of the dust cover and withdraw the dust cover from the balljoint.

7   Fill the new dust cover with grease and locate it over the joint. Fit the retaining clip and push it into place using a socket or tube of suitable diameter if necessary.

8   Refit the balljoint to the steering knuckle, tighten the nut to the specified torque and secure with a new split pin.

9   Refit the roadwheel and lower the car to the ground.

Steering tie-rod outer balljoint

10 Jack up the front of the car and support it on stands. Remove the front roadwheel.

11 Extract the split pin, then undo the balljoint retaining nut.

12 Using a suitable balljoint separator, release the balljoint from the steering knuckle arm.

13 The procedure is now the same as described previously in paragraphs 6 to 9 inclusive.

13 Rear hub and bearing – renewal

1   The rear hub and bearing are serviced as an assembly. The bearing is sealed for life and requires no lubrication or attention. If bearing renewal is required, it will be necessary to renew the hub and bearing assembly complete.

2   Jack up the rear of the car and support it on stands. Remove the rear roadwheel and the hub cap.

3   Refer to Chapter 9 (Section 6) if necessary and remove the brake drum.

4   Tap up the staking on the hub retaining nut and unscrew the nut from the stub axle. Remove the thrust washer (photo).

5   Using a suitable puller if necessary draw the hub assembly off the stub axle (photo).

6   Fit the new hub assembly followed by the thrust washer, then screw on a new hub retaining nut.

7   Tighten the nut to the specified torque, then stake the edge of the nut into the stub axle groove using a small punch (photo).

8   Refit the brake drum, hub cap and roadwheel, then lower the car to the ground.

13.4 Rear hub thrust washer removal

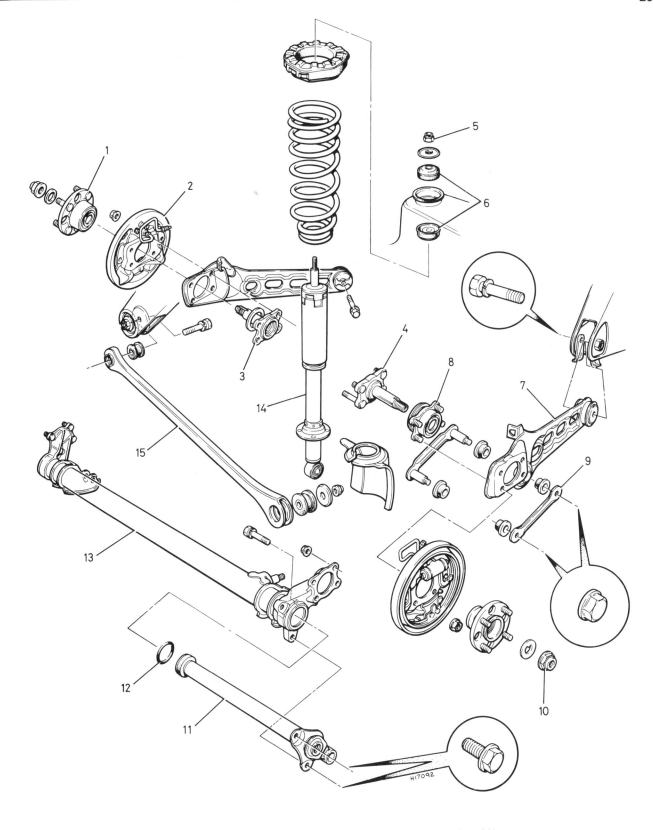

Fig. 10.10 Exploded view of the rear suspension (Secs 13 to 21)

1 Bearing hub unit	5 Shock absorber upper	8 Swing bearing unit	12 Stabilizer rubber seal
2 Back plate	mounting nut	9 Control arm	13 Rear axle beam
3 Stub axle	6 Upper mounting cushions	10 Hub unit nut	14 Shock absorber
4 Stub axle	7 Trailing arm	11 Anti-roll stabilizer assembly	15 Panhard rod

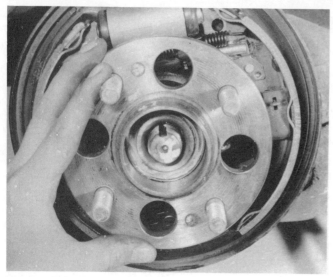

13.5 Removing the rear hub

13.7 Staking the hub nut after tightening

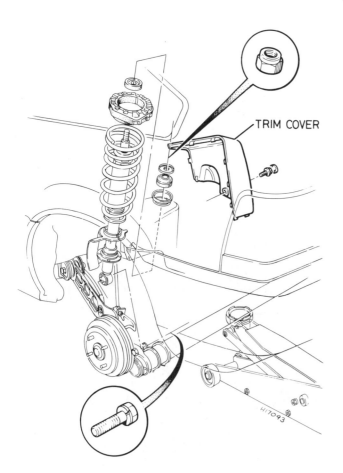

TRIM COVER

H17043

Fig. 10.11 Rear strut removal details (Sec 14)

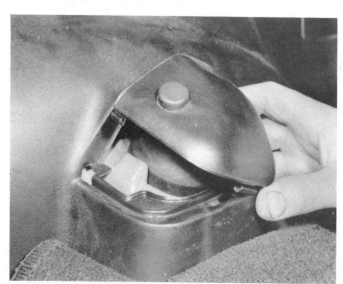

14.3A Remove the trim cover ...

14.3B ... and protective cap ...

14 Rear strut assembly – removal and refitting

1　Jack up the rear of the car and support it on stands. Remove the rear roadwheel.

2　Place a jack beneath the rear axle beam and take its weight.

3　From within the luggage compartment remove the trim cover and

14.3C ... for access to the shock absorber upper mounting

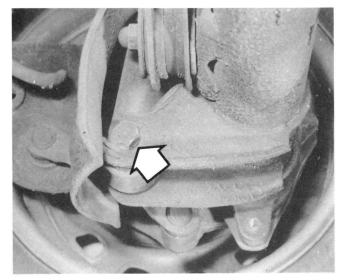

14.6 Shock absorber lower mounting (arrowed)

protective cap to gain access to the shock absorber upper mounting (photos).
4   Unscrew the self-locking nut from the spindle and take off the rubber cushion and retaining plate. Hold the spindle against rotation by inserting an Allen key in its socket.
5   Gently lower the axle beam jack until all tension is relieved in the coil spring.
6   Unbolt the shock absorber lower mounting and then lower the jack again. Withdraw the shock absorber and spring from the car (photo).
7   Remove the spring and the shock absorber protective shield.
8   Prise off the split collar and remove the sleeve upwards from the shock absorber.
9   Remove the bump stop.
10 Grip the shock absorber lower mounting in the jaws of a vice and holding the unit vertically, fully extend and retract it several times. If there is any jerkiness, seizure or lack of resistance, renew the shock absorber complete.
11 Refitting is the reverse sequence to removal bearing in mind the following points:

  (a) The smaller diameter spring coils are at the lower end
  (b) Tighten the upper mounting nut and lower mounting bolt to the specified torque with the weight of the car standing on its wheels.

15 Rear suspension trailing arm – removal and refitting

1   Jack up the rear of the car and support it on stands. Remove the rear roadwheel.
2   Refer to Section 13 and remove the rear hub.
3   Clamp the rear flexible brake hose using a brake hose clamp or self-locking wrench with protected jaws.
4   Unscrew the brake pipe-to-hose union, then extract the clip and withdraw the hose from the trailing arm bracket. Protect the pipe and hose ends against dirt ingress.
5   Refer to Chapter 9 and remove the brake shoes. With the brake shoes removed, withdraw the disconnected handbrake cable from the trailing arm.
6   Undo the four retaining nuts and remove the brake backplate.
7   If working on the right-hand side, undo the two nuts and remove the control arm inner and outer parts from the trailing arm and anti-roll stabilizer.
8   Undo the trailing arm front mounting bolt and remove the arm from under the car.

9   Refitting is the reverse sequence to removal bearing in mind the following points:

  (a) Renew the trailing arm front mounting bolt if the self-locking insert offers little resistance to tightening
  (b) Tighten all nuts and bolts to the specified torque, but tighten the front mounting bolt with the weight of the car standing on its wheels
  (b) Bleed the brake hydraulic system as described in Chapter 9.

16 Panhard rod – removal and refitting

1   Jack up the rear of the car and support it on stands.
2   Unscrew and remove the panhard rod upper mounting bolt, and lower the mounting nut and flat washer (photos).
3   Slide the rod off the lower mounting stud and withdraw it from its upper location.
4   Refitting is the reverse sequence to removal. Tighten the mountings to the specified torque and renew the self-locking nut and bolt if they offer little resistance to tightening.

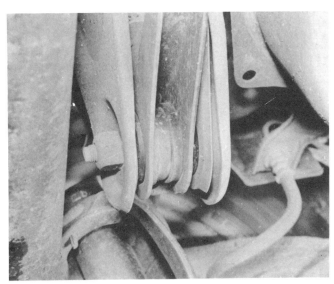

16.2A Panhard rod upper mounting bolt ...

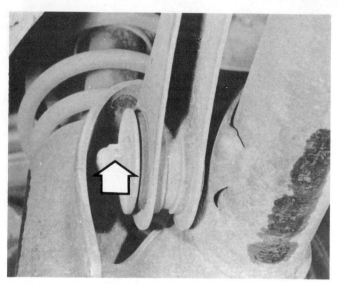

16.2B ... and lower mounting nut

17.5 Control arm retaining nuts (arrowed)

17 Rear axle beam – removal and refitting

1   Jack up the rear of the car and support it on stands. Remove both rear roadwheels.
2   Undo both shock absorber lower mountings.
3   Disconnect the Panhard rod from the axle beam.
4   Remove the left-hand rear hub (Section 13), then undo the four nuts securing the brake backplate, trailing arm and stub axle to the axle beam studs.
5   On the right-hand side undo the two nuts and remove the control arm inner and outer parts from the trailing arm and anti-roll stabilizer (photo).
6   Undo the four bolts securing the right-hand stub axle to the axle beam.
7   With the axle beam supported on a jack, move it sideways to disengage the stub axle studs, then lower the assembly to the ground.
8   Refitting is the reverse sequence to removal. Tighten all nuts and bolts to the specified torque and renew any self-locking nuts that offer little resistance when tightening.

18 Rear stub axle – removal and refitting

Left-hand side

1   Refer to Section 17 and remove the rear axle beam. The stub axle can now be withdrawn from the brake backplate and trailing arm.
2   Refitting is the reverse sequence to removal.

Right-hand side

3   Jack up the rear of the car and support it on stands. Remove both rear roadwheels.
4   Remove the right-hand rear hub (Section 13), then undo the four nuts securing the brake backplate and trailing arm to the swing bearing unit.
5   Remove the rear axle beam using the procedure described in Section 17, paragraphs 2 to 7 inclusive.
6   With the axle beam removed, withdraw the stub axle and swing bearing assembly from the backplate and trailing arm.
7   The swing bearing can be removed as described in Section 19.
8   Refitting is the reverse sequence to removal.

19 Swing bearing unit – removal and refitting

Note: *The swing bearing unit must be renewed complete after removal, as to facilitate removal the bearing is rendered unserviceable.*
1   Remove the right-hand stub axle as described in Section 18.

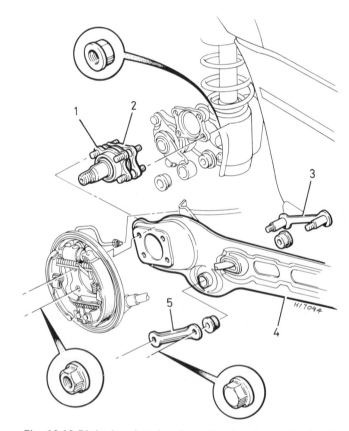

Fig. 10.12 Right-hand stub axle, swing bearing and related components (Secs 18 and 19)

1   *Swing bearing unit*   4   *Trailing arm*
2   *Stub axle*   5   *Control arm*
3   *Control arm*

2   Support the underside of the swing bearing unit and press out the stub axle. The bearing will come apart during this operation and the inner race will remain in position on the stub axle. To remove the inner race, use a bearing remover or two or three legged puller. To facilitate removal, use the U-shaped piece from an exhaust clamp located in the ball track of the inner race and engage the puller legs behind this.

3   The swing bearing unit must now be renewed complete, as this operation renders the bearing unserviceable.

4   Support the inner race of the swing bearing and press the stub axle in from the rear.

5   The unit can now be refitted to the car as described in Section 18.

20 Rear anti-roll stabilizer assembly – removal and refitting

1   Jack up the rear of the car and support it on stands. Remove both rear roadwheels.

2   Remove both rear hubs (Section 13), then remove the rear brake shoes on both sides (Chapter 9).

3   Clamp the flexible brake hoses on both sides using brake hose clamps on self-locking wrenches with protected jaws.

4   Undo the brake pipe-to-hose unions and protect the pipes against dirt ingress.

5   Undo the four brake backplate retaining nuts each side and remove the backplates.

6   On the right-hand side, undo the two nuts and remove the control arm inner and outer parts from the trailing arm and anti-roll stabilizer.

7   Extract the cap from the left-hand end of the axle beam.

8   Undo the two bolts securing the stabilizer to the axle beam.

9   Insert a long dowel into the axle beam from the left-hand end, and using a mallet, tap out the stabilizer.

10 Refitting is the reverse sequence to removal bearing in mind the following points:

   (a) Tighten all nuts and bolts to the specified torque
   (b) Renew any self-locking nuts that offer little resistance when tightening
   (c) The two bolts securing the stabilizer to the axle beam should be tightened after the control arm has been fitted
   (d) Bleed the brake hydraulic system as described in Chapter 9

21 Suspension flexible bushes – renewal

1   Worn or hardened flexible bushes can be renewed using a press or long bolt or stud with a nut, thick washers, and distance pieces of suitable length and diameter. A wide opening vice is also suitable for pressing out flexible bushes and pressing in new ones using sockets, tubes or mandrels of different diameters.

2   When refitting bushes they should be liberally coated with silicone grease.

3   Where the bushes are bonded to a steel backing, considerable force will be required and it is likely that a press will be necessary for removal and refitting.

22 Steering rack rubber gaiter – renewal

1   Jack up the front of the car and support it on stands. Remove the front roadwheel.

2   Release the tie-rod outer balljoint locknut by unscrewing it one quarter of a turn only (photo).

3   Extract the split pin and unscrew the nut securing the balljoint to the steering knuckle arm.

4   Release the balljoint using a suitable balljoint extractor tool.

5   Hold the tie-rod and unscrew the balljoint.

6   Release the retaining clips and slide the rubber gaiter off the rack housing and tie-rod.

7   Extend the rack fully on the side being worked on and liberally coat the rack teeth with multi-purpose grease. Centralise the rack.

8   Slide on the new gaiter and secure with new retaining clips.

9   Screw on the balljoint to its original position, where the locknut will only require one quarter of a turn back to lock it.

10 Reconnect the balljoint to the steering knuckle, fit and tighten the retaining nut and secure with a new split pin.

11 Refit the roadwheel and lower the car to the ground.

12 The front wheel alignment should be checked and if necessary adjusted as described in Section 38.

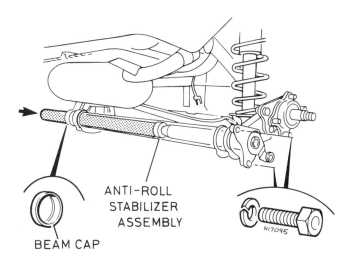

Fig. 10.13 Anti-roll stabilizer removal details (Sec 20)

Arrow shows dowel rod used to remove stabilizer assembly

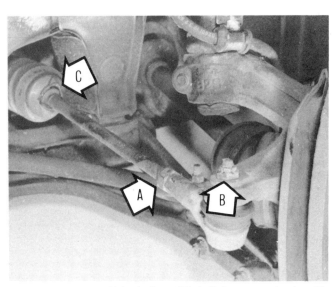

22.2 Tie-rod outer balljoint locknut (A), balljoint-to-steering knuckle nut (B) and gaiter outer clip (C)

23 Tie-rod outer balljoint – removal and refitting

The procedure is covered in detail as part of the steering rack rubber gaiter renewal procedure, and reference should be made to Section 22, paragraph 1 to 5 and 9 to 12.

24 Steering wheel – removal and refitting

1   Using a small screwdriver, prise out the blanking plate from the centre of the steering wheel hub (photo).

2   Check that the front roadwheels are in the straight-ahead position and mark the steering wheel hub-to-spindle relationship.

3   Unscrew the retaining nut and pull off the steering wheel. If the wheel is tight on the splines, jar it lightly with the hands located at opposite sides at the rear of the wheel rim.

4   The horn pad can be removed to expose the contact plate after extracting the screws from the rear face of the steering wheel hub.

24.1 Removing the steering wheel blanking plate

5   Refitting is a reversal of removal. Tighten the retaining nut to the specified torque. It is important that, as the steering wheel is pushed onto its shaft, the direction indicator lugs engage in the cut-outs on the steering wheel hub boss.

25 Steering column intermediate shaft – removal and refitting

Note: *The steering column intermediate shaft can only be removed separately on certain UK models. On North American models and some UK models the intermediate shaft is an integral part of the steering column (see Section 26).*

1   Remove the cover from the base of the intermediate shaft.
2   Unscrew the pinch-bolts from the intermediate shaft universally-jointed couplings.
3   Centralise the steering with the front roadwheels in the straight-ahead position.
4   Remove the intermediate from the pinion shaft and steering shaft.
5   Refitting is a reversal of removal, but make sure that the pinch-bolt holes are aligned with the shaft groove and flat when pushing the couplings onto the splines.
6   Tighten the pinch-bolts to the specified torque.

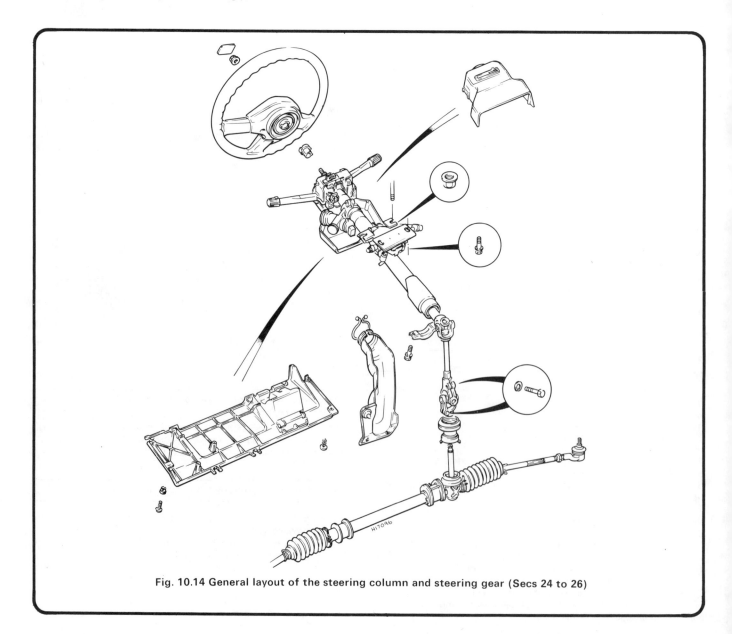

Fig. 10.14 General layout of the steering column and steering gear (Secs 24 to 26)

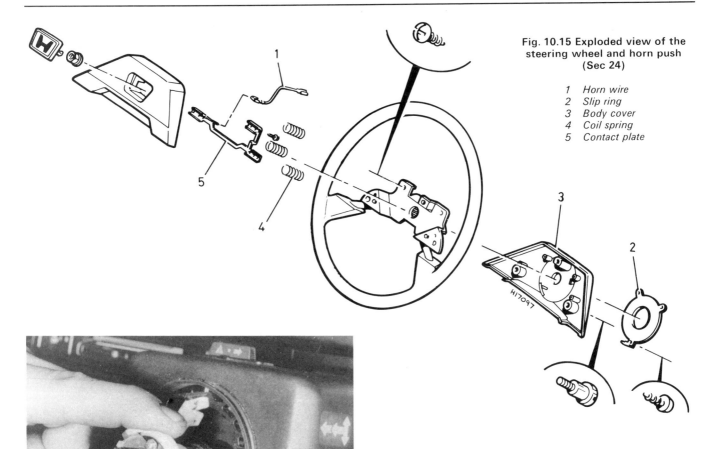

Fig. 10.15 Exploded view of the
steering wheel and horn push
(Sec 24)

1   Horn wire
2   Slip ring
3   Body cover
4   Coil spring
5   Contact plate

26.3 Removing the direction indicator self-cancelling sleeve

26 Steering column – removal, overhaul and refitting

Note: *The steering column may be conventional or incorporate a tilt mechanism according to model. The following procedure describes the tilt type. The conventional column is similar but ignore all references to the tilt mechanism.*

1   Disconnect the battery negative terminal.
2   Remove the steering wheel as described in Section 24.
3   Withdraw the direction indicator self-cancelling sleeve (photo).
4   Extract the retaining ring securing the column upper and lower shrouds (photo).
5   Undo the three lower shroud retaining screws and remove both shrouds (photo).

26.4 Column upper and lower shroud retaining ring   26.5 Removing the lower shroud

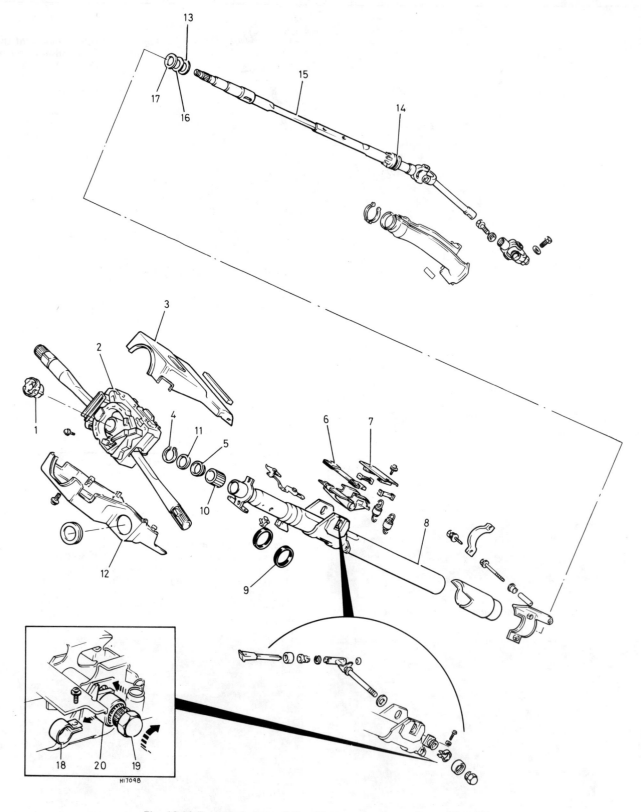

Fig. 10.16 Exploded view of the tilt type steering column (Sec 26)

1	Cancelling sleeve	6	Bending plate	11	Washer	16	Dished washer
2	Combination switch assembly	7	Bending plate guide	12	Lower shroud	17	Flat washer
3	Upper shroud	8	Steering column	13	Spacer	18	Stopper clip
4	Circlip	9	Rubber band	14	Hanger bushing	19	Domed lock nut
5	Column thrust ring	10	Steering column bushing	15	Steering shaft	20	Stopper collar

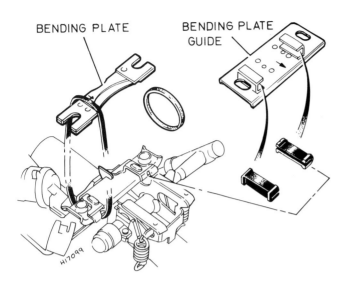

BENDING PLATE   BENDING PLATE
                        GUIDE

H17099

Fig. 10.17 Arrangement of the steering column bending plate components – tilt type steering (Sec 26)

6   Undo the two screws securing the combination switch to the column.
7   Disconnect the wiring harness connectors and slide the combination switch off the column.
8   Remove the cover from the base of the intermediate shaft, and the cover panel from below the column.
9   Unscrew the intermediate shaft lower universal joint pinch bolt.
10 Unbolt the steering column lower bracket.
11 Undo the nuts and bolts securing the bending plate guide and bending plate, then withdraw the column assembly from the car.
12 Release the rubber bands, then remove the column bracket bending plate and bending plate guide.
13 Turn the ignition switch to the 'I' position.
14 Prise the horn contact from the column.
15 At the top of the steering shaft extract the circlip and washer, and pull the shaft down and out of the column.
16 Remove the spacer, dished spring washer and flat washer from the top of the shaft.
17 To renew the column lower hanger bushing, remove the plastic collar and extract the bushing. Fit a new bushing, then push the plastic collar over the column until the projection engages with the column hole.
18 To renew the top bush, withdraw the thrust ring and extract the bush. Fit a new bush and push in the thrust ring.
19 If the tilt mechanism requires attention on models so equipped, refer to Section 27.
20 Reassembly is the reverse sequence to dismantling, but lubricate the shaft and bushings with multi-purpose grease and ensure that the dished washer behind the shaft circlip is fitted with its concave side towards the steering wheel.
21 To refit the column reverse the removal operations. Make sure that the bending plate is not distorted, and renew it if it is. Fit the bending plate and guide with their arrows uppermost and pointing towards the bottom of the column. Tighten all nuts and bolts to the specified torque.

27 Steering column tilt mechanism – overhaul

1   With the steering column removed from the car, take off the hanger springs and rubber bands which retain the bending and holder plates.
2   Release the screw and remove the stopper clip from the tilt mechanism.
3   Unscrew and remove the domed locknut, collar, and stopper. *Note that the locknut has a left-hand thread.*
4   Remove the adjuster lever assembly.

5   Lubricate the sliding surfaces with grease, assemble the lever, stopper and collar without damaging the O-ring.
6   Fit the hanger springs and domed locknut, tightening to 7.0 Nm (5.0 lbf ft), with the collar pushed towards the locknut.
7   Check the force required to operate the adjustment lever. This should be between 5.9 and 9.0 kg (11.0 and 20.0 lb) when checked on a spring balance. If not as specified, slide the collar towards the stopper and slightly tighten or slacken the domed locknut.
8   Finally slide the collar towards the locknut and fit the stopper clip.
9   Fit the bending and holder plates with their spring and rubber bands.

28 Steering column lock – removal and refitting

1   Remove the steering column as described in Section 26.
2   Secure the column in the jaws of a vice and remove the lock fixing bolts. Do this by drilling them out or using a screw extractor. To remove the ignition switch from the lock, refer to Chapter 12.
3   Locate the new lock on the column and tighten the new shear head bolts finger tight. Check that the steering lock is correctly aligned with the hole in the column.
4   Insert the key into the lock and check for smooth operation of the lock tongue on the column cut-out.
5   Tighten the bolts until their heads shear off.

29 Steering rack damper – adjustment

1   If knocking from the steering is heard when traversing rough surfaces consistent with excessive steering free play, or if the steering is excessively stiff, check the rack damper adjustment as follows.
2   Jack up the front of the car and support it on stands with the roadwheels hanging free.
3   Attach a spring balance to the outer end of a steering wheel spoke and check the pull required to turn the steering wheel. This should not exceed 1.5 kg (3.3 lb). A figure just below this is ideal.
4   To adjust, centralise the steering, slacken the rack damper locknut and tighten the adjuster screw until it is felt to contact the coil spring. Check the steering wheel pull as previously described, adjusting the screw by a quarter turn at a time until the specified pull is obtained.
5   Tighten the locknut without altering the position of the adjuster screw.
6   Lower the car to the ground.

30 Rack and pinion steering gear (manual steering) – removal and refitting

1   Jack up the front of the car and support it on stands. Remove the front roadwheels.
2   Remove the cover from the base of the steering column and unscrew the pinch bolt from the intermediate shaft lower universal joint.
3   Pull the universal joint up to release it from the steering gear pinion.
4   Separate both tie-rod outer balljoints from the steering knuckle arms as described in Section 23.
5   On manual transmission models disconnect the gearchange torque rod at the transmission, then move the safety clip aside and drive out the remote control rod roll pin. Slide the remote control rod off the selector shaft. On automatic transmission models, remove the selector cable guide from the floor and pull the selector cable down by hand.
6   Undo the two self-locking nuts, then remove the bolts and tension springs at the exhaust front pipe flexible joint. Separate the joint and pull the front pipe down.
7   Turn the steering gear onto full left-hand lock by pulling on the right-hand tie-rod.
8   Undo the bolts and remove the two steering gear mounting brackets (photo).
9   Drop the unit until the pinion is clear of the entry hole in the floor. Manipulate the steering gear so that it can be lowered clear of the exhaust, then remove the assembly sideways from under the car.

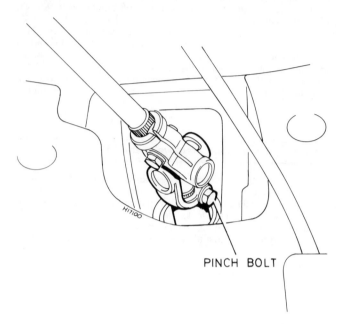

Fig. 10.18 Intermediate shaft lower universal joint pinch bolt (Sec 30)

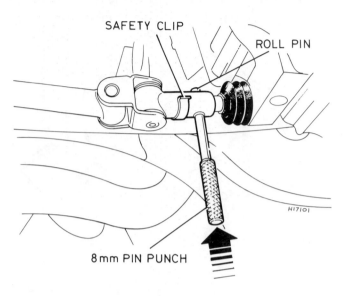

Fig. 10.19 Disconnecting the gearchange mechanism at the manual transmission (Sec 30)

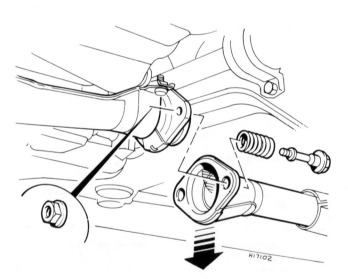

Fig. 10.20 Disconnecting exhaust flexible joint (Sec 30)

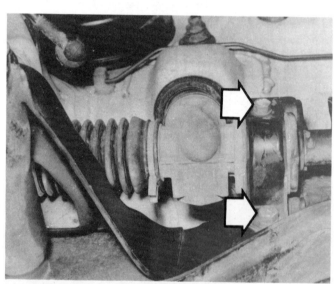

30.8 Steering gear mounting bracket bolts (arrowed)

10 Refitting is the reverse sequence to removal, but centralise the rack and steering wheel before connecting the intermediate shaft universal joint. Tighten all nuts and bolts to the specified torque.

31 Rack and pinion steering gear (manual steering) – overhaul

1 If the steering gear is worn, it is recommended that a new or factory reconditioned unit is fitted. If overhaul of the existing unit is to be undertaken, check the availability of replacement parts before proceeding.
2 Remove the steering gear from the car as described in Section 30. Clean away external dirt and mount the unit in a vice with protected jaws.

3 Release the gaiter clips and pull them away from the rack housing.
4 Release the tie-rod lockwasher tabs. Hold the rack still by means of its flats and unscrew the tie-rods.
5 Unscrew the locknut and remove the rack damper components.
6 Extract the pinion dust seal and the circlip, then withdraw the pinion shaft from the housing.
7 Slide the rack out of the pinion gear end of the rack housing.
8 Remove the mounting insulator followed by the rack end bush.
9 Clean and renew all components which appear worn.
10 Reassembly is a reversal of dismantling. Pack the pinion bearing with multi-purpose grease and smear grease onto the inner surface of the rack end bush. Do not fill the outer slots with grease or the air passages will be restricted.
11 The mounting insulator bush should be positioned between 1.0 and 3.0 mm from the end of the rack housing.
12 Apply grease to the teeth of the rack and then insert the rack from the pinion gear end of the housing.

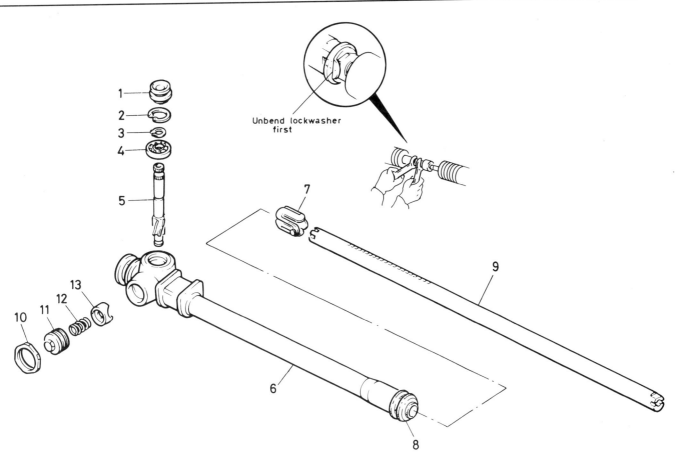

Fig. 10.21 Exploded view of the rack and pinion steering gear (Sec 31)

1 Pinion dust seal	5 Pinion	8 Mount bushing	11 Rack damper screw
2 Circlip	6 Rack housing	9 Rack	12 Rack damper spring
3 Circlip	7 Rack end bushing	10 Damper screw lock nut	13 Rack damper
4 Ball bearing			

13 Liberally grease the pinion shaft opening. Insert the pinion, and fit the circlip and dust seal.

14 Reassemble the rack damper components having been smeared with grease.

15 Reconnect the tie-rods to the rack using a new lock washer and stop washer.

16 Partially fill the gaiters with grease and fit them with their clips. Release one clip so that any air can be removed from the gaiters by gently squeezing them.

32 Power-assisted steering – general

1 Due to the complex nature of the power-assisted steering gear, overhaul is considered beyond the scope of the average diy enthusiast. The relevant Sections of this manual and therefore limited to the servicing, removal and refitting instructions for the various components.

2 Should a fault develop, it is recommended that the advice of a dealer or power steering specialist is sought.

33 Power-assisted steering fluid – level checking

1 The fluid level in the steering pump reservoir should be checked with the car parked on level ground and with the engine switched off.

2 Wipe clean the filler cap and the filler neck of the pump reservoir.

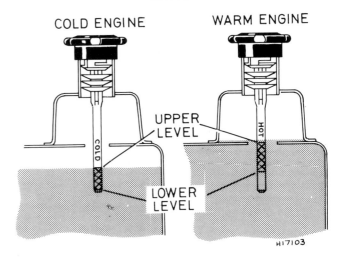

Fig. 10.22 Power-assisted steering pump fluid levels (Sec 33)

Unscrew the cap, wipe the dipstick, then refit the cap fully. Unscrew the cap once more and note the level on the dipstick which should be within the cross-hatched portion on the side marked 'HOT' if the engine is warm, or 'COLD' if the engine is cold.

3   If topping-up is necessary, add the specified type of fluid through the filler neck until the level is correct. Take care not to overfill the reservoir. Refit the cap on completion.

34 Power-assisted steering fluid – renewal

1   Jack up the front of the car and support it on stands with the front wheels hanging free.
2   Disconnect the fluid return hose at the pump (Fig. 10.23) and place its end in a suitable container. Plug the outlet on the pump.
3   Start the engine and allow it to idle. Turn the steering wheel from lock-to-lock several times. When fluid stops running out of the hose, switch off the engine.
4   Discard the expelled fluid.
5   Remove the plug and refit the return hose to the pump.
6   Fill the pump reservoir with the specified fluid to the upper mark on the dipstick (see Section 33).
7   Start the engine, and with it idling turn the steering from lock-to-lock several times to bleed the system.
8   Switch the engine off, recheck the fluid level and top up if necessary.
9   Lower the car to the ground.

35 Power-assisted steering pump drivebelt – adjustment, removal and refitting

1   To check the drivebelt adjustment, press the belt using firm thumb pressure at a point midway between the two pulleys. The belt should deflect by between 18.0 and 22.0 mm (0.7 and 0.86 in).
2   If adjustment is necessary, slacken the four pump mounting bolts and carefully lever the pump upwards to increase, or downwards to decrease, the tension. Hold the pump in position and tighten the bolts.
3   To renew the belt, unscrew the four pump mounting bolts, withdraw the pump and remove the belt.
4   Fit the new belt over the pulleys and refit the pump and mounting bolts. Adjust the belt tension as previously described.
5   If the drivebelt has been renewed, start the engine, allow it to idle and turn the steering from lock-to-lock several times. Switch off and recheck the adjustment.

36 Power-assisted steering pump – removal and refitting

1   Disconnect the fluid hoses at the pump, noting their locations. Cap the hoses after removal.
2   Undo the four bolts and withdraw the pump. Slip off the drivebelt and remove the pump from the engine.
3   Refitting is the reverse sequence to removal. Adjust the drivebelt as described in Section 35, then fill the system with fluid as described in Section 34.

37 Rack and pinion steering gear (power-assisted steering) – removal and refitting

1   The procedure is the same as described in Section 30 for manual steering but with the following additions.
2   Before starting drain the fluid from the pump reservoir as described in Section 34.
3   Disconnect the hydraulic pipe unions at the valve body unit on the rack housing. Clean the unions thoroughly before removal and mark their locations for refitting.
4   After refitting the steering gear, fill the pump with fluid and bleed the system as described in Section 34.

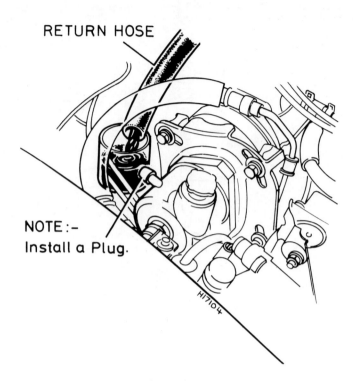

Fig. 10.23 Power-assisted steering return hose disconnected for fluid draining (Sec 34)

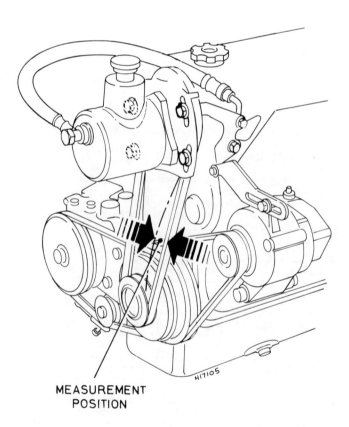

Fig. 10.24 Power-assisted steering pump drivebelt tension checking point (Sec 35)

38 Front wheel alignment and steering angles

1   Accurate front wheel alignment is essential to provide good steering and roadholding characteristics and to ensure slow and even tyre wear. Before considering the steering angles, check that the tyres are correctly inflated, that the front wheels are not buckled, the hub bearings are not worn, and that the steering linkage is in good order, without slackness or wear at the joints.

2   Wheel alignment consists of four factors:

Camber, is the angle at which the road wheels are set from the vertical when viewed from the front or rear of the vehicle. Positive camber is the angle (in degrees) that the wheels are tilted outwards at the top from the vertical.

Castor, is the angle between the steering axis and a vertical when viewed from each side of the vehicle. Positive castor is indicated when the steering axis is inclined towards the rear of the vehicle at its upper end.

Steering axis inclination, is the angle when viewed from the front or rear of the vehicle between a vertical and an imaginary line drawn between the top and bottom strut mountings.

Toe, is the amount by which the distance between the front inside edges of the roadwheel rims differs from that between the rear inside edges. If the distance between the front edges is less than that at the rear, the wheels are said to toe-in. If the distance between the front inside edges is greater than that at the rear, the wheels toe-out.

3   Owing to the need for precision gauges to measure the small angles of the steering and suspension settings, it is preferable that measuring of camber and castor is left to a service station having the necessary equipment.

4   The camber, castor and steering axis inclination angles are set in production and cannot be adjusted. Where they differ from those specified, suspect collision damage or gross wear in the steering or suspension components.

5   To check the front wheel alignment, first make sure that the lengths to both tie-rods are equal when the steering is in the straight-ahead position. Adjust if necessary by releasing the tie-rod balljoint locknuts and turning the tie-rods until the lengths of the exposed threads are equal on each side.

6   Obtain a tracking gauge. These are available in various forms from accessory stores or one can be fabricated from a length of steel tubing suitably cranked to clear the sump and bellhousing and having a setscrew and locknut at one end.

7   With the gauge, measure the distance between the two wheel inner rims (at hub height) at the rear of the wheel. Push the vehicle forward to rotate the wheel through 180° (half a turn) and measure the distance between the wheel inner rims, again at hub height, at the front of the wheel. This last measurement should differ from the first by the appropriate toe-in or toe-out according to specification (see Specifications Section).

8   Where the toe-in or toe-out is found to be incorrect, release the tie-rod balljoint locknuts and turn the tie-rods equally. Only turn them a quarter of a turn at a time before re-checking the alignment. Do not grip the threaded part of the tie-rod/balljoint during adjustment and make sure that the gaiter outboard clip is released otherwise the gaiter will twist as the tie-rod is rotated. Turn each tie-rod in the same direction when viewed from the centre line of the car otherwise the rods will become unequal in length. This would cause the steering wheel spoke position to alter and cause problems on turns with tyre scrubbing. On completion, tighten the tie-rod locknuts without disturbing their setting, check that the balljoint is at the centre of its arc of travel and then retighten the gaiter clip.

39 Wheels and tyres – general care and maintenance

Wheels and tyres should give no real problems in use provided that a close eye is kept on them with regard to excessive wear or damage.

To this end, the following points should be noted.

Ensure that tyre pressures are checked regularly and maintained correctly. Checking should be carried out with the tyres cold and not immediately after the vehicle has been in use. If the pressures are checked with the tyres hot, an apparently high reading will be obtained owing to heat expansion. Under no circumstances should an attempt be made to reduce the pressures to the quoted cold reading in this instance, or effective underinflation will result.

Underinflation will cause overheating of the tyre owing to excessive flexing of the casing, and the tread will not sit correctly on the road surface. This will cause a consequent loss of adhesion and excessive wear, not to mention the danger of sudden tyre failure due to heat build-up.

Overinflation will cause rapid wear of the centre part of the tyre tread coupled with reduced adhesion, harsher ride, and the danger of shock damage occurring in the tyre casing.

Regularly check the tyres for damage in the form of cuts or bulges, especially in the sidewalls. Remove any nails or stones embedded in the tread before they penetrate the tyre to cause deflation. If removal of a nail *does* reveal that the tyre has been punctured, refit the nail so that its point of penetration is marked. Then immediately change the wheel and have the tyre repaired by a tyre dealer. Do *not* drive on a tyre in such a condition. In many cases a puncture can be simply repaired by the use of an inner tube of the correct size and type. If in any doubt as to the possible consequences of any damage found, consult your local tyre dealer for advice.

Periodically remove the wheels and clean any dirt or mud from the inside and outside surfaces. Examine the wheel rims for signs of rusting, corrosion or other damage. Light alloy wheels are easily damaged by 'kerbing' whilst parking, and similarly steel wheels may become dented or buckled. Renewal of the wheel is very often the only course of remedial action possible.

The balance of each wheel and tyre assembly should be maintained to avoid excessive wear, not only to the tyres but also to the steering and suspension components. Wheel imbalance is normally signified by vibration through the vehicle's bodyshell, although in many cases it is particularly noticeable through the steering wheel. Conversely, it should be noted that wear or damage in suspension or steering components may cause excessive tyre wear. Out-of-round or out-of-true tyres, damaged wheels and wheel bearing wear/maladjustment also fall into this category. Balancing will not usually cure vibration caused by such wear.

Wheel balancing may be carried out with the wheel either on or off the vehicle. If balanced on the vehicle, ensure that the wheel-to-hub relationship is marked in some way prior to subsequent wheel removal so that it may be refitted in its original position.

General tyre wear is influenced to a large degree by driving style – harsh braking and acceleration or fast cornering will all produce more rapid tyre wear. Interchanging of tyres may result in more even wear, but this should only be carried out where there is no mix of tyre types on the vehicle. However, it is worth bearing in mind that if this is completely effective, the added expense of replacing a complete set of tyres simultaneously is incurred, which may prove financially restrictive for many owners.

Front tyres may wear unevenly as a result of wheel misalignment. The front wheels should always be correctly aligned according to the settings specified by the vehicle manufacturer.

Legal restrictions apply to the mixing of tyre types on a vehicle. Basically this means that a vehicle must not have tyres of differing construction on the same axle. Although it is not recommended to mix tyre types between front axle and rear axle, the only legally permissible combination is crossply at the front and radial at the rear. When mixing radial ply tyres, textile braced radials must always go on the front axle, with steel braced radials at the rear. An obvious disadvantage of such mixing is the necessity to carry two spare tyres to avoid contravening the law in the event of a puncture.

In the UK, the Motor Vehicles Construction and Use Regulations apply to many aspects of tyre fitting and usage. It is suggested that a copy of these regulations is obtained from your local police if in doubt as to the current legal requirements with regard to tyre condition, minimum tread depth, etc.

40 Fault diagnosis – suspension and steering

Note: *Before attempting to diagnose suspension or steering faults, be sure that the trouble is not due to incorrect tyre pressures, a mixture of tyre types, or binding brakes*

Symptom	Reason(s)
Vehicle pulls to one side	Incorrect wheel alignment Wear in suspension or steering components Accident damage to steering or suspension components Faulty tyre
Steering stiff or heavy	Lack of steering gear lubricant Incorrect rack damper adjustment Incorrect wheel alignment Steering rack or column bent Broken or incorrectly adjusted pump drivebelt (power-assisted steering) Power-assisted steering pump faulty (where applicable)
Excessive play in steering	Wear in steering or suspension components Wear in intermediate shaft universal joints Worn rack and pinion assembly Incorrect rack damper adjustment
Wheel wobble and vibration	Roadwheels out of balance Roadwheels buckled or distorted Faulty or damaged tyre Worn shock absorber (suspension struts) Worn steering or suspension joints Wheel nuts loose See also Fault diagnosis – driveshafts (Chapter 8)
Tyre wear uneven	Incorrect wheel alignment Worn steering or suspension components Roadwheels out of balance Accident damage
Excessive pitching and rolling on corners and during braking	Worn or faulty shock absorbers (suspension struts) Worn or broken anti-roll bar mountings
Excessive noise from steering gear (power-assisted steering)	Drivebelt slipping Insufficient fluid in pump reservoir Worn or faulty power-assisted steering pump
Jerky steering, intermittent loss of power assistance (power-assisted steering)	Drivebelt slipping Faulty power-assisted steering pump Kinked or restricted fluid hose Insufficient fluid in pump reservoir Fluid leakage Faulty rack and pinion assembly

Chapter 11 Bodywork and fittings

Contents

Specifications

Torque wrench settings

	Nm	lbf ft
Door hinge bolts	22	16
Front and rear seat track bolts	22	16
Seat belt anchor bolts	32	23
Bumper mounting bolts	22	16
Bonnet, boot and tailgate hinge bolts	10	7
Air conditioning compressor mounting bolts	46	33
Air conditioning compressor adjuster pulley nut	46	33

1 General description

The bodyshell and underframe is of all-steel welded construction, incorporating progressive crumple zones at the front and rear and a rigid centre safety cell. To facilitate accident damage repair, many of the main body panels are supplied as part-panel replacements and are bolted rather than welded in place, particularly at the front of the vehicle.

Honda Civic models covered by this manual are available in three-door Hatchback, five-door Shuttle/Wagon (estate), four-door Sedan (North America only) and three-door CRX coupe body styles.

This sequence of photographs deals with the repair of the dent and paintwork damage shown in this photo. The procedure will be similar for the repair of a hole. It should be noted that the procedures given here are simplified — more explicit instructions will be found in the text

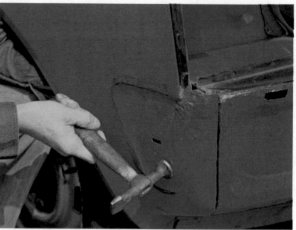

In the case of a dent the first job — after removing surrounding trim — is to hammer out the dent where access is possible. This will minimise filling. Here, the large dent having been hammered out, the damaged area is being made slightly concave

Now all paint must be removed from the damaged area, by rubbing with coarse abrasive paper. Alternatively, a wire brush or abrasive pad can be used in a power drill. Where the repair area meets good paintwork, the edge of the paintwork should be 'feathered', using a finer grade of abrasive paper

In the case of a hole caused by rusting, all damaged sheet-metal should be cut away before proceeding to this stage. Here, the damaged area is being treated with rust remover and inhibitor before being filled

Mix the body filler according to its manufacturer's instructions. In the case of corrosion damage, it will be necessary to block off any large holes before filling — this can be done with aluminium or plastic mesh, or aluminium tape. Make sure the area is absolutely clean before ...

... applying the filler. Filler should be applied with a flexible applicator, as shown, for best results; the wooden spatula being used for confined areas. Apply thin layers of filler at 20-minute intervals, until the surface of the filler is slightly proud of the surrounding bodywork

Initial shaping can be done with a Surform plane or Dreadnought file. Then, using progressively finer grades of wet-and-dry paper, wrapped around a sanding block, and copious amounts of clean water, rub down the filler until really smooth and flat. Again, feather the edges of adjoining paintwork

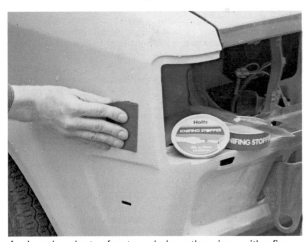

Again, using plenty of water, rub down the primer with a fine grade wet-and-dry paper (400 grade is probably best) until it is really smooth and well blended into the surrounding paintwork. Any remaining imperfections can now be filled by carefully applied knifing stopper paste

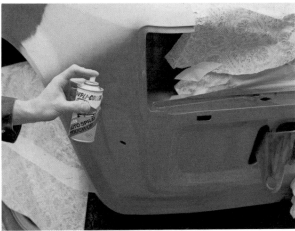

The top coat can now be applied. When working out of doors, pick a dry, warm and wind-free day. Ensure surrounding areas are protected from over-spray. Agitate the aerosol thoroughly, then spray the centre of the repair area, working outwards with a circular motion. Apply the paint as several thin coats

The whole repair area can now be sprayed or brush-painted with primer. If spraying, ensure adjoining areas are protected from over-spray. Note that at least one inch of the surrounding sound paintwork should be coated with primer. Primer has a 'thick' consistency, so will find small imperfections

When the stopper has hardened, rub down the repair area again before applying the final coat of primer. Before rubbing down this last coat of primer, ensure the repair area is blemish-free – use more stopper if necessary. To ensure that the surface of the primer is really smooth use some finishing compound

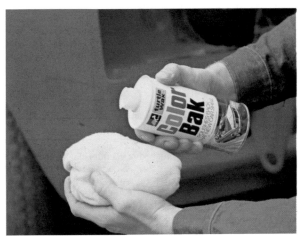

After a period of about two weeks, which the paint needs to harden fully, the surface of the repaired area can be 'cut' with a mild cutting compound prior to wax polishing. When carrying out bodywork repairs, remember that the quality of the finished job is proportional to the time and effort expended

2 Maintenance – bodywork and underframe

The general condition of a vehicle's bodywork is the one thing that significantly affects its value. Maintenance is easy but needs to be regular. Neglect, particularly after minor damage, can lead quickly to further deterioration and costly repair bills. It is important also to keep watch on those parts of the vehicle not immediately visible, for instance the underside, inside all the wheel arches and the lower part of the engine compartment.

The basic maintenance routine for the bodywork is washing – preferably with a lot of water, from a hose. This will remove all the loose solids which may have stuck to the vehicle. It is important to flush these off in such a way as to prevent grit from scratching the finish. The wheel arches and underframe need washing in the same way to remove any accumulated mud which will retain moisture and tend to encourage rust. Paradoxically enough, the best time to clean the underframe and wheel arches is in wet weather when the mud is thoroughly wet and soft. In very wet weather the underframe is usually cleaned of large accumulations automatically and this is a good time for inspection.

Periodically, except on vehicles with a wax-based underbody protective coating, it is a good idea to have the whole of the underframe of the vehicle steam cleaned, engine compartment included, so that a thorough inspection can be carried out to see what minor repairs and renovations are necessary. Steam cleaning is available at many garages and is necessary for removal of the accumulation of oily grime which sometimes is allowed to become thick in certain areas. If steam cleaning facilities are not available, there are one or two excellent grease solvents available which can be brush applied. The dirt can then be simply hosed off. Note that these methods should not be used on vehicles with wax-based underbody protective coating or the coating will be removed. Such vehicles should be inspected annually, preferably just prior to winter, when the underbody should be washed down and any damage to the wax coating repaired. Ideally, a completely fresh coat should be applied. It would also be worth considering the use of such wax-based protection for injection into door panels, sills, box sections, etc, as an additional safeguard against rust damage where such protection is not provided by the vehicle manufacturer.

After washing paintwork, wipe off with a chamois leather to give an unspotted clear finish. A coat of clear protective wax polish will give added protection against chemical pollutants in the air. If the paintwork sheen has dulled or oxidised, use a cleaner/polisher combination to restore the brilliance of the shine. This requires a little effort, but such dulling is usually caused because regular washing has been neglected. Care needs to be taken with metallic paintwork, as special non-abrasive cleaner/polisher is required to avoid damage to the finish. Always check that the door and ventilator opening drain holes and pipes are completely clear so that water can be drained out. Bright work should be treated in the same way as paint work. Windscreens and windows can be kept clear of the smeary film which often appears by the use of a proprietary glass cleaner. Never use any form of wax or other body or chromium polish on glass.

3 Maintenance – upholstery and carpets

Mats and carpets should be brushed or vacuum cleaned regularly to keep them free of grit. If they are badly stained remove them from the vehicle for scrubbing or sponging and make quite sure they are dry before refitting. Seats and interior trim panels can be kept clean by wiping with a damp cloth. If they do become stained (which can be more apparent on light coloured upholstery) use a little liquid detergent and a soft nail brush to scour the grime out of the grain of the material. Do not forget to keep the headlining clean in the same way as the upholstery. When using liquid cleaners inside the vehicle do not over-wet the surfaces being cleaned. Excessive damp could get into the seams and padded interior causing stains, offensive odours or even rot. If the inside of the vehicle gets wet accidentally it is worthwhile taking some trouble to dry it out properly, particularly where carpets are involved. *Do not leave oil or electric heaters inside the vehicle for this purpose.*

4 Minor body damage – repair

The photographic sequences on pages 218 and 219 illustrate the operations detailed in the following sub-sections.
Note: *For more detailed information about bodywork repair, the Haynes Publishing Group publish a book by Lindsay Porter called The Car Bodywork Repair Manual. This incorporates information on such aspects as rust treatment, painting and glass fibre repairs, as well as details on more ambitious repairs involving welding and panel beating.*

Repair of minor scratches in bodywork

If the scratch is very superficial, and does not penetrate to the metal of the bodywork, repair is very simple. Lightly rub the area of the scratch with a paintwork renovator, or a very fine cutting paste, to remove loose paint from the scratch and to clear the surrounding bodywork of wax polish. Rinse the area with clean water.

Apply touch-up paint to the scratch using a fine paint brush; continue to apply fine layers of paint until the surface of the paint in the scratch is level with the surrounding paintwork. Allow the new paint at least two weeks to harden: then blend it into the surrounding paintwork by rubbing the scratch area with a paintwork renovator or a very fine cutting paste. Finally, apply wax polish.

Where the scratch has penetrated right through to the metal of the bodywork, causing the metal to rust, a different repair technique is required. Remove any loose rust from the bottom of the scratch with a penknife, then apply rust inhibiting paint to prevent the formation of rust in the future. Using a rubber or nylon applicator fill the scratch with bodystopper paste. If required, this paste can be mixed with cellulose thinners to provide a very thin paste which is ideal for filling narrow scratches. Before the stopper-paste in the scratch hardens, wrap a piece of smooth cotton rag around the top of a finger. Dip the finger in cellulose thinners and then quickly sweep it across the surface of the stopper-paste in the scratch; this will ensure that the surface of the stopper-paste is slightly hollowed. The scratch can now be painted over as described earlier in this Section.

Repair of dents in bodywork

When deep denting of the vehicle's bodywork has taken place, the first task is to pull the dent out, until the affected bodywork almost attains its original shape. There is little point in trying to restore the original shape completely, as the metal in the damaged area will have stretched on impact and cannot be reshaped fully to its original contour. It is better to bring the level of the dent up to a point which is about ⅛ in (3 mm) below the level of the surrounding bodywork. In cases where the dent is very shallow anyway, it is not worth trying to pull it out at all. If the underside of the dent is accessible, it can be hammered out gently from behind, using a mallet with a wooden or plastic head. Whilst doing this, hold a suitable block of wood firmly against the outside of the panel to absorb the impact from the hammer blows and thus prevent a large area of the bodywork from being 'belled-out'.

Should the dent be in a section of the bodywork which has a double skin or some other factor making it inaccessible from behind, a different technique is called for. Drill several small holes through the metal inside the area – particularly in the deeper section. Then screw long self-tapping screws into the holes just sufficiently for them to gain a good purchase in the metal. Now the dent can be pulled out by pulling on the protruding heads of the screws with a pair of pliers.

The next stage of the repair is the removal of the paint from the damaged area, and from an inch or so of the surrounding 'sound' bodywork. This is accomplished most easily by using a wire brush or abrasive pad on a power drill, although it can be done just as effectively by hand using sheets of abrasive paper. To complete the preparation for filling, score the surface of the bare metal with a screwdriver or the tang of a file, or alternatively, drill small holes in the affected area. This will provide a really good 'key' for the filler paste.

To complete the repair see the Section on filling and re-spraying.

Repair of rust holes or gashes in bodywork

Remove all paint from the affected area and from an inch or so of the surrounding 'sound' bodywork, using an abrasive pad or a wire brush on a power drill. If these are not available a few sheets of abrasive paper will do the job just as effectively. With the paint removed you will be able to gauge the severity of the corrosion and therefore decide whether to renew the whole panel (if this is possible) or to repair the affected area. New body panels are not as expensive as most people think and it is often quicker and more satisfactory to fit a new panel than to attempt to repair large areas of corrosion.

Remove all fittings from the affected area except those which will act as a guide to the original shape of the damaged bodywork (eg headlamp shells etc). Then, using tin snips or a hacksaw blade, remove all loose metal and any other metal badly affected by corrosion. Hammer the edges of the hole inwards in order to create a slight depression for the filler paste.

Wire brush the affected area to remove the powdery rust from the surface of the remaining metal. Paint the affected area with rust inhibiting paint; if the back of the rusted area is accessible treat this also.

Before filling can take place it will be necessary to block the hole in some way. This can be achieved by the use of aluminium or plastic mesh, or aluminium tape.

Aluminium or plastic mesh is probably the best material to use for a large hole. Cut a piece to the approximate size and shape of the hole to be filled, then position it in the hole so that its edges are below the level of the surrounding bodywork. It can be retained in position by several blobs of filler paste around its periphery.

Aluminium tape should be used for small or very narrow holes. Pull a piece off the roll and trim it to the approximate size and shape required, then pull off the backing paper (if used) and stick the tape over the hole; it can be overlapped if the thickness of one piece is insufficient. Burnish down the edges of the tape with the handle of a screwdriver or similar, to ensure that the tape is securely attached to the metal underneath.

Bodywork repairs – filling and re-spraying

Before using this Section, see the Sections on dent, deep scratch, rust holes and gash repairs.

Many types of bodyfiller are available, but generally speaking those proprietary kits which contain a tin of filler paste and a tube of resin hardener are best for this type of repair. A wide, flexible plastic or nylon applicator will be found invaluable for imparting a smooth and well contoured finish to the surface of the filler.

Mix up a little filler on a clean piece of card or board – measure the hardener carefully (follow the maker's instructions on the pack) otherwise the filler will set too rapidly or too slowly. Using the applicator apply the filler paste to the prepared area; draw the applicator across the surface of the filler to achieve the correct contour and to level the filler surface. As soon as a contour that approximates to the correct one is achieved, stop working the paste – if you carry on too long the paste will become sticky and begin to 'pick up' on the applicator. Continue to add thin layers of filler paste at twenty-minute intervals until the level of the filler is just proud of the surrounding bodywork.

Once the filler has hardened, excess can be removed using a metal plane or file. From then on, progressively finer grades of abrasive paper should be used, starting with a 40 grade production paper and finishing with 400 grade wet-and-dry paper. Always wrap the abrasive paper around a flat rubber, cork, or wooden block – otherwise the surface of the filler will not be completely flat. During the smoothing of the filler surface the wet-and-dry paper should be periodically rinsed in water. This will ensure that a very smooth finish is imparted to the filler at the final stage.

At this stage the 'dent' should be surrounded by a ring of bare metal, which in turn should be encircled by the finely 'feathered' edge of the good paintwork. Rinse the repair area with clean water, until all of the dust produced by the rubbing-down operation has gone.

Spray the whole repair area with a light coat of primer – this will show up any imperfections in the surface of the filler. Repair these imperfections with fresh filler paste or bodystopper, and once more smooth the surface with abrasive paper. If bodystopper is used, it can be mixed with cellulose thinners to form a really thin paste which is ideal for filling small holes. Repeat this spray and repair procedure until you are satisfied that the surface of the filler, and the feathered edge of the paintwork are perfect. Clean the repair area with clean water and allow to dry fully.

The repair area is now ready for final spraying. Paint spraying must be carried out in a warm, dry, windless and dust free atmosphere. This condition can be created artificially if you have access to a large indoor working area, but if you are forced to work in the open, you will have to pick your day very carefully. If you are working indoors, dousing the floor in the work area with water will help to settle the dust which

would otherwise be in the atmosphere. If the repair area is confined to one body panel, mask off the surrounding panels; this will help to minimise the effects of a slight mis-match in paint colours. Bodywork fittings (eg chrome strips, door handles etc) will also need to be masked off. Use genuine masking tape and several thicknesses of newspaper for the masking operations.

Before commencing to spray, agitate the aerosol can thoroughly, then spray a test area (an old tin, or similar) until the technique is mastered. Cover the repair area with a thick coat of primer; the thickness should be built up using several thin layers of paint rather than one thick one. Using 400 grade wet-and-dry paper, rub down the surface of the primer until it is really smooth. While doing this, the work area should be thoroughly doused with water, and the wet-and-dry paper periodically rinsed in water. Allow to dry before spraying on more paint.

Spray on the top coat, again building up the thickness by using several thin layers of paint. Start spraying in the centre of the repair area and then, using a circular motion, work outwards until the whole repair area and about 2 inches of the surrounding original paintwork is covered. Remove all masking material 10 to 15 minutes after spraying on the final coat of paint.

Allow the new paint at least two weeks to harden, then, using a paintwork renovator or a very fine cutting paste, blend the edges of the paint into the existing paintwork. Finally, apply wax polish.

Plastic components

With the use of more and more plastic body components by the vehicle manufacturers (eg bumpers, spoilers, and in some cases major body panels), rectification of damage to such items has become a matter of either entrusting repair work to a specialist in this field, or renewing complete components. Repair by the DIY owner is not really feasible owing to the cost of the equipment and materials required for effecting such repairs. The basic technique involves making a groove along the line of the crack in the plastic using a rotary burr in a power drill. The damaged part is then welded back together by using a hot air gun to heat up and fuse a plastic filler rod into the groove. Any excess plastic is then removed and the area rubbed down to a smooth finish. It is important that a filler rod of the correct plastic is used, as body components can be made of a variety of different types (eg polycarbonate, ABS, polypropylene).

If the owner is renewing a complete component himself, he will be left with the problem of finding a suitable paint for finishing which is compatible with the type of plastic used. At one time the use of a universal paint was not possible owing to the complex range of plastics encountered in body component applications. Standard paints, generally speaking, will not bond to plastic or rubber satisfactorily. However, it is now possible to obtain a plastic body parts finishing kit which consists of a pre-primer treatment, a primer and coloured top coat. Full instructions are normally supplied with a kit, but basically the method of use is to first apply the pre-primer to the component concerned and allow it to dry for up to 30 minutes. Then the primer is applied and left to dry for about an hour before finally applying the special coloured top coat. The result is a correctly coloured component where the paint will flex with the plastic or rubber, a property that standard paint does not normally possess.

---

5 Major body damage – repair

1 This sort of work should be left to your Honda dealer or specialist body repair works.
2 It is essential to have the body aligned on special jigs to ensure that the specified steering and suspension settings are maintained during repair.
3 This is of course beyond the scope of the home mechanic and if not carried out correctly will give rise to unroadworthy behaviour and severe tyre wear.

---

6 Front bumper – removal and refitting

1 Remove the splash panels from under the front of the car.
2 Remove the radiator grille as described in Section 9.

3   Remove the front direction indicator lamp units and disconnect the wiring connectors.
4   Refer to the accompanying illustration and undo the bumper bracket mount bolts and lower mount bolts.
5   Slide the bumper forward and remove it from the car.
6   Refitting is the reverse sequence to removal.

7   Bonnet – removal and refitting

1   Open the bonnet and support it on its stay.
2   Mark the position of the hinges on the underside of the bonnet. Use a pencil or masking tape to prevent scoring the paint, as this could encourage rust (photo).

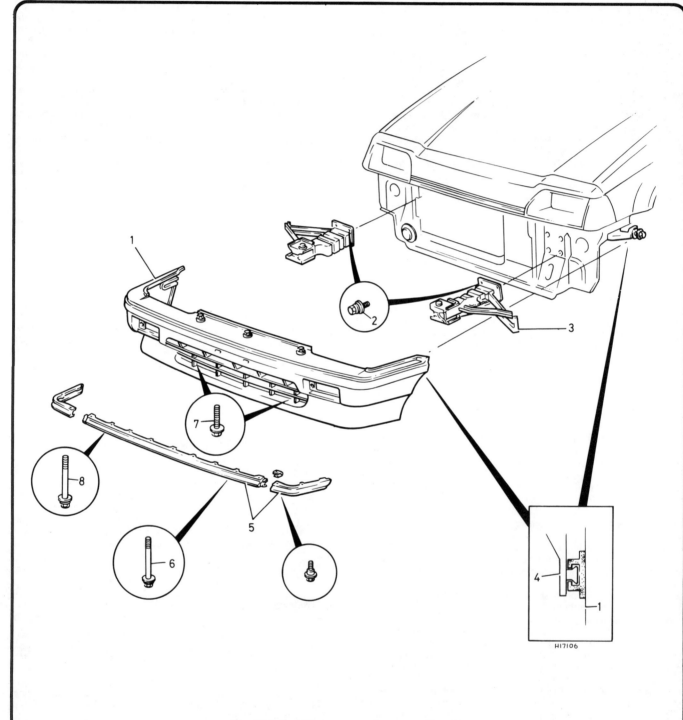

Fig. 11.1 Front bumper components (Sec 6)

1 Front bumper	3 Bumper bracket	5 Front spoiler	7 Bumper lower mount bolts
2 Bumper bracket mount bolt	4 Body	6 Bumper mount bolt	8 Bumper mount bolt

H17106

7.2 Bonnet hinge and retaining bolts

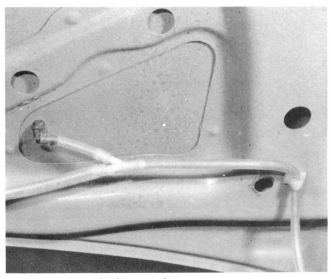

7.3 Windscreen washer hose attachments

3   Release the washer hose from its clip and disconnect it. With the help of an assistant, unscrew the hinge bolts, disconnect the stay and lift the bonnet from the car (photo).
4   Refitting is a reversal of removal, but do not fully tighten the hinge bolts until the bonnet has been gently lowered and its alignment checked. There should be an equal gap at each side between wing and bonnet. Move the bonnet if necessary after releasing the hinge bolts.
5   It is acceptable to fit shims under the hinges to make the near end of the bonnet flush with the wing top surfaces.
6   Adjust the bonnet lock and bump stops to provide firm positive closure as described in the next Section.

8   Bonnet lock and cable – adjustment, removal and refitting

1   The bonnet lock may be moved within the limits of its elongated bolt holes so that the bonnet shuts smoothly and positively. This should be carried out in conjunction with adjusting the rubber bump stops. These should be screwed in or out so that the bonnet will be flush with the tops of the wings and not rattle when closed.

2   The bonnet cable is not adjustable, but may be renewed after disconnecting it from the lock and release lever and withdrawing it through the bulkhead grommet into the engine compartment.

9   Radiator grille – removal and refitting

1   Extract the retaining screws from between the slots of the grille (photo).
2   Ease the grille from the retaining tags and remove it from the car (photo).
3   Refitting is the reverse sequence to removal.

10 Front wing – removal and refitting

1   Remove the front bumper (Section 6).
2   Refer to Chapter 12 and remove the headlamp unit and sidelight lens unit.

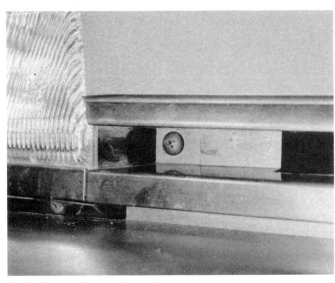

9.1 Radiator grille retaining screw

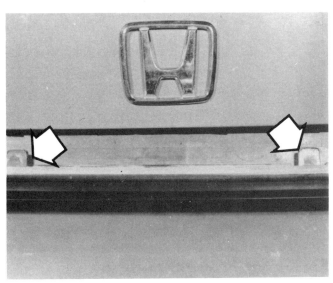

9.2 Radiator grille retaining tags (arrowed)

3   Raise the front of the car and remove the roadwheel. Remove the underwing protective plastic shield.

4   Open the bonnet (if not already done).

5   Unscrew the row of bolts from the top edge of the wing.

6   Open the front door and remove the wing upper fixing bolt which is accessible between the rear edge of the wing and the leading edge of the door.

7   Extract the fixing screw from the front and rear lower edges of the wing.

8   Remove the wing and recover the rubber buffer from halfway down the rear edge. If the wing is stuck tight, cut along the mastic joint using a sharp knife.

9   Before fitting the new wing, clean away all old jointing mastic and apply a bead of new material.

10   Once the wing has been fitted, apply protective coating to its underside and finish the outer surface to match the body colour.

11   Front upper body panel – removal and refitting

1   Refer to Chapter 12 and remove the headlamp unit.

2   According to model, remove the headlamp bracket or garnish if this restricts removal of the body panel.

3   Remove the radiator grille as described in Section 9.

4   Undo the upper and side mounting bolts and withdraw the panel from the front of the car.

5   Refitting is the reverse sequence to removal.

12   Door interior trim panel – removal and refitting

1   Extract the screws and remove the armrest. On some CRX models only, the armrest upper part is removed. On the front and rear doors of all other models the complete armrest is removed (photo).

2   Extract the screw and remove the escutcheon plate from the remote control handle (photo).

3   Extract the spring clip and take off the window regulator handle. The clip can be removed using a length of wire with a hook on its end, or a strip of rag pulled around the handle boss (photo). Refit the clip to the handle after removal (photo). When refitting, push the handle firmly onto the regulator spindle to re-engage the clip.

4   Extract the retaining screws around the panel and, where fitted, around the speaker grille if working on the front door (photo).

5   Insert a broad, blunt blade between the panel and the door, then slide it sideways until it contacts a retaining clip. Pull it up sharply to release the clip, then continue until all the clips are released (photo).

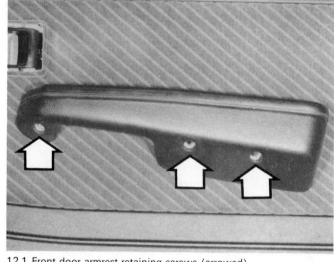

12.1 Front door armrest retaining screws (arrowed)

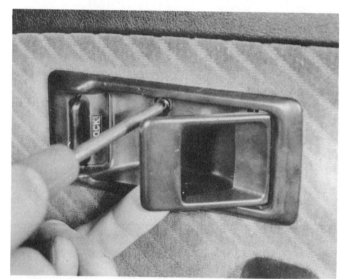

12.2 Removing the remote control handle escutcheon

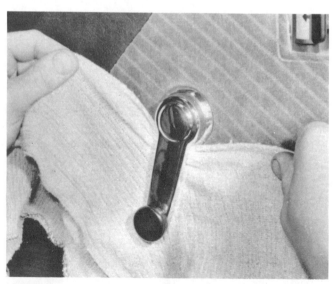

12.3A Using a rag to release the regulator handle spring clip

12.3B Spring clip (arrowed) refitted to regulator handle

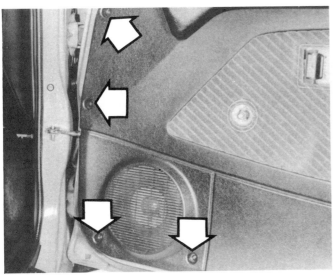

12.4 Speaker grille and trim panel front retaining screws (arrowed)

12.5 Removing the door interior trim panel

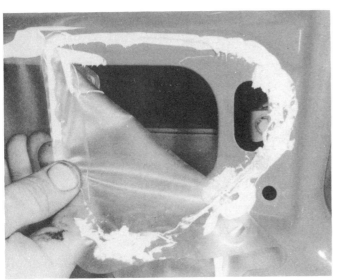

12.7 Removal of the waterproof sheet for access to the door internal components

6   Lift the panel upwards and off the window sill.
7   To gain access to the door internal components, carefully peel back the waterproof sheet as necessary (photo).
8   Refitting is the reverse sequence to removal.

13 Front door – dismantling and reassembly

Window glass
1   Remove the exterior rear view mirror as described in Section 29.
2   Remove the interior trim panel as descibed in Section 12.
3   Remove the door waist outer moulding by peeling away the end of the door lower weatherstrip slightly, then pulling the moulding up and off the sill. On CRX models undo the two retaining screws first.
4   Remove the front speaker from the door (where fitted), and on CRX models, the door panel bracket.
5   On CRX models remove the two bolts and stabilizers from the door waist edge.
6   Temporarily refit the regulator handle and lower the glass until the bolts (or nuts) securing the glass to the regulator are accessible. Remove the nuts or bolts while supporting the glass (photos).
7   Tilt the glass forward slightly, then slide it up and out of the door.

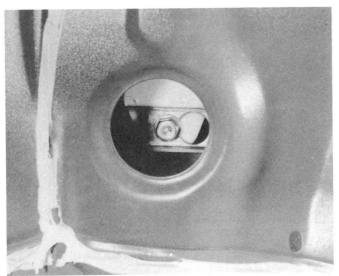

13.6A Door glass front retaining bolt ...

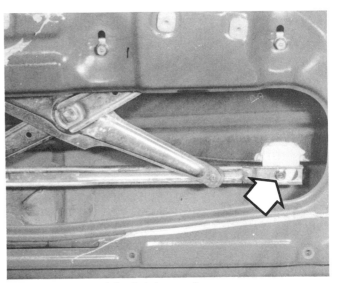

13.6B ... and rear retaining bolt (arrowed)

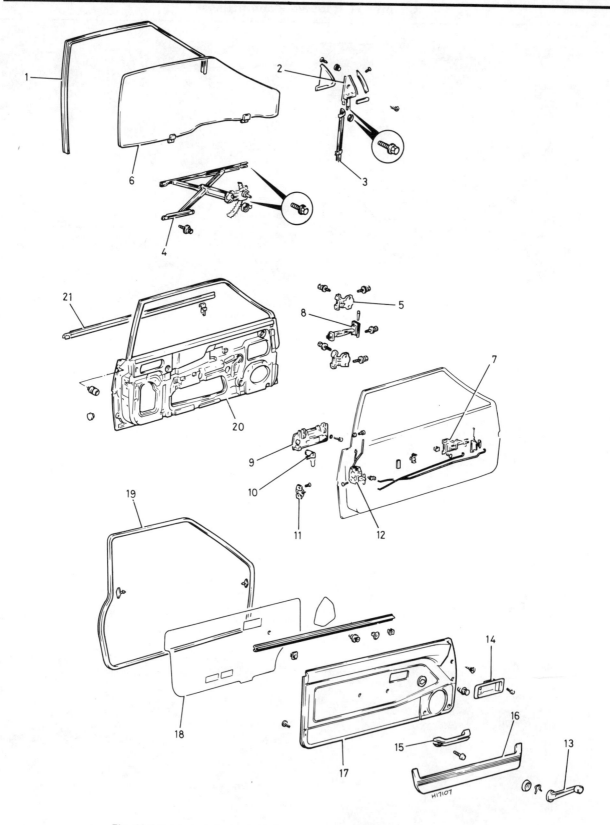

Fig. 11.2 Exploded view of the front door – Hatchback models (Sec 13)

1	Glass run channel	7	Inside door handle	12	Latch assembly	17	Door panel
2	Front sash	8	Detent rod	13	Regulator handle	18	Plastic shield
3	Front channel	9	Outside door handle	14	Inside handle trim plate	19	Weatherstrip
4	Regulator	10	Lock cylinder	15	Arm rest	20	Door
5	Door hinge	11	Striker	16	Door pocket	21	Outer moulding
6	Glass						

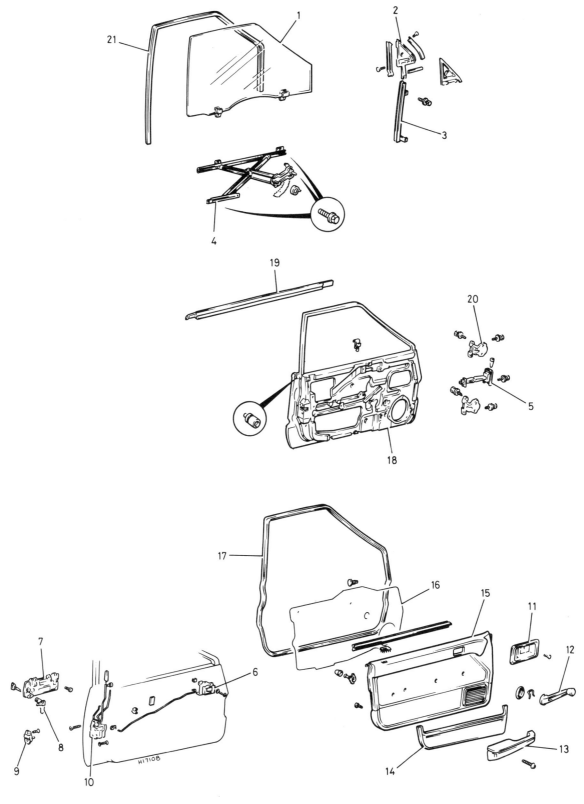

Fig. 11.3 Exploded view of the front door – Sedan models (Sec 13)

1	Glass	7	Outside door handle	12	Regulator handle
2	Front sash	8	Lock cylinder	13	Arm rest
3	Front channel	9	Striker	14	Door pocket
4	Regulator	10	Latch assembly	15	Door panel
5	Detent rod	11	Inside handle trim plate	16	Plastic shield
6	Inside door handle				

17	Weatherstrip
18	Door
19	Outer moulding
20	Door hinge
21	Glass run channel

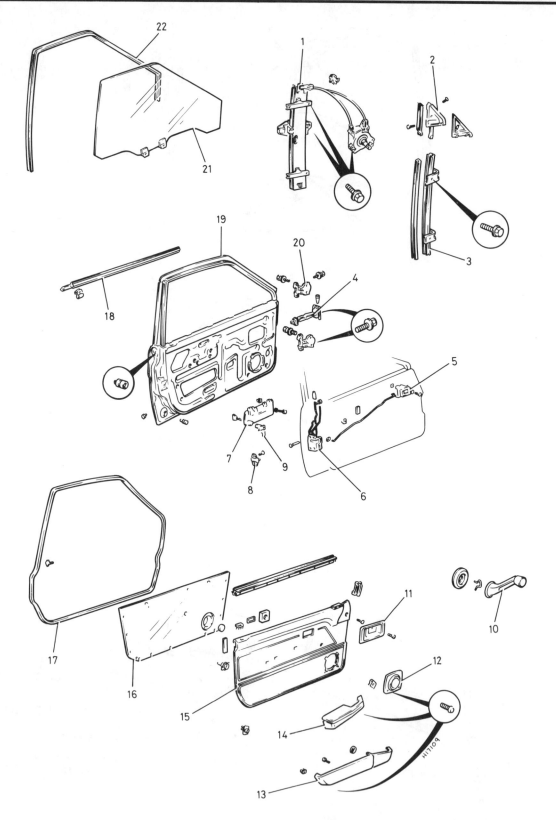

Fig. 11.4 Exploded view of the front door – Shuttle and Wagon models (Sec 13)

1	Regulator	7	Outside door handle	13	Door pocket	18	Outer moulding
2	Front sash	8	Striker	14	Arm rest	19	Door
3	Front channel	9	Lock cylinder	15	Door panel	20	Door hinge
4	Detent rod	10	Regulator handle	16	Plastic shield	21	Glass
5	Inside door handle	11	Inside handle trim plate	17	Weatherstrip	22	Glass run channel
6	Latch assembly	12	Speaker cover				

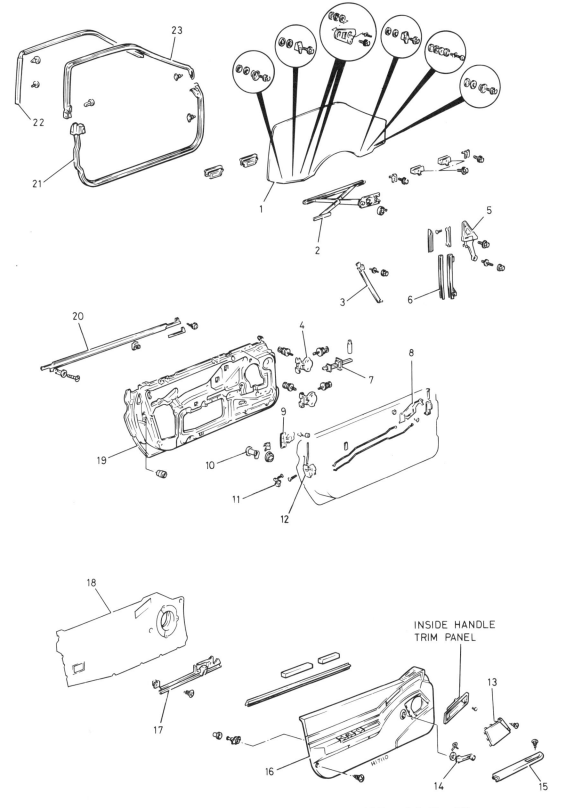

Fig. 11.5 Exploded view of the front door – UK CRX models (Sec 13)

1	Glass	7	Detent rod	13	Speaker grille	19	Door
2	Regulator	8	Inside door handle	14	Regulator handle	20	Outer moulding
3	Door glass guide	9	Outside door handle	15	Arm rest	21	Lower weatherstrip
4	Door hinge	10	Lock cylinder	16	Door panel	22	Retainer
5	Front sash	11	Striker	17	Door panel bracket	23	Upper weatherstrip
6	Front channel	12	Latch assembly	18	Plastic shield		

INSIDE HANDLE
TRIM PANEL

Window winder regulator

8 With the window glass removed as previously described, unscrew the regulator mounting bolts and manoeuvre the regulator out through the lower aperture in the door (photos).

Door lock

9 Unscrew the exterior handle bolts (or nuts) which are accessible from inside the door.
10 Pull out the forked spring retainer and take out the lock cylinder, at the same time disconnecting the link rod.
11 Extract the screws from the edge of the door and push the latch and rod inside the door (photo).
12 Undo the screws and release the interior handle from the door (photo).
13 Measure the length of exposed thread on the latch rod and unscrew the exterior handle from it.
14 Withdraw the latch and interior handle from the door.

Reassembly

15 Refitting is a reversal of removal but observe the following points.
16 When screwing the exterior handle onto the latch rod, set it so that the original length of thread is exposed. Check for full movement of the handle and unscrew it or screw it further onto the rod to achieve this.
17 When refitting the glass on all models except CRX, set it centrally between the side channels then tighten the regulator mounting bolts. The regulator mounting holes are oversize so slight adjustment to achieve this condition is possible.
18 Adjustment of the window glass is slightly more involved on CRX models. Five positonal adjustments are possible as shown in Fig. 11.6. Adjustment is largely a matter of trial and error until a uniform fit and seal of the glass is achieved. The adjustments are as follows:

(a) **Inclinaton adjustment:** *Carried out by altering the position of the regulator roller guide so that the glass moves vertically and has a uniform fit all round when closed.*

(b) **Forward/backward adjustment:** *Carried out by moving the door glass guide forward or backward until the rear edge of the glass, when raised with the door closed, is approximately 10 mm (0.39 in) from the weatherstrip retainer*

(c) **Vertical adjustment:** *Controlled by altering the position of the upper stoppers*

(d) **Window-to-weatherstrip seal adjustment:** *Carried out by slackening the lock nuts and turning the door glass guide adjusters as necessary, then tightening the locknuts. Mark the position of the guide bolts first, otherwise the forward/backward adjustment will be upset if they move*

(e) **Front sash angle adjustment:** *Altered by slackening the front sash locknut and moving the sash to follow the contour of the glass. Tighten the locknut after adjustment*

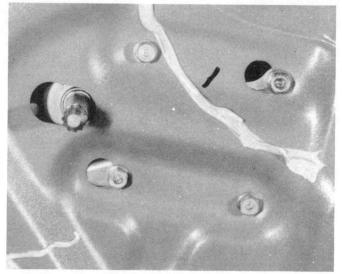

13.8A Door glass regulator and mounting bolts

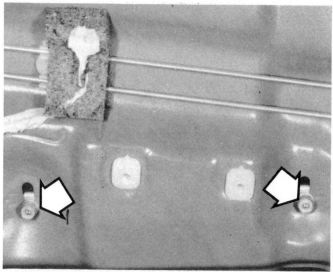

13.8B .. and regulator roller retaining bolts (arrowed)

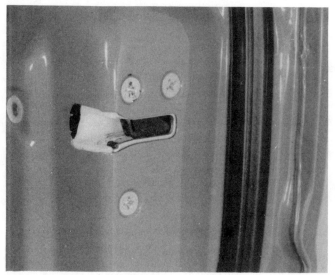

13.11 Door latch retaining screws

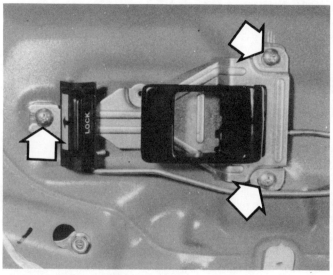

13.12 Door interior handle retaining screws (arrowed)

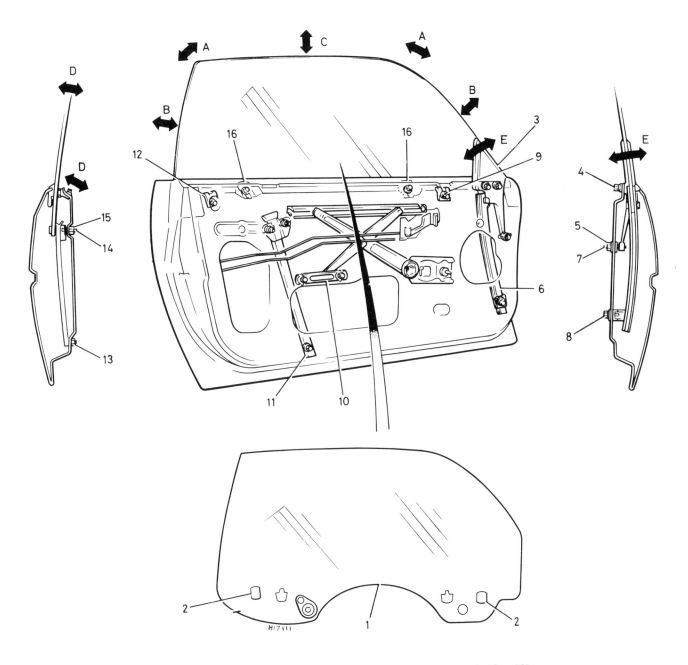

Fig. 11.6 Window glass adjustment details – UK CRX models (Sec 13)

1 Glass	6 Front channel	12 Upper stopper	B Forward/backward
2 Glass stopper	7 Adjuster	13 Nut	adjustment
3 Front sash	8 Bolt	14 Adjuster	C Vertical adjustment
4 Fixing bolt	9 Upper stopper	15 Lock nut	D Window-to-weatherstrip
5 Lock nut	10 Regulator roller guide	16 Stabilizers	seal adjustment
	11 Door glass guide	A Inclination adjustment	E Front sash angle adjustment

14 Rear door – dismantling and reassembly

Window glass

1 Remove the trim panel as described in Section 12.
2 Lower the glass fully.
3 Extract the sash screws, tilt the sash and remove the quarter-light.
4 Adjust the position of the glass by temporarily fitting the regulator handle until the glass-to-regulator fixing screws are visible. Extract the screws and manoeuvre the glass up and out of the door waist slot.

Window regulator

5 With the door glass removed as previously described, unbolt the regulator and remove it through the lower aperture of the door.

Door lock

6 Working throught the door cavity, unscrew the door exterior handle fixing bolts.
7 Remove the lock crank and disconnect the link rods.
8 Extract the latch screws from the door edge and push the latch and rods inside the door. Measure the length of exposed thread on the latch

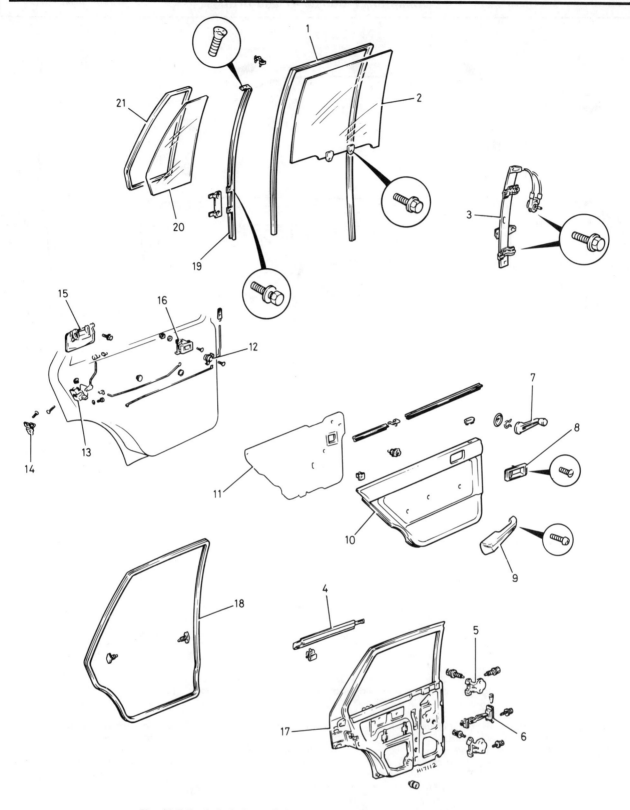

Fig. 11.7 Exploded view of the rear door – Sedan models (Sec 14)

1	Glass run channel	7	Regulator handle	12	Lock crank	17	Door
2	Glass	8	Inside handle trim plate	13	Latch assembly	18	Weatherstrip
3	Regulator	9	Arm rest	14	Striker	19	Centre channel
4	Outer moulding	10	Door panel	15	Outside door handle	20	Quarter glass
5	Door hinge	11	Plastic shield	16	Inside door handle	21	Quarter weatherstrip
6	Detent rod						

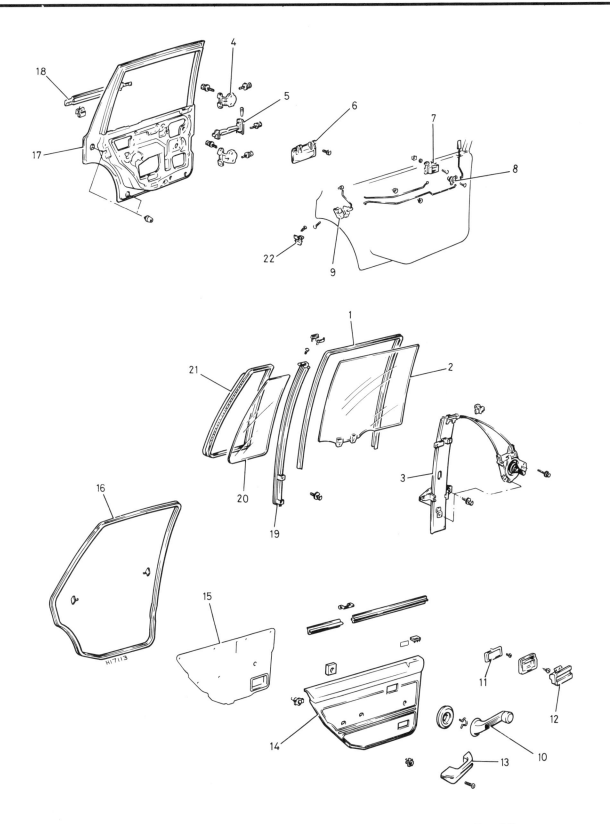

Fig. 11.8 Exploded view of the rear door – Shuttle and Wagon models (Sec 14)

1 Glass run channel	7 Inside door handle	13 Arm rest	18 Outer moulding
2 Glass	8 Lock crank	14 Door panel	19 Centre channel
3 Regulator	9 Latch assembly	15 Plastic shield	20 Quarter glass
4 Door hinge	10 Regulator handle	16 Weatherstrip	21 Quarter weatherstrip
5 Detent rod	11 Inside handle trim plate	17 Door	22 Striker
6 Outside door handle	12 Ashtray		

rod and then withdraw the exterior handle until it can be usncrewed from the latch rod.
9   Remove the latch and rods from the door.

Reassembly

10   Refitting is a reversal of removal, but observe the following points.
11   When fitting the glass, centralise it between the side channels before tightening the bottom slide channel-to-regulator bolts.
12   When screwing the exterior handle onto the latch rod, set it so that the original length of thread is exposed, then check for full operation of the handle and unscrew it or screw it further onto the rod to achieve this.

15 Door – removal and refitting

1   Remove the interior trim panel as described in Section 12.
2   Where fitted, disconnect the wiring to the door speaker and remove the wiring harness.
3   Drive out the pin from the check strap detent rod.
4   Support the door securely on jacks or blocks, well protected with rags.
5   Undo the bolts securing the hinges to the door, and lift away the door.
6   If necessary undo the bolts and remove the hinges.
7   Refitting is the reverse sequence to removal. Check that the door is a flush fit with the body and if necessary, slacken the hinge-to-door bolts to move the door in or out, or slacken the hinge-to-body bolts to move the door forward or backward. After adjustment, check the closure of the door and operation of the latch. Adjust the position of the lock striker plate to achieve proper closing without slamming.

16 Boot lid (Sedan) – removal and refitting

1   Open the lid fully and mark the positon of the hinges on the underside of it.
2   With the help of an assistant, support the weight of the lid, unscrew the hinge bolts and remove the lid from the car.
3   Refitting is a reversal of removal, but do not fully tighten the hinge bolts until the lid has been closed gently and checked for alignment. If an equal gap does not exist on both sides of the lid, move it as necessary within the limits of the elongated hinge bolt holes and then tighten the bolts.
4   As the lid is closed, the lock should engage smoothly and positively. If it does not, released the striker or lock bolts or both and adjust for alignment and closure.
5   If for any reason the boot lid counterbalance torsion rod must be removed, then the end of the rod must be released from its anchorage slot. Do this using a large adjustable spanner or a long lever. *Exercise caution as the rod is under considerable torsion.*

17 Tailgate – removal and refitting

1   Open the tailgate and remove the interior trim panel.
2   Disconnect the washer hose at the connector (where fitted).
3   Disconnect the rear window and wiper motor wiring (as applicable), then pull the wiring harness out of the tailgate. To facilitate refitting tie a string to the end of the harness and pull this through as the harness is withdrawn.
4   Support the tailgate and undo the two bolts each side securing the support struts (photo).
5   Undo the bolts securing the hinges to the tailgate and remove the tailgate (photo).
6   Refitting is the reverse sequence to removal but do not fully tighten the hinge bolts until the tailgate has been closed gently and checked for alignment. If an equal gap does not exist on both sides of the tailgate, move it as necessary within the limits of the elongated hinge bolt holes and then tighten the bolts.
7   As the tailgate is closed, the lock should engage smoothly and positively. If it does not, release the striker plate bolts and adjust for closure.

18 Boot lid (Sedan) and tailgate lock and controls – removal and refitting

Lock

1   Working in the luggage compartment, remove the trim panel to gain access to the lock.
2   Refer to Fig. 11.9 and disconnect the release cable.
3   Undo the lock retaining screws, withdraw the lock until the link rod from the lock cylinder can be disconnected and the lock removed from the car.
4   If required the lock cylinder can be removed after extracting the retainer.

Control cable and lever

5   Working inside the car, remove the release lever cover and housing from the side of the driver's seat.
6   Unbolt the lever bracket and disconnect the control cable from the lever.
7   Remove the rear seat cushion (Section 27) and the sill mouldings from the front and rear right-hand door openings (Section 31).
8   Peel back the floor carpet to expose the control cable.
9   Remove the fixing tape and pull the cable through into the luggage boot. Disconnect the cable from the lock and its locating clips.

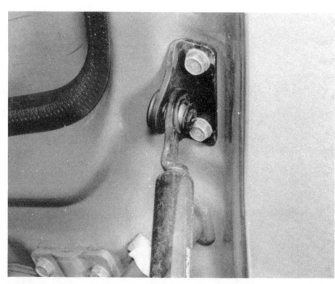

17.4 Tailgate support strut upper retaining bolts

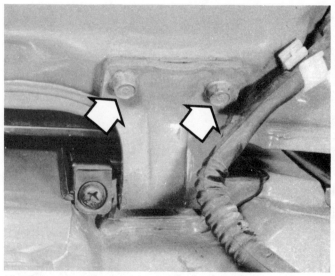

17.5 Tailgate-to-hinge retaining bolts (arrowed)

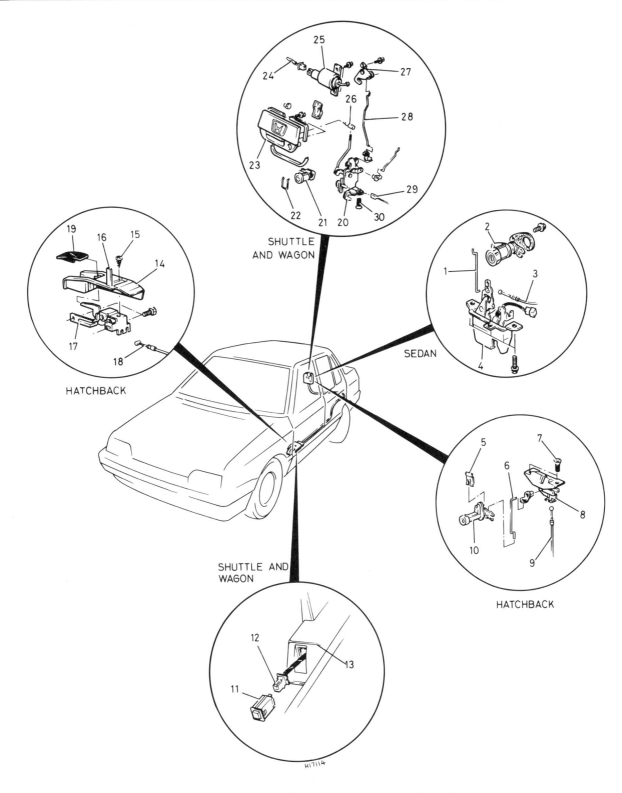

Fig. 11.9 Boot lid and tailgate lock and controls (Sec 18)

1 Lock rod	9 Opener cable	17 Opener	24 Wire connector
2 Lock cylinder	10 Lock cylinder	18 Tailgate cable	25 Tailgate opener solenoid
3 Opener cable	11 Tailgate opener switch	19 Release lever	26 Joint
4 Latch	12 Wire harness	20 Latch	27 Lock link
5 Retainer	13 Seat side trim	21 Lock cylinder	28 Release rod
6 Lock rod	14 Opener cover	22 Retainer	29 Ground cable
7 Screw	15 Screw	23 Tailgate handle	30 Screw
8 Latch	16 Cap		

Refitting
10 Refitting of compoents is the reverse sequence to removal.

19 Tailgate support struts – removal and refitting

1 Open the tailgate and have an assistant support it in the open position.
2 Undo the upper and lower mounting bolts and remove the strut from the car.
3 Refitting is the reverse sequence to removal.
4 The struts are gas-pressurised and should not be punctured or subjected to excess heat.

20 Fuel filler flap lock and controls – removal and refitting

1 The control cable for the fuel filler flap lock runs along the same route as the one for the boot lid or tailgate release, and removal and refitting procedures are as described in Section 18.
2 To remove the cable release lock tongue, open the flap, pull out the forked retaining clip and withdraw the assembly into the luggage compartment.
3 The lock cylinder can be removed after extracting the retaining clip.

21 Rear bumper – removal and refitting

1 Where fitted remove the mudflaps.
2 On models with rear foglights mounted in the bumper, remove the foglights and disconnect the wiring connectors.
3 Undo the two bumper mount bolts or, on Shuttle and Wagon models, the eight bumper mount screws.

4 Slide the bumper to the rear, disconnect the number plate light wiring and remove the bumper.
5 Refitting is the reverse sequence to removal.

22 Windscreen, rear window and fixed window glass – removal and refitting

1 On all models the windscreen, rear window and fixed window glass is flush mounted and bonded in position.
2 Removal and refitting is a specialist operation and should only be undertaken by a dealer or specialist equipped for glass replacement of this type.

23 Rear quarter-light glass (Hatchback) – removal and refitting

1 From inside the car carefully prise out the latch mounting cover.
2 At the forward end of the quarter-light, undo the two screws and remove the quarter-pillar moulding.
3 Undo the latch mounting screws and the two hinge mounting screws, and remove the quarter-light glass.
4 Refitting is the reverse sequence to removal.

24 Centre console – removal and refitting

1 Remove the gear lever knob (manual transmission) or the selector lever handle (automatic transmission).
2 If a front console is fitted, remove the mounting screws and lift out the console box and front console.

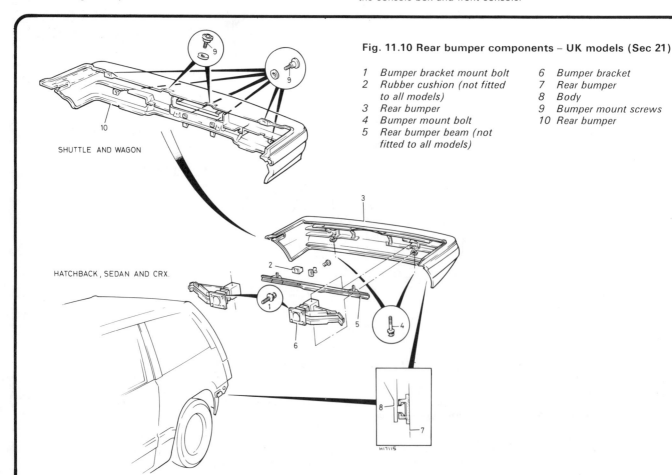

Fig. 11.10 Rear bumper components – UK models (Sec 21)

1 Bumper bracket mount bolt	6 Bumper bracket
2 Rubber cushion (not fitted to all models)	7 Rear bumper
3 Rear bumper	8 Body
4 Bumper mount bolt	9 Bumper mount screws
5 Rear bumper beam (not fitted to all models)	10 Rear bumper

SHUTTLE AND WAGON

HATCHBACK, SEDAN AND CRX.

24.3A Removing the centre console rear lid

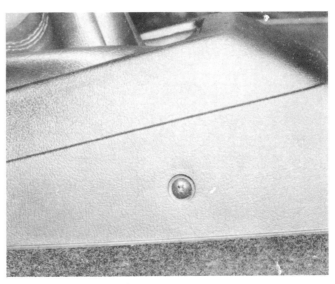

24.3B Console side retaining screw ...

24.3C ... top front ...

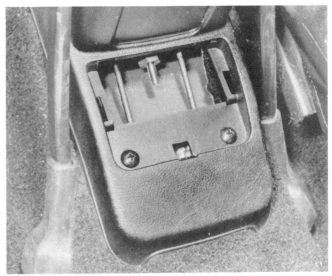

24.3D ... and top rear retaining screws

3   Prise out the centre cap and rear lid, then remove the side and top retaining screws (photos).
4   Lift the console up and where fitted, disconnect the radio speaker balance control wiring connector.
5   Withdraw the console over the handbrake lever and gear lever/selector, then remove it from the car.
6   Refitting is the reverse sequence to removal.

25 Roof console – removal and refitting

1   Disconnect the battery negative terminal.
2   Remove the interior rear view mirror and interior light from the console.
3   Undo the two screws and remove the rear plate.
4   Undo the screws securing the mirror base and the two screws at the rear, under the rear plate.
5   Disconnect the wiring connectors and remove the console.
6   Refitting is the reverse sequence to removal.

26 Facia panel – removal and refitting

1   Disconnect the battery negative terminal.
2   Remove the steering wheel (Chapter 10).
3   Remove the facia undercover access panel from around the steering column by extracting the screws.
4   Extract the screws and remove the glovebox and, where fitted, the glovebox undertray.
5   Remove the ashtray.
6   Remove the radio (Chapter 12).
7   Where fitted, prise out the clock and disconnect the wiring.
8   Refer to Chapter 12 and remove the instrument panel.
9   On all models except CRX, extract the screw which secures the bonnet release lever to the bracket and move the lever to one side.
10 On Hatchback and Sedan models remove the side caps from both ends of the facia panel. Do this by prising them out sideways.
11 On CRX models remove the side air vents.
12 On Shuttle and Wagon models remove the side defroster garnish and lower side caps.

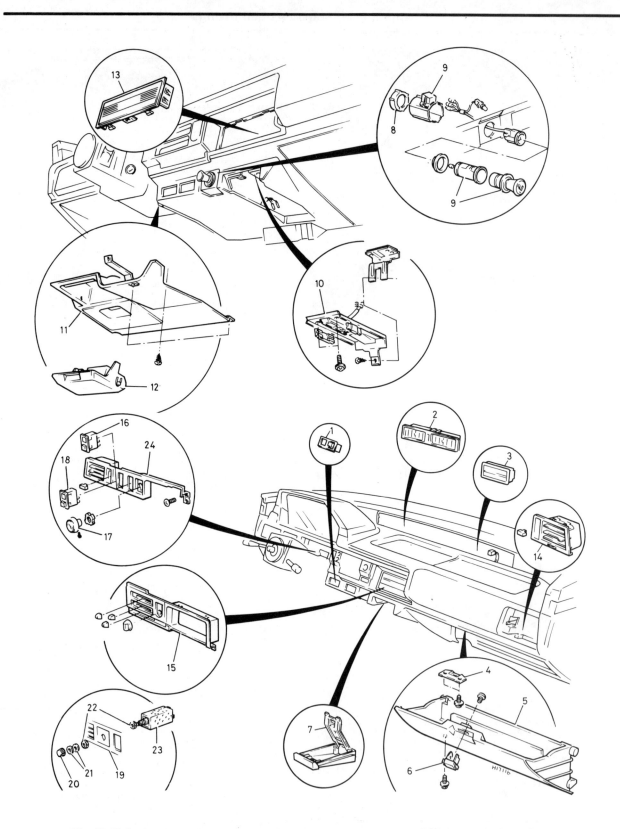

Fig. 11.11 Facia trim and accessory attachments – Hatchback and Sedan models (Sec 26)

1	Headlight wiper switch	8	Ring nut	14	Side air vent	20	Knob
2	Centre air vent	9	Cigarette lighter assembly	15	Heater control face plate	21	Washers
3	Clock	10	Ashtray holder	16	Rear defroster switch	22	Ring nuts
4	Striker	11	Facia lower panel	17	Choke knob	23	Dashlight brightness control
5	Glove box	12	Coin box	18	Rear fog light switch		switch
6	Latch	13	Radio panel	19	Side facia panel	24	Side face panel
7	Ashtray						

13 On Hatchback and Sedan models remove the centre air vent, on all other models remove the cover over the centre bolt.

14 On UK carburettor models, release the choke cable from the facia as described in Chapter 3.

15 On all models except CRX, pull off the heater control lever knobs and release the heater control escutcheon plate retainers. Withdraw the plate until the illumination bulb can be disconnected. Extract the screws and separate the heater control lever mounting base from the facia.

16 Mark the position of the wiring harness connectors at the fusebox and disconnect them. Similarly disconnect the remaining facia wiring connectors.

17 Disconnect the steering column bracket earth lead and, on tilt type steering columns, set the column at its lowest position.

18 Unscrew all the facia retaining bolts, and with the help of an assistant lift the facia up off the centre guide pin and remove it from the car.

19 Refitting is the reverse sequence to removal.

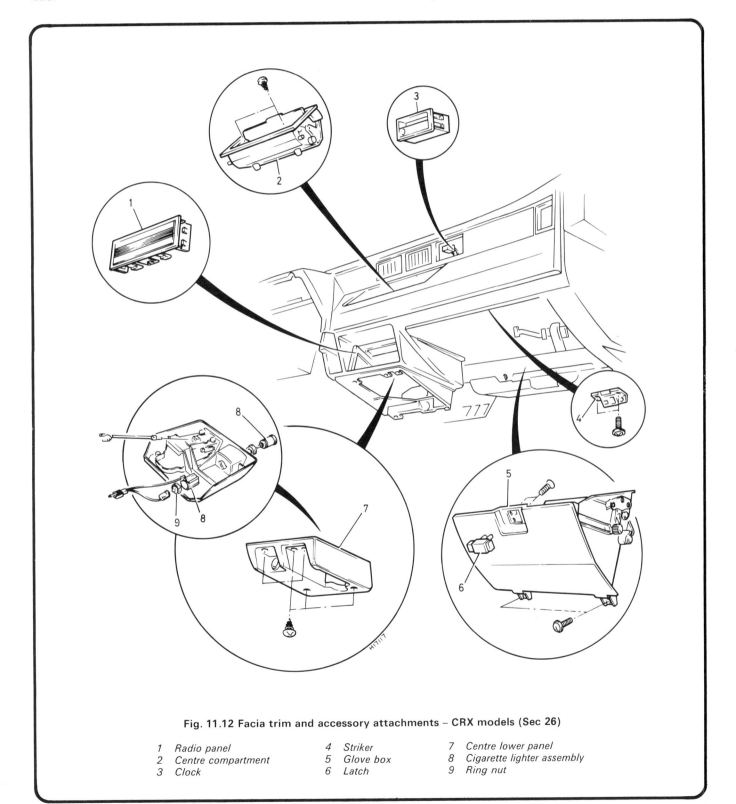

Fig. 11.12 Facia trim and accessory attachments – CRX models (Sec 26)

1	Radio panel	4	Striker	7	Centre lower panel
2	Centre compartment	5	Glove box	8	Cigarette lighter assembly
3	Clock	6	Latch	9	Ring nut

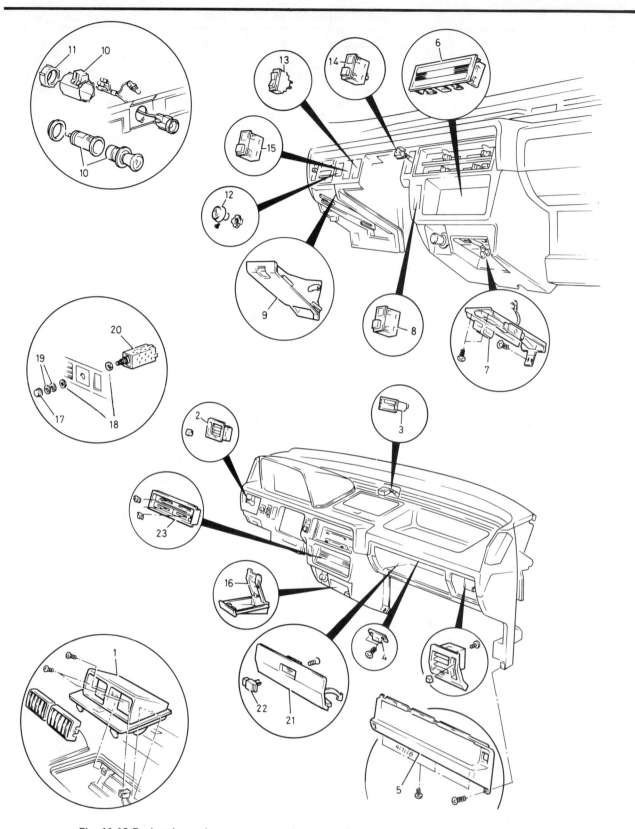

Fig. 11.13 Facia trim and accessory attachments – Shuttle and Wagon models (Sec 26)

1	Pop-up centre air vent
2	Side air vent
3	Clock
4	Striker
5	Under tray
6	Radio panel
7	Ashtray holder
8	Headlight wiper switch
9	Coin box
10	Cigarette lighter assembly
11	Ring nut
12	Choke knob
13	Sunroof switch
14	Rear defroster switch
15	Rear fog light switch
16	Ashtray
17	Knob
18	Ring nuts
19	Washers
20	Dashlight brightness control switch
21	Glove box lid
22	Latch
23	Heater control face plate

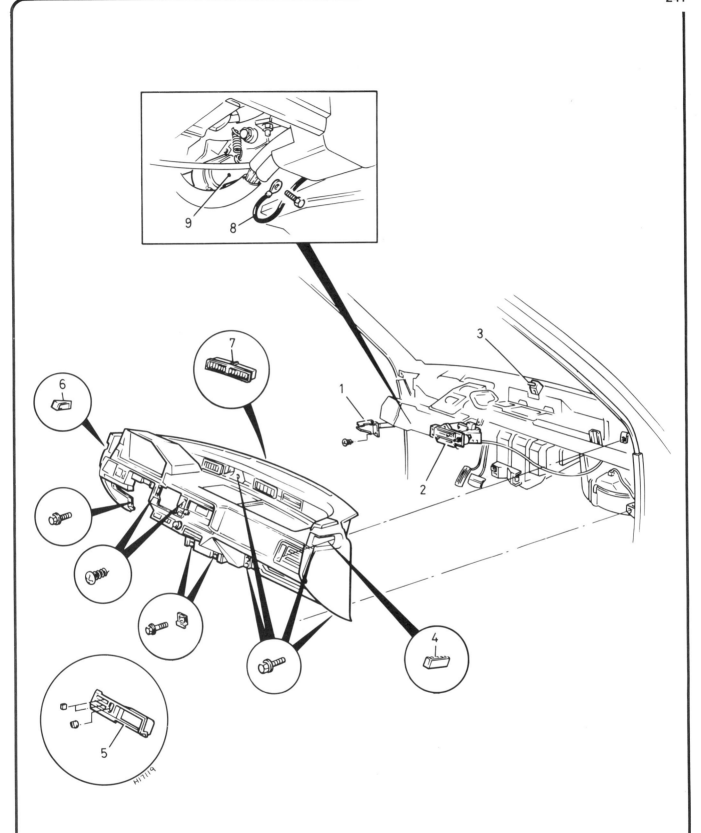

Fig. 11.14 Facia mounting details – Hatchback and Sedan models (Sec 26)

1 Hood opener	4 Side cap	7 Centre air vent
2 Heater control panel	5 Heater control face plate	8 Ground cable
3 Guide pin	6 Side cap	9 Steering column

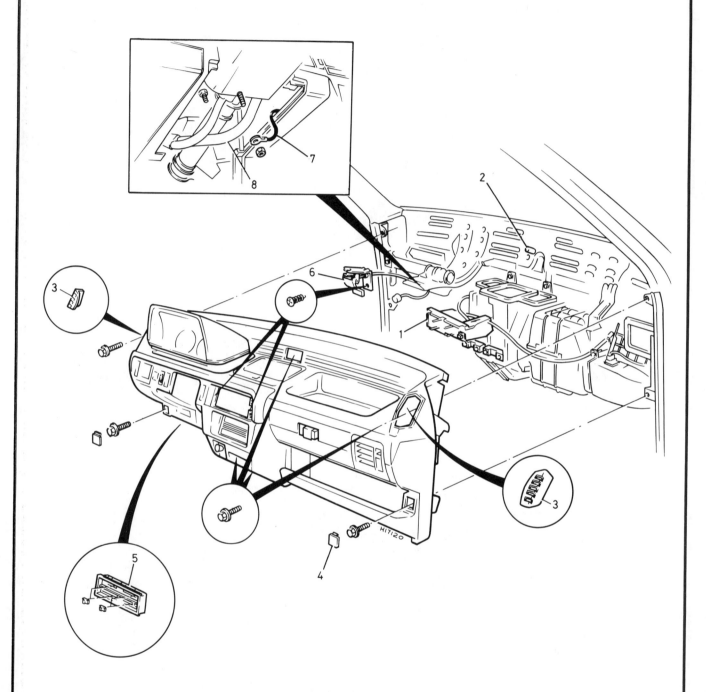

Fig. 11.15 Facia mounting details – Shuttle and Wagon models (Sec 26)

1	Heater control pad	4	Side cap	7	Ground cable
2	Guide pin	5	Heater control face plate	8	Steering column
3	Side defroster garnish	6	Hood opener		

243

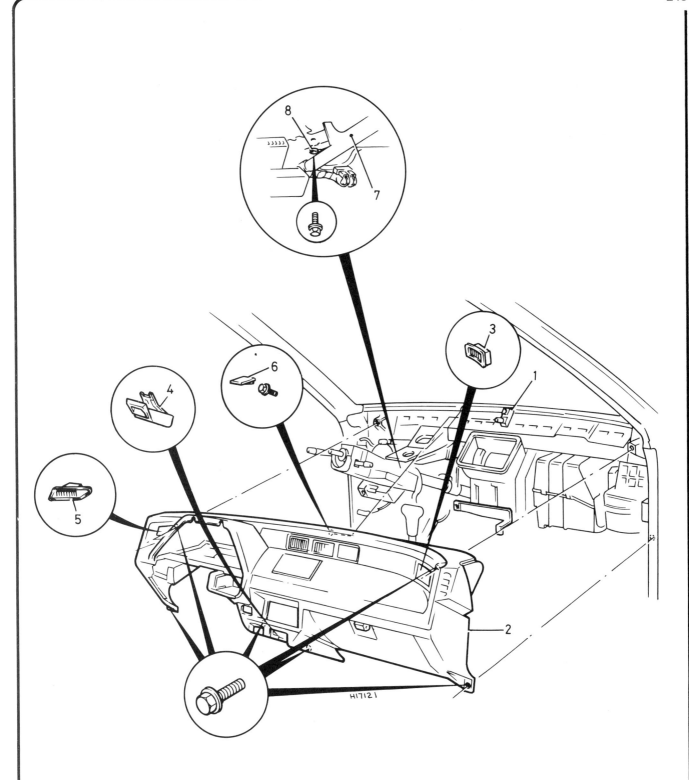

Fig. 11.16 Facia mounting details – CRX models (Sec 26)

1	Guide pin	4	Ashtray	7	Steering column
2	Dashboard	5	Side air vent	8	Ground cable
3	Side air vent	6	Centre bolt cover		

27 Front and rear seats – removal and refitting

Front seats

1   Push the seat fully forwards and unscrew the bolts which hold the rear end of the seat track to the floor.
2   Push the seat fully back and unscrew the track front end bolts.

3   Lift the seat from the car.
4   Refitting is a reversal of removal.

Rear seats

5   Removal and refitting of the rear seats varies considerably according to model. The procedure is however straightforward and only entails releasing the relevant retaining bolts or catches. Full details are shown in Figs. 11.19 to 11.23.

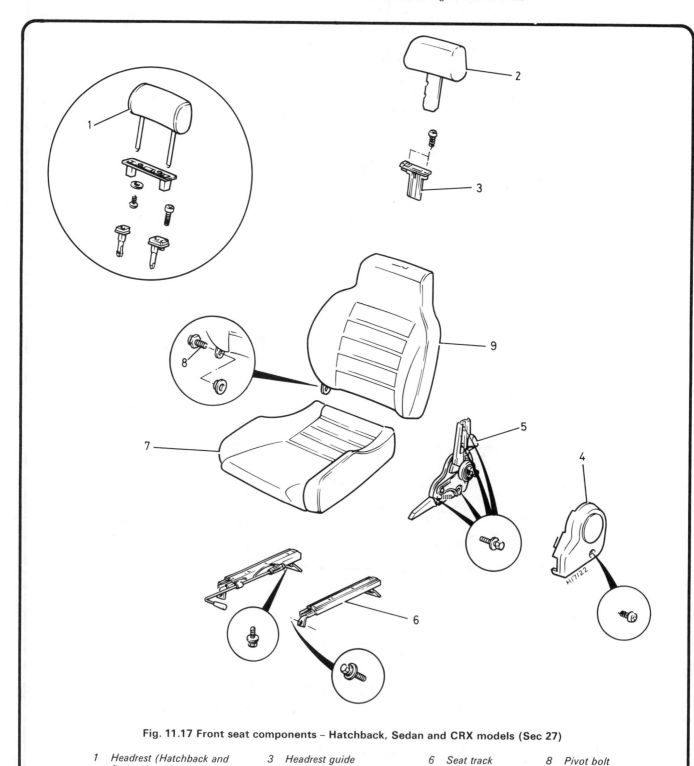

Fig. 11.17 Front seat components – Hatchback, Sedan and CRX models (Sec 27)

1 Headrest (Hatchback and Sedan)	3 Headrest guide	6 Seat track	8 Pivot bolt
2 Headrest (CRX)	4 Reclining adjuster cover	7 Seat cushion	9 Seat back
	5 Reclining adjuster		

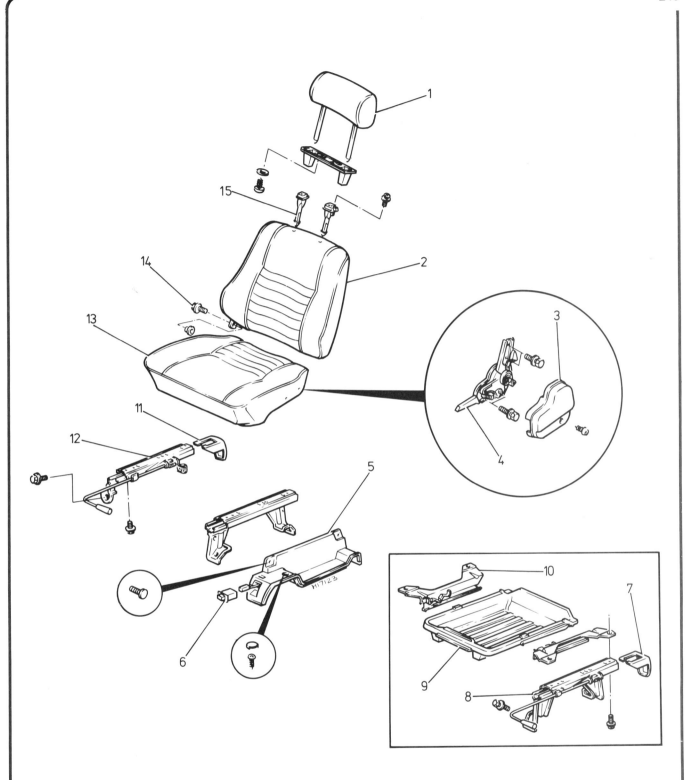

Fig. 11.18 Front seat components – Shuttle and Wagon models (Sec 27)

1 Headrest	6 Tailgate opener switch	11 Rear track cover
2 Seat back	7 Rear track cover	12 Seat track
3 Reclining adjuster cover	8 Seat track	13 Seat cushion
4 Reclining adjuster	9 Under seat tray	14 Pivot bolt
5 Seat side trim	10 Tray guide	15 Headrest guide

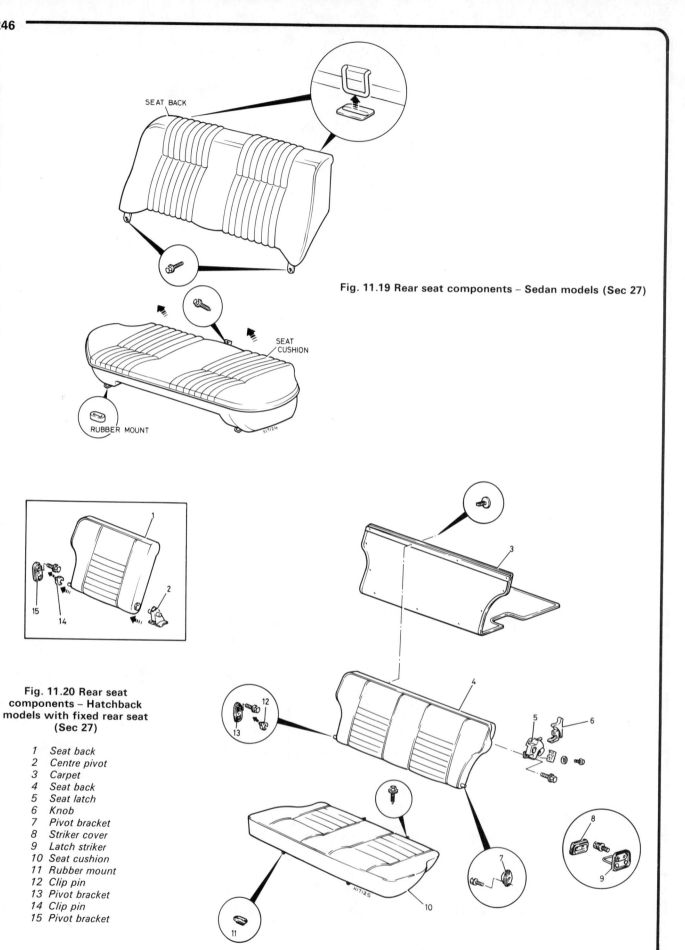

SEAT BACK

Fig. 11.19 Rear seat components – Sedan models (Sec 27)

SEAT CUSHION

RUBBER MOUNT

Fig. 11.20 Rear seat
components – Hatchback
models with fixed rear seat
(Sec 27)

1 Seat back
2 Centre pivot
3 Carpet
4 Seat back
5 Seat latch
6 Knob
7 Pivot bracket
8 Striker cover
9 Latch striker
10 Seat cushion
11 Rubber mount
12 Clip pin
13 Pivot bracket
14 Clip pin
15 Pivot bracket

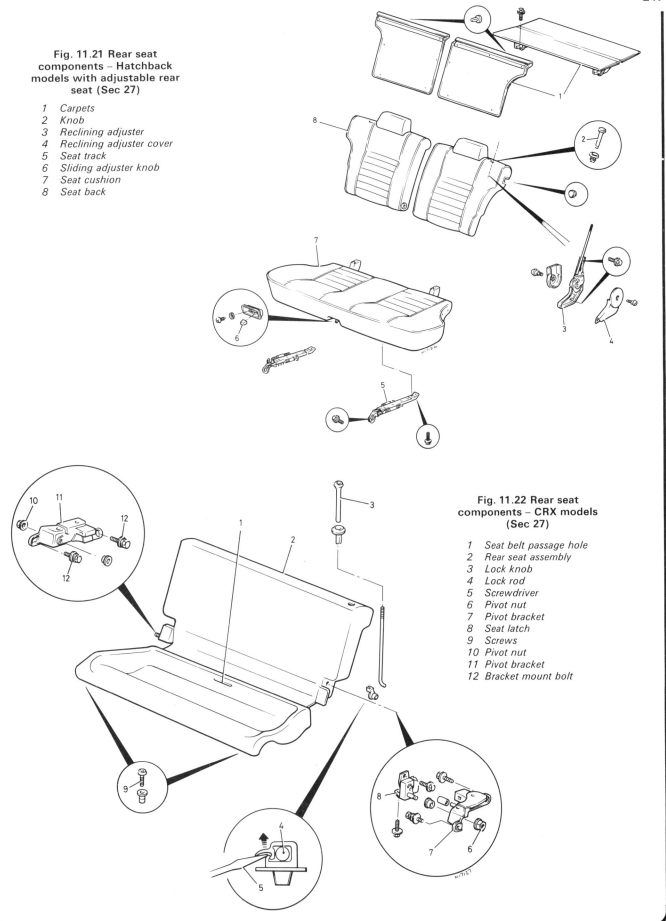

Fig. 11.21 Rear seat components – Hatchback models with adjustable rear seat (Sec 27)

1 Carpets
2 Knob
3 Reclining adjuster
4 Reclining adjuster cover
5 Seat track
6 Sliding adjuster knob
7 Seat cushion
8 Seat back

Fig. 11.22 Rear seat components – CRX models (Sec 27)

1 Seat belt passage hole
2 Rear seat assembly
3 Lock knob
4 Lock rod
5 Screwdriver
6 Pivot nut
7 Pivot bracket
8 Seat latch
9 Screws
10 Pivot nut
11 Pivot bracket
12 Bracket mount bolt

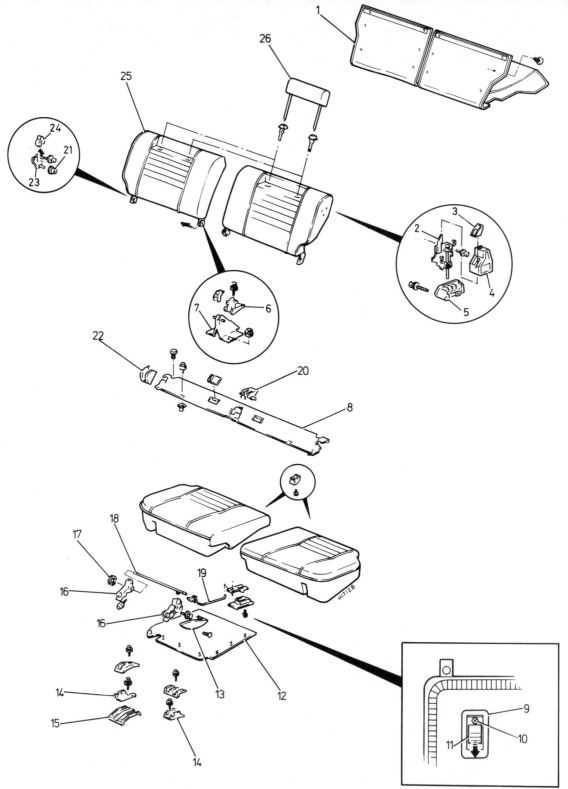

Fig. 11.23 Rear seat components – Shuttle and Wagon models (Sec 27)

1 Carpet	8 Seat belt garnish	15 Body	21 Spacer bush
2 Seat latch	9 Slide knob cover	16 Seat hinge	22 Side pivot cover
3 Knob	10 Mount screw	17 E-clip	23 Side pivot
4 Seat latch cover	11 Slide knob	18 Link	24 Clip pin
5 Latch striker	12 Cushion carpet	19 Rod	25 Seat back
6 Seat cushion latch	13 Hinge cover	20 Seat cushion latch cover	26 Headrest
7 Centre pivot	14 Seat hinge base		

28 Seat belts – maintenance, removal and refitting

1   Periodically inspect the seat belts for fraying or other damage. If evident, renew the belt.
2   The belts may be cleaned using warm water and liquid detergent. Do not use solvents of any kind.
3   If the car is involved in a front end collision and the belts have restrained the front or rear seat occupants, renew the belts.
4   Before unbolting the seat belt anchor bolts, remove the trim panels as necessary (Section 31).
5   When refitting, always maintain the original fitted sequence of washers and spacers.
6   Set the floor stalk at 45° to the floor before tightening its bolt.

29 Rear view mirrors – removal and refitting

Interior
1   If the mirror incorporates a plastic trim cover over its base, prise off the cover, undo the two screws and remove the mirror.
2   If the mirror arm is a one-piece moulding, slide the mirror rearwards to remove it from the base. The base can be removed after undoing the two screws.
3   Refitting is the reverse sequence to removal.

Exterior
4   Slide the mirror control knob from the operating rod (photo).
5   Prise out the triangular escutcheon plate, to expose the mirror fixing screws (photos).

6   Remove the screws and take off the mirror.
7   Refitting is a reversal of removal.

30 Sunroof – general

1   According to model the sunroof fitted may be a detachable panel, or manually or electrically-operated sliding panel.
2   All types are maintenance-free, but adjustment, fault tracing and removal and refitting are involved operations requiring special tools, and are beyond the scope of the Manual. In the event of problems occuring with the sunroof, the work should be entrusted to a dealer.

31 Interior trim panels – removal and refitting

1   All interior surfaces in the car are covered by moulded plastic trim panels secured with screws, push fasteners and clips.
2   Many of the panels engage with each other and it is necessary to remove them in a set sequence to avoid damage.
3   Removal entails extracting the caps over the retaining screws, then undoing them, or carefully prising out the push fasteners (photos). For the panels around the door frame, the rubber sealing weatherstrip must be released in the areas around the panel. Once this is done the panel clips can be released and the panels removed. Figs. 11.24 to 11.27 show the panels and fastener locations.
4   Refitting is a reversal of removal.

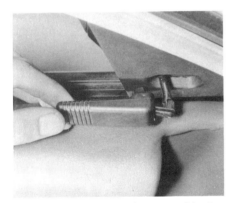
29.4 Removing exterior mirror control knob

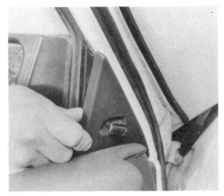
29.5A Removing the mirror escutcheon plate ...

29.5B ... to gain access to the fixing screws (arrowed)

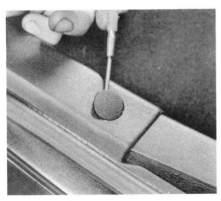
31.3A Extracting interior trim retaining screw cap ...

31.3B ... and screw

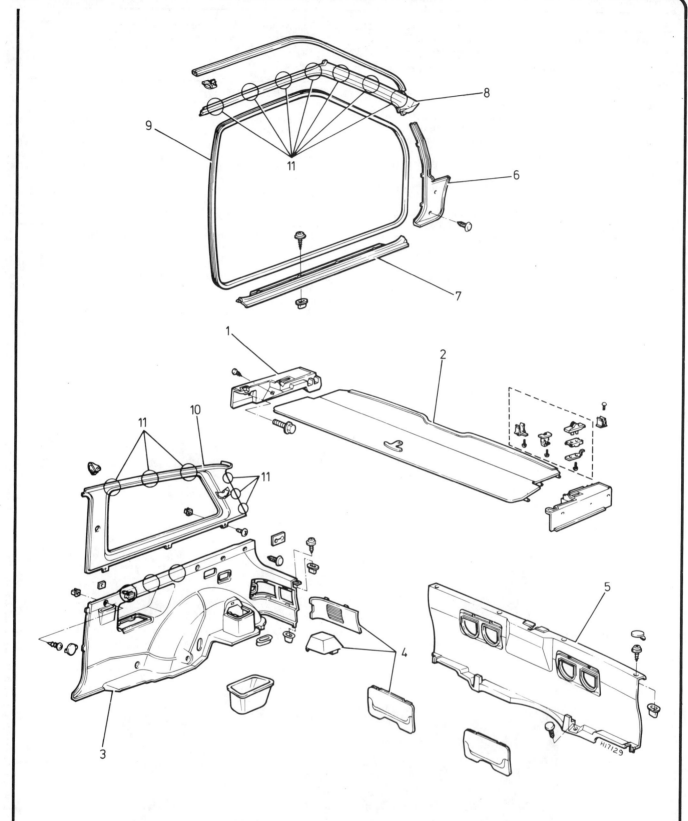

Fig. 11.24 Interior trim panel attachments – Hatchback models (Sec 31)

1 Side shelf	4 Maintenance doors	7 Door sill moulding	10 Quarter window trim
2 Rear shelf	5 Rear trim panel	8 Front pillar trim	11 Clip locations
3 Quarter trim panel	6 Kick panel	9 Door trim	

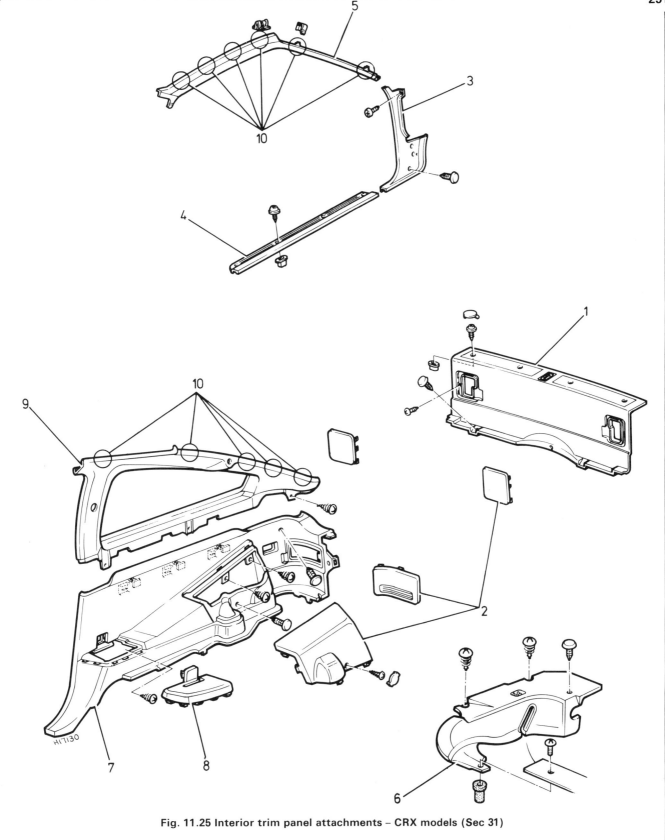

Fig. 11.25 Interior trim panel attachments – CRX models (Sec 31)

1	Rear trim panel	4	Door sill moulding	7	Quarter trim panel	9	Quarter window trim
2	Maintenance doors	5	Front pillar trim	8	Seat belt anchor cover	10	Clip locations
3	Kick panel	6	Rear seat side trim				

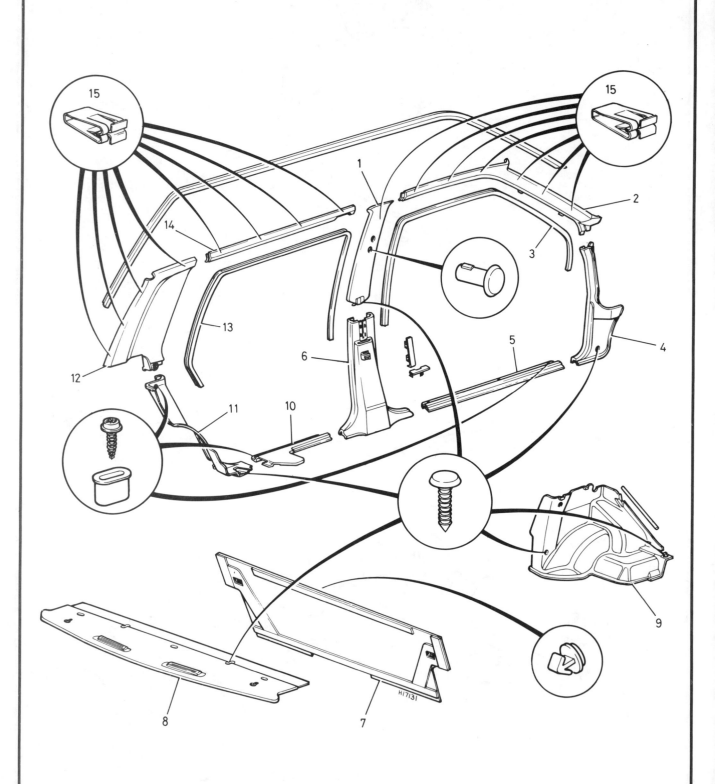

Fig. 11.26 Interior trim panel attachments – Sedan models (Sec 31)

1 Centre pillar upper trim	6 Centre pillar lower trim	11 Quarter trim panel
2 Front pillar trim	7 Rear bulkhead insulator	12 Rear pillar trim panel
3 Door trim	8 Rear shelf	13 Door trim
4 Kick panel	9 Trunk side panel	14 Headliner side moulding
5 Front door sill moulding	10 Rear door sill moulding	15 Clip locations

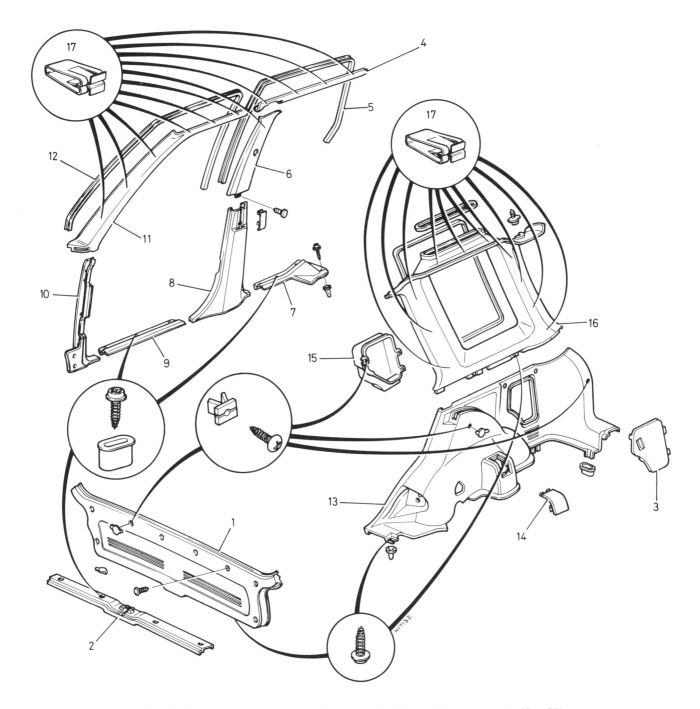

Fig. 11.27 Interior trim panel attachments – Shuttle and Wagon models (Sec 31)

1 Tailgate trim panel	6 Centre pillar upper trim	11 Front pillar trim	14 Damper maintenance lid
2 Tailgate sill moulding	7 Rear door sill moulding	12 Door trim	15 Side compartment
3 Side compartment cover	8 Centre pillar lower trim	13 Luggage compartment side	16 Quarter window trim
4 Headliner side moulding	9 Front door sill moulding	trim panel	17 Clip locations
5 Door trim	10 Kick panel		

32 Heater – removal and refitting

1 Disconnect the battery negative terminal.
2 Drain the cooling system as described in Chapter 2.
3 Refer to Section 26 and remove the facia.
4 Working within the engine compartment, disconnect the heater hoses at the bulkhead.

5 Remove the nut from the large stud in the centre of the engine compartment rear bulkhead.
6 Carefully prise out the plastic pins which hold the air duct to the blower motor and heater casings, and withdraw the air duct. Disconnect the blower motor wiring plug.
7 Release the recirculation control outer cable from its fixing clip and the inner cable from the operating lever.

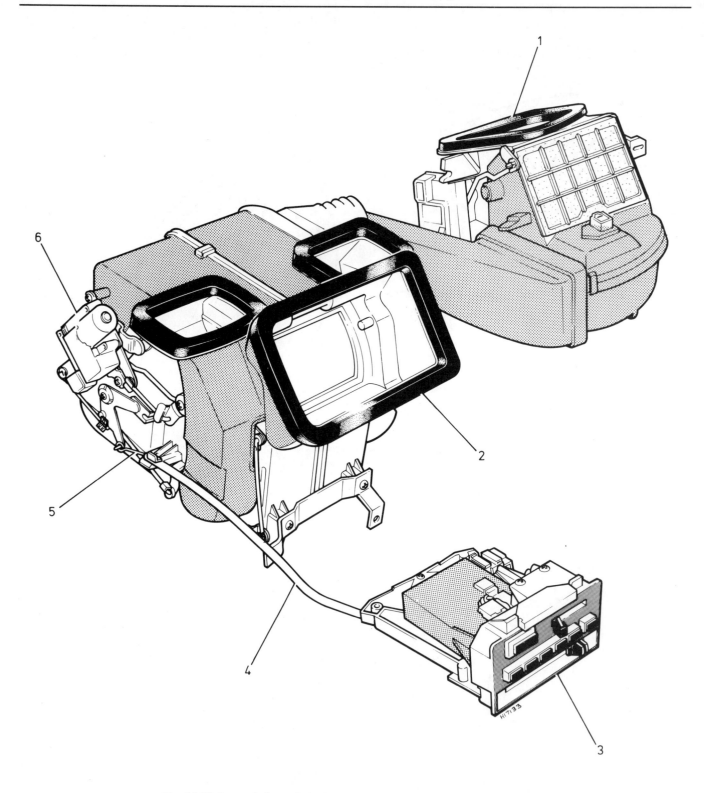

Fig. 11.28 General view of the heater components – UK models (Sec 32)

1	Blower	3	Heater controller	5	Heater valve cable
2	Heater	4	Air mix cable	6	Mode control motor

8   Disconnect the remaining control cables in a similar way.

9   Release the wiring harness from its clips.

10 Unscrew and remove the two upper heater mounting bolts, pull the heater from the bulkhead and lift it away.

11 The casing may be dismantled for access to the matrix. If the matrix is clogged, try reverse flushing it. If the matrix is leaking, leave repairs to a specialist or exchange it for a new one.

12 Refitting is a reversal of removal. Adjust the control cables as described in Section 35.

13 Refill the cooling system, reconnect the battery.

33 Heater blower – removal and refitting

1   Disconnect the battery negative terminal.
2   Refer to Section 26 and where applicable remove the glovebox and frame.
3   Carefully prise out the plastic pins which hold the air duct to the blower motor and heater casings, withdraw the air duct.
4   Disconnect the multi-plugs from the motor casings and the blower motor (photos).
5   Disconnect the recirculation control cable.

6   Unscrew the three nuts and withdraw the blower motor and casing.
7   Disconnect the corrugated hose from the blower motor.
8   Unscrew the motor cover screws and then withdraw the motor/fan assembly.
9   If dismantling is necessary, unscrew the fan nut and pull the fan from the motor shaft. Retrieve the washer.
10 Refitting is a reversal of removal, but use a new gasket on the motor mounting flange.
11 Adjust the recirculation control as described in Section 35. Reconnect the battery.

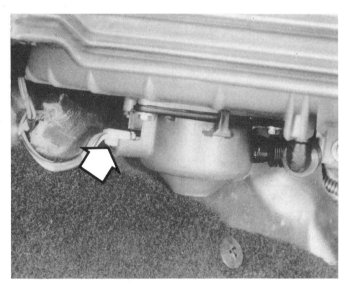

33.4A Heater blower wiring multi-plug at the motor (arrowed)

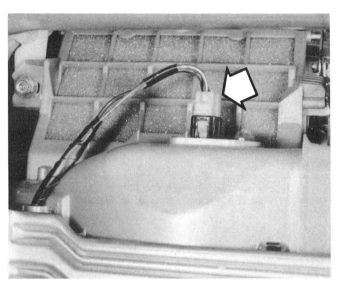

33.4B ... and motor casing (arrowed)

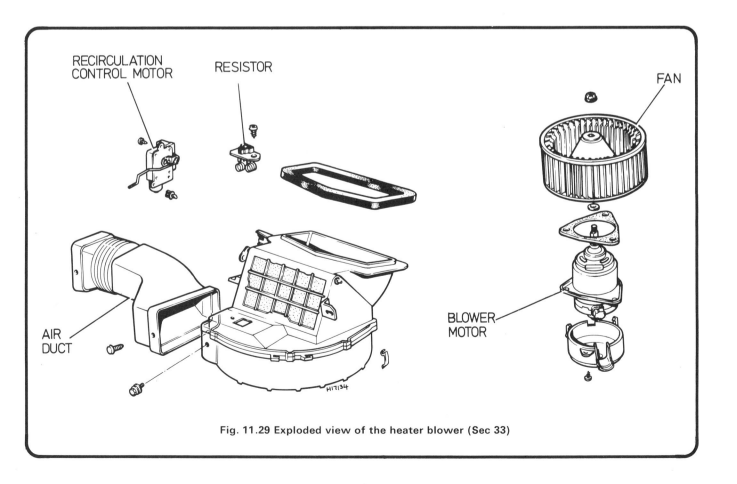

Fig. 11.29 Exploded view of the heater blower (Sec 33)

34 Heater control panel – removal and refitting

1 Disconnect the battery negative terminal.
2 Refer to Section 26 and its accompanying illustrations and remove the facia attachments as necessary to gain access to the panel.
3 Prise out the heater control escutcheon plate.
4 Unscrew the nut and release the blower motor switch from the control unit panel.
5 Release the recirculation control cable from the blower motor casing and the control arm.
6 Disconnect the other control cables in a similar way.
7 Extract the heater control panel fixing screws, withdraw the panel and disconnect the multi-plug from the rear of the panel.
8 Refitting is a reversal of removal. Adjust the control cables as described in Section 35.
9 Reconnect the battery.

35 Heater control cables and rods – removal, refitting and adjustment

1 The removal and refitting of all rods and cables is simply a matter of unclipping and releasing from the control lever and operating arm.
2 It is important to adjust each control cable or rod carefully in the following way if it has been disturbed, or its operation is incorrect.
3 It will be necessary to remove parts of the facia to gain access and reference should be made to Section 26 and its accompanying illustrations.

Air mix cable
4 Slide the temperature control to 'COLD'.
5 Close the air mix door, connect the cable end to the arm and secure the cable with the clip.
6 Operate the control lever and check that the air mix door opens fully with the lever in the 'HOT' position and closes fully when at 'COLD'.

Mode control cable
7 Slide the mode control lever to the 'DEF' position.
8 With the mode control arm in the 'DEF' position, attach the cable to the function control arm and secure with the clip. Check for smooth operation of the linkage.

Heater valve cable
9 Position the cable so that its outer sheath is 5 mm (0.2 in) from the end of the clamp boss and secure with the clip.
10 Connect the cable end to the heater valve control arm.
11 Move the temperature control lever to 'COLD'.
12 Close the heater valve fully, then connect the cable end to the valve arm. Secure with the clip.

Recirculation cable
13 Move the control lever to the 'FRESH' position.
14 Open the recirculation door.

15 Connect the cable to the recirculation arm and secure with the clip.
16 Check for smooth operation of the linkage.

36 Air conditioning system – description

1 Air conditioning is an option on certain models and consists of a belt-driven compressor, a condenser mounted ahead of the radiator, a receiver drier and an evaporator.

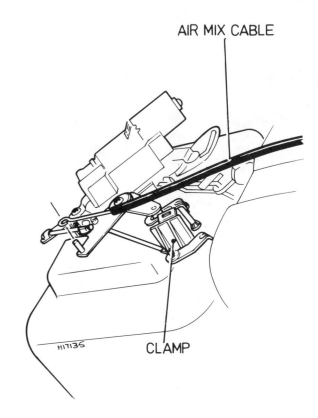

Fig. 11.30 Heater air mix cable fittings (Sec 35)

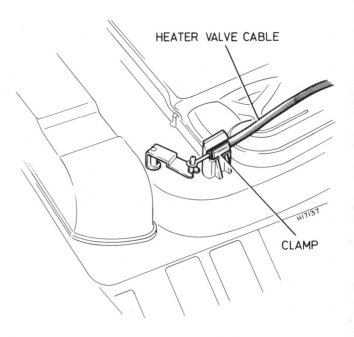

Fig. 11.32 Heater valve cable fittings at heater end (Sec 35)

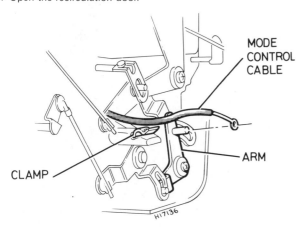

Fig. 11.31 Heater mode control cable fittings (Sec 35)

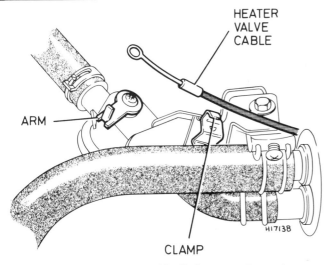

HEATER
VALVE
CABLE

ARM

CLAMP

H17138

Fig. 11.33 Heater valve cable fittings at valve end
(Sec 35)

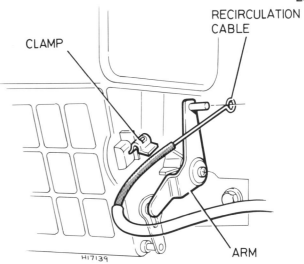

CLAMP

RECIRCULATION
CABLE

ARM

H17139

Fig. 11.34 Heater recirculation cable fittings (Sec 35)

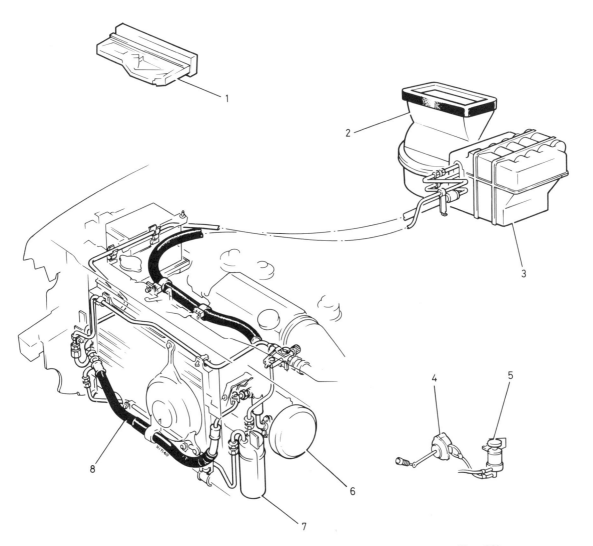

Fig. 11.35 General layout of the air conditioning system components (Sec 36)

1	Heater and air conditioning control panel	3	Evaporator	5	Idle control solenoid	7	Receiver and filter/drier
2	Blower	4	Idle boost diaphragm	6	Compressor	8	Condenser

Compressor

2   This circulates refrigerant through the system and incorporates an electro-magnetic clutch to engage or disengage the compressor according to pressure and temperature requirements.

3   While the compressor is running, the idle control solenoid permits vacuum to be applied on the idle boost diaphragm which moves the throttle linkage to compensate for the increased engine load at idle speed.

Condenser

4   This receives vaporised refrigerant from the compressor and by cooling it, converts the vapour into liquid.

Receiver drier

5   This is located at the side of the condenser and collects moisture from the system to prevent freezing of the components.

Evaporator

6   From the receiver drier, the refrigerant flows through the sight glass to give an indication of refrigerant charge.

7   The refrigerant is then vaporised by the pressure drop as it passes through an expansion valve and passes into the evaporator. Air flow through the fins of the evaporator is cooled before it is distributed inside the car. The refrigerant is then drawn back into the compressor to start a new cycle.

37 Air conditioning system compressor drivebelt – tensioning and renewal

Note: *On models equipped with power-assisted steering the steering pump drivebelt must be removed (Chapter 10) to allow renewal of the compressor drivebelt.*

1   Slacken the tensioner pulley nut and move the pulley by turning the adjusting bolt until the tension is correct. This is when the total deflection at the mid-point of the longest run is between 7.0 and 9.0 mm (0.28 and 0.35 in).

2   Tighten the tensioner pulley nut to the specified torque.

3   If the compressor drivebelt is to be renewed, slacken the tensioner pulley and ease the belt over the rim of the pulley. If it is difficult to remove, apply a spanner to the crankshaft pulley bolt, turn it while prising the belt up and over the pulley rim.

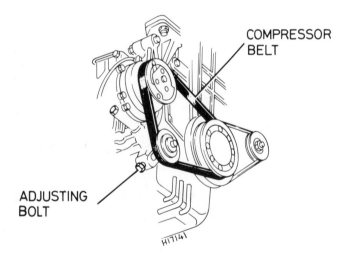

Fig. 11.36 Air conditioning compressor drivebelt adjusting bolt (Sec 37)

4   Fit the new belt, again turning the crankshaft pulley while prising the belt over the pulley rim and into its groove.

5   Tension the belt, run the engine for five munutes and then re-tension it as described in paragraph 1.

38 Air conditioning system components – removal and refitting

Warning: *Before removing or refitting any component have the system discharged by your dealer or refrigerant engineer. Once a component has been removed, cap the ends of open pipelines or couplings to prevent the entry of moisture.*

Compressor

1   Disconnect the battery and the compressor clutch stator lead.

2   Disconnect the compressor hoses and plug all openings.

3   Remove the drivebelt as described in Section 37.

4   Unscrew and remove all the mounting bolts and lift the compressor from the engine compartment.

5   If a new compressor is being fitted, then 30 cc (1.0 fl. oz) of refrigerant oil must be added to the low pressure fitting on the compressor.

6   Refitting is a reversal of removal. Tension the drivebelt as previously described and have the system charged by your dealer or refrigeration engineer.

Condenser

7   Disconnect the battery.

8   Refer to Section 6 and remove the front bumper.

9   Disconnect the high pressure pipe from the receiver and the low pressure hose from the condenser. Plug the openings.

10 Disconnect the condenser fan switch leads, remove the condenser mounting bolts and lift the condenser from the car. If required, the condenser fan can be detached from the condenser.

11 If a new condenser is being fitted, pour 10 cc (0.33 fl. oz) of refrigerant oil into the condenser.

12 Refitting is a reversal of removal. Have the system charged by your dealer or refrigeration engineer.

Evaporator, expansion valve and thermostat

13 Disconnect the battery.

14 Disconnect the low pressure hose and the receiver pipe from the evaporator. Extract the O-ring seals and then plug or cap all opnings.

15 Remove the protective sleeve from the low pressure hose. Also remove the grommet and retainer plate.

16 Refer to Section 26 and remove the glovebox and glovebox frame.

17 Refer to Section 33 and remove the blower unit. Slacken the sealing band which secures the evaporator to the heater.

18 Disconnect the drain hose and the electrical leads.

19 Unscrew the mounting bolts and lift away the evaporator assembly.

20 Release the fixing clips and remove the bottom half of the evaporator casing.

21 If the expansion valve must be removed, take off the tape and release the capillary tube from the low pressure pipe, then remove the expansion valve and extract the O-rings. Plug or cap all openings.

22 If the thermostat must be removed, withdraw the capillary tube from the evaporator fins and remove the thermostat.

23 The evaporator can be withdrawn from its casing after extracting the screws from the casing upper section.

24 If a new evaporator is being fitted, pour 30 cc (1.0 fl oz) of refrigerant oil into it.

25 Refitting is a reversal of removal. Apply sealant around the bulkhead grommet.

26 Reconnect the battery, have the system charged by your dealer or refrigeration engineer.

Chapter 12 Electrical system

Contents

Specifications

General
System type	12 volt, negative earth
Battery	47 Ah low maintenance or maintenance-free

Alternator
Output at 14 volts and 6000 alternator rpm	55 A
Minimum brush length:	
Nippon Denso	5.0 mm (0.20 in)
Mitsuba	8.0 mm (0.31 in)
Minimum brush spring tension:	
Nippon Denso	200 g (7.05 oz)
Mitsubishi	210 g (7.41 oz)

Starter motor
Type	Nippon Denso, Hitachi or Mitsuba
Minimum brush length:	
Nippon Denso 0.8 kW	10.0 mm (0.39 in)
Hitachi 0.8 kW	12.0 mm (0.47 in)
Nippon Denso 1.0 and 1.4 kW	8.5 mm (0.33 in)
Mitsuba 1.0 and 1.4 kW	9.3 mm (0.37 in)

Fusible links
Number and rating .... 1 x 55A, 2 x 45 A

Bulbs
Headlamps: **Wattage**
UK models 60/55
North American models 65/55
Front and rear sidelights/side marker lights 5
Front and rear direction indicators 21
Direction indicator side repeaters 5
Number plate lamps 5
Reversing lights 21
Stop/tail lights 21/5
Rear fog lights 21
Interior light 5
Luggage compartment light 3.4
Instrument panel illumination 3.4
Instrument panel warning lamps 1.4
Switch warning lamps 1.4
Heater control illumination 1.4

Torque wrench settings

	Nm	lbf ft
Alternator mounting bolt	45	33
Alternator adjusting link	24	17
Starter motor mounting bolts	45	32

1 General description

The electrical system is of the 12 volt negative earth type, and consists of a 12 volt battery, alternator, starter motor and related electrical accessories, components and wiring. The battery is of the low maintenance or maintenance-free, 'sealed for life' type and is charged by an alternator which is belt-driven from the crankshaft pulley. The starter motor is of the pre-engaged type incorporating an integral solenoid. On starting, the solenoid moves the drive pinion into engagement with the flywheel ring gear before the starter motor is energised. Once the engine has started, a one-way clutch prevents the motor armature being driven by the engine until the pinion disengages from the flywheel.

Further details of the major electrical systems are given in the relevant Sections of this Chapter.

Caution: *Before carrying out any work on the vehicle electrical system, read through the precautions given in Safety First! at the beginning of this manual and in Section 2 of this Chapter.*

2 Electrical system – precautions

It is necessary to take extra care when working on the electrical system to avoid damage to semi-conductor devices (diodes and transistors), and to avoid the risk of personal injury. In addition to the precautions given in Safety First! at the beginning of this manual, observe the following items when working on the system.

1 *Always remove rings, watches, etc before working on the electrical system.* Even with the battery disconnected, capacitive discharge could occur if a component live terminal is earthed through a metal object. This could cause a shock or nasty burn.

2 *Do not reverse the battery connections.* Components such as the alternator or any other having semi-conductor circuitry could be irreparably damaged.

3 If the engine is being started using jump leads and a slave battery, connect the batteries *positive to positive* and *negative to negative*. This also applies when connecting a battery charger.

4 Never disconnect the battery terminals, or alternator wiring, when the engine is running.

5 The battery leads and alternator wiring must be disconnected before carrying out any electric arc-welding on the car.

6 Never use an ohmmeter of the type incorporating a hand cranked generator for circuit or continuity testing.

3 Maintenance and inspection

1 At regular intervals (see 'Routine Maintenance') carry out the following maintenance and inspection operations on the electrical system components.

2 Check the operation of all the electrical equipment, ie wipers, washers, lights, direction indicators, horn etc. Refer to the appropriate Sections of this Chapter if any components are found to be inoperative.

3 Visually check all accessible wiring connectors, harnesses and retaining clips for security, or any signs of chafing or damage. Rectify any problems encountered.

4 Check the alternator drivebelt for cracks, fraying or damage. Renew the belt if worn or, if satisfactory, check and adjust the belt tension. These procedures are covered in Section 6.

5 Check the condition of the wiper blades and if they are cracked or show signs of deterioration, renew them as described in Section 21. Check the operation of the windscreen and tailgate washers (if fitted).

6 On low maintenance batteries top up the battery using distilled water to the upper mark on the battery case. Always maintain the level in all the cells between the upper and lower marks (photo).

7 Check the battery terminals, and if there is any sign of corrosion disconnect and clean them thoroughly. Smear the terminals and battery posts with petroleum jelly before refitting the plastic covers. If there is any corrosion on the battery tray, remove the battery, clean the deposits away and treat the affected metal with an anti-rust preparation. Repaint the tray in the original colour after treatment.

8 Top up the windscreen washer reservoir and check the security of the pump wires and water pipes.

9 It is advisable to have the headlight beam adjusted using optical beam setting equipment.

10 While carrying out a road test, check the operation of all the instruments and warning lights, and the operation of the direction indicator self-cancelling mechanism.

4 Battery – removal and refitting

1 The battery is located on the right-hand side of the engine compartment.

2 To remove the battery, slacken the negative terminal clamp bolt and lift the terminal off the battery post (photo).

3 Lift the plastic cover from the positive terminal, slacken the clamp bolt and lift the terminal off the battery post.

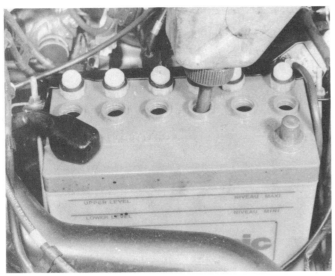

3.6 Topping-up the battery

4.2 Battery negative terminal disconnected

4   Slacken the clamp plate retaining nuts, noting the wiring harness clip location (photo).
5   Remove the clamp plate and lift the battery out of its tray.
6   Refitting is the reverse sequence to removal, but make sure that the polarity is correct before connecting the leads, and do not overtighten the clamp bolts.

5   Battery – charging

1   It is possible that in winter, when the load on the battery cannot be recuperated during normal driving time, external charging may be necessary.
2   Charging should be done at a trickle rate of about 1 to 1.5 amps overnight. Alternatively, if a more sophisticated charger is available then this should be set to charge at 10% of the battery's capacity over a 10 hour period ie for a 47 amp hour battery, charge at 4.7 amps for 10 hours from a fully discharged state.
3   Before connecting the battery charger ensure that the electrolyte level is correct. Top up with distilled water if necessary (except on maintenance-free batteries) to bring the level between the upper and lower markings on the battery case. Disconnect the battery negative terminal and make sure that the charging takes place in a well ventilated area. Do not smoke or allow naked flame anywhere near the battery during charging.

6   Alternator drivebelt – renewal and adjustment

Note: *On cars equipped with air conditioning and/or power-assisted steering, it will be necessary to remove the steering pump drivebelt (Chapter 10) and air conditioning compressor drivebelt (Chapter 11) to facilitate renewal of the alternator drivebelt.*

1   Regularly inspect the condition of the alternator drivebelt and if frayed or cut, renew it. To do this, slacken the alternator mounting and adjuster link bolts and move the alternator as far as it will go towards the engine. Slip the belt off the pulleys. If it is tight, press the belt against the rim of a pulley while the crankshaft pulley bolt is turned. The belt will then ride up the pulley rim and come off.
2   Fit the new belt using the same method.
3   To tension the drivebelt, pull the alternator away from the engine as far as it will come and nip up the adjuster link bolt. At the mid-point of the longest run of the belt, it should deflect 12.7 mm (0.5 in) under moderate finger pressure. If further tension is required, prise the alternator away from the engine using a piece of wood or the handle of a hammer. Keep the prising force applied while the adjuster link bolt is tightened (photos).

4.4 Clamp plate retaining nut (arrowed) and wiring harness clip

6.3A Alternator drivebelt adjustment

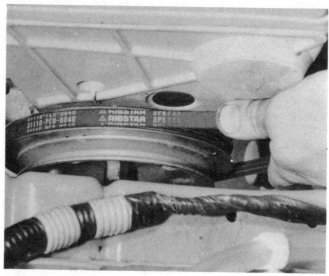

6.3B Checking drivebelt tension

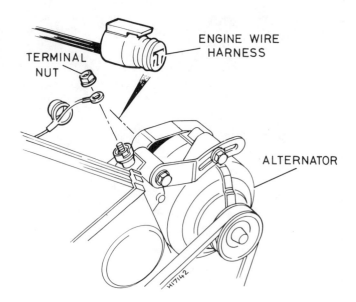

Fig. 12.1 Alternator wiring connections (Sec 7)

4   Once the belt tension is correct, tighten the alternator mounting bolt.
5   Drivebelt tension should be checked and adjusted at the intervals specified in 'Routine Maintenance'. If a new belt has been fitted, check its tension after the first few miles of operation.

7 Alternator – removal and refitting

1   Disconnect the battery negative terminal.
2   Remove the drivebelt as described in Section 6.
3   Disconnect the wiring at the rear of the alternator.
4   Remove the alternator mounting and adjuster link bolts and remove the unit from the engine (photo).
5   Refitting is the reverse sequence to removal. Adjust the drivebelt as described in Section 6.

8 Alternator – overhaul

1   Renewal of the brushes should be the limit of overhaul work to the alternator. If the unit has covered a high mileage, exchange it for a new or factory-reconditioned assembly. Renewal of several internal components will prove more expensive than the price of a complete alternator.
2   To renew the brushes, unscrew the nuts and take off the rear cover.
3   Remove the brush holder with brushes. If the brushes have worn down to or nearly down to their limit (see Specifications) then the brush holder assembly must be renewed (photos).
4   While the brush holder is out, take the opportunity to clean the slip rings with a fuel-soaked rag or very fine glasspaper if they are severely discoloured.
5   Fit the brush holder and the rear cover.

9 Starter motor – testing in the car

1   If the starter motor fails to operate, first check the condition of the battery by switching on the headlamps. If they glow brightly then gradually dim after a few seconds, the battery is in an unchrged condition.
2   If the battery is satisfactory, check the starter motor main terminal and the engine earth cable for security. Check the terminal connections on the starter solenoid – located on top of the starter motor.
3   If the starter still fails to turn, use a voltmeter, or 12 volt test lamp and leads, to ensure that there is battery voltage at the solenoid main

7.4 Removing alternator mounting bolt

terminal (containing the cable from the battery positive terminal).
4   With the ignition switched on and the ignition key in position III, check that voltage is reaching the solenoid terminal with the spade connector, and also the starter main terminal.
5   If there is no voltage reaching the spade connector, there is a wiring or ignition switch fault. If voltage is available, but the starter does not operate, then the starter or solenoid is likely to be at fault.

10 Starter motor – removal and refitting

1   Disconnect the battery negative terminal.
2   For better access disconnect the air intake ducts and move the wiring harness aside.
3   Disconnect the wiring at the rear of the solenoid.
4   Unscrew the mounting bolts and withdraw the starter motor from the flywheel or torque converter housing.
5   Refitting is the reverse sequence to removal.

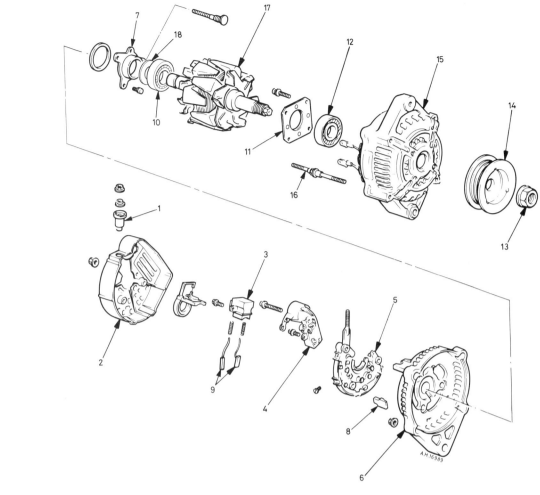

Fig. 12.2 Exploded view of the alternator (Sec 8)

1	Terminal	6	Rear housing	11	Bearing retainer	15 Stator assembly/drive end
2	Rear end cover	7	Bearing mount	12	Front bearing	housing
3	Brush holder	8	Insulator sleeve	13	Pulley lock nut	16 Stator through bolt
4	IC regulator	9	Brushes	14	Pulley	17 Rotor
5	Diode (rectifier) assembly	10	Rear bearing			18 Spacer ring

8.3A Removing alternator brush holder

8.3B Alternator brush holder with brushes

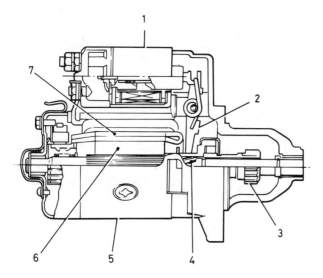

11 Starter motor – overhaul

1   Six different starter motors are used on Civic models according to engine size, transmission type and country of export.

2   The starter motors are extremely reliable, and overhaul should be confined to renewal of the brushes and an inspection of the rest of the parts. If more extensive repair is required, such as renewal of the bearings, drive components, armature or field windings, then it will probably be more economical to renew the complete unit for a new or factory-reconditioned starter.

3   Brush renewal is described in the following paragraphs. If more extensive dismantling is necessary, this can be carried out with reference to the accompanying illustrations.

4   Where fitted, prise off the dust cover from the centre of the starter motor end cover. On some versions the dust cover is retained by two screws.

5   Where fitted, remove the circlip or lock plate and washers from the armature.

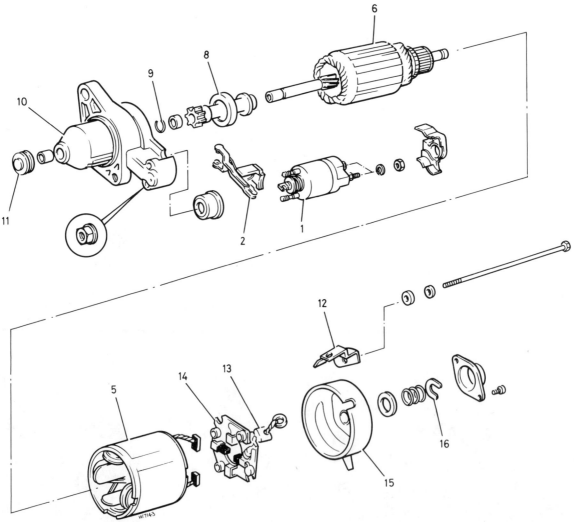

Fig. 12.3 Exploded view of the Nippon Denso 0.8 kW starter motor (Sec 11)

1 Starter solenoid	5 Field winding (armature) housing	8 Clutch assembly	13 Brush
2 Solenoid lever		9 Spring clip	14 Brush holder
3 Pinion gear (drive gear)	6 Armature	10 Gear housing	15 End cover
4 Overrunning clutch	7 Field winding	11 Shaft cover	16 Lock plate
		12 Harness clip	

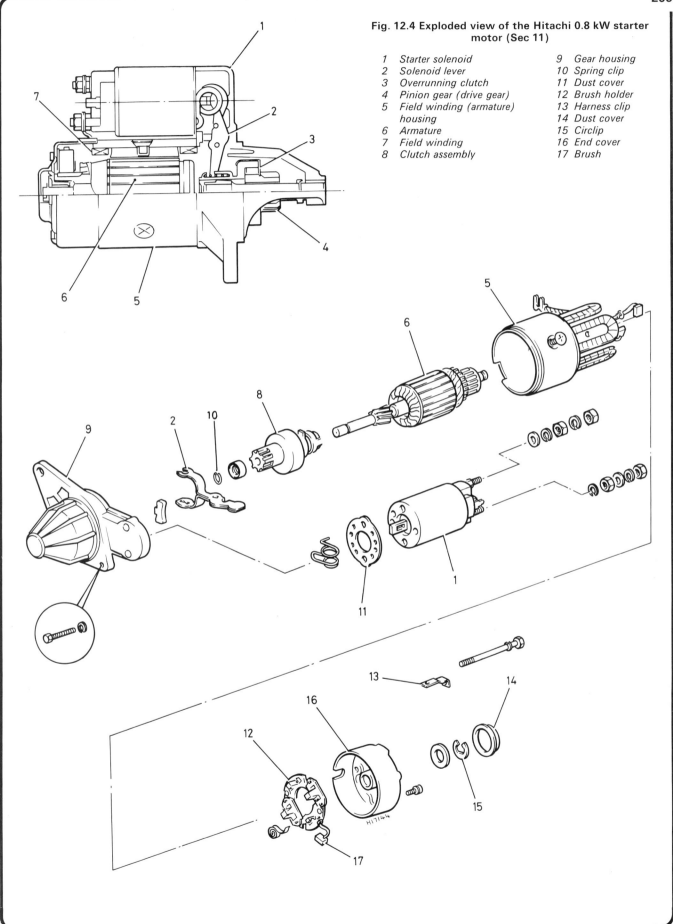

Fig. 12.4 Exploded view of the Hitachi 0.8 kW starter motor (Sec 11)

1 Starter solenoid
2 Solenoid lever
3 Overrunning clutch
4 Pinion gear (drive gear)
5 Field winding (armature) housing
6 Armature
7 Field winding
8 Clutch assembly
9 Gear housing
10 Spring clip
11 Dust cover
12 Brush holder
13 Harness clip
14 Dust cover
15 Circlip
16 End cover
17 Brush

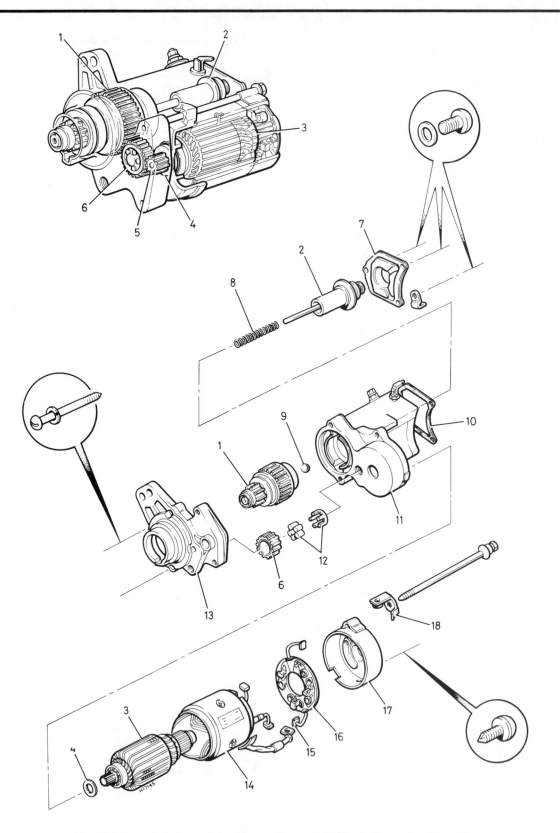

Fig. 12.5 Exploded view of the Nippon Denso 1.0 kW starter motor (Sec 11)

1	Overrunning clutch assembly	5	Pinion gear	10	Gasket
2	Starter solenoid	6	Idler gear	11	Solenoid housing
3	Armature	7	Cover	12	Roller bearing and cage
4	Felt seal	8	Spring	13	Reduction gear housing
		9	Steel ball	14	Field winding/armature housing

15	Brush
16	Brush holder
17	End cover
18	Harness clip

6   Unscrew the retaining bolts and remove the end cover.
7   Lift off the brush holder and remove the bushes.
8   Inspect the brushes for condition and length and check the springs for tension. If the brushes have worn down to below the specified minimum length they must be renewed. Renewal of the brushes entails unsoldering the old brushes and soldering on new ones. When using the soldering iron on the field brushes use a pair of pliers as a heat sink and to prevent solder running up the brush lead.

9   Inspect the commutator – if discoloured, clean it with a petrol-moistened cloth, or if very dirty use very fine glasspaper.
10 Reassembly is a reversal of dismantling. Make sure that the bushes slide freely in their holders.

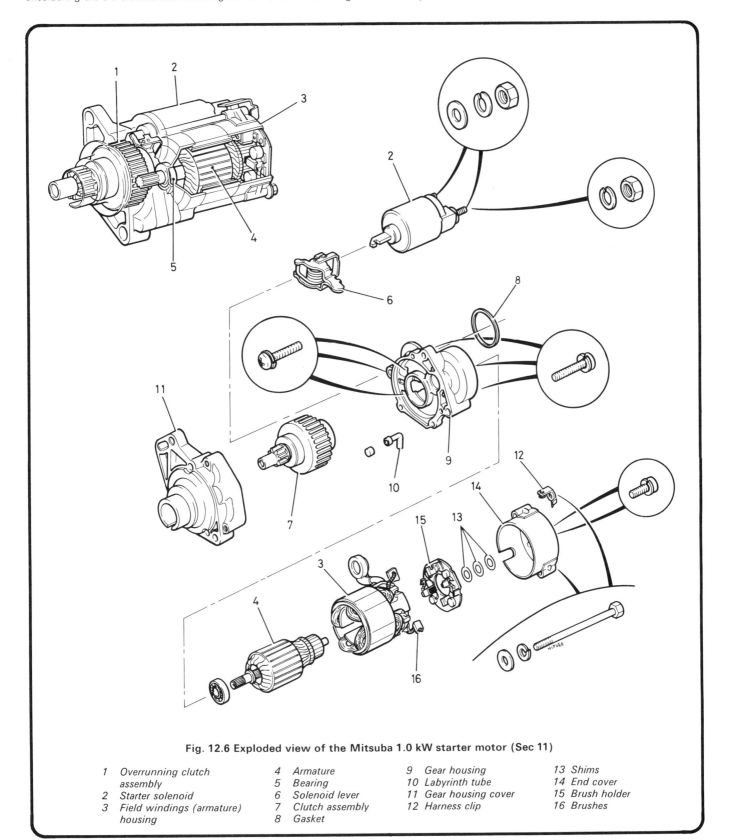

Fig. 12.6 Exploded view of the Mitsuba 1.0 kW starter motor (Sec 11)

1	Overrunning clutch assembly	4 Armature	9 Gear housing	13 Shims
2	Starter solenoid	5 Bearing	10 Labyrinth tube	14 End cover
3	Field windings (armature) housing	6 Solenoid lever	11 Gear housing cover	15 Brush holder
		7 Clutch assembly	12 Harness clip	16 Brushes
		8 Gasket		

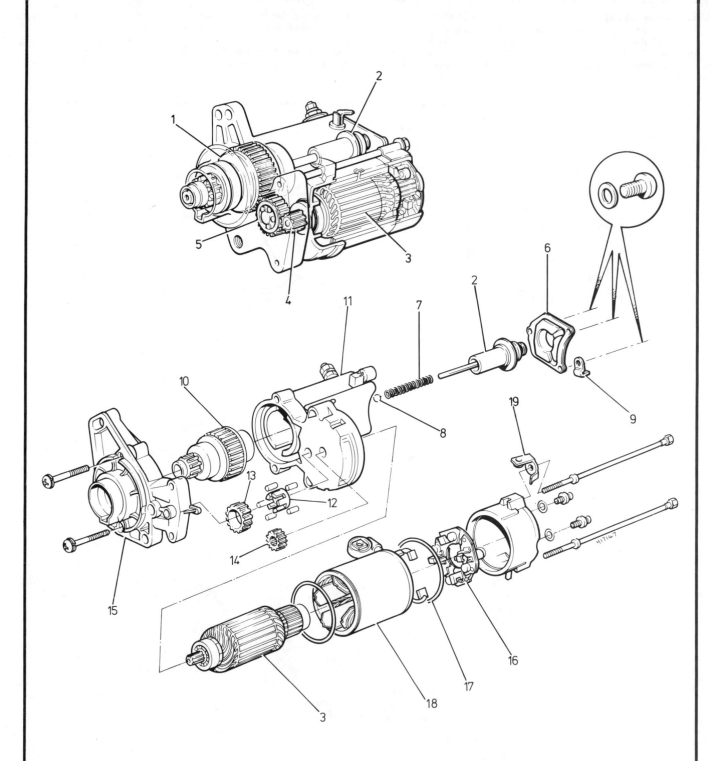

Fig. 12.7 Exploded view of the Nippon Denso 1.4 kW starter motor (Sec 11)

1 Overrunning clutch assembly	8 Steel ball	15 Reduction gear housing
2 Starter solenoid	9 Harness clip	16 Brush holder
3 Armature	10 Clutch assembly	17 Brush
4 Pinion gear	11 Solenoid housing	18 Field winding/armature housing
5 Idler gear	12 Roller bearings and cage	19 Harness clip
6 Cover	13 Idler gear	
7 Spring	14 Pinion gear	

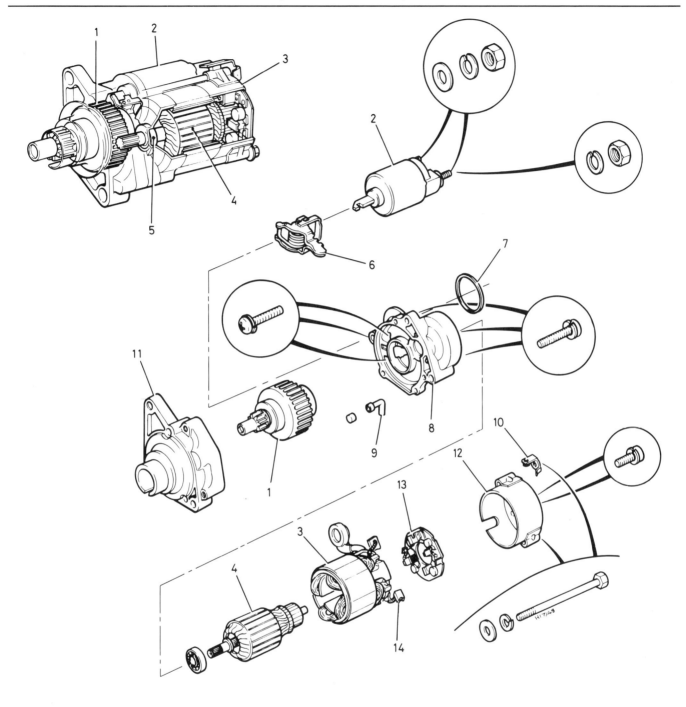

Fig. 12.8 Exploded view of the Mitsuba 1.4 kW starter motor (Sec 11)

1	Overrunning clutch assembly	4 Armature	8 Gear housing	12 End cover
2	Starter solenoid	5 Bearing	9 Labyrinth tube	13 Brush holder
3	Field windings (armature) housing	6 Solenoid lever	10 Harness clip	14 Brush
		7 Gasket	11 Gear housing cover	

12 Fuses and relays

1   Three main fusible links are located in a box in the engine compartment. Should one of these blow at any time, do not renew it until the charging circuit has been checked and tested by your dealer or an auto electrical engineer (photo).

2   The fuses which protect all the other electrical circuits in the car are located in the fusebox under the facia panel (photo).

3   The fuse ratings and circuits protected are shown on the fusebox cover (photo).

4   If a fuse blows, renew it with one of identical rating. Never substitute anything for the correct type of fuse. If the new fuse blows immediately, check and rectify the problem, usually shorting of a wire due to chafed insulation.

5   Relays for intermittent windscreen wiper and hazard warning systems are plugged into the fusebox. Other relays are located behind the fusebox, under the facia, or in the engine compartment.

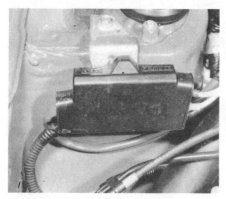

12.1 Wiring harness fusible link box location

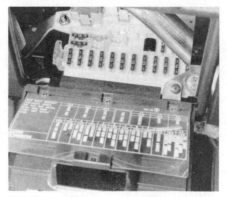

12.2 Fusebox location under facia

12.3 Fuse ratings and circuits protected shown on cover

These include, where applicable:

> *Main fuel-injection system relay*
> *Heated rear window relay*
> *Sunroof relay*
> *Side marker light relay*
> *Brake check relay*
> *Alternator control unit*
> *Seat belt timer/buzzer*
> *Radiator fan control unit*
> *Air conditioning system relays*

13 Switches – removal and refitting

Steering column combination switch

1   Disconnect the battery negative terminal then remove the steering wheel as described in Chapter 10.
2   Pull the direction indicator cancelling sleeve from the steering shaft (photo).
3   Undo the steering column shroud retaining screws, extract the retaining ring and remove the shrouds (photos).
4   Undo the two screws and withdraw the switch (photo).
5   Disconnect the wiring plugs and remove the switch from the steering column (photo).

6   When refitting, make sure that the cancelling sleeve is pushed fully home.
7   When refitting the steering wheel, check that the lugs engage correctly with the cut-outs in the cancelling cam before tightening the retaining nut.

Heated rear window switch

8   Disconnect the battery negative lead.
9   Carefully prise the switch from the facia panel. Disconnect the multi-plug from the switch.
10   Refitting is a reversal of removal.

Rear fog warning lamp switch

11   The operations are as described for the heated rear window switch.

Instrument panel lamp dimmer switch (rheostat)

12   Disconnect the battery and remove the facia panel access undercover.
13   Reach up behind the switch and disconnect the multi-plug.
14   Prise off the switch knob and remove the plain washer.
15   Unscrew the bezel nut and remove the switch from the facia panel.
16   Refitting is a reversal of removal.

Ignition switch

17   Disconnect the battery and remove the steering column shrouds.
18   Insert the ignition key into the lock.
19   Disconnect the wiring harness plug.

13.2 Direction indicator cancelling sleeve (arrowed)

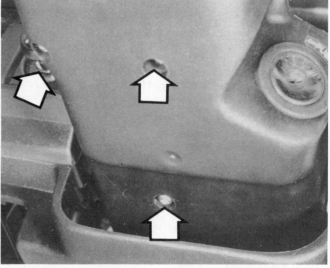

13.3A Steering column shroud retaining screws (arrowed) ...

13.3B ... and shroud retaining ring removal

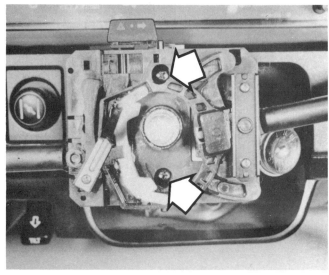

13.4 Combination switch retaining screws (arrowed)

13.5 Combination switch wiring plugs (arrowed)

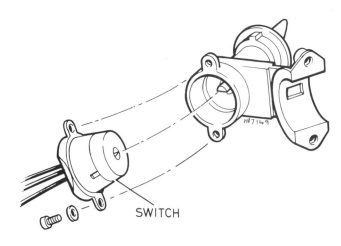

Fig. 12.9 Ignition switch renewal (Sec 13)

20 Extract the two switch fixing screws and remove the switch from the lock.

21 Refitting is a reversal of removal, but make sure that as the switch is fitted to the lock, the tang on the lock barrel enters the recess in the switch.

Heater blower switch
22 This is described in Chapter 11.

Courtesy lamp switch
23 These are of sliding type and control the interior lamp (photo).
24 Extract the screw which holds the switch to the body pillar, withdraw the switch and disconnect the leads.
25 Tape the leads to the body to prevent them from slipping into the pillar interior.
26 When refitting the switch, smear the contacts with petroleum jelly to prevent corrosion.
27 Access is obtained by removing the glovebox. Disconnect the wiring plugs and pull the switch from its mounting bracket while holding the retaining tags squeezed inwards.

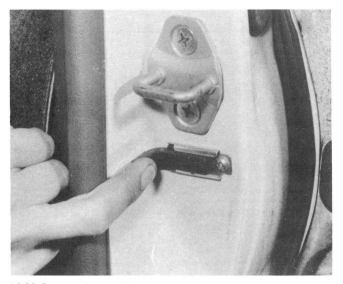

13.23 Courtesy lamp switch

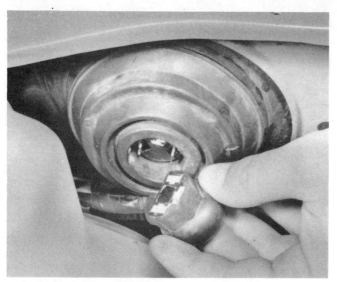

14.2 Headlamp bulb wiring plug

14.3A Release the spring retaining clips ...

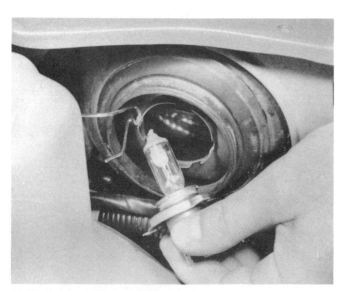

14.3B ... and remove the headlamp bulb

14 Exterior bulbs – renewal

Headlamp (bulb type)
1   Open the bonnet.
2   Disconnect the wiring plug at the rear of the bulb (photo).
3   Prise back the spring clips and remove the bulb (photos).
4   Fit the new bulb, avoiding touching the glass with the fingers. If it is inadvertently touched, clean it with methylated spirit.
5   Fit the spring clips and the wiring plugs.

Headlamp (sealed beam type)
6   Open the bonnet.
7   Disconnect the wiring plug at the rear of the bulb.
8   Undo the screws in the headlamp trim and headlamp retaining ring and withdraw the sealed beam unit.
9   Refitting is the reverse sequence to removal.

Front sidelight (UK models), front parking/side marker light (North American models)
10 Extract the lens retaining screws and pull the lens gently from the car (photo).

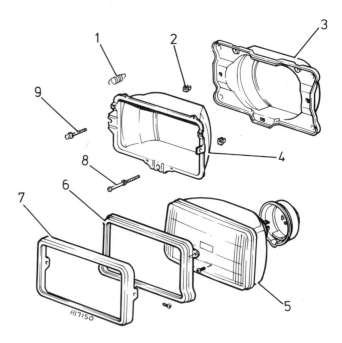

Fig. 12.10 Sealed beam headlamp and mounting components (Sec 14)

1   Spring
2   Nylon nut
3   Headlight mounting panel
4   Mount ring
5   Sealed beam

6   Retaining ring
7   Headlight trim
8   Horizontal adjusting screw
9   Vertical adjusting screw

11 Twist the bulbholder to remove it, then renew the bulb which is a push fit in the holder (photo).
12 Refit the bulbholder and lens.

Front direction indicator lamp
13 Undo the two screws and remove the lens (photo).
14 Push and turn the bayonet fitting bulb to renew.
15 Refit the lens.

14.10 Sidelight lens retaining screws

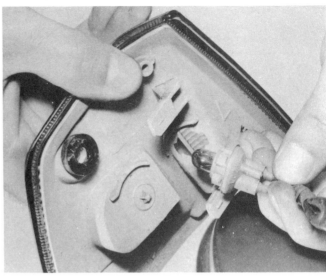

14.11 Sidelight bulb and holder

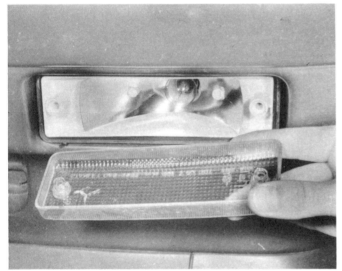

14.13 Removing front direction indicator lens

Direction indicator side repeater lamp

16 Carefully prise out the lens and bulbholder using a screwdriver (photo).
17 Twist the bulbholder to remove it, then remove the bulb which is a push fit in the holder (photo).
18 Refit the bulbholder to the lens and push the unit carefully into its hole.

Rear lamp cluster bulbs

19 Release the trim panels, which are retained by catches or thumb screws according to model, and are accessible from inside the luggage compartment (photo).
20 Twist the bulbholder to remove it, then renew the bayonet type bulbs (photo).
21 Refit the bulbholder and trim panels.

Rear number plate lamp

22 Undo the screws and withdraw the lens (photo).
23 Renew the bulb(s) which are a bayonet fitting in the holders (photo).
24 Refit the lens.

14.16 Using a screwdriver to release side repeater lamp

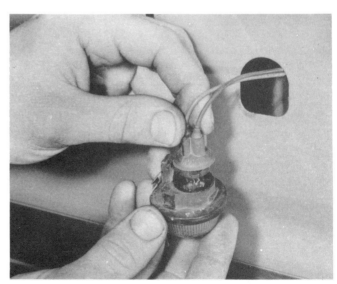

14.17 Side repeater lamp bulb and holder

14.19 Removing rear lamp cluster trim panel

14.20 Rear lamp cluster bulb renewal

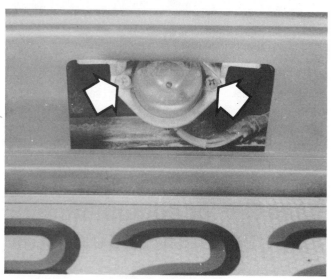

14.22 Number plate lamp lens retaining screws (arrowed)

14.23 Number plate lamp bulb renewal

15 Interior bulbs – renewal

Interior lamps
1   Prise the lens carefully from the lamp (photo).
2   Renew the festoon type bulb by pulling it from its contacts.
3   Refit the lens.

Switch illuminating lamps
4   Reach up behind the relevant switch and push it out of its location.
Alternatively, carefully prise the switch from the facia.
5   Pull off the wiring plug and turn the bulbholder anti-clockwise to
remove it.
6   Renew the bulb then refit the bulbholder and switch.

Cigarette lighter/ashtray lamp
7   Remove the facia centre lower panel.
8   Remove the ring nut, then withdraw the bulholder.
9   Renew the bulb then refit the bulbholder and facia panel.

15.1 Interior lamp lens and bulb

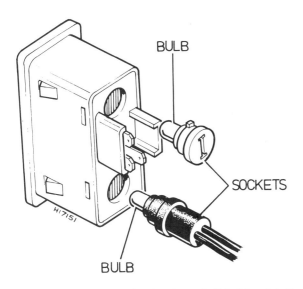

Fig. 12.11 Switch illuminating lamp bulbholder details (Sec 15)

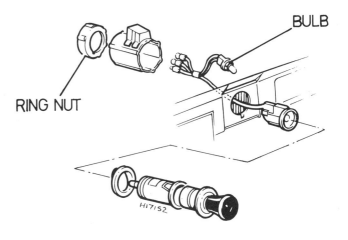

Fig. 12.12 Cigarette lighter and lamp details (Sec 15)

Warning and instrument panel lamps
10 The instrument panel must be released and pulled forward for access to these lamps (see Section 18). Some upper bulbs are accessible after removal of the instrument panel hood (photos).

Glove compartment lamp
11 Open the glove compartment and prise out the lens.
12 Renew the bulb and refit the lens.

16 Headlamp – removal and refitting

1 Refer to Chapter 11 and remove the radiator grille and the front bumper.
2 Remove the front sidelight lens as described in Section 14.
3 Raise the bonnet if not already done.
4 Disconnect the bulb wiring connector.
5 On bulb type headlamps extract the two lower and two upper headlamp retaining screws and remove the unit.

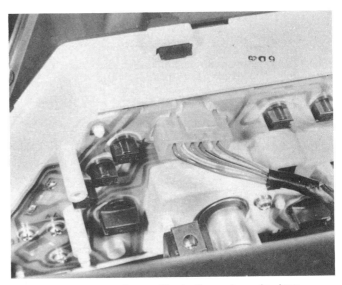

15.10A Instrument panel upper illumination and warning lamp bulbholders

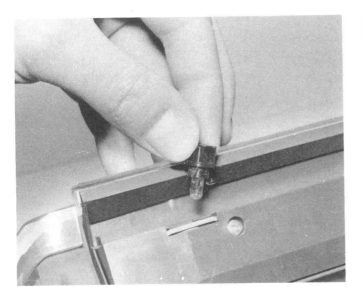

15.10B Renewing instrument panel illumination bulb

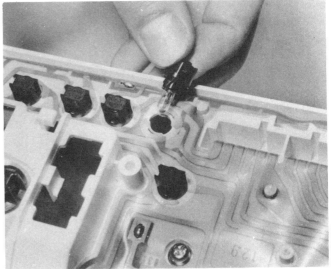

15.10C Renewing instrument panel warning lamp bulb

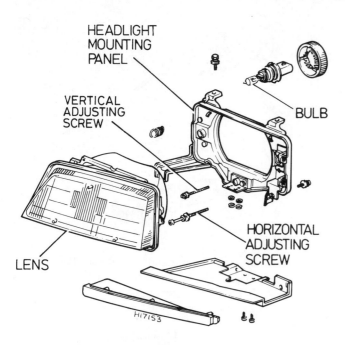

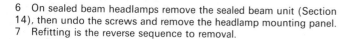

Fig. 12.13 Headlamp lens and mounting panel details – bulb type headlamps (Sec 16)

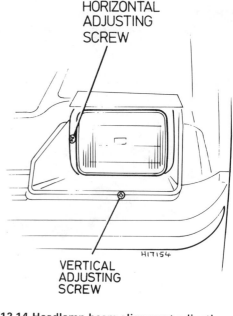

Fig. 12.14 Headlamp beam alignment adjusting screw (Sec 17)

6   On sealed beam headlamps remove the sealed beam unit (Section 14), then undo the screws and remove the headlamp mounting panel.
7   Refitting is the reverse sequence to removal.

17 Headlamp beam – alignment

1   This should be carried out by a dealer or service station using optical beam setting equipment, except in emergency.
2   The vertical and horizontal adjusting screws are accessible through the front of the headlamp (Fig 12.14).

18 Instrument panel – removal and refitting

1   Prise out the blanking plates which cover the hood securing srews. These are brittle so exercise care (photos).
2   Extract the screws now exposed and remove the hood (photos).
3   Disconnect the battery.
4   Reach behind the instrument panel, press the arm of the speedometer cable retaining clip and disconnect the cable from the speedometer head (photo).
5   Extract the instrument panel fixing screws (photo).
6   Raise the instrument panel until the wiring multi-plugs can be disconnected.
7   Remove the panel.
8   The instrument panel may be dismantled in the following way.
9   Prise the trip reset knob from its spindle.
10 Release the plastic clips and separate the panel and lens.

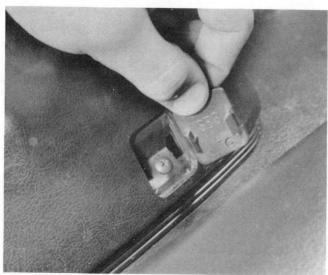

18.1A Instrument panel hood upper blanking plate ...

18.1B ... and front blanking plate

18.2A Extracting instrument panel hood front retaining screw ...

18.2B ... and upper screw

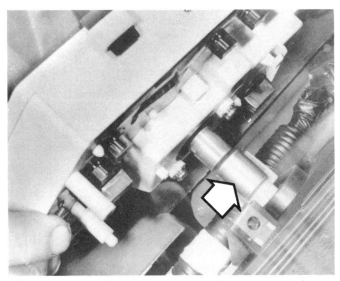

18.4 Speedometer cable attachment at rear of instrument panel (arrowed)

18.5 Instrument panel fixing screw locations (arrowed)

11 Unscrew the nuts or screws and remove the instruments as necessary (photo). Handle the printed circuit with care using clean hands.

12 Refitting is a reversal of removal.

19 Speedometer cable – removal

1 Disconnect the battery.

2 Remove the instrument panel hood as described in the preceding Section.

3 Reach behind the instrument panel and disconnect the cable from the speedometer head.

4 Working under the facia panel, remove the access undercover panel and release the speedometer cable grommet and boot from the bulkhead.

5 Feed the speedometer cable through the bulkhead into the engine compartment.

6 Working at the transmission, pull the boot up the cable and extract the spring clip which retains the cable. On no account remove the bolt or lockplate or the pinion might drop into the transmission.

7 Fit the new cable by reversing the removal operations.

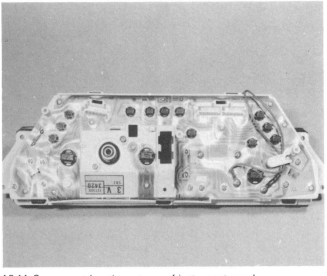

18.11 Component locations at rear of instrument panel

20 Clock – removal and refitting

1 Disconnect the battery.
2 Using a small screwdriver, carefully prise the clock from the facia panel until the wiring harness can be disconnected.
3 Refit the clock by reversing the removal operations.
4 The clock normally only displays when the ignition is on, but if the ignition is off, it will display if the button cover panel is pressed in.
5 To set the clock, depress the centre 'MIN' button until the minutes are correct.
6 Depress the left-hand 'HOUR' button until the hour is correct.
7 If it is wished to synchronise the clock with a radio time signal or another clock, set the car clock to within a few minutes before the hour. As the time signal is heard, depress the reset button on the car clock.

21 Wiper blades and arms – removal and refitting

1 The wiper blades should be renewed as soon as they cease to clean the glass without leaving streaks.
2 Lift the wiper arm from the screen until it locks.
3 Turn the blade through 90°, depress the retaining tab with the thumb nail and slide the blade down the arm until it can be withdrawn over the hook of the arm (photo).
4 On certain models the tailgate wiper blade is a ball-and-socket push-fit in the arm, and is withdrawn by carefully prising it free.
5 Refit the new blade, pushing it fully into place until it locks.
6 To remove a wiper arm, have the arm in the parked position. Run some masking tape along the edge of the blades on the glass as a guide to refitting the arms.
7 Unscrew the domed nut and remove the wiper arm from the splined spindle (photo).
8 Refit by reversing the removal procedure.

22 Windscreen wiper motor and linkage – removal and refitting

1 Remove the wiper arms as described in the preceding Section.
2 Open the bonnet and pull off the rubber weatherstrip from the front edge. The weatherstrip incorporates plastic pins which serve to hold the front edge of the scuttle plastic cover (air scoop) (photo).
3 Prise out the circular plastic blanking plates just below the windscreen and extract the exposed screws (photo).
4 Remove the scuttle plastic cover (air scoop) (photo).

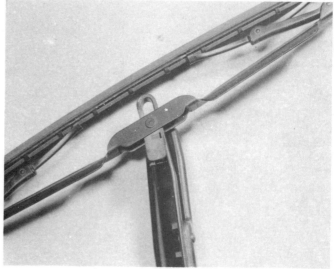

21.3 Wiper blade-to-arm connection

21.7 Removing wiper arm retaining nut

22.2 Rubber weatherstrip locating pin (arrowed)

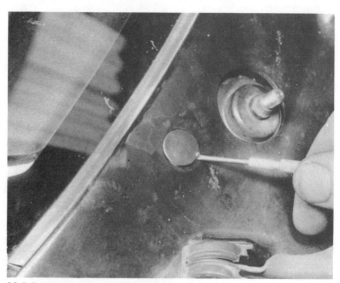

22.3 Prising out scuttle blanking plates

22.4 Removing the scuttle cover

22.6A Windscreen wiper link rod balljoint ...

22.6B ... and motor cover

23.2 Tailgate cover trim retaining screws

5   Disconnect the wiper motor multi-plug.
6   Prise the crank arm-to-link rod balljoint apart. Remove the wiper motor cover (photos).
7   Unbolt and remove the wiper motor.
8   Remove the wheelbox fixing bolts and withdraw the complete wiper linkage.
9   Refitting is a reversal of removal.

23 Tailgate wiper motor and linkage – removal and refitting

1   Remove the wiper arm as described in Section 21.
2   Open the tailgate and remove the cover trim to gain access to the motor (photo).
3   Disconnect the wiring harness from the motor and retaining clips.
4   Refer to Fig. 12.15 or 12.16 and remove the spindle nut, washers and spacers according to model.

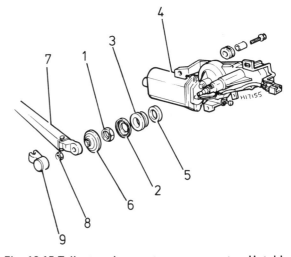

Fig. 12.15 Tailgate wiper motor components – Hatchback, Shuttle and Wagon models (Sec 23)

1	Special nut	6	Pivot cover
2	Washer	7	Wiper arm
3	Rubber cushion	8	Nut
4	Wiper motor	9	Cover
5	Spacer		

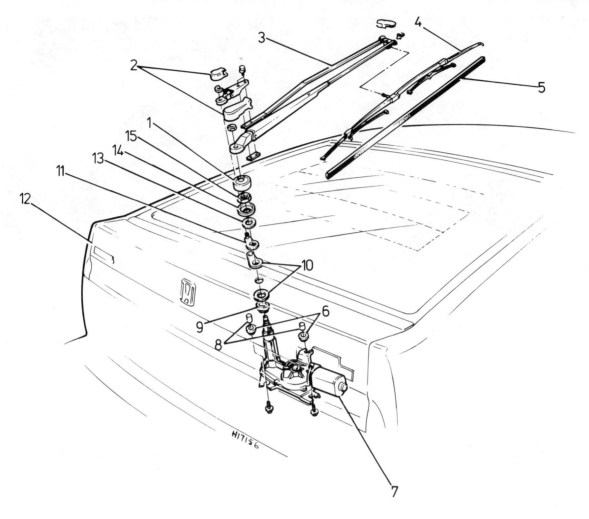

Fig. 12.16 Tailgate wiper motor components – CRX models (Sec 23)

1 Pivot cap	5 Blade rubber	9 Spacer	13 Rubber
2 Covers	6 Mounting rubbers	10 Rubber	14 Washer
3 Wiper arm	7 Wiper motor	11 Link plate	15 Special nut
4 Wiper blade	8 Collar	12 Hatch	

5   From inside the tailgate undo the bolts and remove the motor assembly (photo).

6   Refitting is the reverse sequence to removal.

24 Washer system – general

1   Depending on model, a windscreen washer system may be fitted only, or a combined windscreen and tailgate window washer system may be used.

2   The reservoir capacity differs between the two systems and two independent electric pumps are used where a windscreen and tailgate washer are fitted.

3   The pumps are detachable from the reservoir after disconnecting the wiring plugs and tubes. When removing a tube from a pump or jet nozzle, warm the tube with a rag soaked in boiling water, otherwise the nozzle may fracture.

4   The jets may be adjusted by inserting a pin into the nozzles.

5   Do not use household detergent or cooling system antifreeze in the washer reservoir or the pumps and car paintwork will be damaged.

6   In very cold weather, a little methylated spirit may be added to the reservoir in addition to the normal mixture of water and screen cleaning fluid.

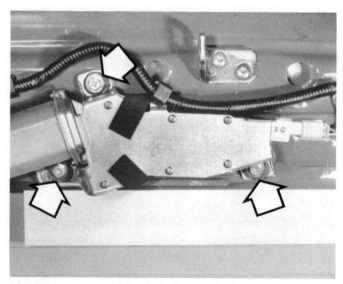

23.5 Tailgate wiper retaining bolts (arrowed)

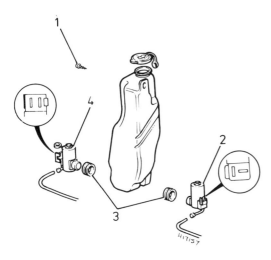

Fig. 12.17 Washer reservoir and pump components (Sec 24)

1 Mounting screw	*3 Grommets*
2 Rear washer motor	*4 Front washer motor*

26.2 Removing aerial mounting base screws

25 Radio/cassette player – removal and refitting

1   All models are supplied with a windscreen pillar aerial and either a radio or radio/cassette player depending upon the particular vehicle specifications.
2   The leads and connecting plugs at the back of the radio are accessible without having to remove the receiver if the facia panel undercover is removed and the hand inserted round behind the radio.
3   To remove the radio/cassette player, carry out the following operations.
4   Pull off the control knobs and bezels from the radio.
5   Unscrew the retaining nuts and take off the escutcheon plate.
6   Push the unit slighly into the facia and remove the mounting plate.
7   Pull the radio towards you until the aerial, feed, speaker and earth plugs can be disconnected.
8   Refitting is a reversal of removal.

26 Aerial – removal and refitting

1   Remove the facia undercover from the side on which the aerial is located.
2   Extract the screws from the aerial mounting base at the top of the windscreen pillar (photo).
3   Reach behind the radio and disconnect the aerial lead.
4   Withdraw the aerial and lead upwards out of the pillar. A length of cord should be securely taped to the end of the aerial lead so that it can be drawn through the pillar and used to guide the new aerial lead through the pillar cavity (photo).
5   If a new aerial is fitted, always adjust the aerial trim. This is done by tuning in to a station with low signal strength on the medium wave band. Using a small screwdriver turn the trim screw provided in the radio in or out until the loudest volume is obtained.

26.4 Removing the aerial

27 Horns – general

1   The horns are located below the headlamps within the bumper.
2   Although the horns normally require no attention, if they must be removed, then the headlamps and front bumper must be removed (Section 16). See also Chapter 11.

Fault diagnosis overleaf

28 Fault diagnosis – electrical system

Symptom	Reason(s)
Starter fails to turn engine	Battery discharged or defective Battery terminal and/or earth leads loose Starter motor connections loose Starter solenoid faulty Starter brushes worn or sticking Starter commutator dirty or worn Starter field coils earthed Starter inhibitor switch faulty (automatic transmission only)
Starter turns engine very slowly	Battery discharged Starter motor connections loose Starter brushes worn or sticking
Starter spins but does not turn engine	Pinion or flywheel ring gear teeth broken or badly worn Starter pinion sticking
Starter noisy	Pinion or flywheel ring gear teeth badly worn Mounting bolts loose
Battery will not hold charge for more than a few days	Battery defective internally Battery terminals loose Alternator drivebelt slipping Alternator or regulator faulty Short circuit
Ignition light stays on	Alternator faulty Alternator drivebelt broken
Ignition light fails to come on	Warning bulb blown Indicator light open circuit Alternator faulty
Instrument readings increase with engine speed	Faulty instrument voltage stabilizer
Fuel or temperature gauge gives no reading	Wiring open circuit Sender faulty Faulty instrument voltage stabilizer
Fuel or temperature gauge gives continuous maximum reading	Wiring short circuit Sender faulty Faulty instrument voltage stabilizer Faulty gauge
Lights inoperative	Bulb blown Fuse blown Fusible link blown Battery discharged Switch faulty Relay faulty Wiring open circuit Bad connection due to corrosion
Failure of component motor	Commutator dirty or burnt Armature faulty Brushes sticking or worn Armature bearings dry or misaligned Field coils faulty Fuse blown Relay faulty Fusible link blown Poor or broken wiring connections
Failure of an individual component	Fuse blown Relay faulty Fusible link blown Poor or broken wiring connections Switch faulty Component faulty

Explanatory notes for wiring diagrams

Where a circled number appears on an auxiliary diagram a corresponding number will be found on the main wiring diagram identifying the point at which the relevant circuits connect.

Where a number appears in a triangle, this indicates a connecting point within a main diagram (ie, a corresponding number should be found elsewhere within the same diagram).

Wiring diagram colour codes

Bl	Black
Y	Yellow
Bu	Blue
G	Green
R	Red
W	White
Br	Brown
O	Orange
Lb	Light blue
Lg	Light green
P	Pink
Gr	Grey
Sw	Switch
Pl	Pilot light

Wiring diagrams commence overleaf

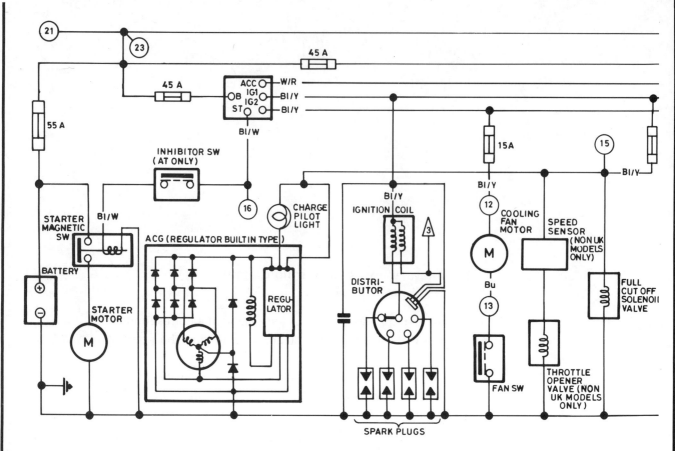

Fig. 12.18 Main wiring diagram – UK Hatchback models

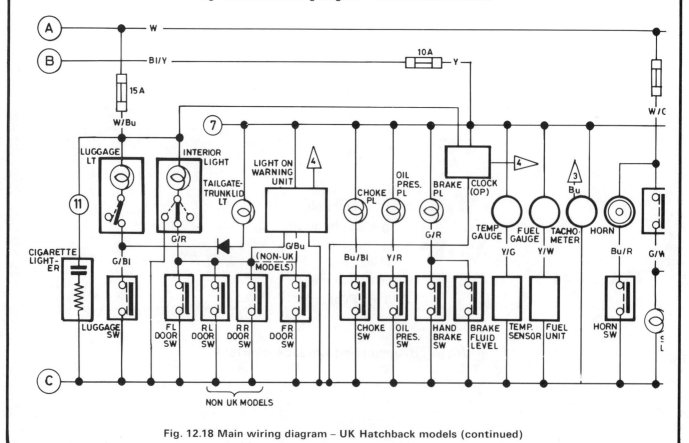

Fig. 12.18 Main wiring diagram – UK Hatchback models (continued)

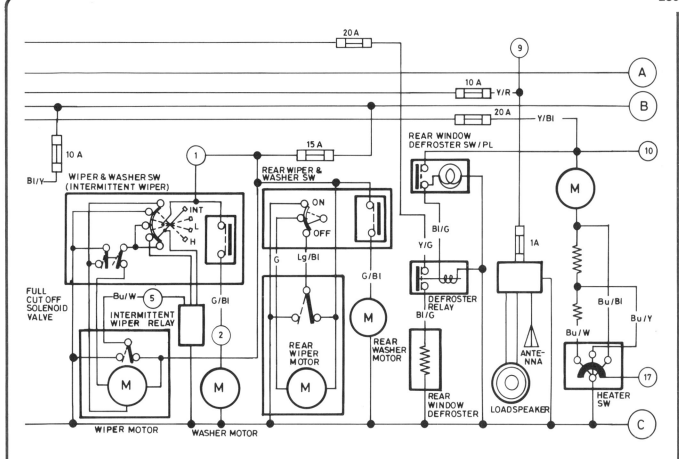

Fig. 12.18 Main wiring diagram – UK Hatchback models (continued)

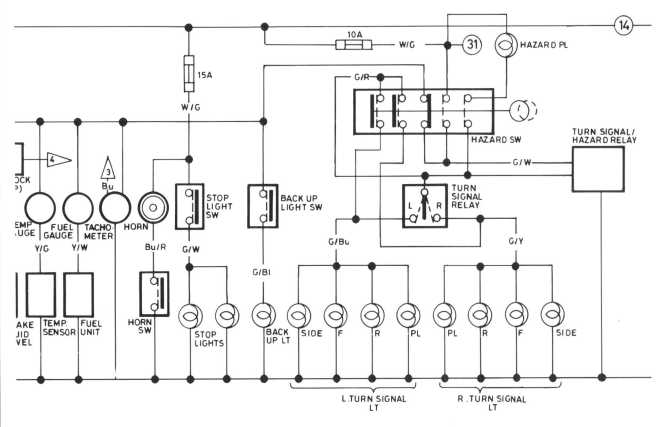

Fig. 12.18 Main wiring diagram – UK Hatchback models (continued)

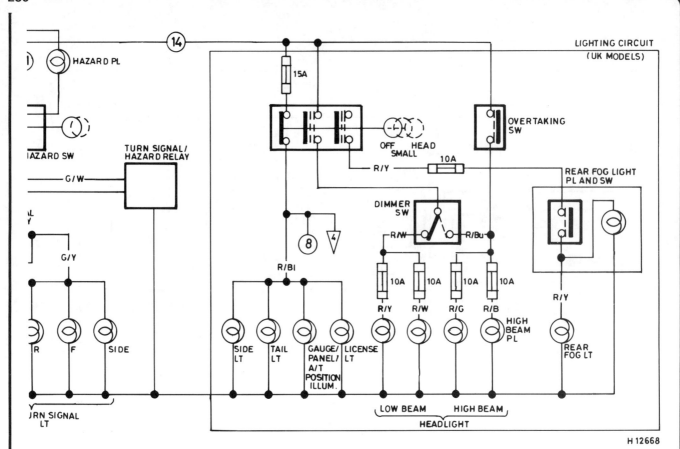

Fig. 12.18 Main wiring diagram – UK Hatchback models (continued)

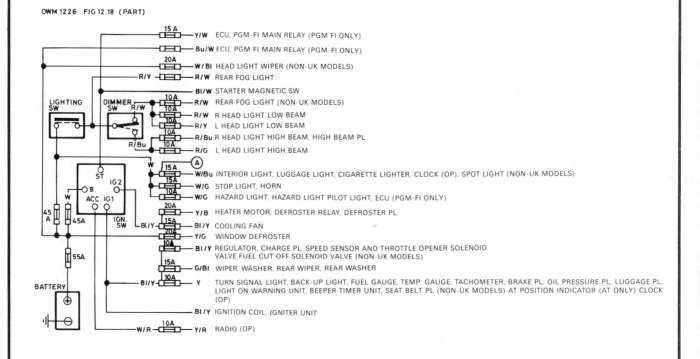

Fig. 12.18 Main wiring diagram – UK Hatchback models (continued)

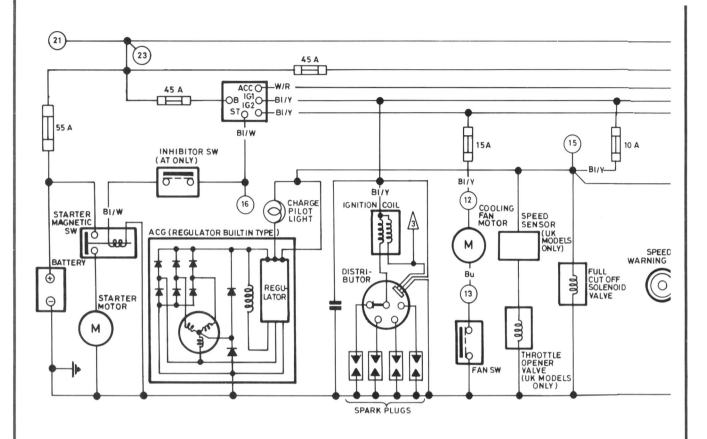

Fig. 12.19 Main wiring diagram – UK Shuttle models

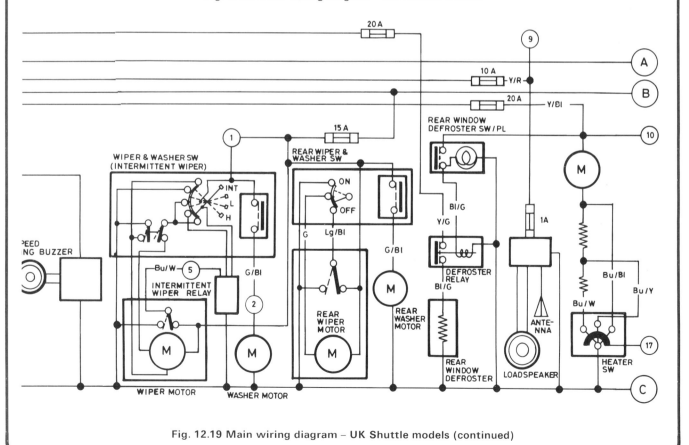

Fig. 12.19 Main wiring diagram – UK Shuttle models (continued)

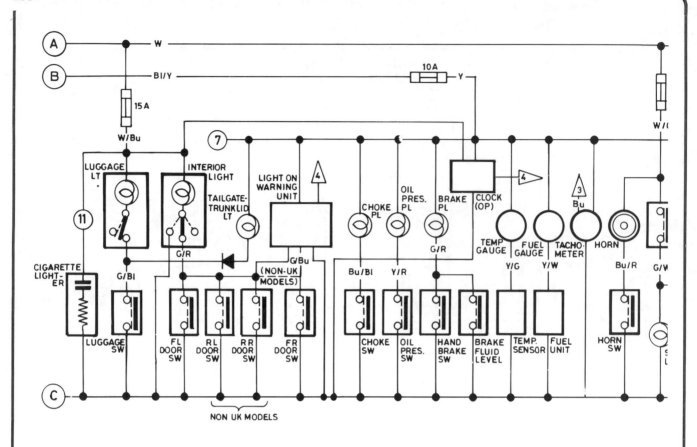

Fig. 12.19 Main wiring diagram – UK Shuttle models (continued)

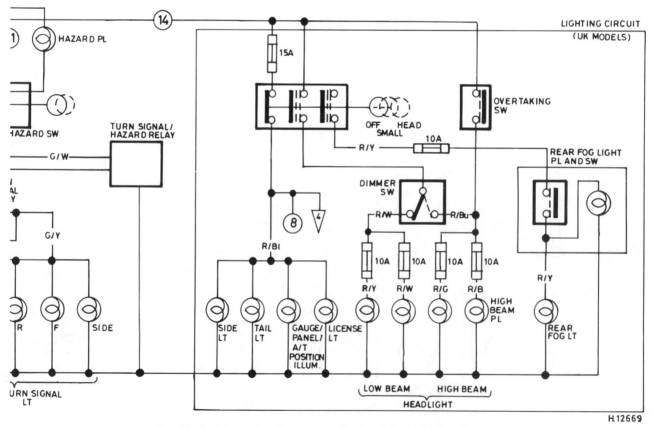

Fig. 12.19 Main wiring diagram – UK Shuttle models (continued)

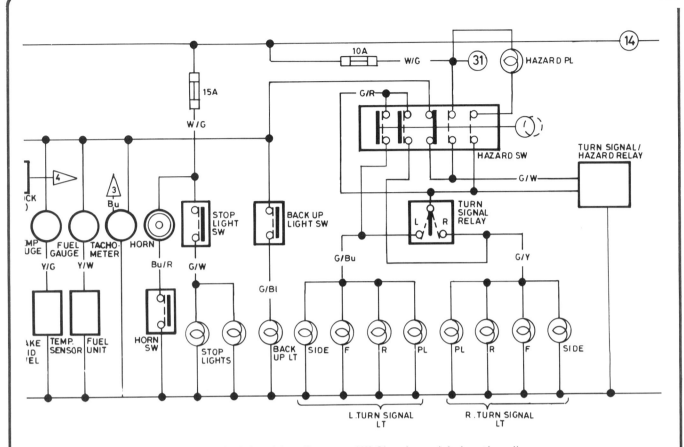

Fig. 12.19 Main wiring diagram – UK Shuttle models (continued)

Fig. 12.19 Main wiring diagram – UK Shuttle models (continued)

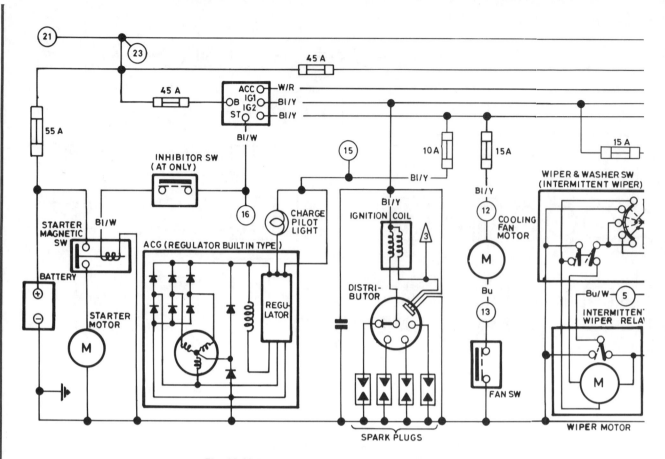

Fig. 12.20 Main wiring diagram – UK CRX models

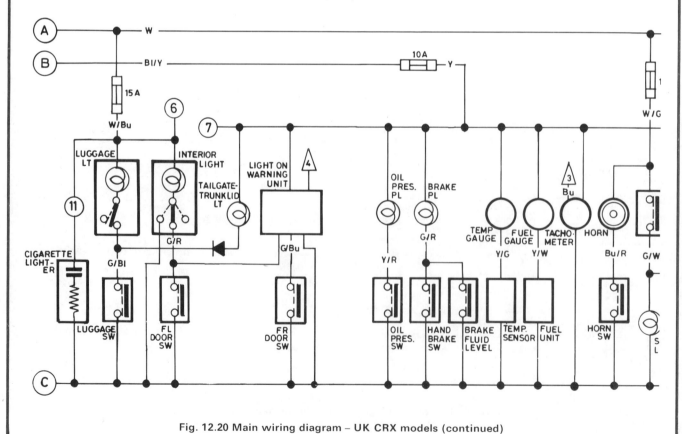

Fig. 12.20 Main wiring diagram – UK CRX models (continued)

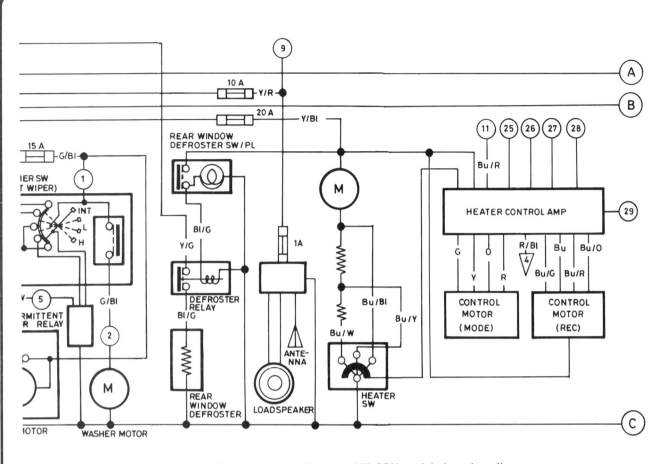

Fig. 12.20 Main wiring diagram – UK CRX models (continued)

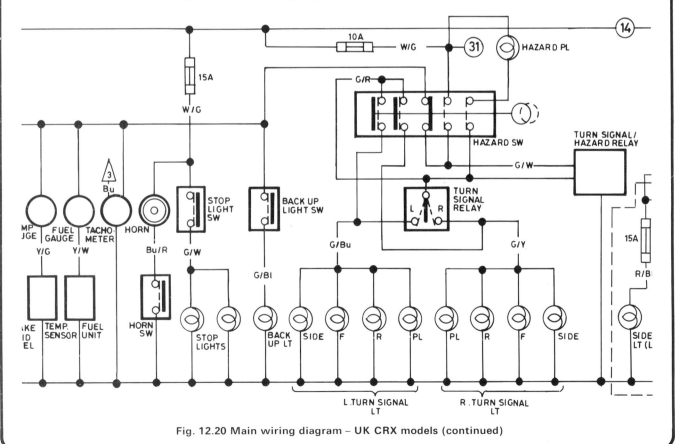

Fig. 12.20 Main wiring diagram – UK CRX models (continued)

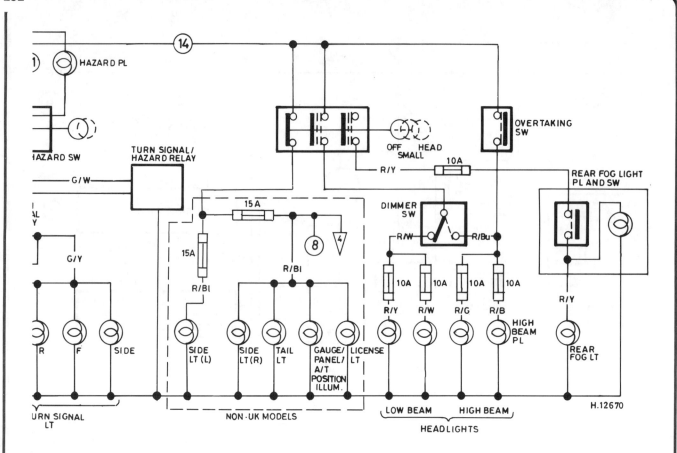

Fig. 12.20 Main wiring diagram – UK CRX models (continued)

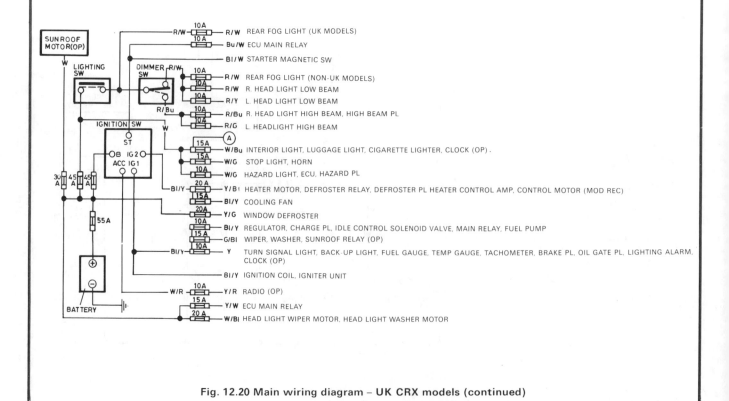

Fig. 12.20 Main wiring diagram – UK CRX models (continued)

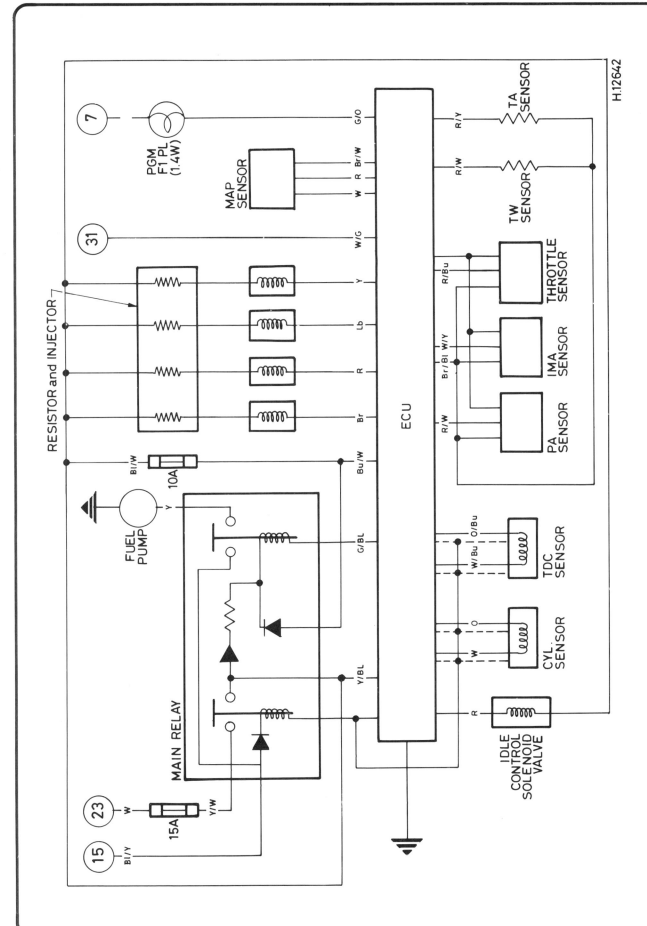

Fig. 12.21 Wiring diagram – fuel-injection circuit (UK models)

H.12642

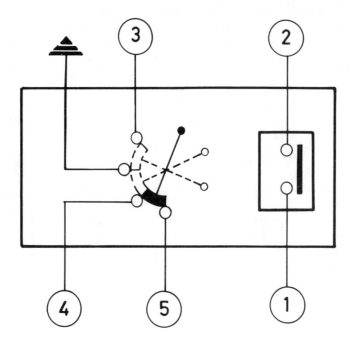

Fig. 12.22 Wiring diagram – wiper/washer circuit (UK models)

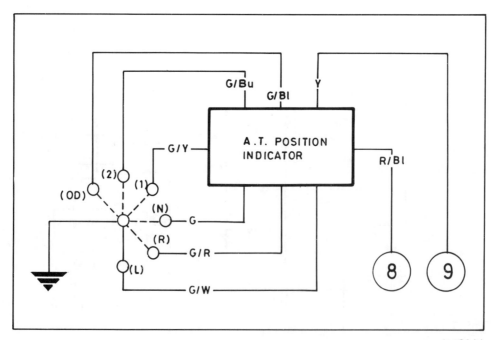

H.12644

Fig. 12.23 Wiring diagram – automatic transmission selector position indicator (UK models)

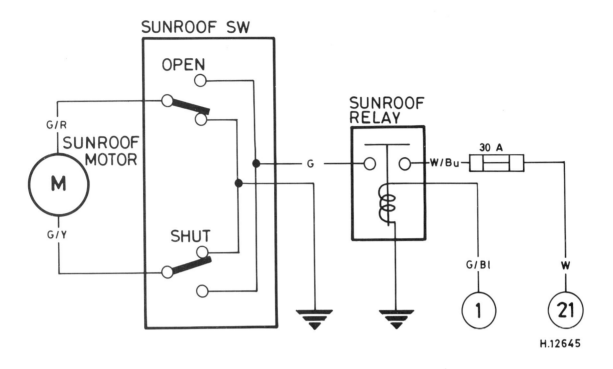

Fig. 12.24 Wiring diagram – electric sunroof (UK models)

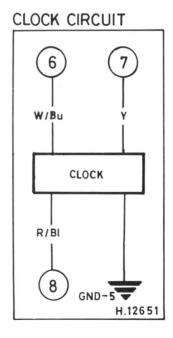

Fig. 12.25 Wiring diagram – clock (UK models)

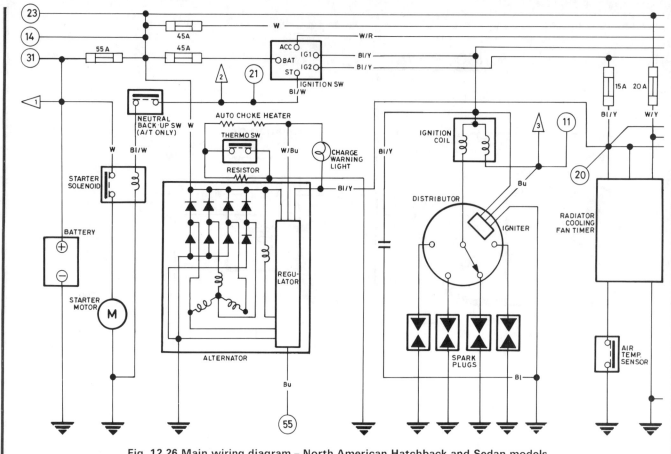

Fig. 12.26 Main wiring diagram – North American Hatchback and Sedan models

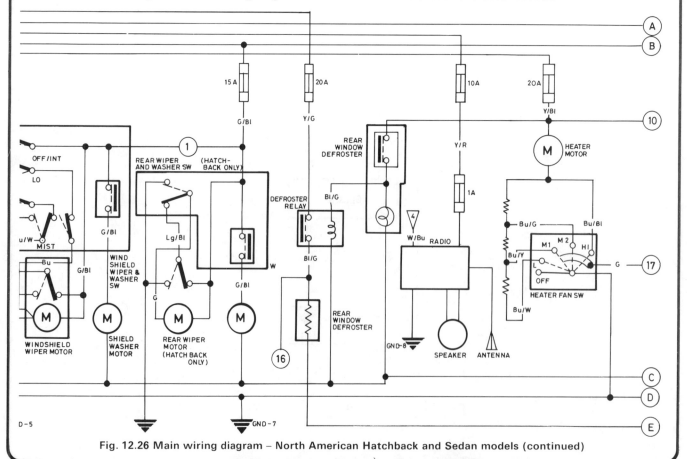

Fig. 12.26 Main wiring diagram – North American Hatchback and Sedan models (continued)

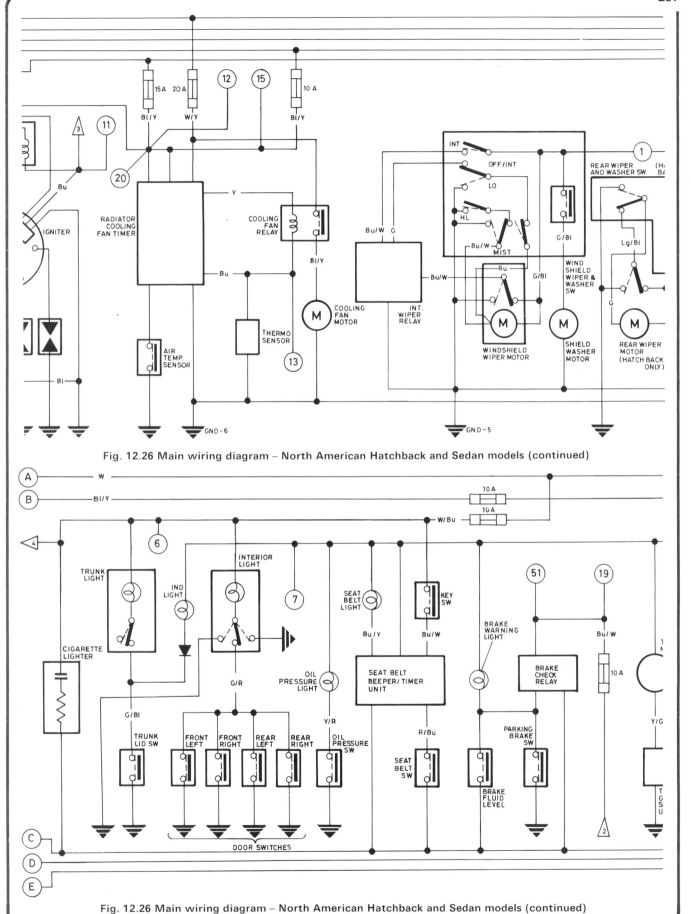

Fig. 12.26 Main wiring diagram – North American Hatchback and Sedan models (continued)

Fig. 12.26 Main wiring diagram – North American Hatchback and Sedan models (continued)

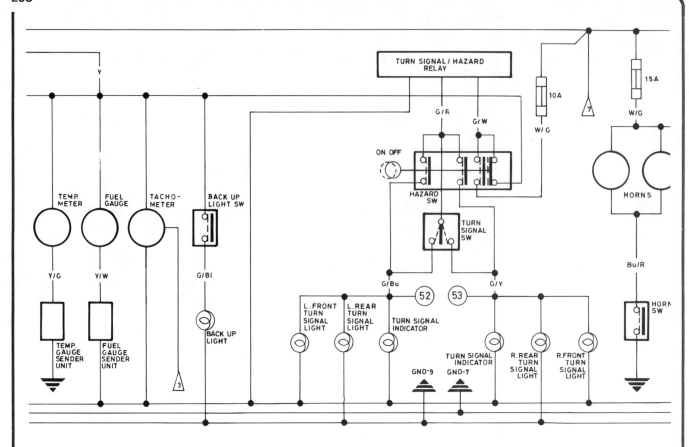

Fig. 12.26 Main wiring diagram – North American Hatchback and Sedan models (continued)

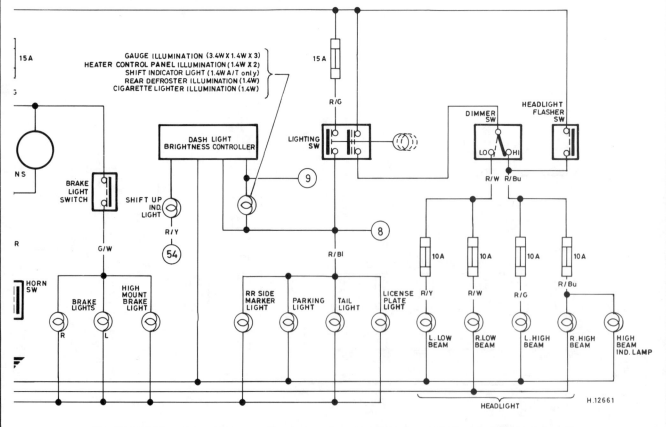

Fig. 12.26 Main wiring diagram – North American Hatchback and Sedan models (continued)

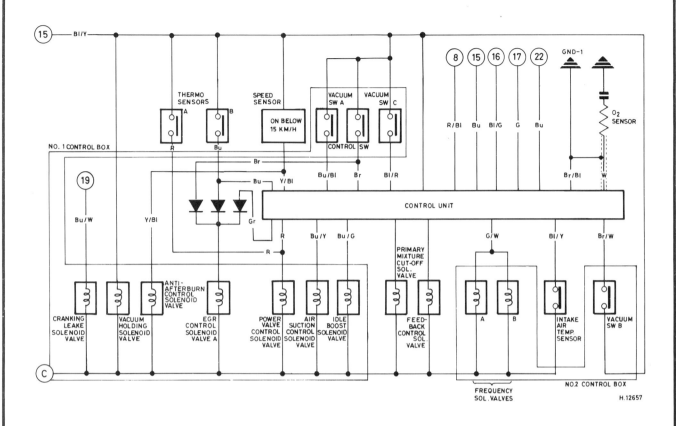

Fig. 12.27 Auxiliary wiring diagrams – North American Hatchback and Sedan models

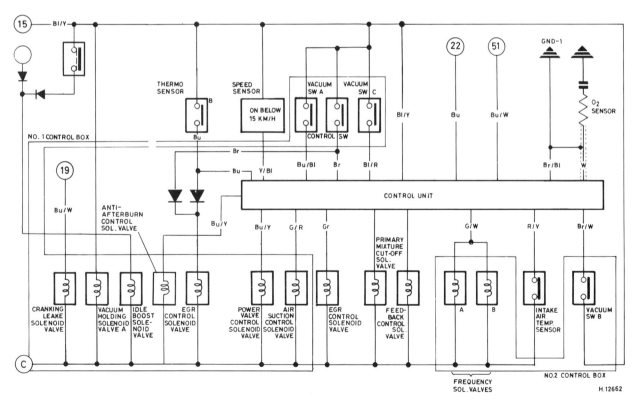

Fig. 12.27 Auxiliary wiring diagrams – North American Hatchback and Sedan models (continued)

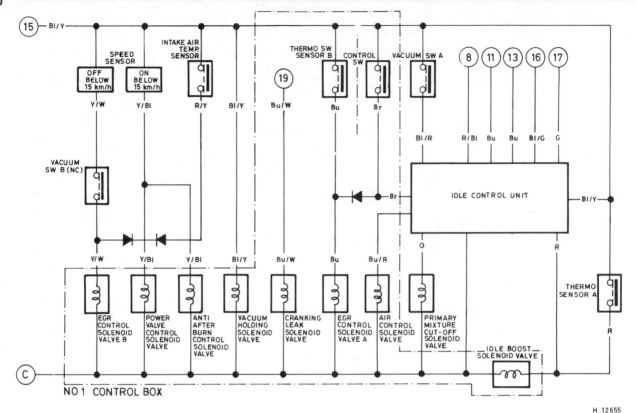

Fig. 12.27 Auxiliary wiring diagrams – North American Hatchback and Sedan models (continued)

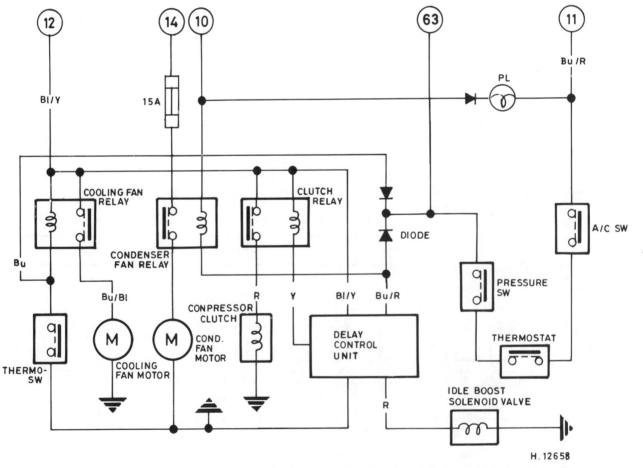

Fig. 12.27 Auxiliary wiring diagrams – North American Hatchback and Sedan models (continued)

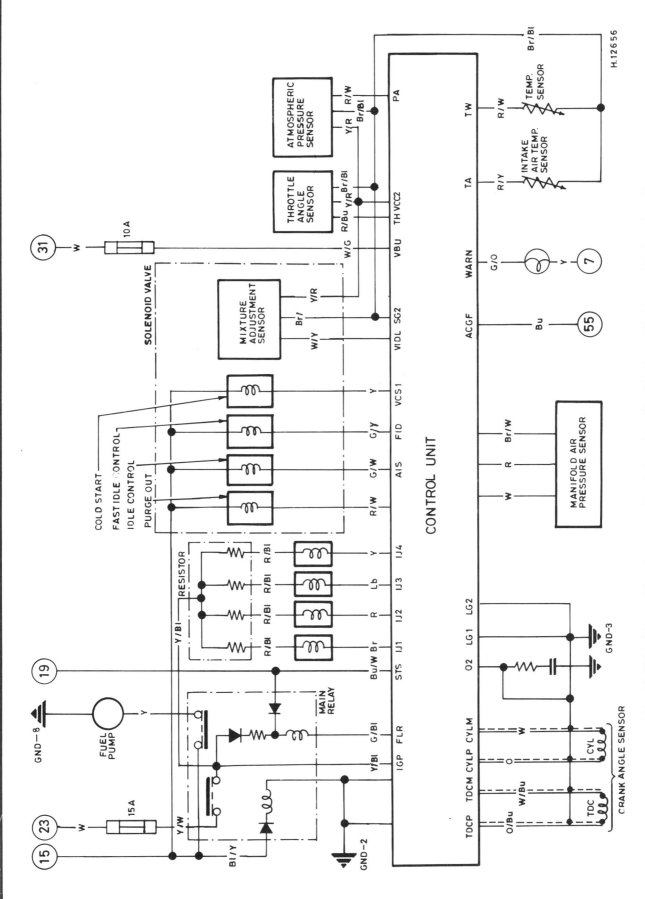

Fig. 12.27 Auxiliary wiring diagrams – North American Hatchback and Sedan models (continued)

AIR CONDITIONER CIRCUIT (Carb)

CLOCK CIRCUIT

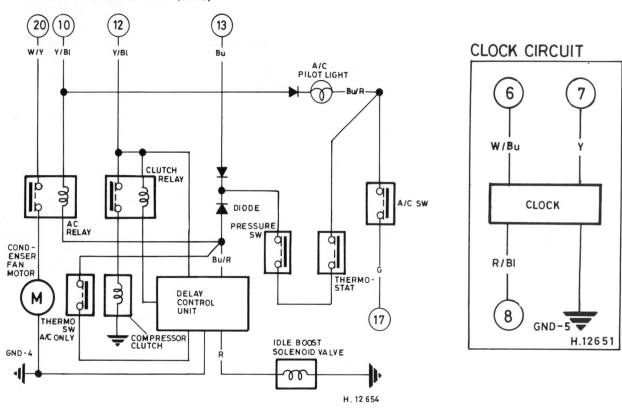

Fig. 12.27 Auxiliary wiring diagrams – North American Hatchback and Sedan models (continued)

SIDE MARKER, FLASHER CIRCUIT

WINDSHIELD WIPER AND WASHER CIRCUIT (1300 ONLY)

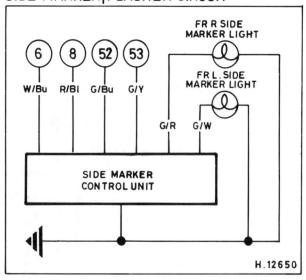

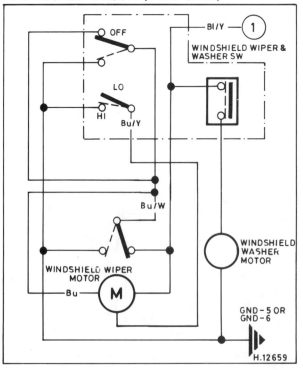

Fig. 12.27 Auxiliary wiring diagrams – North American Hatchback and Sedan models (continued)

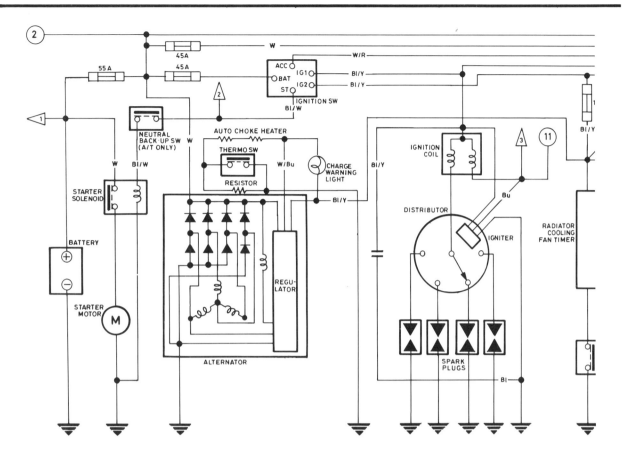

Fig 12.28 Main wiring diagram – North American Wagon models

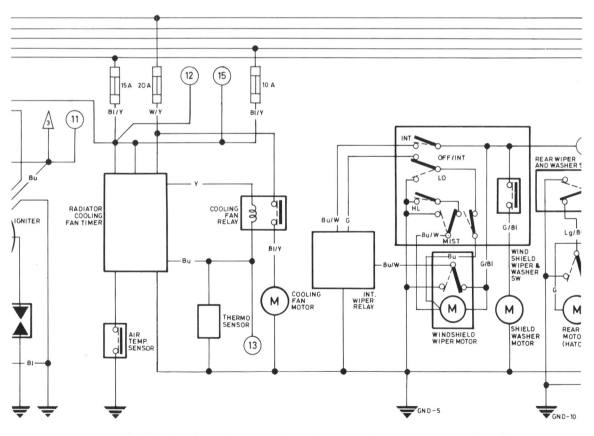

Fig. 12.28 Main wiring diagram – North American Wagon models (continued)

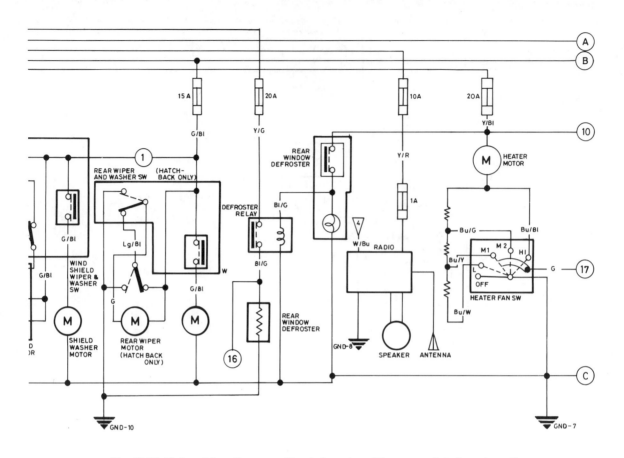

Fig. 12.28 Main wiring diagram – North American Wagon models (continued)

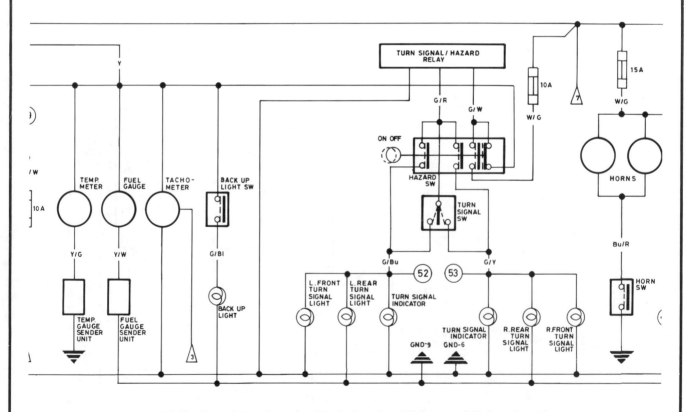

Fig. 12.28 Main wiring diagram – North American Wagon models (continued)

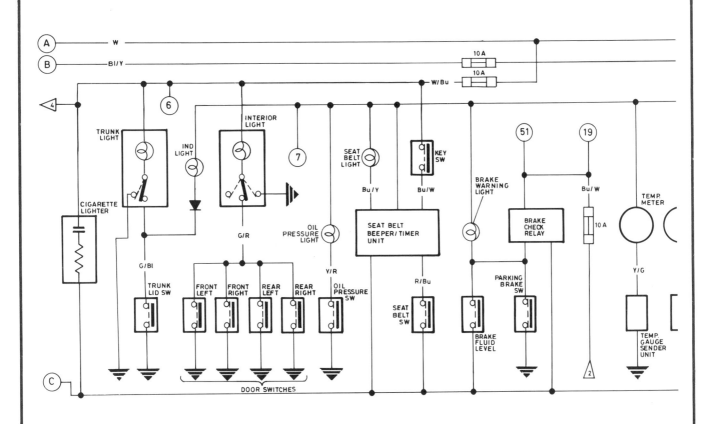

Fig. 12.28 Main wiring diagram – North American Wagon models (continued)

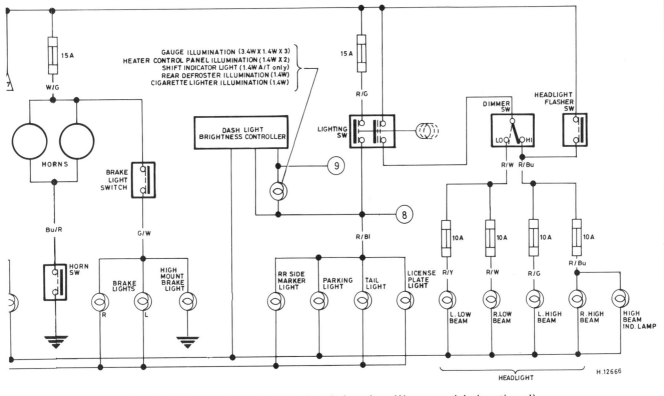

Fig. 12.28 Main wiring diagram – North American Wagon models (continued)

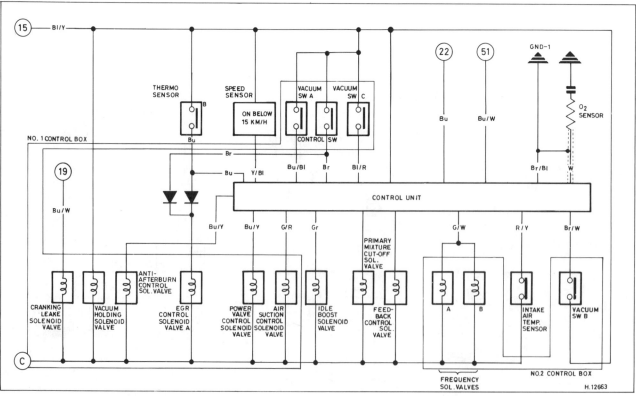

EMISSION CONTROL CIRCUIT (MT)

Fig. 12.29 Auxiliary wiring diagrams – North American Wagon models

EMISSION CONTROL CIRCUIT (A/T)

Fig. 12.29 Auxiliary wiring diagrams – North American Wagon models (continued)

AIR CONDITIONER CIRCUIT

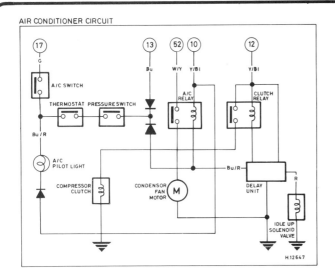

SIDE MARKER, FLASHER CIRCUIT

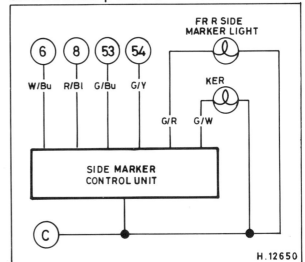

SUNROOF CIRCUIT

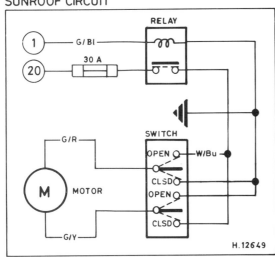

TAILGATE OPENER CIRCUIT

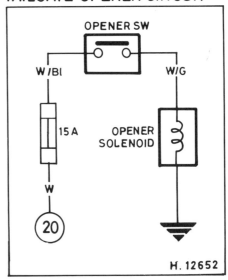

CLOCK CIRCUIT

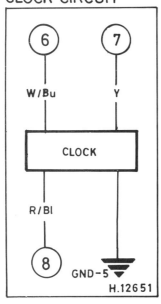

4 WD CIRCUIT

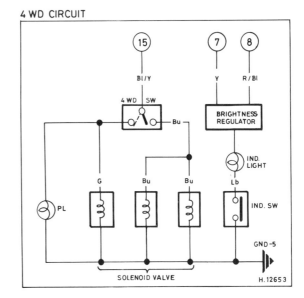

Fig. 12.29 Auxiliary wiring diagrams – North American Wagon models (continued)

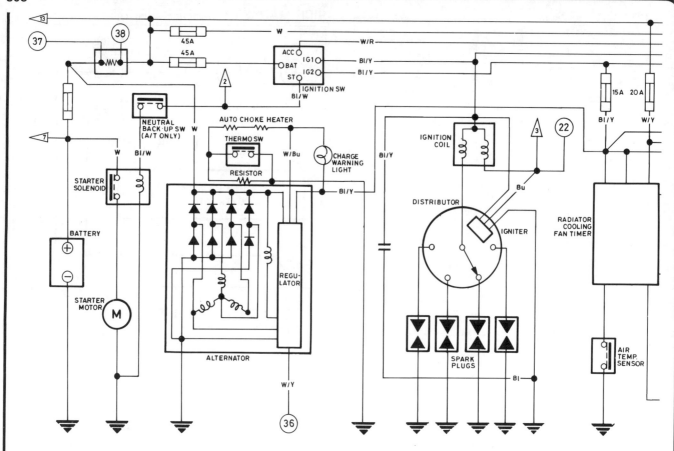

Fig. 12.30 Main wiring diagram – North American CRX (carburettor) models

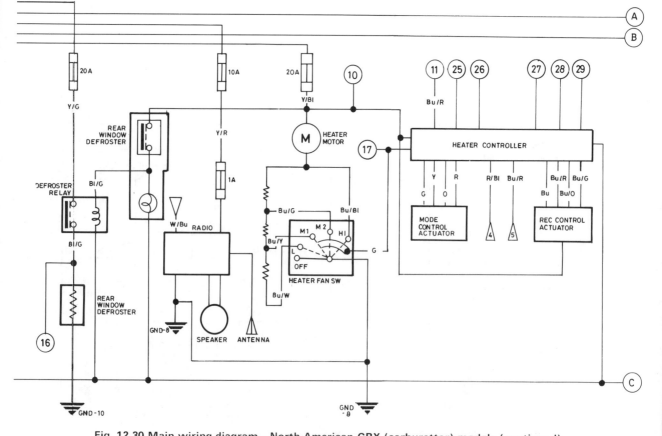

Fig. 12.30 Main wiring diagram – North American CRX (carburettor) models (continued)

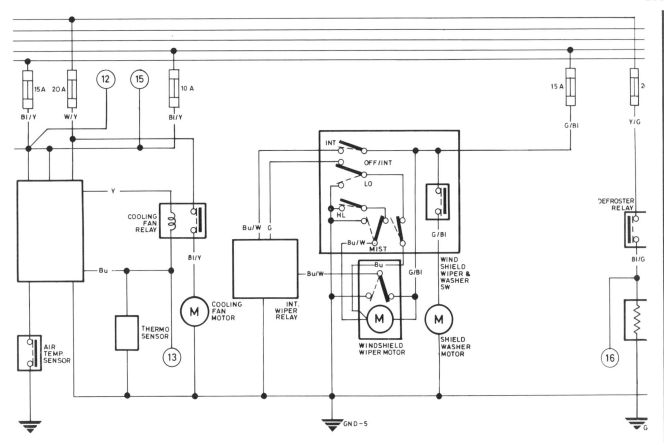

Fig. 12.30 Main wiring diagram – North American CRX (carburettor) models (continued)

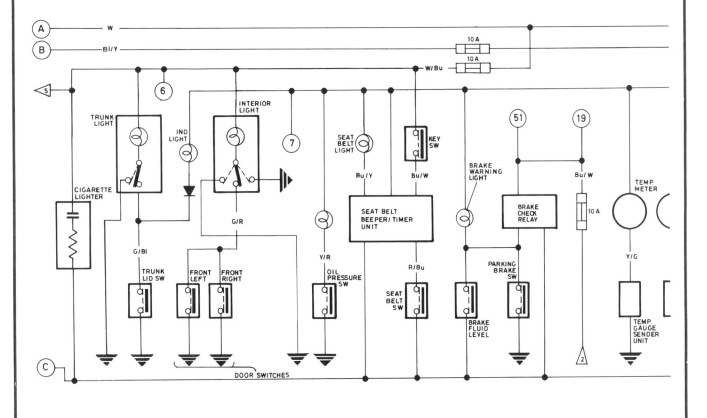

Fig. 12.30 Main wiring diagram – North American CRX (carburettor) models (continued)

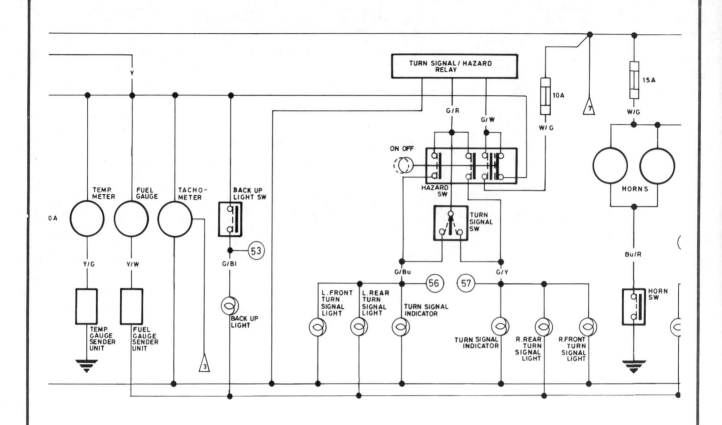

Fig. 12.30 Main wiring diagram – North American CRX (carburettor) models (continued)

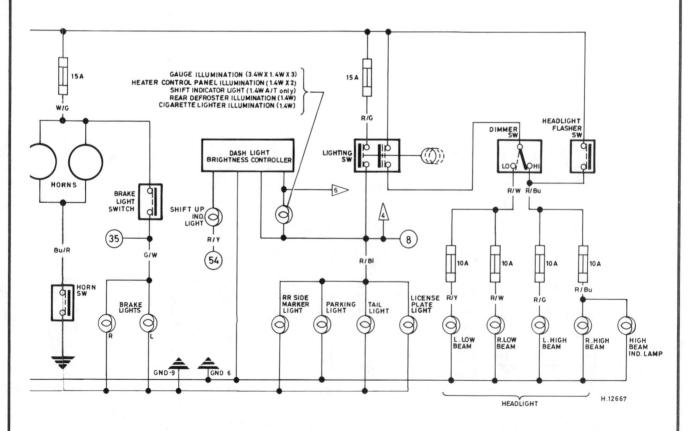

Fig. 12.30 Main wiring diagram – North American CRX (carburettor) models (continued)

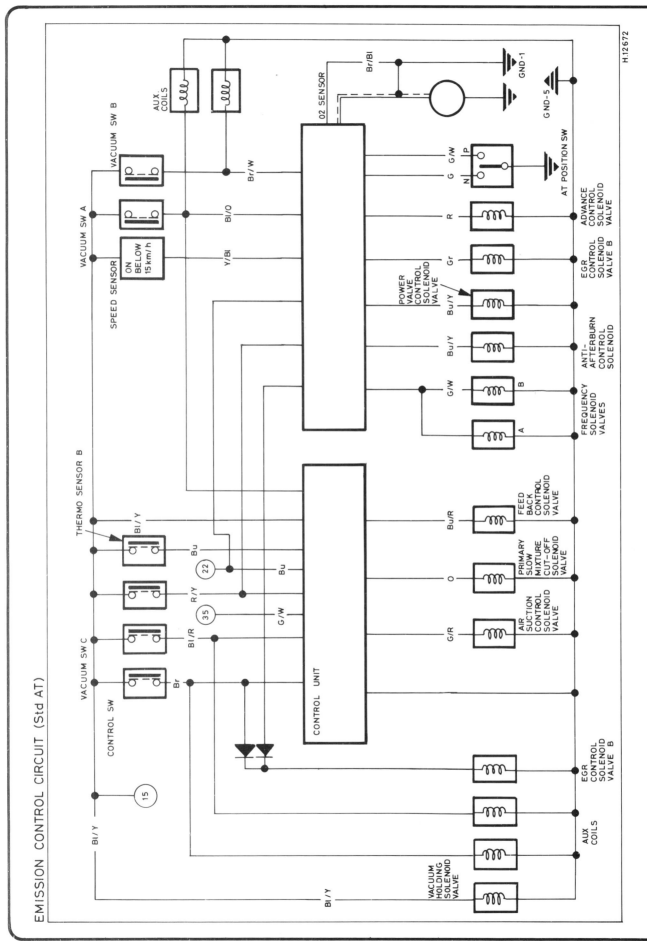

Fig. 12.31 Auxiliary wiring diagrams – North American CRX (carburettor) models

EMISSION CONTROL CIRCUIT (HI & 49 ST HF)

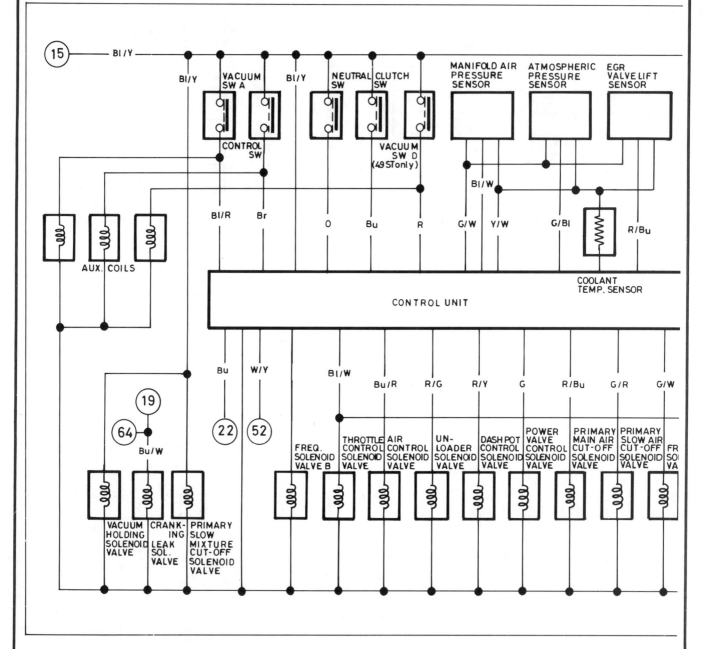

Fig. 12.31 Auxiliary wiring diagrams – North American CRX (carburettor) models (continued)

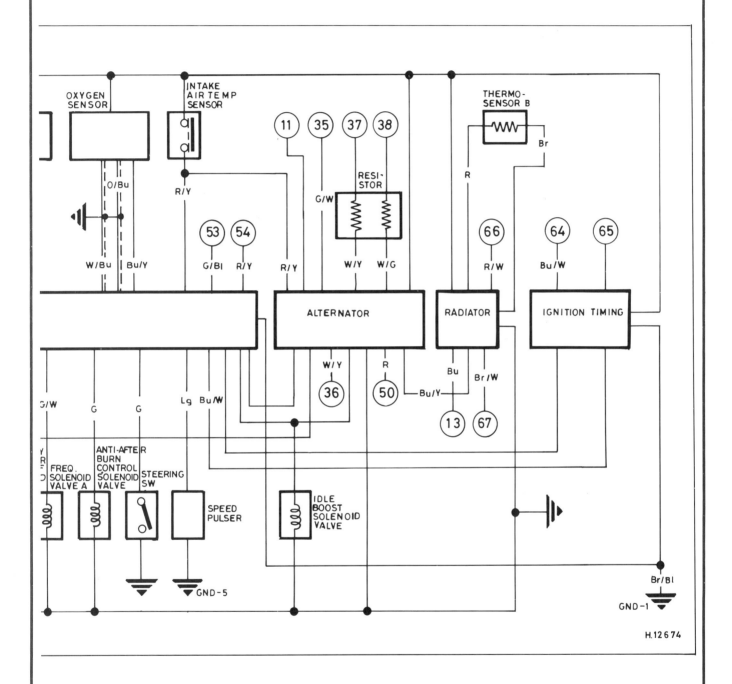

Fig. 12.31 Auxiliary wiring diagrams – North American CRX (carburettor) models (continued)

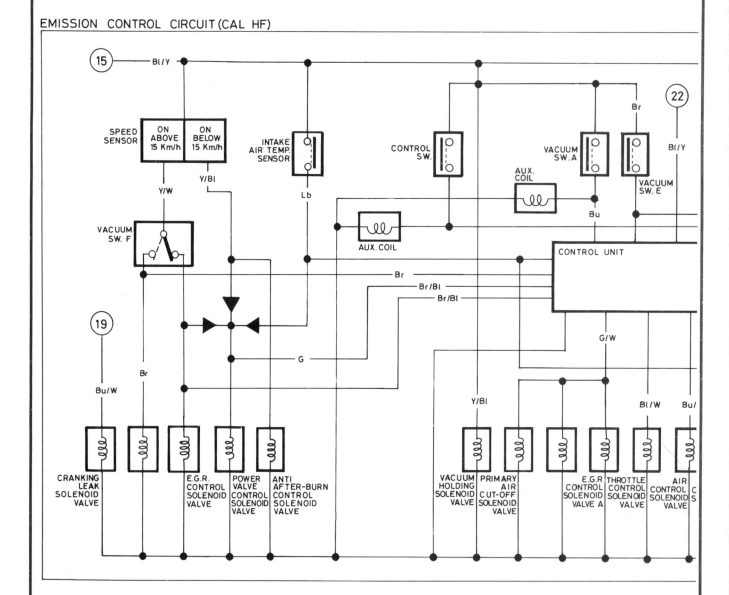

Fig. 12.31 Auxiliary wiring diagrams – North American CRX (carburettor) models (continued)

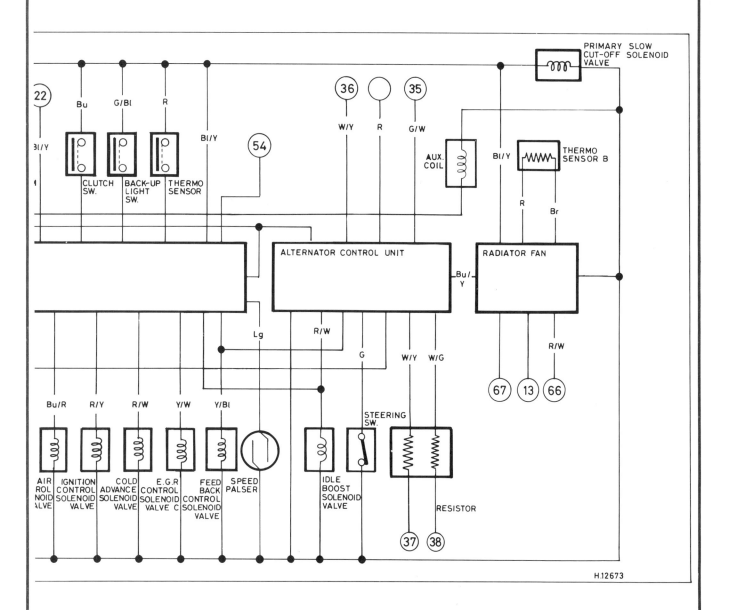

Fig. 12.31 Auxiliary wiring diagrams – North American CRX (carburettor) models (continued)

EMISSION CONTROL CIRCUIT (Std MT)

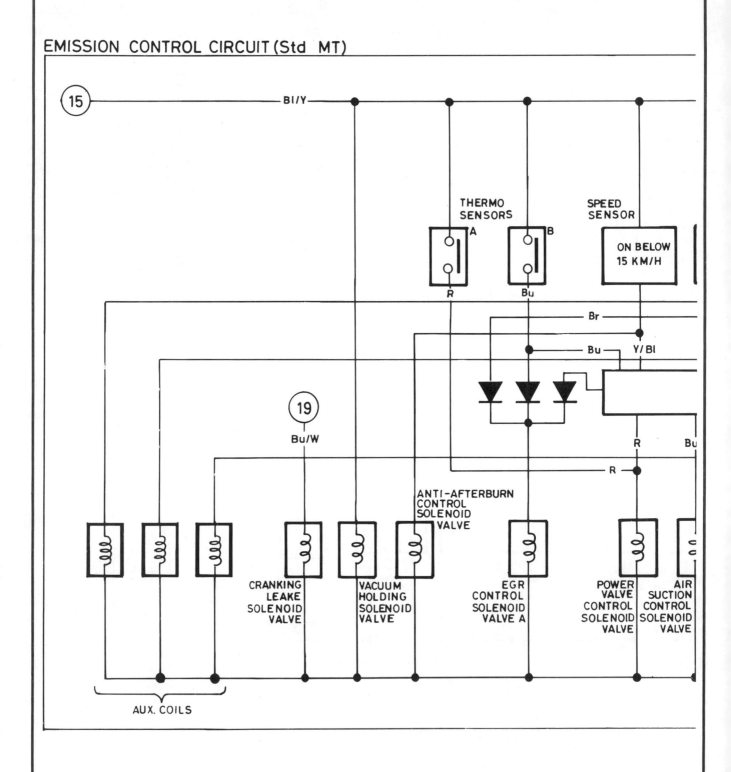

Fig. 12.31 Auxiliary wiring diagrams – North American CRX (carburettor) models (continued)

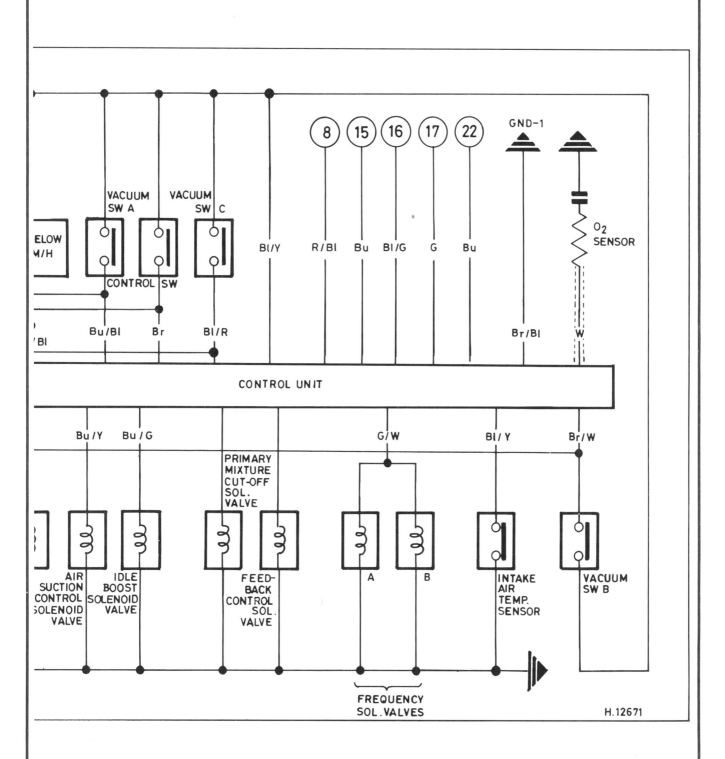

Fig. 12.31 Auxiliary wiring diagrams – North American CRX (carburettor) models (continued)

AIR CONDITIONER CIRCUIT (Std)

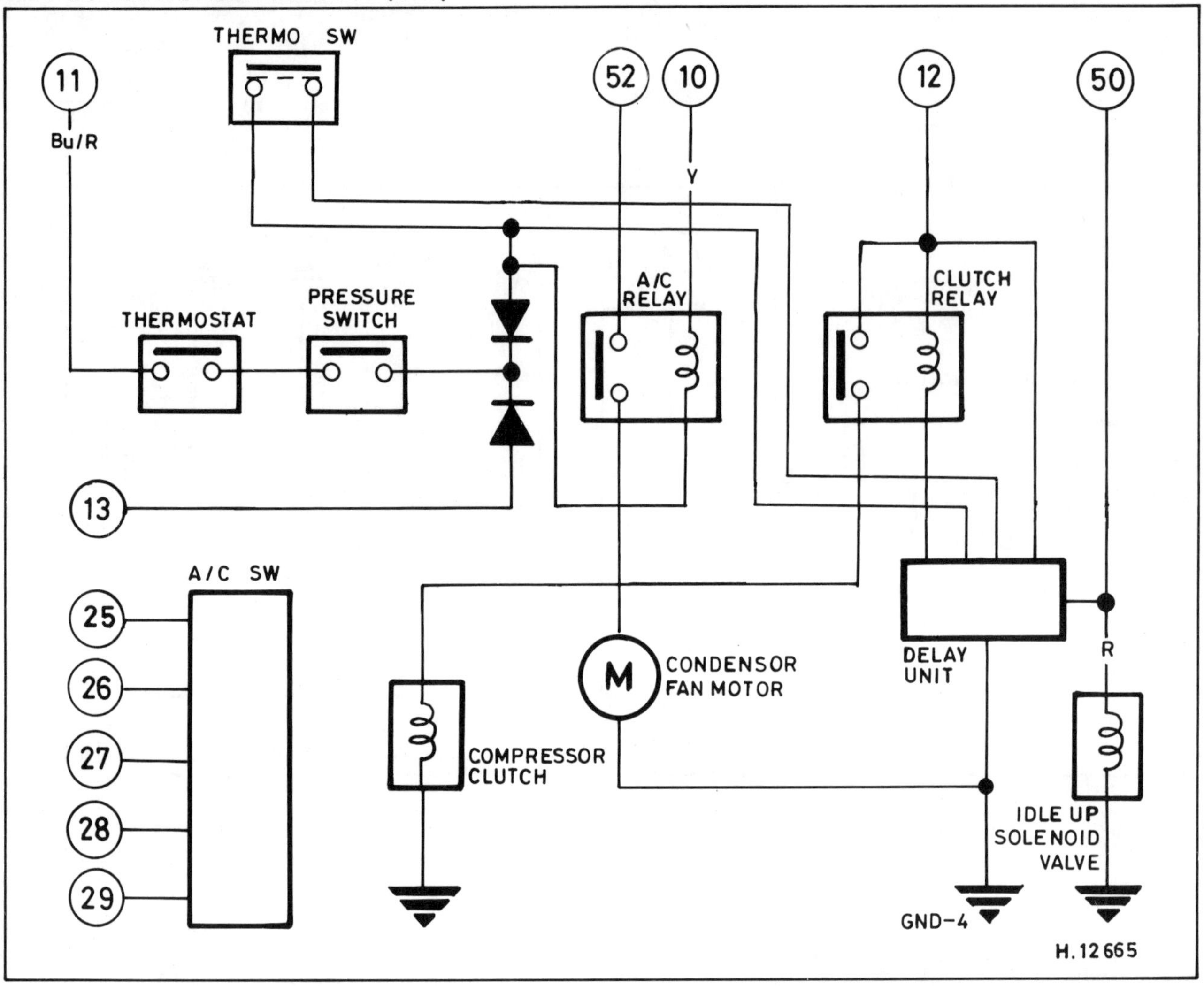

THERMO SW

(11)
Bu/R

THERMOSTAT

PRESSURE SWITCH

A/C RELAY

CLUTCH RELAY

(52) (10) (12) (50)

Y

(13)

A/C SW

(25)

(26)

(27)

(28)

(29)

COMPRESSOR CLUTCH

M CONDENSOR FAN MOTOR

DELAY UNIT

R

IDLE UP SOLENOID VALVE

GND-4

H.12665

AIR CONDITIONER CIRCUIT (HF)

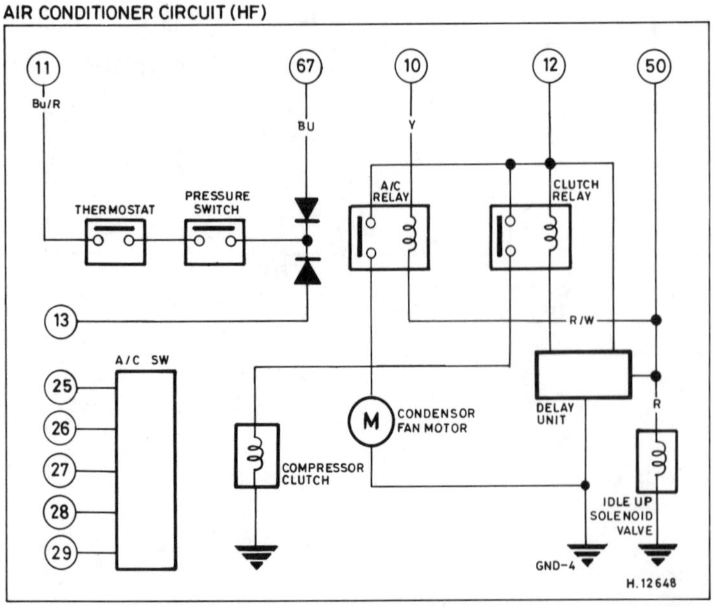

(11)
Bu/R

(67)
BU

(10)
Y

(12)

(50)

THERMOSTAT

PRESSURE SWITCH

A/C RELAY

CLUTCH RELAY

(13)

A/C SW

(25)

(26)

(27)

(28)

(29)

COMPRESSOR CLUTCH

M CONDENSOR FAN MOTOR

R/W

DELAY UNIT

R

IDLE UP SOLENOID VALVE

GND-4

H.12648

CLOCK CIRCUIT

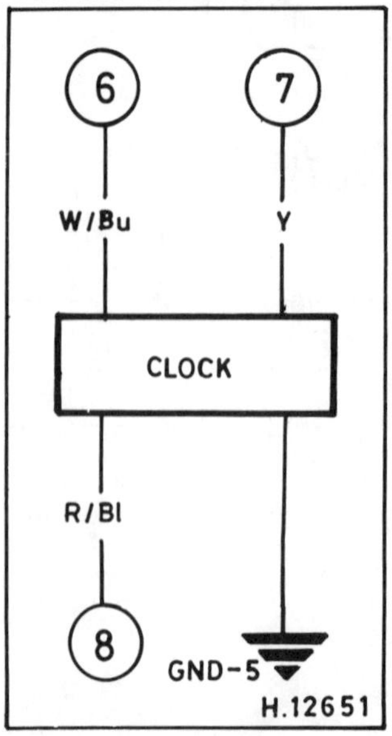

(6)
W/Bu

(7)
Y

CLOCK

R/Bl

(8)

GND-5

H.12651

Fig. 12.31 Auxiliary wiring diagrams – North American CRX (carburettor) models (continued)

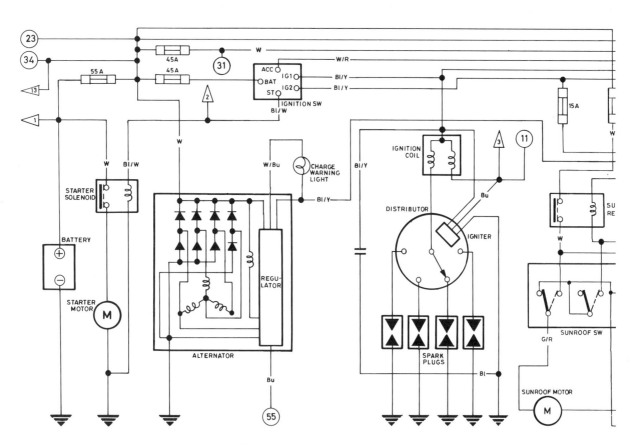

Fig. 12.32 Main wiring diagram – North American CRX (fuel-injection) models

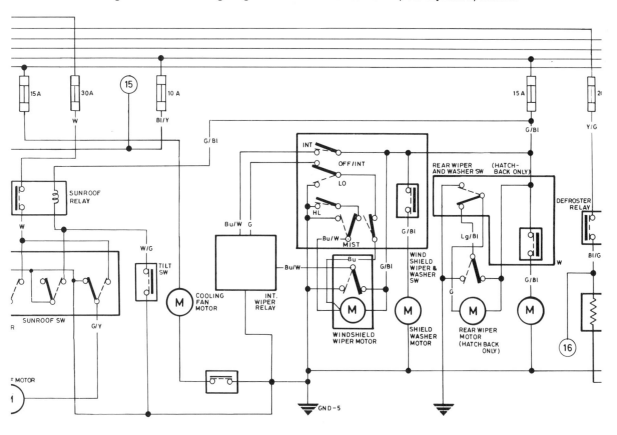

Fig. 12.32 Main wiring diagram – North American CRX (fuel-injection) models (continued)

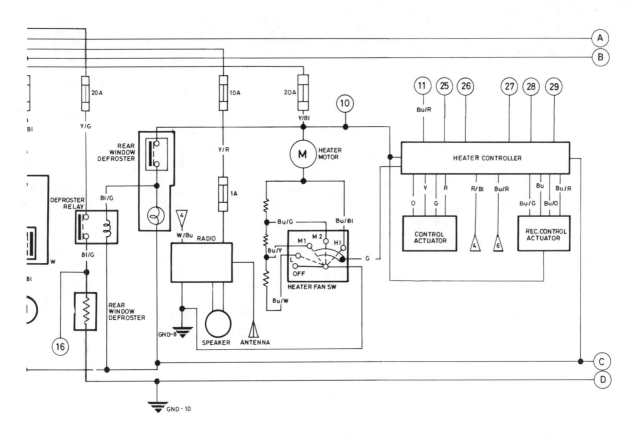

Fig. 12.32 Main wiring diagram – North American CRX (fuel-injection) models (continued)

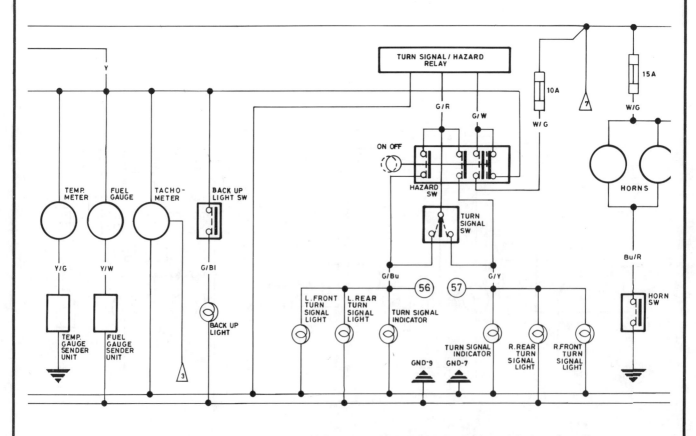

Fig. 12.32 Main wiring diagram – North American CRX (fuel-injection) models (continued)

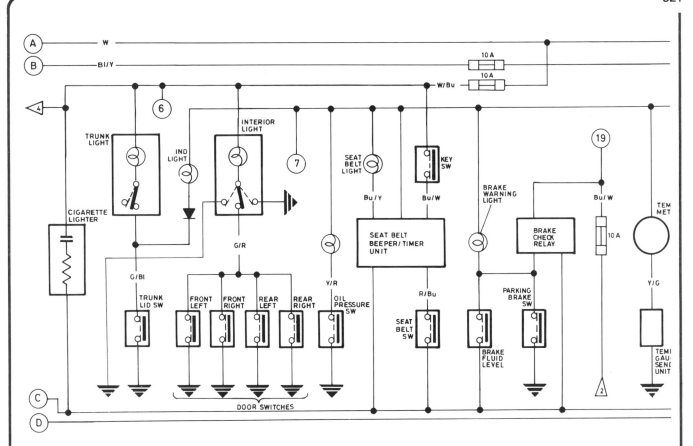

Fig. 12.32 Main wiring diagram – North American CRX (fuel-injection) models (continued)

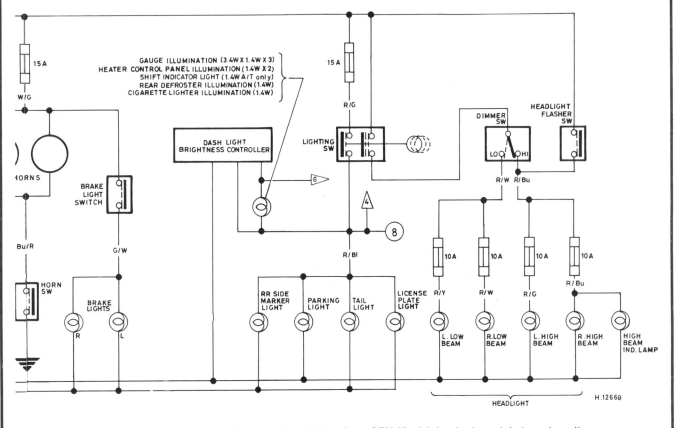

Fig. 12.32 Main wiring diagram – North American CRX (fuel-injection) models (continued)

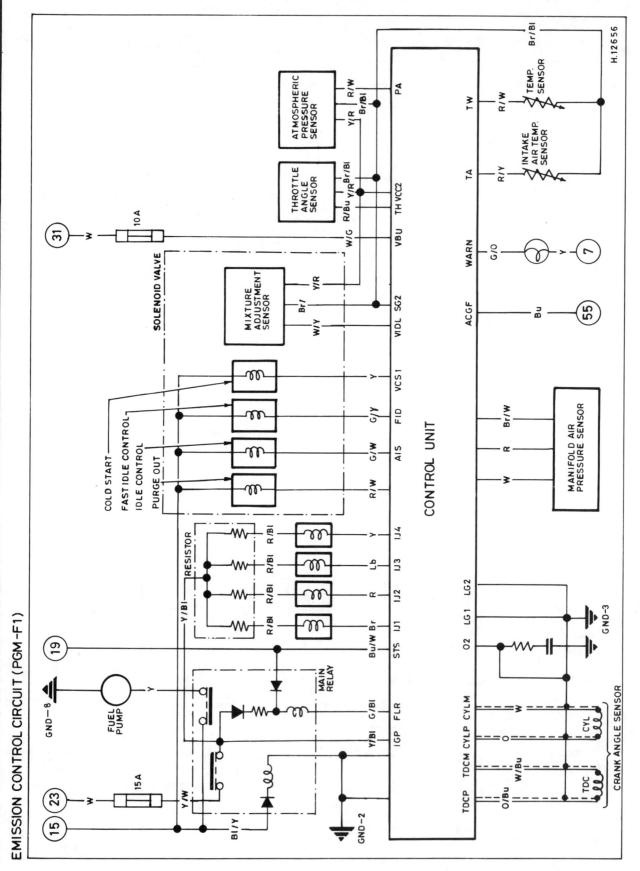

Fig. 12.33 Auxiliary wiring diagrams – North American CRX (fuel-injection) models

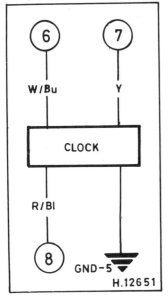

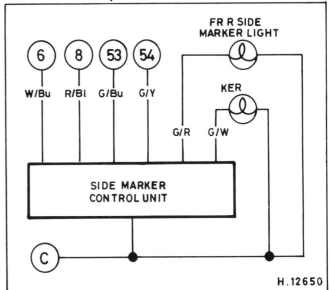

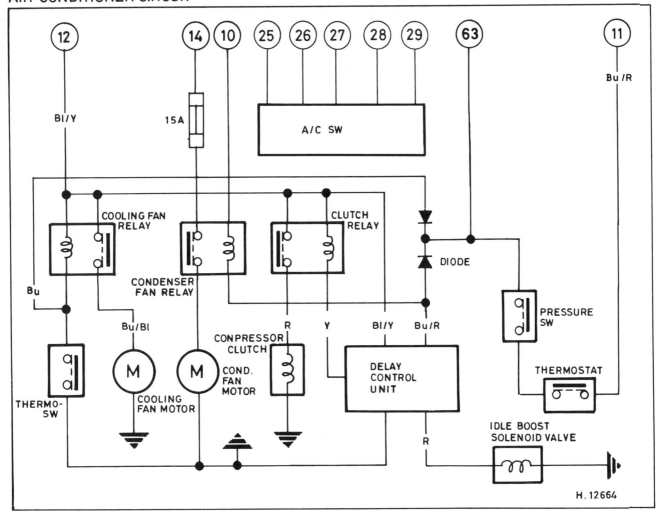

Fig. 12.33 Auxiliary wiring diagrams – North American CRX (fuel-injection) models (continued)

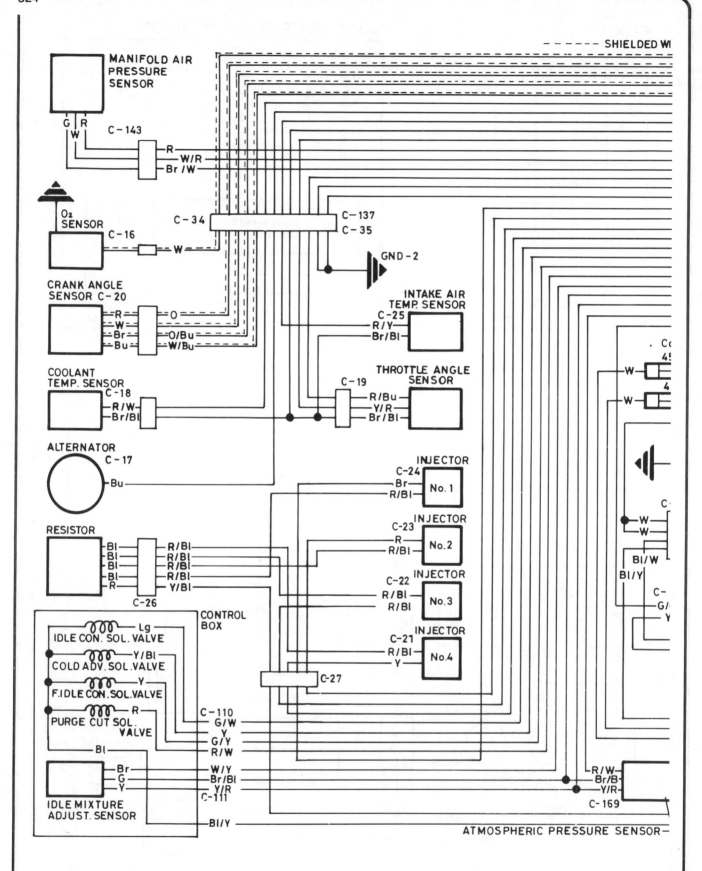

Fig. 12.34 Wiring diagram – North American fuel-injection system

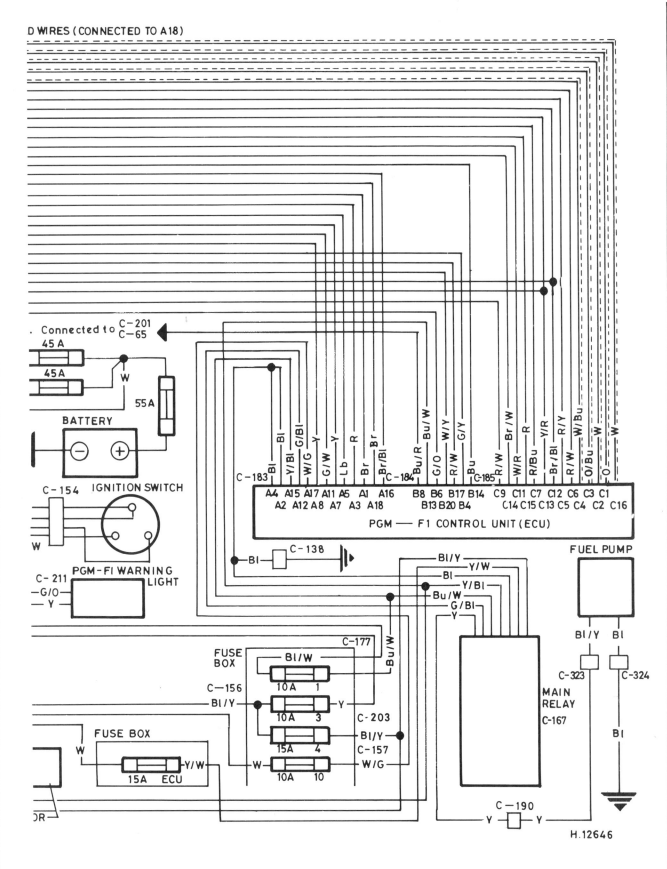

Fig. 12.34 Wiring diagram – North American fuel-injection system (continued)

Index